MARGARET BEAUFORT

LAUREN JOHNSON is a public historian and author of works including the critically acclaimed *Shadow King: The Life and Death of Henry VI*. Lauren received an MSt in medieval historical research from the University of Oxford, and is currently studying for an AHRC-funded collaborative doctorate with Manchester Metropolitan University and the National Archives. With a passion for restoring marginalised narratives to our history, she has worked in heritage since 2008 and acted as historical consultant for Historic Royal Palaces, Wellcome Library, Sky History, Dante or Die and the Royal Shakespeare Company.

MARGARET BEAUFORT

SURVIVOR, REBEL, KINGMAKER

LAUREN JOHNSON

HEAD
of ZEUS

An Apollo Book

First published in the UK in 2025 by Head of Zeus Ltd,
part of Bloomsbury Publishing Plc

9 7 5 3 1 2 4 6 8

A catalogue record for this book is available from the British Library.

ISBN (HB): 9781789541649
ISBN (E): 9781789541632

Typeset by Siliconchips Services Ltd UK

Printed and bound in Great Britain by
Clays Ltd, Elcograf S.p.A.

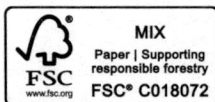

MIX
Paper | Supporting
responsible forestry
FSC® C018072
FSC
www.fsc.org

Bloomsbury Publishing Plc
50 Bedford Square, London, WC1B 3DP, UK
Bloomsbury Publishing Ireland Limited,
29 Earlsfort Terrace, Dublin 2, D02 AY28, Ireland

HEAD OF ZEUS LTD
5–8 Hardwick Street
London EC1R 4RG

To find out more about our authors and books
visit www.headofzeus.com

For product safety-related questions contact productsafety@bloomsbury.com

For Willow

For her three siblings, who were with me for however
short a time during the writing of this book

And for Anne, Irene, Margaret and Anne.
Foundations of my patchwork family.

Contents

II

'HIGH AND MIGHTY PRINCESS'

III

'ALTERA SECURITAS'

Dramatis Personae

Note: Names are listed alphabetically by the most commonly used form in the text, whether Christian name or noble title. For instance, Margaret Beaufort would be listed as 'Margaret' not under Beaufort, countess of Richmond or king's mother.

Bernard ANDRÉ (*c.*1450–1522). French-born cleric who came to England with Henry Tudor and became his official poet and historian.

ARTHUR Tudor, Prince of Wales (1486–1502). First-born child of Henry Tudor and Elizabeth of York, Arthur's birth united the warring roses of York and Lancaster.

John BEAUFORT, 1st duke of Somerset (1404–44). Margaret's father, who died before her first birthday.

Edmund BEAUFORT, 2nd duke of Somerset (1406–55). Margaret's paternal uncle, governor of English-held France and the power behind Henry VI's throne. His ascendancy was bitterly resented by the duke of York.

Henry BEAUFORT, 3rd duke of Somerset (1436–64). Eldest son of Edmund Beaufort, the angry young nobleman became an inveterate enemy of the Yorkists.

Edmund BEAUFORT, 4th duke of Somerset (*c.*1438–71). Younger son of the second duke of Somerset who attempted to win his cousin Margaret back to the Lancastrian cause.

Reynald BRAY (*c*.1440–1503). Margaret's low-born and straight-talking receiver-general was her right-hand man, at the heart of every conspiracy she masterminded.

Anne Neville/Stafford, duchess of BUCKINGHAM (d. 1480). Margaret's mother-in-law was the guiding light of the Stafford clan – and Margaret herself – throughout the tumultuous 1460s.

Humphrey Stafford, duke of BUCKINGHAM (1402–60). Margaret's father-in-law vainly tried to keep the peace in the early years of the Wars of the Roses and died defending Henry VI.

Henry Stafford, duke of BUCKINGHAM (1455–83). The grandson of Anne, duchess of Buckingham became duke at four years old. He championed Richard III's accession – until a better offer came his way through Margaret.

Edward Stafford, duke of BUCKINGHAM (1478–1521). Heir of Henry Stafford and Katherine Woodville. As children, he and his brother Henry were Margaret's wards.

Charles the Bold, duke of BURGUNDY (1433–77). Husband of Margaret of York and ruler of the Burgundian Low Countries.

Margaret, duchess of BURGUNDY (1446–1503). The youngest sister of Edward IV and wife of Charles the Bold caused persistent trouble for the Tudors from her base in the Low Countries.

Philip the Fair, duke of BURGUNDY (1478–1506). Philip's Low Countries territories, and his pretensions to the Spanish throne, made him a crucial international ally to Henry VII.

Isabella of CASTILE (1451–1504). The 'Catholic monarch' ruled Spain with her husband, Ferdinand of Aragon. She gained international renown for her *Reconquista* of Muslim Granada.

Joanna of CASTILE (1479–1555). The wife of Philip the Fair was, in her own right, heir to Castile, but that did not save her from the jealous schemes of her husband's courtiers.

CECILY Neville, duchess of York (1415–95). One of the twenty-three children of Ralph, earl of Westmorland; wife of Richard, duke of York; mother of Edward IV and Richard III. Cecily exerted considerable influence, and became a role model for Margaret.

CECILY, princess of York (1469–1507). The second-eldest child of Edward IV became one of Margaret's closest friends and protégés. Margaret arranged Cecily's marriage to her half-brother John Welles.

Thomas, duke of CLARENCE (1387–1421). The younger brother of Henry V and – after marrying Margaret Holland – stepfather of the Beaufort dukes of Somerset. Killed in the French wars.

George, duke of CLARENCE (1449–78). The abilities of the middle Yorkist son did not match his ambition. His marriage to Isabel Neville, daughter of Warwick the Kingmaker, put him on a collision course with his brother Edward IV.

'Crowland Chronicler' (fl. *c.*1486). Anonymous author of a continuation of the chronicle compiled at Crowland Abbey in Lincolnshire, who wrote of Richard III's reign shortly after it ended. States that he was a former councillor of Edward IV with links to Richard's court and therefore eyewitness to events.

Alice (née Chaucer) and William DE LA POLE, duchess and duke of Suffolk (*c.*1404–75 and 1396–1450). The architects of Margaret's first marriage, to their son – an arrangement that accelerated their disgrace.

John DE LA POLE, duke of Suffolk (1442–92). Margaret's first, short-lived, marriage ended before she and John really began a relationship. John's mother then arranged his union with the duke of York's daughter Elizabeth.

John DE LA POLE, earl of Lincoln (*c.*1460–87). The eldest son of Elizabeth and John de la Pole became a leading Ricardian.

Edmund DE LA POLE, earl of Suffolk (*c.*1472–1513). Cousin of Queen Elizabeth of York, who ultimately rebelled against the Tudors.

Thomas Grey, marquess of DORSET (*c.*1455–1501). Elizabeth Woodville's eldest son (from her first marriage) was a man of mediocre abilities but considerable pride.

EDWARD IV, aka earl of March (1442–83). First Yorkist monarch. Handsome, charismatic and militarily daring, in the end the only thing that could destroy Edward's regime was himself.

EDWARD V (1470–83?). Heir of Edward IV. One of the two 'Princes in the Tower' usurped by their uncle Richard, duke of Gloucester. Their disappearance incited rebellion, but they were never seen alive again.

ELIZABETH of York (1466–1503). The eldest child of Edward IV and Elizabeth Woodville was as beautiful and accomplished as her parents, but considerably more submissive. Throughout much of her marriage, Elizabeth worked and lived at court with her mother-in-law, Margaret, and for the most part enjoyed a close relationship.

FERDINAND of Aragon (1452–1516). With his wife, Isabella of Castile, Ferdinand ruled Spain, and was an important (if unreliable) ally to the Tudors.

HENRY VI of Lancaster (1421–71). 'Holy King Henry' was an abysmal failure as ruler: vacillating, eager to please and terrified of conflict.

HENRY Tudor, earl of Richmond/Henry VII (1457–1509). Margaret's only child and, in later life, the crucible of her hopes.

William HERBERT, earl of Pembroke (d. 1469). Edward IV's 'lock key in Wales' caused the death of Margaret's second husband and became the guardian of her son, but still managed to work with Margaret for their mutual benefit.

Anne Devereux, Lady HERBERT (c.1433–c.86). Anne brought up Henry Tudor at Raglan Castle, and saved him from the violence of 1469–70, an act Margaret never forgot.

KATHERINE of Aragon (1485–1536). The younger daughter of Ferdinand and Isabella of Spain was betrothed to Arthur Tudor from infancy. This Anglo-Spanish alliance was the lynchpin of Tudor diplomacy, but Katherine was left in limbo after Arthur's death.

Francis, Viscount LOVELL (c.1457–c.88). Richard III's loyal 'dog' grew up, like him, in the care of Warwick the Kingmaker and refused to bow to the Tudors.

MARGUERITE of Anjou (1430–82). French princess Marguerite was the effective leader of the Lancastrian regime from 1453, and proved considerably more adept – and ruthless – than her saintly husband, Henry VI.

Thomas MORE (1478–1535). Humanist lawyer who wrote a famous 'history' of Richard III c.1513–18. A protégé of John Morton, some of More's work may have been gleaned from first-hand testimony, but much was a rhetorical exercise in tyrannical kingship.

John MORTON (1420–1500). A champion of Marguerite of Anjou who shared her exile for years, Morton nonetheless made his peace with the Yorkist regime after Henry VI's death. His political sagacity and Church connections proved essential to the Tudor cause.

Anne NEVILLE, Queen (1456–85). The second daughter of Warwick the Kingmaker enjoyed a large northern following, which bolstered the rule of her husband, Richard, duke of Gloucester.

John de Vere, earl of OXFORD (1442–1513). The daredevil earl never fully made peace with the Yorkists, and was implicated in one rebellion after another.

Margaret Plantagenet, Lady POLE (1473–1541). The daughter of George, duke of Clarence inherited the Yorkist royal claim, and was safely absorbed into Margaret's family through marriage to her nephew.

Sir Richard POLE (1462–1504). Margaret's nephew was a Tudor loyalist who served as councillor to three generations of her family.

RICHARD, duke of Gloucester/Richard III (1452–85). Schooled in warfare and intrigue from childhood, Richard served as his brother's right hand in the north, where he often clashed with the Stanleys.

Prince RICHARD of York (duke of Norfolk) (1473–83?). The younger 'Prince in the Tower' disappeared in summer 1483. Under Henry VII, Perkin Warbeck of Tournai assumed the prince's identity, and garnered enough support to seriously endanger the Tudor regime.

Sir Harry STAFFORD (c.1425–71). Margaret's third husband, and first lasting relationship. A younger son of the duke of Buckingham, with ongoing ill health which may have contributed to his and Margaret's inability to have children.

Margaret Beauchamp, dowager duchess of SOMERSET (c.1410–82). Margaret's mother was widowed three times by war, both French and civil, leaving her to raise seven children alone. She taught Margaret to be astute – and sometimes unscrupulous – to survive.

Lord Thomas STANLEY, earl of Derby (1435–1503). Margaret's fourth and last husband was the turncoat warlord of much of Cheshire and Lancashire. Thomas stood aloof from the violence of the Wars of the Roses and thus outlived most of his rivals.

Sir William STANLEY (*c.*1435–95). Thomas's younger brother was a Yorkist through and through, serving both Edward IV and V.

George STANLEY, Lord Strange (1460–1503). Thomas Stanley's heir and leading commander, who owed his title and some of his northern estate to his wife, Joan.

James STANLEY (1465–1515). Although always intended for the Church, Margaret's stepson (and eventual bishop of Ely) lived a disreputable early life, gambling and maintaining a mistress. Nonetheless, he and Margaret were close throughout their lives.

Tom STANLEY, earl of Derby (d. 1521). Thomas's grandson, a contemporary of Prince Arthur, who remained close to Margaret long after she separated from Thomas.

Owen TUDOR/Owain ap Maredudd ap Tudur (d. 1461). The second husband of Queen Catherine Valois was a lowly Welsh servant, who fathered Edmund and Jasper Tudor.

Edmund TUDOR, earl of Richmond (*c.*1430–56). The eldest son of Queen Catherine Valois and Owen Tudor. He married his ward Margaret when she was twelve.

Jasper TUDOR, earl of Pembroke (*c.*1431–95). The Welsh powerhouse and younger brother of Edmund Tudor risked everything to defend the House of Lancaster.

Polydore VERGIL (*c.*1470–1555). Italian priest and writer who came to England in 1502 as a papal agent and celebrity in cultured circles. Wrote a history of England that is an important source for fifteenth- and sixteenth-century events, much of it gathered from first-hand testimony.

Perkin WARBECK. See Prince RICHARD of York.

Richard Neville, earl of WARWICK aka Warwick the Kingmaker (1428–71). Commander of the port of Calais and the steel core of the Yorkist regime.

Edward, earl of WARWICK (1475–99). The only son of George, duke of Clarence and Isabel Neville spent most of his life in prison.

John WELLES (c.1450–98). Margaret's youngest half-sibling and Tudor loyalist.

Elizabeth WOODVILLE (1437–92). The first English-born Queen of England since the Norman Conquest came from a large family. Her rampant nepotism made her and her relatives deeply unpopular.

Katherine WOODVILLE, duchess of Buckingham and Bedford (1457/8–97). Younger sister of Queen Elizabeth, her marriage was arranged to Henry, duke of Buckingham – a union he found socially disdainful. A second arranged marriage (this time to Jasper Tudor) appears to have been even less affectionate.

Richard, duke of YORK (1411–60). The proud and ambitious York was acutely aware of his status as Henry VI's closest adult heir. He was on the point of gaining the throne when killed in battle.

Margaret's main homes ◆

Battles ✕

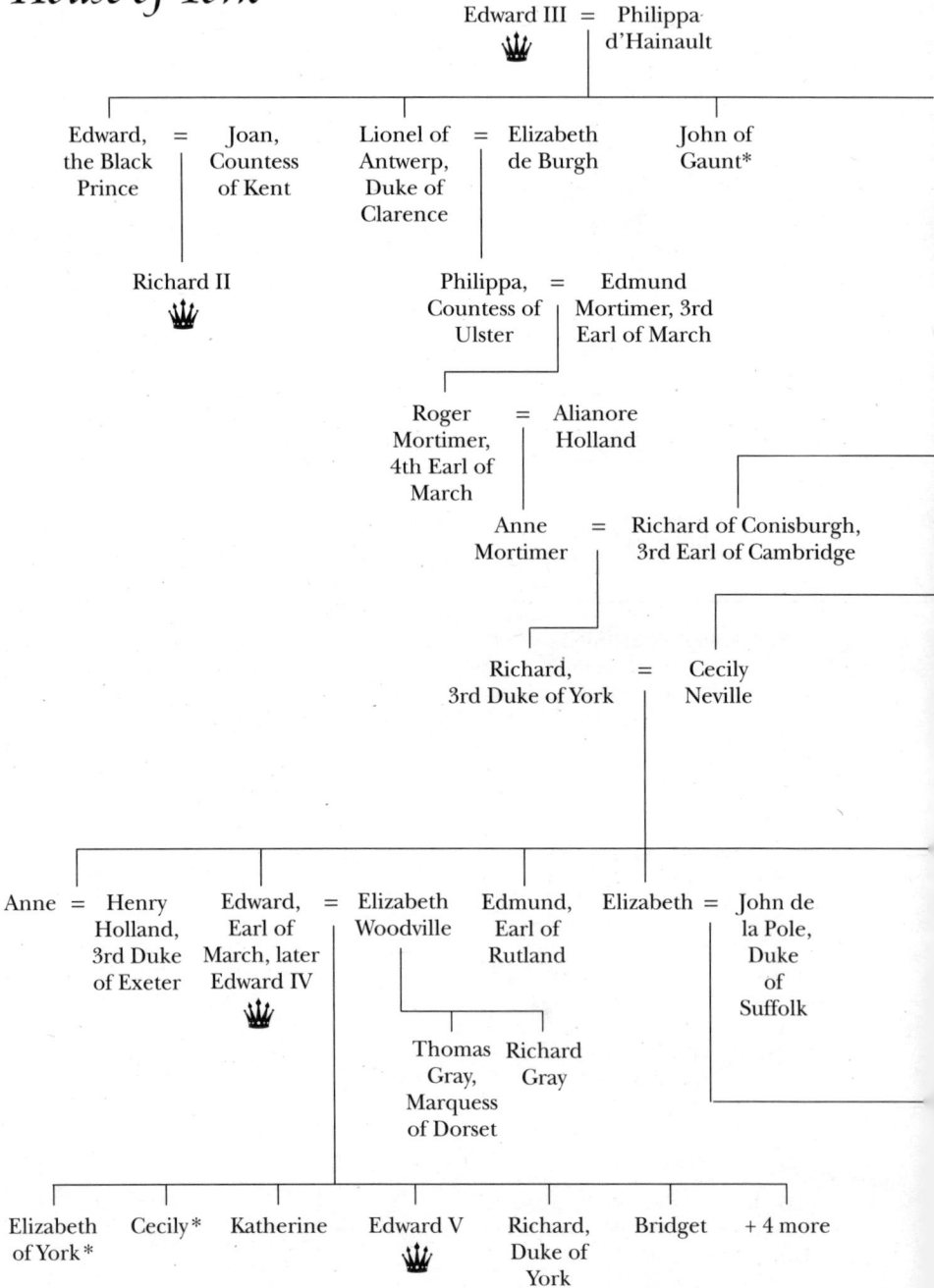

House of York

Edward III = Philippa d'Hainault
👑

Edward, the Black Prince = Joan, Countess of Kent

Lionel of Antwerp, Duke of Clarence = Elizabeth de Burgh

John of Gaunt*

Richard II 👑

Philippa, Countess of Ulster = Edmund Mortimer, 3rd Earl of March

Roger Mortimer, 4th Earl of March = Alianore Holland

Anne Mortimer = Richard of Conisburgh, 3rd Earl of Cambridge

Richard, 3rd Duke of York = Cecily Neville

Anne = Henry Holland, 3rd Duke of Exeter

Edward, Earl of March, later Edward IV 👑 = Elizabeth Woodville

Edmund, Earl of Rutland

Elizabeth = John de la Pole, Duke of Suffolk

Thomas Gray, Marquess of Dorset

Richard Gray

Elizabeth of York*

Cecily*

Katherine

Edward V 👑

Richard, Duke of York

Bridget

+ 4 more

Edmund of = Isabella of
Langley,   Castile
1st Duke of
York

Thomas of = Eleanor
Woodstock,   de Bohun
1st Duke of
Gloucester

Joan
Beaufort*

Anne Neville = Humphrey
Stafford,
Duke of
Buckingham

Richard Neville, = Alice
5th Earl of   Montacute
Salisbury

Sir Harry = Margaret
Stafford*   Beaufort

Richard,   John   George
Earl of   Neville, 1st Neville,
Warwick   Marquess of   Bishop of
=   Montagu   Exeter,
Anne   Archbishop
Beauchamp   of York

George,   Richard, Duke
Duke of   of Gloucester,
Clarence   later
              Richard III
              ♔

Margaret = Charles, Duke
           of Burgundy

George = Isabel
(Duke of
Clarence)

Edward of = Anne = Richard
Lancaster* 1   2 (Duke of
                   Gloucester)

John de   Edmund   Richard
la Pole,   de la Pole,   de la Pole
Earl of   Earl of
Lincoln   Suffolk

= Marriage
♔ Monarch
* See "Margaret's Family" tree

Margaret's Family

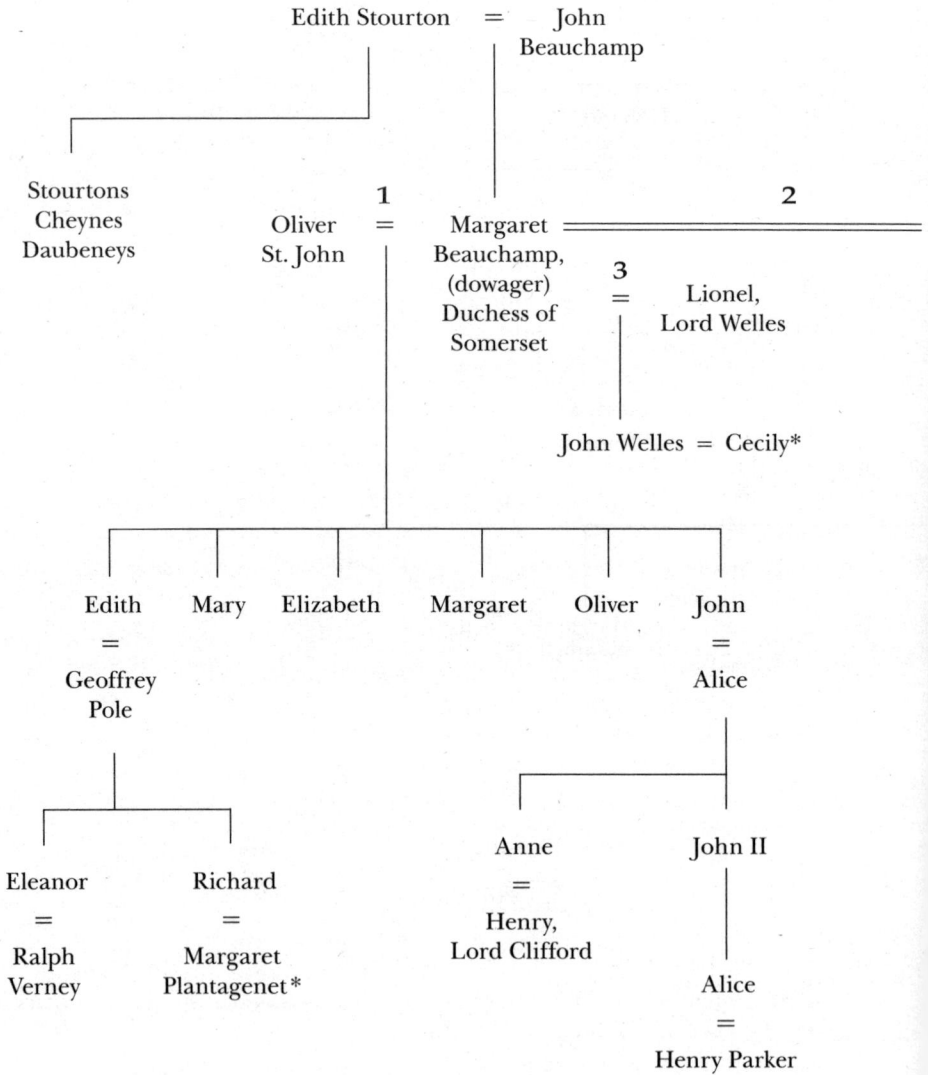

Edith Stourton = John Beauchamp

Stourtons
Cheynes
Daubeneys

1

Oliver
St. John
=

Margaret
Beauchamp,
(dowager)
Duchess of
Somerset

2

3
=
Lionel,
Lord Welles

John Welles = Cecily*

Edith
=
Geoffrey
Pole

Mary

Elizabeth

Margaret

Oliver

John
=
Alice

Eleanor
=
Ralph
Verney

Richard
=
Margaret
Plantagenet*

Anne
=
Henry,
Lord Clifford

John II

Alice
=
Henry Parker

=   Marriage

♛   Monarch

*   See "House of York"

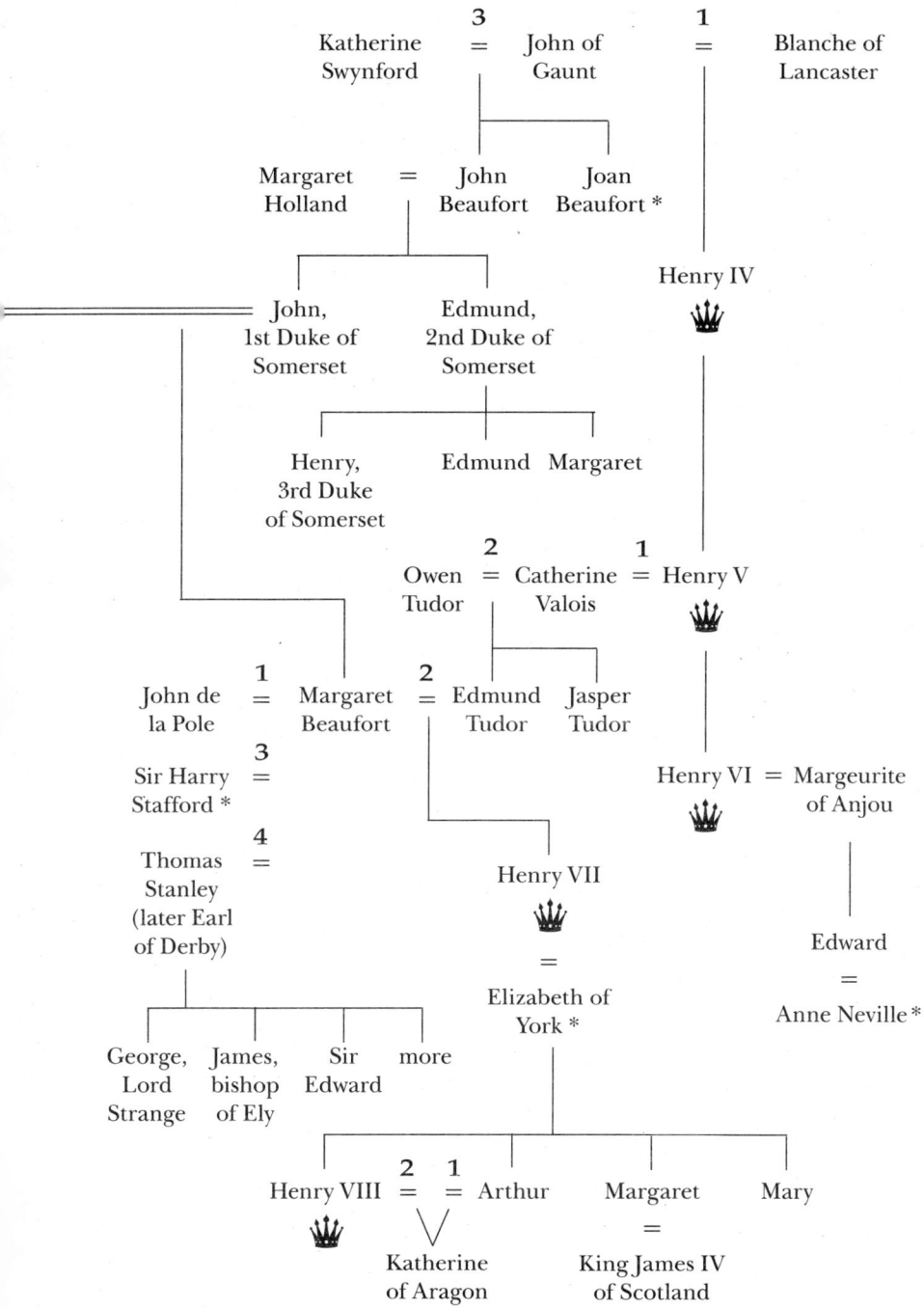

3   **1**
            Katherine   =   John of   =   Blanche of
            Swynford   Gaunt   Lancaster

            Margaret   =   John   Joan
            Holland   Beaufort   Beaufort *

                                                                   Henry IV
                                                                      ♛

======================= John,   Edmund,
                        1st Duke of   2nd Duke of
                        Somerset   Somerset

                                    Henry,   Edmund   Margaret
                                    3rd Duke
                                    of Somerset

                                                   2   **1**
                                    Owen   =   Catherine   =   Henry V
                                    Tudor   Valois   ♛

                1   **2**
        John de   =   Margaret   =   Edmund   Jasper
        la Pole   Beaufort   Tudor   Tudor

                3
        Sir Harry =   Henry VI = Margeurite
        Stafford *   ♛   of Anjou

                4
        Thomas   =
        Stanley   Henry VII
        (later Earl   ♛
        of Derby)
                                             =

                                           Elizabeth of   Edward
                                           York *   =
                                                                     Anne Neville *
        George,   James,   Sir   more
        Lord   bishop   Edward
        Strange   of Ely

                                    2   **1**
                Henry VIII   =   =   Arthur   Margaret   Mary
                    ♛   ∨   =
                            Katherine   King James IV
                            of Aragon   of Scotland

Prologue

*

Five hundred years after she died, she lives. So diminutive in life, here she is transformed, painted inside an almost two-metre frame. The prayer book in front of her lies unclasped on a pillow, the carefully written Latin text opening with a red circle 'O', perhaps: *Obsecro te* (I beseech thee) or *O Intemerata* (O undefiled one). She, too, is conspicuously undefiled, her hair bound up in a white headdress, her body swathed in black fabric that merges into the shadows on the floor. Her only visible features are a benign face, gazing into the next world, and a pair of pale hands studded with gold rings, lightly pressed together in supplication.

She is pious. She is rich. She is old. All three qualities stand testament to incredible good fortune – and her own formidable persistence. Pushing seventy, she has far surpassed the thirty-something life expectancy of most of her contemporaries. Repeated childbearing, the desperate thrusting quest for an heir, carried away many of the women she knew at a young age. Beyond the misfortunes of being female and aristocratic – a sorry combination – there were the specific calamities of her own existence. Born into a century of conflict, and deprived of her father while she lay in her crib; she was married at twelve, widowed and in labour at thirteen; her only child born into a plague-stricken war zone. Then two more husbands followed and, like so many women struggling to assert their rights against a predatory ruling regime, she conspired and rebelled, not once or twice but ultimately four times. She would become the mother and grandmother of kings, part of a usurping dynasty whose rivals were legion and whose tragic pattern of infant mortality deprived it of heirs.

Yet none of this experience is conveyed by the painting of the nun-like figure beneath her golden canopy of estate.

She is pious. She is rich. She is old.

But how did she get that way?

THIS PORTRAIT OF MARGARET BEAUFORT, MATRIARCH OF THE Tudor dynasty, hangs in St John's College, Cambridge. At 180 cm tall by 122 cm wide, it is one of the earliest large-scale portraits of a single individual in the country, and the first of its size of any Englishwoman. Other surviving portraits of contemporary women show them alongside men or accompanied by religious figures. But in this portrait Margaret Beaufort is, exceptionally, alone. Her solitariness makes this an utterly misleading image. For in life, Margaret was almost never physically alone – at prayer, she was with a confessor or priest; asleep, she was attended by ladies of the bedchamber or occasionally, one presumes, a husband – and her world was constantly peopled. Her dependents were almost beyond counting: almspeople, servants, solicitors, petitioners, tenants, farmers, retainers. Unlike in her portrait, Margaret would never have been viewed in life divorced from her surroundings, or from other people. Context is key to understanding Margaret Beaufort – to making sense of how she emerged from a period of terrible warfare, against the odds, to assume her unassailable position of authority in the dawn of the Tudor age. Too often, Margaret has been viewed through a lens of exceptionalism – and she was in many ways exceptional. She would not be such an interesting topic for a biography were she not. But emphasising that exceptionalism can be misleading. We need to repopulate her world to find the real woman behind the painting.

This is not the first biography of Margaret, and I must acknowledge my debt to the work of Margaret's historians who came before me. However, one element has been consistently missing from Margaret's story: her womanhood. Not just her status as a woman, but her place in a network of women that extended across generations, counties and ultimately inter-national borders. Historians have been obsessed with Margaret's relationship with her only (male) child – which is fair enough, since Margaret was obsessed with him too – but the Wars of the Roses suffer from this androcentric myopia: we recite the battles that men won or lost, we scroll through the parliamentary rolls that only men wrote. The challenge of locating women in an era when female identity, and especially autonomy, is often concealed and sometimes eradicated hardly needs reciting. Married women were so 'covered' by their husband's existence that they were forbidden to write wills – bequeathing *their* pos-sessions – without said husband's permission.

But the past decades of research by diligent and patient histor-ians have revealed, time and again, the presence of women in our archives. The issue has not been a lack of evidence of women's activities, but a failure to read the sources in a way that revealed them. We can too easily forget that when men rode to war, they did so having discussed their choice with their female relatives, especially the wife who would be most immediately affected by that choice. We can be so befuddled by the intricacies of legal or accounting sources that we do not investigate the subtle ways in which women protected themselves and their loved ones from deprivation. A suit for illegally escheated jointure is less immedi-ately enticing than hearing about someone being hacked to death in battle, but for fifteenth-century survivors the former was likely to be much more important in the long term. We can even some-times forget that, because men were so often absent making war or attending court, it was women who actually did the hard work of running their homes. 'Homes' in this context potentially meant mile after mile of land, servants in the household, tenant farmers working the land, travellers using the roads or bridges they main-tained, merchants supplying their provisions and fellow Christians being baptised, married or buried in the churches they supported.

All of this was understood implicitly by Margaret Beaufort. She was acutely aware of her responsibility as a 'lord' – in her case, a female lord – to her dependents, and she learned that responsibility from the women around her. She passed on her knowledge to her daughter-in-law, her sister-in-law, her granddaughters, her servants, her cousins, distant relatives and friends. It would be ridiculous to insist that Margaret existed in female isolation. She actively chose to live a public life, which meant in many ways a male life. Her senior servants were men, as too were many of the leading influences in her life – but not all. By interpreting Margaret as an anomaly, whether the Perfect Pious Patron or the original Mother-in-Law from Hell, we have done her and her contemporaries a huge disservice. We need to restore Margaret to the world in which she lived. A world that was half female.

Margaret has enabled us to do this because of the extraordinary resources she left, which have been preserved by archivists for five centuries, particularly her household accounts. The years where we lack these accounts – frustratingly, the very years that marked her political ascendancy – are desperately bare by comparison. These sources reveal her personal networks and concerns like nothing else. They humanise a woman who can otherwise appear monumental.

Margaret's was a remarkable life, and it makes a compelling story. But it begins a century before the tree that provided the boards for her portrait was felled, when its branches still stretched to the sky and its leaves turned towards the sun.

It begins with a child born to grief.

Money, Time and Distance

BEFORE DECIMALISATION, ENGLISH MONEY WAS CALCULATED IN pounds, shillings and pence: twelve pennies made up a shilling, and twenty shillings (240 pennies) a pound. Where modern financial equivalents appear for sums, I have used the National Archives' Currency Converter.

Hours and minutes existed in the fifteenth century, but seconds did not. The year was measured in various ways and might begin on Lady Day (25 March), the accession date of the king (22 August for Henry VII), the date of election of the mayor (in London chronicles), and occasionally from New Year's Day (1 January). All my years are dated from 1 January.

Distances have been calculated using Google Maps's 'walking' function. Where possible, I have checked the time taken for individual journeys against contemporary descriptions, particularly in Margaret's household accounts.

Names and Titles

IN THE FIFTEENTH CENTURY, NOBLEMEN AND -WOMEN WERE referred to by their highest-ranking title. Thus, Margaret was the 'Countess of Richmond' or 'my Lady Countess' until she became 'my lady the King's Mother'. Her own mother, Margaret Beauchamp, continued to enjoy the title 'Duchess of Somerset' even after she had married Sir Lionel Welles following the death of her husband the duke, and even though another duchess of Somerset (Eleanor Talbot-Beaufort) had stepped onto the political stage. Inevitably, this can cause confusion, especially in the tumultuous Wars of the Roses when titles passed between different families, depending on the whim of the ruling regime. The earldom of Pembroke, for instance, passed from Jasper Tudor to William Herbert, then back to Jasper, while later Charles Beaufort (aka Charles Somerset) was made Lord Herbert, despite not being a Herbert. Spelling was also inconsistent, with 'Richmond' rendered often as 'Rychemonde' and Elizabeth variously as 'Elysabet', etc.

In naming the historical characters peopling this book, I have therefore prioritised narrative clarity over strict historical accuracy. Thus, Queen Margaret of Anjou is called by her French name, Marguerite, even though this was not used in England during her queenship. Elizabeth Woodville continues to be given her birth name, even though she was at various stages of her life known as 'Lady Grey' or 'the Queen'. This helps distinguish her from her daughter (Princess) Elizabeth of York.

For nominal variety, the various dukes of Somerset are usually referred to by their Christian names (Henry/Edmund/John Beaufort) while the Yorkist princes take their ducal titles

(York/Clarence/Gloucester). In an era where Johns, Henrys, Richards and Margarets are legion, my choices are made for the ease of the reader – with all due apologies to any fifteenth-century aristocrats who are thereby demoted.

I

'MOTHER OF THE KING'S GREAT REBEL AND TRAITOR'

I

'The stain of so great a disgrace'[1]

✳

S he was born on the feast day of St Petronilla the virgin, 31 May
1443. There could be no doubt of the day[2] for the birth was recorded in the family prayer book. Margaret could find the note in
the calendar of saint days, under the flourished *Sanctis* in blue and
red ink, right on the thin, red line that ended the month. '*Natale
domine Margarete...*' it began: 'The birth of lady Margaret, daughter of the illustrious Lord John, duke of Somerset, Anno Domini
1443'. Four lines above, in darker ink, were scrawled: 'Death of
John, duke of Somerset, 27 May 1444'.[3]

Margaret's birth and the death of her father – triumph and
tragedy – were closely interwoven in the revolving calendar of
family anniversaries. The family prayer book did not record the
cause of his death but other contemporaries were less circumspect.
The monks of Crowland, recipients of Beaufort patronage and
well placed to know the truth, reported that John Beaufort had
died by his own hand – a terrible sin for a Christian. Whether suicide or natural causes ended her father's life, there was no denying
that he died in disgrace. His disastrous military endeavours had
damaged his pride and made his dishonour unbearable.

Therefore, even before her first birthday, Margaret Beaufort had
been taught an important lesson in the transience and danger of
fifteenth-century life. Joy was fleeting and honour all too easily destroyed. Even the highest-born were prey to the whims of Fortune.
It was a lesson that Margaret never forgot.

★

LIKE ALL FIFTEENTH-CENTURY PRINCESSES, MARGARET'S SENSE of self-worth was rooted in her family history and it is impossible to understand her world without looking back at her family tree. It was in the footprints of her ancestors that Margaret placed her own halting steps and her bloodline determined how she was treated and which doors opened before her. In a court packed with noble families, the question of precedent – quite literally, who stood nearest the king and queen, who handled their clothes, who entered a room first – were symbols of power and jealously guarded. When precedent was ignored, it was not uncommon for blood to be spilled. Margaret would have been alive to the names and deeds of her ancestors, their tombs and heraldry, the records of births, marriages and deaths. So, while Margaret never knew her father, she would have known a great deal about him. Unfortunately, little of it was good.

John Beaufort was 'a man full of pride and self-importance', wrote the contemporary chronicler Thomas Basin, 'but in reality vain and incapable'.[4] He was also crippled by a misplaced instinct for secretiveness, so anxious to keep his own counsel that he once told his soldiers that 'if the linen shirt on his skin learnt of his intentions, he would burn it'.[5] By the time John Beaufort came to prominence, the Beauforts were already famed for their arrogance and avarice. Like all noble families they sought self-enrichment at the expense of their rivals and jealously guarded their good name and their reputation – that intangible, yet vital, fifteenth-century concept of honour. They had more cause than most for sensitivity to such concerns, for they were little more than royal bastards.

The roots of the Beaufort family lay in the illicit liaison of John of Gaunt, third surviving son of Edward III, and the Lincolnshire governess Katherine Swynford in the last decades of the fourteenth century. Both Katherine and John of Gaunt were already married to other people when their affair began in 1371 but that did not stop them producing a full nursery of children: three boys and a girl. The children were given the honorific surname 'Beaufort', after part of John of Gaunt's estate in northern France. This neatly distinguished them from John's legitimate children, who took their name from his Lancastrian estates.

It was only in 1396, when both his and Katherine's spouses were dead, that John took the unusual step of legitimising their offspring by marrying his mistress. Contemporaries blinked in surprise at the decision, not least because John and Katherine's eldest child was by then twenty-four years old. However, although John of Gaunt persuaded both the Pope and the English parliament to retrospectively legitimise his Beaufort children, the taint of bastardy lingered, especially for their eldest son, Margaret Beaufort's paternal grandfather, John the elder. He had been born before Katherine was widowed and while a nobleman's adultery could be winked at, a woman's was more troubling. Thanks to the timing of his birth, there was an uncomfortable possibility that John the elder was not a Beaufort at all, but a Swynford.[6]

The Beauforts' royal half-blood was another sensitive issue. In 1399, John of Gaunt's legitimate heir – and the Beauforts' half-brother – Henry of Lancaster usurped their cousin, Richard II, of the house of Plantagenet. The unpopular King Richard was starved to death in Pontefract Castle and Henry IV assumed the throne as head of a new Lancastrian dynasty. The Beauforts carefully fostered their loyalty to the new regime, but all the same, their close kinship made their status in the line of succession a delicate one – what if they grasped for the throne as their half-brother had done? To quell any such anxieties, in 1407, at their own request, the Beaufort royal rights were exemplified by parliament. A new clause was inserted into their statute of legitimisation, entitling the Beauforts to inherit from their parents but explicitly denying them 'the dignity of the crown' (*excepta dignitate regali*).[7]

Such circumspection was rewarded by the grateful Henry IV. By the time Margaret's grandfather John the elder died in 1410, he had been created earl of Somerset, royal chamberlain and a chief counsellor of the king. So closely had Lancastrian and Beaufort fortunes entwined that John asked to be buried at Canterbury as close as possible to the tomb of his king. He left his widow, Margaret Holland, to bring up six children, including Margaret's father, John the younger. Capable, intelligent, and a patron of literature and religion, Margaret Holland knew that the best way to provide for her children's future was to maintain the Lancastrian alliance by the primary means at her disposal: marriage. Thus, in 1412 she remarried Thomas, duke of Clarence, younger son of Henry IV and brother of the future Henry V. After decades of uncertainty and illegitimacy, this royal match finally gave the Beauforts just cause for pride.

Out of respect for his wife, Thomas took his stepsons under his wing, and when he was appointed Henry V's second-in-command in Normandy, he chose to take the Beaufort boys with him.* These were the glory days of the Hundred Years War and a good time for a young nobleman like John – then only fifteen – to test his military worth. In 1415, Henry V had won a momentous victory at the Battle of Agincourt, but there was little glorious about the campaigns that Thomas and the Beauforts endured. In 1418–19, Henry V laid siege to Normandy's capital, Rouen, for six months. As supplies in the city ran out, the citizens began to kill and eat their own pets: first horses and dogs, and eventually any rats or cats they could lay their hands on. In desperation, the garrison ejected all their women, children, sick and elderly, hoping that Henry V would let them seek refuge elsewhere. But Henry was not inclined to show mercy. The Rouennais citizens were forbidden to pass the English encampment, and cowered in the sodden ditches, slowly starving to death. The English besiegers fared little better. As autumn advanced towards winter, conditions were persistently wet and cold. John's eldest brother, Henry Beaufort, died on 25 November. When the English finally took Rouen on 19 January 1419, its streets were strewn with the dead and dying.[8]

John managed to escape these horrors, arriving in Rouen in late 1419 just in time to enjoy Christmas festivities with the royal court. That winter he and his younger brothers, Thomas and Edmund Beaufort, were knighted by Henry V himself. As the adolescent Beauforts stood proud in their red silken mantles before the

---

* The duchy of Normandy in what is now northern France was contested between the kings of France and England.

king, they shared in the chivalric ideal of warfare.[9] But this would be the highpoint of John Beaufort's military experience.

What young warrior lords in training like John really sought was not a siege but a battle in the open, like Henry V had won at Agincourt. The English had gained a reputation for military prowess in the field and it was blithely assumed that they could triumph in any pitched battle with the French. On 22 March 1421, they had their wish. In a boggy marshland close to Baugé, in what is now the Pays de la Loire, John Beaufort and his stepfather, Thomas, intercepted a Franco-Scottish force and attempted to bar their route through Anjou. Not realising – or unconcerned by – the numerical disadvantage of his own forces, Thomas ignored his captains' advice and launched a headlong assault on the enemy. His army was annihilated by Scottish archers and Thomas himself killed. It was the first time an English army had been defeated in battle in France for a generation. The seventeen-year-old John Beaufort was dragged from the battlefield into French captivity.

Margaret's father had the unfortunate distinction of being the most valuable English prisoner of war in French control, and in the following years was reduced to the status of pawn in an international game of chess. His younger brother, Thomas, taken hostage in the same battle, was ransomed and released by 1430, but John remained in captivity for seventeen years – the longest imprisonment of any English nobleman in the entire Hundred Years War. His gaoler was Marie, duchess of Bourbon, whose own husband had been captured by the English at Agincourt and – ominously for John – died still an English prisoner twenty years later in 1434. Noble captives were treated well, kept under a form of house arrest as guests of their captors, and John had sufficient liberty to father a child, Tacyn, during his imprisonment. But he was a prisoner nonetheless and, as the years gnawed away his youth and his prospects, his position became intolerable. Despite the unfailing efforts of his mother and kinsmen, John began to despair of ever being freed. In 1427, six years into his captivity, he wrote to the English parliament of his sufferings and pleaded with them to secure his liberty. He was to remain a prisoner for another decade.[10]

It was late summer 1438 before John's release was finally

secured. His ransom was set at £24,000, the entire value of his and
his mother's inheritance combined.[11] He returned to England as a
ghost from a lost age of military optimism, with a bastard daughter, crippling debts and a bitter sense of grievance against a world
that had robbed him of twenty years of opportunity. He found
England much changed. In 1422, John's cousin Henry V had died of
dysentery, contracted during a siege of the northern French fortress
of Meaux. For the past sixteen years, England had been ruled by
a child: Henry's son, Henry VI, who had inherited the thrones of
England and France before his first birthday. By the time of John's
return, the young king was finally emerging from his minority and
beginning to rule for himself, but there was little indication that
he would become the towering warrior his father had been. The
devout and virginal Henry VI had an almost pathological fear of
conflict and promoted a peace policy that was completely at odds
with the regime under which John Beaufort had grown up. Henry
and his councillors reluctantly realised that war for the French
crown could no longer be sustained. The English treasury was
empty and the expense of campaigning on multiple fronts had
ground the English commons into disobedience and lawlessness.

The dynamics of the Beaufort family had also changed during
John's exile. He was now eclipsed by his last surviving brother,
Edmund.* Edmund Beaufort was a handsome military hero who
once had a short-lived romance with Henry V's widow, Catherine
of Valois. He was now married to the widowed heiress Eleanor
Beauchamp, daughter of the earl of Warwick. By contrast, John's
estate was so encumbered by his ransom that the only respectable bride he could persuade into marriage was a knight's widow
who already had six children: Eleanor's distant relative Margaret
Beauchamp of Bletsoe in Bedfordshire.† Margaret Beauchamp's
first husband, Oliver St John, had died in France in 1437, but while
her fortune may have been lacking, her strong personality was
more than a match for her husband. She took pride in her noble

* Their only other brother, Thomas Beaufort, had died at the siege of Louviers in
1431.
† Through Margaret's West Country relations she had connections to John's
powerful uncle Cardinal Beaufort and also, distantly, to the Beauchamp earls of
Warwick.

ancestry, and her experience of marriage and widowhood had made her a capable administrator with a keen sense of her rights at law. Her proven ability to bear children also gave John hope that he could promptly sire a legitimate heir of his own.[12] Together, John and Margaret set about stamping their authority on John's estates, so zealously that they immediately enflamed local tensions. John's neighbour, the Abbot of Crowland, lamented that no sooner was John back in the country than he was violently asserting his right to the manor of Market Deeping, which neighboured his wife's estates, levying illicit tolls, blocking roads and rustling cattle in order to undermine the abbot's local power.[13]

But, no matter how ruthlessly John harangued his neighbours, he could not wring enough money from his lands to make a dint in the debts he owed for his ransom. Not even close. When his mother died in 1439, she left him a substantial inheritance, but still he was humiliatingly poor. And, without money, his high birth counted for nothing. For impoverished noblemen in John's position there was really only one option. A mere five years after his release, he was forced to go to war again.

By 1443, very few lords remained willing to front the expense, effort and physical danger of long campaigns in France. Sensing an opportunity, John Beaufort offered to command a royal army himself – but demanded a high price for his services. He insisted on being promoted from an earl to a duke – the highest rank below prince – with accompanying lands worth 600 marks to maintain his estate.* He also haughtily demanded a command independent of the existing governor of English-held Normandy and France, Richard, duke of York, and the governments of the continental territories of Anjou and Maine, even though Maine had already been granted to his brother Edmund. There was some justification for John's high-handedness. For while he was negotiating with the crown, his wife Margaret Beauchamp was preparing to give birth to their first child. It was an anxious time for the prospective parents. Margaret Beauchamp had already lost one husband to the French wars and John knew well the bitter consequences of

---

* John had originally demanded lands worth 1,000 marks, but was bargained down.

imprisonment. Thus, the last demands he made of King Henry VI were to protect his wife and children in the event he did not return. John's illegitimate daughter Tacyn, who was probably living under Margaret Beauchamp's care by this point, was made a denizen of England, enabling her to inherit some of John's English lands. The bulk of his inheritance, however, John sought to safeguard for his and Margaret's legitimate, unborn child.[14] The couple feared that, if John died, his heir would become royal property, their wardship sold to whoever happened to be in favour at court. So, John insisted that in the event of his death the 'keeping' of his heir would be granted to his wife Margaret 'since she should by nature have [the child] in more tenderness than any other creature'. The soft-hearted Henry VI agreed, since 'it should be to her too great an heaviness, the lack of her husband and also of her said issue'.[15] Indeed, Henry agreed to every single one of John's demands. Confident he had done everything possible to protect Margaret and their children, John readied himself to take ship to France that summer.

But something was wrong. As artillery and ordnance were carried along the Thames towards the South Downs, where arms were stockpiled to ferry across to Cherbourg, John Beaufort failed to appear. Early in 1443 he had been sufficiently unwell – 'diseased and not in bodily health' – that the king had dispatched councillors to investigate if he was up to the task of commanding an army.[16] John had persuaded Henry of his capability, but, as the day of his departure neared, he prevaricated and made excuses, absenting himself from one muster after another. Before his army had even left the country there were rumours of financial malpractice and military misconduct.

It was an unusually hot summer and tempers flared as the king and his council tired of Beaufort's excuses. Finally, on 9 July, Henry VI sent an uncharacteristically acerbic last message to John: the king 'marvelleth greatly', he wrote, 'and not without cause the long abode of his said cousin on this side the sea... to the king's full great hurt, harm and charge'. Now he chastised John, 'all excusions ceasing', to lead his army to France within a fortnight or face extreme royal displeasure.[17]

In the midst of these anxieties, John's heir was born on 31 May 1443, possibly at Corfe Castle.[18] No doubt to his disappointment, it was a girl. Daughters had an important place in noble powerplay due to their marriage potential, but they carried their estates to their husbands, away from the direct line of their fathers. Instead of a third generation of proud 'John Beauforts', John had to make do with another Margaret, no doubt named for John's wife and mother. It must have been hoped that, in the fullness of time, she would be supplanted by a male heir. In August, John finally left for France, swearing 'that he would do great and marvellous things'.[19] It was a promise he could not keep.

IN THE NEW YEAR OF 1444, JOHN BEAUFORT RETURNED TO his family in the West Country, a ruined man. The disorder and ineptitude that had characterised John's preparations in England had worsened after he crossed the Channel. His army meandered through Anjou and Maine, apparently unaware of exactly what their plan of attack was. Some suspected that John's notorious secrecy concealed the fact that he really had no plan at all. This was not quite fair: his intention was clearly to force the French to meet his army in battle, but as autumn turned to winter, his bored soldiers began ravaging the countryside. John's sole military success was the seizure of the town of La Guerche, which was technically within the territory of England's ally the Duke of Brittany, and therefore incited a major diplomatic incident. A fruitless siege of the neighbouring town of Pouancé was abandoned and, by December 1443, John admitted defeat and marched his army back to England, apparently trusting to the king's gentle nature to forgive him for such a futile and costly campaign.

John had hoped that this military campaign would restore his fortunes but instead he was banished from court, a figure of mockery and derision. There were even whispers that he would be charged with treason.[20] The ill health from which he had suffered a year earlier returned. It was not uncommon for noblemen confronted with public falls from grace to suffer sudden, terminal declines, and the chronicler Thomas Basin believed this was what ailed John: 'He took such chagrin at [his disgrace], that his petulance and pride could not support such criticisms and he fell sick.'[21] On 27 May 1444, four days before his daughter Margaret's first birthday, John Beaufort died.

To die in political disgrace was bad enough, but rumours soon circulated that John had taken his own life. The chronicler of Crowland Abbey, which had so recently endured John's mercenary attentions, reported:

> The noble heart of a man of such high rank... was moved to extreme indignation, and being unable to bear the stain of so great a disgrace, he accelerated his death by putting an end to his existence, it is generally said; preferring thus to cut short his sorrow, rather than pass a life of misery, laboring under so disgraceful a charge.[22]

If John had taken his own life, he would have been committing a felony. To kill yourself was to defy God's will; suicide was believed to have been the fate of the biblical arch-villains Judas and Herod, who languished in Hell. The goods of a suicide were confiscated under English law, including, grimly, the tool of suicide itself, but, most alarmingly for Christians, suicides were denied the rites and burial place of the Church.[23]

If John had indeed hastened his end, his family must have concealed the fact, for he received burial in Wimborne Minster in Dorset, where a priest was paid £10 for two days of prayers for his soul. A small commemorative window was erected there in his honour.[24] Decades later, Margaret founded a chantry chapel and grammar school at Wimborne in memory of her parents. Perhaps, after all, the rumours of her father's suicide were no more than that. What was certain was that his surviving family would suffer from his death. When John died, the dowager duchess of Somerset was pregnant again and Margaret was still a baby. They both now faced an uncertain future.

2

'Right studious she was in books'[1]

✳

It takes a village to raise a child, it is said, and it took a household staff to raise a noble child in the fifteenth century. As Margaret Beaufort lay swaddled in her cradle at John's family seat in the West Country – perhaps Corfe Castle, or Wimborne Minster – she was attended not merely by her mother, the dowager duchess of Somerset, but by an entourage of servants and kinfolk. Her nursery was staffed with nurses and rockers, supervised by an older, respectable gentlewoman who would eventually become Margaret's governess. She was probably fed by a wet nurse, for, although it was not unknown for noblewomen to breastfeed their own children, it was unusual. In the corridors beyond were the myriad servants and retainers of the dowager duchess, their loyalties proudly displayed in the Beaufort livery and badges on their clothing. Such outward expressions of noble ties had become common and, where rivalries existed between neighbouring lords or ladies, these signs of allegiance could incite violence.

When Margaret's father died, her mother had eight children to provide for, including Tacyn, and was pregnant with a ninth. Her six St John children were probably still unmarried, although the eldest, Edith and John, were around fifteen years older than Margaret and therefore an appropriate age to consider betrothal. Tacyn was soon married, to the dowager duchess's neighbour Reginald Grey, Baron Grey de Wilton.[2] The younger children, Mary, Elizabeth, Margaret* and Oliver, were still small enough to grow up alongside Margaret in her nursery. With so many dependents, Margaret's mother could not afford to wallow when she lost her second husband. When a nobleman died out of favour, courtiers moved swiftly to pick at the spoils of his estate, and John's was a substantial prize. At the time of his death, his inheritance and royal grants made his combined wealth over £2,600.† The majority of John's estate passed directly to Margaret as his heir or to her mother as dower, but since John had no surviving son, the Beaufort patrimony passed to his brother Edmund. Thus, Corfe Castle and the rich Surrey manors of Woking and Sutton were lost. The dowager duchess of Somerset had to pack up her household and retrench.[3] Worse, the hard-won endowments that John had gained in return for his military service reverted to the crown, becoming available to anyone who could bend the king's ear. Within days there was a flurry of royal grants and the late duke's acquisitions, from a Kendal lordship to a Lincolnshire meadow, disappeared with a stroke of the royal pen.[4]

But the biggest prize of all for courtiers on the make was Margaret Beaufort herself. At John's death, she too became a royal possession and Henry VI did not uphold John's wishes. On Margaret's first birthday, only four days after her father's death, control over her inheritance and her marriage were granted to the king's chief counsellor, William de la Pole, earl of Suffolk. On 8 June 1444, Henry further promised William that his claims on Margaret's wardship would not be prejudiced even if the widowed duchess of Somerset gave birth to a living child. As it transpired, this grant was unnecessary. We never hear any more of the dowager duchess of Somerset's pregnancy, and whether it ended in miscarriage or stillbirth is uncertain.[5] For now, at least, the dowager duchess was allowed one kindness: her infant daughter was permitted to live with her, rather than being removed into William de la Pole's household. But, whenever William chose to exercise

---

* Margaret Beaufort did indeed have a half-sister called Margaret, as well as a mother, grandmother and cousin.
† More than £1,670,000 in modern terms.

his rights over Margaret, she could be taken from her mother and married off as he saw fit.

Instead of on the lands of her Beaufort predecessors, Margaret would grow up between two manors closely connected with her female relatives: the Bletsoe estate of her mother's Beauchamp forebears in Bedfordshire and Maxey Castle, the fenland fortress in which her grandmother Margaret Holland had lived during her second marriage and widowhood. These maternal inheritances exerted an abiding influence over Margaret, giving her a much-needed sense of stability. Into the Book of Hours she inherited from her mother, which became one of her most treasured possessions, she transcribed the details of her mother's family, tracing it all the way back to her Grandison forebears who had lived at Bletsoe in the early fourteenth century.[6] Bletsoe Castle displayed some of Margaret's fine embroidery work, emblazoned with the arms of her St John half-siblings, long after Margaret herself had died.[7] Here and there, Margaret might catch sight of ghosts from her father's life in a series of tapestries he had owned, including – with mocking irony – one depicting an idealised celebration of military endeavours in France.[8] But she would have had practically no memory of her father and certainly none of his West Country estates.

Like many noblewomen, Margaret grew up with a constantly evolving family circle. Early marriage, widowhood and remarriage were common, and created a patchwork identity of different kinships, estates and retainers from each phase of women's lives. Sometimes bonds were created between mistress and servant, or stepmother and stepchild, that survived decades of turbulence, while at other times a marriage was fleeting, its ties swiftly severed. The one presence in a noblewoman's life that was not constant was her husband. As the early fifteenth-century French author Christine de Pizan noted, a nobleman spent 'the least possible time at his manors and his own estates, for his duties are to bear arms, to attend the court of his prince and to travel'. During these frequent absences, it was up to his wife to 'take his place'.[9] As a result, faithful servants might prove a more permanent feature of noble-women's lives than their spouses.

In 1447, a whole new branch was added to Margaret's family tree when her mother married Lionel, Lord Welles, a Lincolnshire knight with a nineteen-year-old son, Richard.[10] The new couple produced another half-sibling for Margaret: John Welles, who was at least four years her junior and probably shared Margaret's nursery and servants. Boys grew up alongside their sisters until they turned seven, at which point the distinction between the sexes was firmly enforced: boys were handed over to the care of men to learn Latin and martial skills, girls left to whatever informal education their guardians were willing to bestow on them. In the fifteenth century, even at the highest levels of society, education was fundamentally pragmatic.

Materially, Margaret was far more fortunate than any of her half-siblings, for she would eventually inherit an extensive estate from her father, but as a noblewoman rather than a nobleman, her opportunity to exploit that good fortune was limited. The only careers open to her were nun or wife, which were precisely the roles into which her half-sisters fell: all but one married, the other entered a convent.* When Margaret married – and she *would* marry; there never seems to have been any suggestion that she might follow her big sister into the Church – her estate would become the property of her husband, to do with as he thought best. Special arrangements might be made as part of marriage negotiations for a 'jointure' – an estate held jointly by husband and wife – but otherwise a wife had to wait until her husband's death to hold anything independently.[11]

The inferior status of women, even noblewomen, to men was drummed into them from infancy and the pervasive idea that women were mentally and physically weaker legitimised their exclusion from public office. They could not sit in either houses in parliament, they could not serve on juries and there had never been a queen regnant of England.† Margaret was a keen student of religious matters and medicine. She would have understood that a man was the head of a household, and a husband the master of his wife. But she also grew up watching her mother, as first widow

---

* Margaret's half-sister Margaret St John became Abbess of Shaftesbury.
† Although the Empress Matilda had tried in the 1100s.

and then wife, acting in the role of a lord, overseeing vast estates whose lands needed to be profitable and peaceful – and which could only be maintained in that state by constant exertion on the part of the lady of the manor.[12] Even before her husband left for France, the duchess of Somerset had proven the equal of her husband in unscrupulous land acquisition: she and John illegally acquired a range of southern manors without royal licence, in collusion with her cousin John Stourton. After her husband's death, in 1445, the dowager duchess belatedly sued for a royal pardon. The chronicler at Crowland Abbey (nine miles from the duchess's principal seat, Maxey Castle) observed how carefully the dowager duchess oversaw her rights in the locality. She held, as dower land, the same marshland around Market Deeping that had caused the Abbot of Crowland such consternation in the past, and set about 'exacting amercements [fines] for trespasses, levying for repairs of the embankments, and taking poundage* for animals'.[13]

Her actions were not purely mercenary. To protect her family, the dowager duchess had to safeguard their landed interests, for land was the source of noble wealth and honour. It provided the family with rents from tenants, who tilled the soil and tended livestock, tolls from the travellers using her roads, fines arising from the oversight of local justice and myriad other financial extractions like those inflicted on Market Deeping. A title such as 'duke' or 'duchess' was jealously sought, but it meant nothing if you could not afford servants, retainers and lavish displays of hospitality, all of which had to be paid for from the profits of your lands.

In time, Margaret would have to protect her inheritance for herself, so she would need to learn to be a shrewd administrator like her mother. Her education probably began at her mother's knee, tracing words across the pages of a primer or prayer book with her finger. Once she had mastered the skill of reading, she could have been taught religion, writing and languages by a priest or clerk of the household, or she may have shared a tutor in these subjects with her half-siblings. According to her confessor, writing sixty

---

* A charge for impounding stray animals. John Beaufort had commissioned his retainers to drive stray cattle into Deeping, so that he could claim the poundage fee that resulted.

years later in 1509, Margaret was a quick-witted, studious child with a good memory, 'of singular wisdom far surpassing the common rate of women'.[14] She could read and write in both French and English, and became proficient enough to translate French works herself. She amassed a large library of French and English texts on religion, history and chivalric romance – a testament to her schooling. Yet, despite her evident linguistic ability, it was not thought worthwhile to teach her Latin. She understood some Church Latin – the language in which the Mass and all religious ceremony was conducted – but the complexity of the language was beyond her.[15]

As it was, Margaret's education surpassed what some of her contemporaries believed was suitable for a girl. Certain authors argued that girls should not read or write at all.[16] Far more important was for a noblewoman to know how to behave properly. Margaret had a good exemplar in the dowager duchess, for 'her mother was... right noble as well in manners as in blood'.[17] Margaret needed to learn to be dutiful and submissive, restrained in voice and expression, in eating and drinking, and even in where her gaze fell.[18] Chastity was the cardinal virtue for girls, and looking men in the eye, or taking their hand, was considered disturbingly provocative. If Margaret stepped out of line, she would be chastised, physically if necessary.

But, despite this schooling in the appearance of docility, Margaret's education was ultimately an apprenticeship in female lordship. Even where noblewomen were not formally educated, they still needed considerable experience and knowledge to administer their lands. Christine de Pizan wrote an extensive list of recommended areas of knowledge for the ideal noblewoman. She:

> should be well informed... about the legal aspects and local customs [of her lands]... and what financial resources she has and can find... making herself familiar with the accounts... to be a very good manager of the estate and to know all the work on the land and at what time and in which season one ought to perform what operations.[19]

If her estate was threatened by a rival lord, it might even be necessary for a noblewoman 'to know how to use weapons and be familiar with everything that pertains to them, so that she may be ready to command her men if the need arises. She should know how to launch an attack or to defend against one'.[20] Christine's advice ended with a salutary coda: by learning these skills in 'her husband's lifetime… if she is left a widow she will not be found ignorant of the state of her affairs, even if everyone is trying to take advantage of her and grab her inheritance'.[21] This was a lesson that the twice-widowed duchess of Somerset could certainly impart to her daughter.

In short, Margaret's childhood and education were far from extraordinary and there was little to suggest Margaret's life would be exceptional. True, there was the distant legacy of her Lancastrian royal blood, but that was now three generations removed and no more legitimate than it had ever been. Nonetheless, Margaret's relation to King Henry was to entwine her fate with high politics from an early stage. As she neared her seventh birthday, William de la Pole finally acted on his rights as Margaret's guardian: he had decided she must marry.

MARGARET'S MARRIAGE TO JOHN DE LA POLE, ONLY CHILD OF THE newly minted duke of Suffolk,* was agreed as snowdrops breached the frosted earth and England was mired in crisis. It was the beginning of 1450 and for months the rumblings of political discord had disturbed even the distant estates of Margaret's family. An uneasy truce between England and France was shattered in spring 1449, when the French invaded Normandy. It took little over a year for the entire duchy to submit to French control. At Maxey Castle, Margaret and her family had a personal investment in these reversals as the lieutenant-governor of France and Normandy was Margaret's uncle Edmund Beaufort. He, his wife, Eleanor, and their children were living in Rouen at the time and the ignominy of

---

* William de la Pole was raised to the dukedom of Suffolk in 1448.

surrender stalked the family as they fled to England, once again dragging the Beaufort reputation into the mire. Few could have understood their plight better than the household at Maxey.

Fortunately for Edmund, but less so for Margaret, English outrage at the loss of Normandy soon found another target: Henry's chief adviser, and the man about to become Margaret's father-in-law, William de la Pole. Just as Margaret's marriage to John de la Pole was being finalised, William was arrested on charges of treason. Thus, Margaret was united to a family on the verge of destruction. The dowager duchess had spent all of Margaret's life fighting the moment she would lose her daughter, but she now faced a formidable opponent in John de la Pole's mother, Alice. Born Alice Chaucer – a granddaughter of the celebrated poet – the duchess of Suffolk and her husband were close to the king and queen. Indeed, the extent of Alice's influence over Henry VI led to her being singled out in the House of Commons as a malign force who must be banished from court.[22] (In a rare assertion of the royal will, Henry VI insisted Alice remain.) Like the dowager duchess, Alice was fiercely protective of her heir – perhaps even more so, for John de la Pole was Alice's only child. When William was arrested in 1450, Alice hurried to insulate herself and her son from the effects of his downfall. She knew that, if William died, she would lose control of her child, and if he died a condemned traitor all his possessions would be forfeited to the crown, including Margaret's lucrative wardship. Margaret was married to John de la Pole so that he and his mother could keep control of Margaret's wealth even if William was killed. The girl herself was of little consequence.

It was a tragic irony, then, that the de la Poles' move to secure the Beaufort inheritance inadvertently hammered another nail into William's coffin. In popular memory, the Beauforts were still blood royal, whatever some act of parliament forty years ago said about it, and in 1450 that royal claim was doubly dangerous. Henry VI had been married for six years to the French princess, Marguerite of Anjou, but their union had produced no children. There were already rumours that the queen must be infertile. Inevitably, eyes cast around the noble families of England for rival claims to the succession. By marrying his only son to the Beaufort heiress at such a time, it seemed William de la Pole was trying to steal a crown. Alongside his other alleged treasons, this enraged the Commons, who demanded death and would not be denied. Henry attempted to send William into exile to save his life, but, as de la Pole set sail on 2 May 1450, he was ambushed by an English vessel and butchered: his fine robes stripped from his flesh, his head struck from his body and the grisly remains thrown ashore on Dover sands. It was a horrifying way for Margaret's wardship to end, but it probably saved her from absorption into the de la Pole clan.

As William's dismembered corpse was escorted back to his heartbroken family, Margaret was probably still in her mother's care. Although legally Margaret was bound to the son of William and Alice de la Pole, physically she remained with her mother. She thus avoided witnessing William's downfall at first hand, but she could hardly fail to learn the disturbing details of it. It must have made a fearful impression, and, even in one so young, heightened Margaret's awareness of the dangerous potential of her thin royal blood.

3

'By whom she was made mother'[1]

✳

A fateful change in Margaret's circumstances began with a
royal summons at Shrovetide 1453. King Henry wished to
meet his Beaufort cousin. Bidding farewell to her half-siblings
in the Fenlands, Margaret set out, for the first time in her life,
for London. Ever attentive, her mother accompanied her. As she
entered through the gates of the capital, Margaret would have
found a city beyond anything she had ever encountered – far
louder and more odorous than any of her local market towns.
The city streets closed tight around its 60,000 inhabitants, the
cramped and looming tenements jostling against one another as
pigs squealed along the cramped and dirty streets.[2] The city walls
were banked high with rubbish, and the creeks and brooks that
trickled through them were clogged with the natural outcome of
centuries of human and animal settlement. To Margaret's ears,
even the Londoners' speech would have been strange. Alongside
the dialect spoken by the locals, she would have heard more alien
tongues. 'The ships of all nations' docked here, as one contemporary visitor recorded, and migrant merchants and traders from
Italy, Germany, France, the Low Countries and beyond had settled
inside the city walls.[3]

Margaret and her mother moved into the dowager duchess's
townhouse, Le Ryall, between Blackfriars and St Paul's Cathedral,
on the western limits of the city. There, a short walk south of
St Paul's Cross, where preachers cried messages of salvation and
heretics stood half-naked clutching bundles of firewood, Margaret

prepared herself to meet the king. Henry VI had ruled for thirty-one years, but many deemed him as innocent and ineffective a monarch as he had been on the day he took the throne. His major failing was a desire to please everyone – a cardinal sin in a medieval king. Henry was so ill-equipped to control his subjects that he granted almost anything asked of him. On one notorious occasion, as perhaps Margaret had heard from her Beaufort and Stourton cousins in the West Country, Henry had granted the stewardship of the duchy of Cornwall to two men at the same time, simply because they both asked for it.* The result was a civil war that still shattered the peace two decades later.

Henry's tendency to inattentive generosity would have been visible to Margaret as soon as she and her mother entered the precinct of the royal court. It was so bloated that it now numbered into the high hundreds and every one of those mouths must be fed, lodged and kept warm at royal expense. This was bad enough when the court resided in its Thameside palaces, but when it spilled out into the countryside it could be crippling. Communities barely surviving after decades of economic crisis found their storehouses ransacked by royal purveyors. Common thieves dressed up as purveyors – or sometimes as royal musicians – to steal grain from innocent villagers, and even the king's kitchens were not safe from the depredations of chancers who made off with pewterware and beeswax candles.

Parliament had repeatedly tried to persuade Henry to reduce the size of his court, but the king either would not or could not. He did not seem to realise the danger in which he placed his regime by his inattention, even after the butchery inflicted on William de la Pole and several other leading counsellors in 1450. Those around Henry, however, including his queen, Marguerite, were alive to the danger. They knew that Henry needed direction so, with Queen Marguerite's encouragement, into this vacuum of central authority stepped Margaret's uncle Edmund Beaufort.

Charming, handsome and – now in his forties – old enough to act as a mentor to Henry, Edmund was forgiven for the loss

---

* The men were William Bonville and Thomas Courtenay, earl of Devon.

of Normandy with extraordinary haste by a king in dire need of guidance. Many voices grumbled at Edmund's undue elevation, the loudest of them a fellow veteran of the French wars, Richard, duke of York. The proud and bellicose York felt his honour had been tainted by Edmund's hasty capitulation to the French, which had forced York to surrender his own Norman fortresses. Even worse, York was offended that Edmund was promoted above him. It was York's belief that, as a senior member of the extended royal family – indeed, arguably one whose line had a better claim to the throne than the Lancastrians[*] – he ought to be serving as chief adviser, not the inferior Edmund Beaufort.[†]

York's griping fomented tensions within the court, especially once he took up the call for household reforms and thus won a considerable body of support in the Commons. In 1452, his competition with Edmund almost spilled over into open warfare at Dartford, when York attempted, unsuccessfully, to remove Beaufort by force. Yet still Henry would not listen to York's complaints. Henry needed gentle guidance by charismatic figures, and York was simply too loud and aggressive to be his chief counsellor.

How much these tensions were revealed to Margaret as she visited the royal court in 1453 is unclear, but her audience with the king left a profound impression on her. The naïve Henry VI, with his open, full-moon face and large heart, found children considerably easier company than his demanding courtiers, and Margaret was won over by him. She may have been impressed by his deeply held piety, or perhaps, seeing how beset he was on all sides, she just felt sorry for him. Whatever the cause, she would retain her high opinion of Henry as a religious example for the rest of her life.

Similarly impressed by his interview with Margaret, Henry expressed his affection with a lavish present, granting his 'right dear and right well-beloved cousin Margaret' a hundred marks[‡]

---

[*] York was descended from the second son of Edward III, whereas Henry was a descendant of Edward III's *third* son. Unfortunately for York, his claim came through a woman and was therefore seen as inferior to Henry's.
[†] As duke of Somerset, Beaufort's title was lower than York's in the line of noble precedence.
[‡] Almost £43,000 in modern terms.

for new clothing.[4] He also made Margaret a more questionable gift: a new husband. During her stay in London, Margaret was informed that the king intended to break her union with John de la Pole and marry her instead to Henry's half-brother, Edmund Tudor. In the meantime, Edmund would be appointed Margaret's co-guardian along with his brother Jasper, supplanting the de la Poles. This startling change was communicated to both Margaret and her mother, and, although their permission was not required, technically Margaret still had to give her consent for any wedding to be valid.

For the adults surrounding Margaret, this marriage was a clear-cut political decision, but for the serious-minded nine-year-old it was a deeply personal matter. Young as she was, she baulked at her anticipated future being summarily up-ended without her own voice being heard. Demonstrating the strong-willed pragmatism she had learned from her mother, and perhaps a little of that famed Beaufort pride, Margaret insisted that before consenting to the marriage she must spend the night thinking it over, in quiet prayer. The pious King Henry could hardly refuse.

Remarkably, we have surviving testimonial for this night when Margaret hovered between two potential futures, for in later life she would 'tell [the story] many a time'.[5] One of those who heard it wrote down Margaret's memory of events:

> Doubtful in her mind what she were best to do, [Margaret] asked counsel of an old gentlewoman whom she much loved and trusted, which did advise her to commend herself to St Nicholas, the patron and helper of all true maidens and to beseech him to put in her mind what she were best to do.[6]

The advice of this 'old gentlewoman' – perhaps Margaret's governess – to pray to St Nicholas was apt. Nicholas was the patron saint of children, and closely associated with King Henry, who had been born on St Nicholas's feast day (6 December).

Margaret had a considerable change to contemplate. Unlike John de la Pole, Edmund Tudor was a grown man, at least twenty, although his precise date of birth was shrouded in secrecy because of its unusual circumstances. Edmund and King Henry shared a mother: Catherine de Valois, dowager queen of Henry V and a French princess in her own right. But Edmund's father was Catherine's Welsh servant Owain ap Maredudd ap Tudur – or, as the English called him, Owen Tudor. Legend told that Catherine fell in love with Owen after seeing him swim naked, or perhaps after he fell into her lap at a dance. Either way, the attraction between them bore fruit, and by the time of Catherine's death in 1437 there were four Tudor children, of whom Edmund was the eldest. A daughter died young, a son called Owen entered the Church, but Edmund and his brother Jasper were both adopted by King Henry. Henry was a diligent protector of his half-siblings, and of their father. To protect his brothers from the distractions of court, Henry placed Edmund and Jasper in the household of William de la Pole's sister Katherine, abbess of Barking, who was paid £50 for their maintenance. Only when they reached their twenties in January 1453 were the Tudors brought back to court, and ennobled as the earls of Richmond and Pembroke.[7]

Edmund's French royal blood gave him no right to the English throne. But by marrying into Margaret's Beaufort claim, there was the tantalising prospect that should Henry's marriage continue to be childless, Edmund might be able to assert his right to succeed as dual ruler of England and France. Any questionable legitimacy could be overcome by an appeal to parliament and the Pope. At the very least, Edmund and Margaret, and especially any offspring they produced, would have a place in the line of English succession, offering an alternative to the current heir apparent: Henry's bête noire, and Edmund Beaufort's outright nemesis, Richard, duke of York. This marriage, then, had considerable advantages for Henry, Edmund Beaufort and Edmund Tudor. But what would it bring Margaret, besides deeper extrication in the political machinations of her kin?

As Margaret 'lay in prayer' that night, 'whether sleeping or waking she could not be sure', 'a marvellous thing' happened: 'about four o'clock in the morning one appeared unto her arrayed like a bishop and naming unto her Edmund [to] take him unto her husband'.[8] This spectral figure, Margaret believed, was St Nicholas, who in life had been bishop of Myra in Turkey. She had prayed for guidance, and it had come: Margaret informed the king that she consented to marry Edmund. By the end of March 1453, her union with John de la Pole was annulled.[9] She had two years to prepare herself to leave her family and begin a new life. Then, when she reached the age of twelve, she would marry Edmund Tudor.

MARRIAGE FOR THE NOBLY BORN LIKE MARGARET WAS synonymous with crisp, pure white. Not the white of a bridal gown – women tended to wear their finest clothing for their wedding, regardless of colour. Instead, it was the white of fresh linen assembled for the marital household. Linen tablecloths, sweetened with herbs, shaken out and spread neatly across trestle tables in the great hall for the wedding feast; napkins draped over shoulders as celebratory wine and spiced sweetmeats were consumed; sheets laid beneath silken coverlets on the marriage bed, and into which the bride and groom slipped on their wedding night. But, for brides, marriage was also associated with blood: consummation was one of two necessary acts to cement a marriage. The other was consent. On 31 May 1455, Margaret turned twelve years old – the age of consent for girls.* Thus, she could legally assent to her marriage, and was deemed old enough to consummate it.

Ten days before that pivotal date in Margaret's life, blood had splattered the walls and run through the streets of the market town of St Albans in the first real battle between Lancaster and York. The years between Margaret's betrothal and her marriage to Edmund Tudor had brought terrible upheavals to her family and the kingdom. In summer 1453, the last English army campaigning in France had been annihilated at Castillon in Gascony. The sexagenarian commander of the English force, a brother-in-law of Edmund Beaufort, was butchered so brutally in the fighting that his herald could only identify his corpse by feeling inside his mouth for a missing tooth. This battle was, effectively, the end of

---

* For boys, the age of consent was fourteen.

the Hundred Years War, and led to the complete collapse of English rule in Gascony. Henry VI's once vast French realm was reduced to a narrow pale of flatland around Calais.[10] Henry's exhausted mind could not withstand news of his loss and he 'suddenly was taken and smitten with a frenzy and his wit and reason withdrawn'.[11] For almost a year and a half, Henry was incapable not only of the business of government, but of the most rudimentary self-care. He was reduced to puppet-like impotency, unable to walk, talk or recognise those around him. He simply sat, head bowed, as government collapsed into chaos. As senior nobleman of the blood royal, the duke of York manoeuvred successfully to be named Protector – effective ruler during Henry's sickness – while Marguerite of Anjou was understandably distracted by the imminent birth of her first child. It was a sign of how complete Henry's mental collapse was that the arrival of this long-awaited Lancastrian heir in October 1453 went completely unnoticed by him.

Yet, disruptive as Henry's mental breakdown was to government, his apparent recovery at Christmas 1454 was far more damaging. His clumsy attempts to restore Edmund Beaufort to his old position of authority and to oust the duke of York infuriated York and the coterie of allies he had built during his protectorate. Seeing no alternative, the Yorkist faction raised an army against the king and Edmund Beaufort, and attacked the royal party in St Albans on 21 May 1455. King Henry was wounded, struck in the neck by a Yorkist arrow and yanked into a reeking tanner's shop to escape worse. Edmund Beaufort was not so fortunate. He found himself cornered inside a tavern with his nineteen-year-old son. Surrounded by their enemies, Edmund was hacked to pieces and his son so badly wounded that he had to be carried away on a cart. Edmund's wife, Eleanor, fled for sanctuary to Maxey Castle and there related the full horror of events to Margaret's kin. In the wake of St Albans, the traumatised king retreated once more into mental torpor and the duke of York seized control of government.

One of the few frontiers where Lancastrian rule held out against the Yorkists was the Welsh territory presided over by the Tudors: Jasper and his elder brother – now Margaret's husband – Edmund.

For, as soon as she was old enough to legally consent to her union, Margaret was married to Edmund. Unusually, the child-bride – whom contemporaries described as slight and small for her age – was promptly removed from her mother's home to begin her life as a noble wife. Meaning the wedding was swiftly consummated. Perhaps, given the political turmoil engulfing the realm, Edmund felt there was no time to lose. More likely, he was motivated by mercenary impulses.

The very little we know of Edmund Tudor suggests he was more concerned with his own advancement than Margaret's wellbeing. The surest way for a man to possess his wife's estates was to consummate the marriage, as once a child was conceived – no matter how short-lived – the father automatically gained a life interest in his wife's inheritance by the 'courtesy of England'. Margaret's estate was worth about a thousand pounds a year (£624,000 in modern money), so Edmund's motivation to secure her wealth was considerable. But, while his behaviour was perfectly legal, it was morally dubious. Even in fifteenth-century aristocratic circles, where marriages were contracted at a very young age, they were not usually consummated until the bride was fourteen to sixteen years old. Twenty was the average age at which most noblewomen had their first pregnancy.[12] Barely pubescent, Margaret was not sufficiently developed to carry a child safely. Nonetheless, Edmund insisted on his marital rights, taking Margaret with him into Wales where he was striving to assert Lancastrian authority. By November 1455 at the latest, Margaret and Edmund were at the bishop of St David's palace of Lamphey in Pembrokeshire, at the westernmost reaches of Wales.[13] It was the furthest that Margaret had ever been from her mother. Within a few months, still not thirteen, she was also pregnant.[14]

Wales would have been totally new territory to the diminutive countess of Richmond. In the fifteenth century, Wales was a proud region whose native culture had been crushed by an oppressive English presence. English garrisons were maintained across northern Wales at the castles of Caernarfon and Harlech, while the south was left to disintegrate into disorder by absentee English noblemen. Under English rule, native Welshmen were forbidden to serve on juries, hold office under the crown, or acquire property within or near boroughs. They could not marry Englishwomen and no Englishman could be convicted of a crime on the oath of a Welshman. Nonetheless, the Welsh maintained a strong sense of their own identity, and native lords gave patronage to poets who wrote ballads praising them in their own language. Among the Welsh lords so praised were the Tudors, whose paternal Welsh blood made them an ideal fit to assert Henry's vacant lordship there.[15]

Carmarthen Castle in West Wales absorbed Edmund's attentions.[16] In autumn 1456, a Yorkist force of 2,000 men appeared at the gates, led by the duke of York's loyal retainers, William Herbert of Raglan in South Wales and his Herefordshire-born brother-in-law Sir Walter Devereux. The Yorkists seized control of the fortress and imprisoned Edmund. Margaret was probably still at Lamphey Palace when she heard the news. She was now six months pregnant and could not easily travel as winter approached. Worse, plague was abroad in Wales. Perhaps it was from this terrible period that Margaret developed her abiding terror of the plague. The patron saints of the sick, Saints Leonard and Anthony, were venerated in Margaret's chapel until her dying days, and she observed 'peculiar fasts of devotion' on St Anthony's feast day in later life. Margaret also acquired, and personalised, a manuscript filled with 'precautions... against the pestilence', including advice on diet and medicines alongside prayers to be used preventatively.[17] Perhaps some of those prayers were on her lips now, but, in captivity, Edmund had no defence against the spreading sickness. Although he was freed by his Yorkist captors, he was already infected and never made it beyond the walls of Carmarthen. He died of the plague on 1 November 1456.

EDMUND'S DEATH LEFT MARGARET, NOW IN HER THIRD trimester, completely alone. Her mother was at Bletsoe or Maxey, over two hundred miles away. The manner of her husband's death, and the ongoing restlessness across Wales, probably made

Margaret fear that she was no longer safe in the secluded but largely unfortified palace at Lamphey. The closest safe haven was Pembroke Castle, about two miles away, the seat of Edmund's brother Jasper. It was there that Margaret sought sanctuary.

Pembroke Castle was a fortress built more for military might than for comfort. Perched precipitously above a tidal creek, a series of crenellated greystone towers studded its high curtain walls. Here, in January 1457, Margaret prepared to give birth. Almost fifty years later, her confessor John Fisher vividly related Margaret's anxiety at this time, not so much for herself as for her unborn child, who she feared could be carried off by the same plague that had killed his father.[18]

But she must also have feared for herself. Medieval mothers were advised to attend Mass and make confession before entering their confinement – it might, after all, be the last time they could do so. A woman's risk of dying in childbirth was 125 in every 1,000 births, although a recent study of noblewomen found that elite women had around a 1 per cent chance of death with every birth. If they endured a stillbirth, the risk increased.[19] For the child, the danger was even greater: up to two hundred out of every thousand children died before reaching the age of five.[20] Little wonder that the announcement of a woman's pregnancy inspired a stream of good wishes tinged with concern, and the dispatch of holy water and relics to aid her in labour.[21]

At Pembroke, Margaret was housed not in one of the grim towers lining the outer walls of the castle – despite one such today bearing the name of her son – but in a recently constructed, more comfortable double-winged mansion within the outer ward of the fortress.[22] There, she was enclosed in a womb-like environment to await the birth of her child. Although details of Margaret's confinement have not survived, fifteenth-century ordinances of the royal household and the letters of other noble mothers enable us to reconstruct her chambers.[23] Every window but one was closed, to keep out daylight and air, and even the keyholes were blocked. The only light came from flickering candles and the hearth fire. Margaret would have lain in a canopied bed of estate covered in fur-lined counterpanes, while rich cloth of arras (a tapestry-like patterned hanging) bedecked the walls. The footfall of her female attendants was muffled by the carpets laid across every inch of the floor, stretching from the richly dressed cupboard to the altar 'well furnished with relics'.[24] These expensive furnishings could be borrowed from neighbours and relatives, passed from maternal hand to hand to provide a little comfort in the darkness.[25]

No men could enter this cloistered world until a month after the birth, and since all physicians and surgeons were male, this meant that medical care for mother and child was entrusted to one or more midwives, selected for their practical experience and 'small and smooth hands'.[26] The importance of a midwife's hand size becomes clear when one reads medieval gynaecological texts. Where there were difficulties, it was up to the midwife to resolve them, if necessary by physical intervention.

January was an inauspicious time to give birth. The twelfth-century compilation of obstetric writings commonly called *Trotula*, composed in the southern Italian town of Salerno, advised that in winter childbirth could be impeded because 'the coldness of the season' constricted the 'tight orifice of the womb'.[27] To counter this, the *Trotula* advised that a bath be prepared with softening herbs like mallow and fenugreek, and the mother's belly, sides, hips and vagina anointed with oil of violets and roses. To ease labour, it was recommended a woman should eat 'light and readily digestible foods' like egg yolks, young fowl and small game birds.[28] To draw the baby safely out, the midwife should anoint the vulva with musk, ambergris and aloewood, as it was believed that the womb 'follows sweet-smelling substances and flees foul-smelling ones'.* Margaret could also drink ivory shavings, suspend coral from her neck and hold a magnet in her right hand, although the *Trotula* admitted that the reason for the efficacy of this was 'obscure to us'.[29] If all else failed, Margaret could pray to her namesake, St Margaret of Antioch, the patron saint of childbirth who had been martyred, tortured, swallowed

---

* The womb, it was commonly believed, was a freely moving organ that roved the female body. Monica H. Green (ed.), *The Trotula: An English Translation of the Medieval Compendium of Women's Medicine* (Philadelphia, 2002), p. 82.

and burst out of the belly of a dragon. Similar logic presumably lay behind pregnant women's tendency to pray to Jonah, who had been delivered from the belly of a whale.[30]

Frustratingly, the only certain detail that survives of Margaret's labour is the bald fact that on 28 January 1457, she gave birth to a boy. But, over forty years later, both Margaret and her confessor made oblique references to how difficult the labour had been. In 1498, Margaret strongly advised against allowing her granddaughter to be married so young, for fear that her husband 'would not wait [to consummate the union], but injure her, and endanger her health'.[31] Similarly, in a Latin address at Cambridge University around 1506, John Fisher celebrated the almost miraculous survival of mother and child, emphasising that the baby was:

> born in extraordinary circumstances, brought into the light by that noble progenitor [Margaret]... who at that time had not yet reached the age of fourteen... She is (as we see) a woman not of a great stature, but at that time it is said she was much smaller still, to such a degree that it almost seemed a miracle at her age that so little a body could bring forth a child at all.[32]

The labour had a successful outcome in that mother and child survived. However, it seems highly likely that Margaret was irreparably damaged by the birth. Despite her youth, two further long marriages produced no children nor, as far as her household accounts suggest, any hint of pregnancy. This was unusual in a period when the average number of children born to fertile noble couples was four.[33] But the survival of the baby could not be taken for granted, so the little boy was whisked away to be baptised while Margaret recovered.

A sixteenth-century Welsh chronicler called Elis Gruffudd suggests that the baptism was the occasion for a quarrel between Margaret and her in-laws. Gruffudd reported that Jasper Tudor wanted the baby to be named 'Owen' for Jasper's father, but that Margaret insisted the boy bear the name of the king. Margaret's will prevailed and Henry Tudor, infant earl of Richmond, was duly baptised. Even in the darkest moments of her life, Margaret was already demonstrating that she had remarkable reserves of courage, fortitude and sheer willpower. He might not have a father, but Henry Tudor had a mother whose strength of character would determine his future and, if it was in her power, his survival.

4

'Mine entirely beloved wife'[1]

✳

In March 1457, Margaret left her new-born son swaddled at Pembroke Castle and set out on a hundred-mile journey across South Wales. It was less than two months since she had endured a harrowing childbirth, and custom – not to mention sound medical reasoning – dictated that mothers should remain in their confinement for at least five weeks after birth, longer if they had given birth to a boy. But Margaret was determined to regain control over her future in one of the only ways a noblewoman could. She went in search of another marriage.

Margaret's destination was Greenfield Manor near Newport in Gwent, part of the considerable estate of Humphrey Stafford, duke of Buckingham. She travelled with her brother-in-law Jasper, who accompanied her as chaperone and, more cynically, to keep an eye on Tudor interests. Buckingham was one of the most influential men in the country, a veteran of the French wars like Margaret's father and stepfather and, more importantly, a moderate force amid the mounting factionalism of the royal court. He was a crucial ally to court at this moment of vulnerability. Personal experience had taught Margaret that fatherless heirs were the playthings of kings and, as heir to the earldom of Richmond, baby Henry was easy prey. Moreover, now that Margaret was both heiress and widow, she was a valuable commodity and, having already married twice according to the whims of strangers, she was determined to choose her own future. But she had to move quickly to head off royal intervention on behalf of other interested parties.[2]

At Greenfield, Margaret, Jasper and the duke were probably joined by two members of the Stafford family who would be central to Margaret's future: Anne Neville, the influential and astute duchess of Buckingham, and her younger son – Margaret's potential husband – Sir Harry Stafford. Little is known about Harry before this time, but he was at least a decade older than Margaret and considerably her inferior in wealth.[3] As the son of a duke, however, he was her social equal, and he was to prove both respectful and kind. Something of his character may have revealed itself to Margaret at their first meeting. Negotiations moved swiftly and, by 6 April, a dispensation was granted for Margaret and Harry to marry.*

Beyond the political necessity for speed, the extraordinary haste with which Margaret left her baby to arrange her own marriage suggests unease with her new role. Scarcely more than a child herself, in the past two years she had been forced to assume new identities as first wife then widow, and now mother – the most profound transformations that a woman could face. She had been schooled to believe that mothers were supposed to rejoice in their offspring, and anything but joy seemed unnatural rejection, but the maternal role models available to Margaret in Pembrokeshire were non-existent and her experience of motherhood profoundly distressing. Her mother and half-sisters were hundreds of miles away, and the women who attended Margaret during her confinement and beyond looked to her as a mistress, which made confessions of vulnerability hard to express. Lacking real world comfort, Margaret may have turned to iconic medieval images of motherhood: the Virgin Mary and her myriad saintly companions. Images of Mary's cousin St Elizabeth placing her hand on the pregnant belly of the Virgin proliferated in churches across England and Wales. But how was one to live up to a saint, never mind the perfection of the Mother of God?

In one way, Margaret was fortunate: as a noblewoman the innate instinct to protect her child could be met by paid retainers. Indeed, she was so rich, she could provide a whole suite of wet

---

* The dispensation was necessary as Harry and Margaret were second cousins. See the Beaufort family tree.

nurses, rockers and lady governesses for little Earl Henry if need be. There was scarcely any need for her to linger with the infant at all. And perhaps if this baby did remind her, even unconsciously – *especially* unconsciously – of the pain she had experienced when he entered the world, she found it better to be away from him altogether. If Margaret felt any qualms about leaving her son at Pembroke Castle, she could quiet those anxieties by reassuring herself that she was acting in his best interests.

After all, in the fraught circumstances of 1457, there was some urgency to finalising her alliance with the Staffords. In the two years since the Battle of St Albans, the royal court had splintered into two bitterly hostile factions, one entrenched at Coventry around Queen Marguerite (now the effective leader of the Lancastrian regime), and the other centred on the duke of York. Since Edmund Beaufort's death, the duke of Buckingham was one of the last surviving noblemen sufficiently powerful to represent a challenge to York's authority. Crucially, though, while the Staffords shared the distant royal blood that made York and the Beauforts such divisive forces, the duke of Buckingham attempted to find a middle way through this conflict. He was related to both sides of the political divide, which gave him a vested interest in restoring harmony to the realm. His indomitable wife, Anne Neville, was the sister of Cecily, duchess of York, and his half-brothers, the lords Bourchier, were also prominent Yorkists. Yet Buckingham's nephew was the arch-Lancastrian Henry Holland, duke of Exeter, and Buckingham himself a friend of the late Edmund Beaufort. Buckingham's eldest son was also married to Edmund Beaufort's daughter, and the couple had two young children together.[*]

Although Margaret did not personally know the Staffords before the negotiations of spring 1457, her cousin's marriage to the Stafford heir was only one of several long-term family connections to them. Perhaps most importantly, her mother's cousin and councillor, John Stourton, had been steward of Buckingham's estates in Gloucestershire, Hampshire and Wiltshire for over a decade.

---

[*] Confusingly for future historians, she was also called Margaret Beaufort.

Stourton was shrewd enough to have survived as a royal councillor for thirty years, and refused to be drawn into the internecine
feuding that was rending the court. If Margaret sought his political
guidance, she was likely advised to forge an alliance that would
not drag her too close to either faction, which was precisely what
she accomplished by marrying Harry Stafford.[4]

There may have been another incentive for Margaret in the
Stafford match. Harry's base at Bourne in Lincolnshire was less
than ten miles from Maxey Castle. Thus, when Margaret married
Harry on 3 January 1458 (her third marriage before her fifteenth
birthday), she was able to move back close to her maternal family.
From Bourne, Margaret could easily ride under the wide fenland
skies to dine at Maxey with her mother and St John half-siblings.[5]
Shortly after her return, her eldest half-sister Edith St John married
and had her first child. The circumstances of the sisters could not
have been more different, for the adult Edith married a gentleman
called Geoffrey Pole and probably gave birth at their home in
Buckinghamshire, close enough for her mother to attend.[6] This
child, Richard, was to be the first of many, but if Margaret felt
any twinges of jealousy at Edith's happier maternal experiences,
she did not show it. The sisters remained close and Margaret was
a devoted aunt to Richard and his siblings.[7]

Indeed, with the return to Lincolnshire and reconnection with
her family it was almost as if Margaret's marriage to Edmund
Tudor had never happened – and perhaps that she had never
become a mother. For, when Margaret began her new life with Sir
Harry, she left her infant son behind. Five days after Margaret's
marriage, on 8 January 1458, Henry Tudor's wardship was
granted to his uncle Jasper.[8] The boy would remain at Pembroke
Castle, 300 miles from Margaret. While it was not unusual for
a ward to be raised with a guardian rather than their parent, Henry
would thus have a notably different upbringing from Margaret,
who had grown up at her mother's side, surrounded by half-
siblings and cousins. Perhaps Margaret rationalised leaving Henry
because, unlike her, he was a male heir. He needed a role model
from whom to learn the ways of men and Jasper could provide
that. But there is a sense that Margaret, still so young and already

having suffered so much, could not cope emotionally with the responsibility of mothering a child.

Nor did Jasper have much time to concern himself directly with Henry Tudor's upbringing. He had taken over where his brother Edmund left off, consolidating royal authority in Wales, attempting to cow the duke of York's supporters, and to bring to justice Sir William Herbert and Sir Walter Devereux, whom Jasper justly blamed for his brother's death. King Henry and Queen Marguerite of Anjou joined Jasper and the duke of Buckingham to oversee trial proceedings against the Welsh agitators late in March 1457 where, to divide the allies among themselves, Herbert was pardoned and Devereux jailed.[9]

Margaret took no part in these proceedings. She and Harry Stafford were soon settling into the rhythms of life at Bourne, where together they oversaw their small household of around thirty servants. The couple proved well-matched and there is evidence of mutual respect and affection in their arranged union. Their household accounts show that they exchanged gifts at New Year, and celebrated their anniversary with feasts of wildfowl and wine. Although Harry was the head of the household, Margaret's name appears often in their accounts, delivering wages to servants or arranging payments to traders. Harry treated Margaret with due respect, repeatedly referring to her in a will of 1471 as 'mine entirely beloved' and 'best beloved wife'.[10] He understood that Margaret's estate was the basis of their combined wealth. As a younger son, his main source of income was a 400-mark* grant of property from the duke of Buckingham, which was dwarfed by Margaret's inheritance of £1,000 a year.

From the windows of Bourne, Margaret could watch their provisions of beer, ale and salt fish lumber into the castle from the markets of neighbouring Bourne and Stamford; and the outgoing woolfells and hides from the animals in their pastures taken for resale to local merchants. She could descend and cross their two courtyards to ride out with her husband to hunt in the parkland beyond its turreted walls. For someone of her genealogical bent,

---

* £240.

it must have pleased Margaret that Bourne had once belonged to her relatives in the Holland family, and from the roof-gardens of the castle she had a view towards the countryside in which she had spent her childhood. Bourne grew to have such a strong place in Margaret's affections that, when she first wrote her will, in 1472, she asked to be buried with Sir Harry in the neighbouring chapel. She even made arrangements for Edmund Tudor to be exhumed from Carmarthen and brought to Bourne to join them – a ménage à trois that appears ghoulish to our eyes, but was considered respectful in a culture that attached considerable value to one's burial place.[11] Life within Bourne, then, was content and uneventful. But, beyond its walls, the Lancastrian regime was crumbling as the realm dissolved into conflict once more.

It was impossible for Margaret and Sir Harry to stand aloof from the political events unfolding beyond their home, for both had relatives on the front lines. At Blore Heath, Staffordshire, in September 1459, when escalating tensions finally spilled over into open conflict between Yorkist and Lancastrian forces, Margaret's stepfather Lionel, Lord Welles was among the commanders fighting for King Henry – and was lucky to escape with his life after he was captured by Yorkist soldiers. When the king faced down a Yorkist army outside Ludlow on the Welsh Marches later that month, Harry's father, the duke of Buckingham, was at his side. Buckingham could personally tell his daughter-in-law how the duke of York and his chief commanders had crept away the night before battle, leaving their bewildered soldiers in the field and York's wife and youngest children stranded inside Ludlow Castle. The ever-merciful King Henry pardoned Cecily, duchess of York and even gave her an annuity. He did, however, take the precaution of placing her in the keeping of her sister Anne, duchess of Buckingham. According to *Gregory's Chronicle*, Margaret's new mother-in-law showed little sisterly feeling for Cecily in her troubles, keeping her 'full straight and [giving] many a great rebuke'.[12]

Both Buckingham and Jasper Tudor attended the 'Parliament of Devils' in November 1459, when King Henry finally condemned the duke of York and his confederates – including Buckingham's nephews John and Edward Bourchier. The Yorkists suffered the most severe legal penalty in the land; they were 'attainted' as traitors. Attainder was the perpetual disinheritance of the traitor's entire bloodline, depriving it of all property and effectively causing the legal death of the family. It was a sign of how serious the rift in English politics had grown that the soft-hearted Henry VI could be persuaded to impose such a punishment.

Although Henry Tudor was far removed from the fields of battle in England, Margaret could not rest assured of his safety. While his uncle and guardian Jasper Tudor was bringing Denbigh Castle in North Wales to heel, Henry's Pembrokeshire home was threatened by Yorkist vessels that sailed up Milford Haven towards Tenby. York had fled to Ireland, but his ally the earl of Warwick had control of a formidable army, which it was feared would make landfall in Wales.[13]

By summer 1460, even one-time moderates like the duke of Buckingham had grown wroth. During negotiations before the Battle of Northampton on 10 July, Buckingham lost his patience with Yorkist protestations of innocence and refused to allow the earl of Warwick access to the king: 'Forsooth,' said the duke, 'the Earl of Warwick shall not come to the king's presence, and if he come he shall die!'[14]

Buckingham's hot words cost him his life. A turncoat in the Lancastrian camp allowed the Yorkists to breach their defences and driving rain rendered the king's guns useless. Buckingham was killed while standing guard outside King Henry's tent. The king himself was taken hostage by York's men. Queen Marguerite and their son barely managed to escape Yorkist riders, and fled into Wales to seek sanctuary with Jasper Tudor.

At Bourne, and at Maxey Castle, summonses arrived from the fugitive queen to muster against the Yorkists in the north of England. Lionel, Lord Welles was as zealous a Lancastrian as Margaret's Beaufort cousins, and he loyally answered the call, traversing the snow-bound country to assemble in the queen's northern camp. The Lancastrian army enjoyed a considerable morale boost when it defeated the duke of York outside Wakefield Castle on 30 December 1460. York himself was killed in battle, alongside his seventeen-year-old son Edmund, earl of Rutland, and his head was skewered above the gates of the city of York, topped with a mocking paper coronet.

Meanwhile, far to the west, another Lancastrian force under Jasper Tudor and his ally, the infamously handsome earl of Wiltshire, slowly assembled, with French and Breton soldiers joining the native Welsh and English. But, before this polyglot host could unite with the queen's, it had to confront an army under the command of York's son, Edward, earl of March, and the Tudors' old nemesis Sir William Herbert. In battle at Mortimer's Cross, on 2 February 1461, the Lancastrian force was scattered and overthrown. Jasper and the earl of Wiltshire managed to escape into exile, but Margaret's father-in-law, Owen Tudor, was captured. In revenge for York's death, at Hereford marketplace Edward ordered that Owen be stripped of his velvet doublet and led to the executioner's block. 'That head shall lie on the stock,' Owen said, 'that was once wont to lie on Queen Catherine's lap.'[15] In the wake of his victory at Mortimer's Cross, on 4 March 1461, the killer of Owen Tudor and the duke of Buckingham was proclaimed King Edward IV in the City of London.

Having attempted hitherto to maintain a measure of neutrality, it appears a spirit of vengeance now infiltrated Bourne. Harry Stafford had played no recorded part in any of the previous campaigns, but in the wake of Edward IV's accession he finally committed his men to join Lord Welles and the Lancastrian army. Although it was spring, when Harry rendezvoused with the Lancastrian forces mustering on a plain between the Yorkshire villages of Towton and Saxton, snow was swirling into the faces of the soldiers. It was 29 March 1461.

If this was Harry's first experience of warfare, it was an exceptionally unfortunate one. The Battle of Towton is remembered as the bloodiest day of combat on British soil. The Lancastrian forces were routed by the army of the newly proclaimed Edward IV, with contemporary reports of 28,000 killed.* Margaret's neighbours at Crowland Abbey wrote a horrified description of the slaughter that Harry could have witnessed: 'The blood... of the slain, mingling with the snow which at this time covered the whole surface of the earth, afterwards ran down in the furrows and ditches along with the melted snow... for a distance of two or three miles.'[16]

Among the myriad corpses bloodying the Yorkshire snow was Lionel, Lord Welles, widowing Margaret's mother for a third time. The Lancastrian forces scattered. King Henry, Queen Marguerite, their seven-year-old son and a handful of faithful servants fled north into Scotland. Those who, like Jasper Tudor, had been unable to reach the battlefield in time now retreated to fortresses in the furthest reaches of England and Wales, or overseas to the Continent. Many, like Sir Harry Stafford, limped home, bloodied, weary and cowed, ready to consider the impossible: to bend the knee to Edward, earl of March, and proclaim him King Edward IV. For Margaret and Harry, the choice was stark. By fighting against Edward at Towton, Sir Harry had potentially condemned himself as a traitor. He and Margaret must either submit to Edward and embrace the Yorkist future, with its potential for material reward, or risk destruction, dishonour and disadvantage by resisting, yet staying true to their family loyalties.

In the aftermath of Towton, Edward IV proved to be as shrewd as he was militarily courageous. Those who now swore fealty to the House of York were treated with magnanimity regardless of their previous loyalties. In truth, Edward had little choice. So many noble families had fought against him at Towton that, to have any hope of ruling effectively, he needed to win them over to his cause. But, to prove he was no pushover like Henry VI, Edward also made a display of summary justice. Those who continued to defy him were punished. In Edward's first parliament, a broad sweep of Lancastrian rebels was attainted, their entire estates stripped from their families in perpetuity. Among them were Jasper Tudor

---

* Modern estimates are much more conservative, with 4,000 casualties a likelier upper limit.

and Lionel Welles. Lionel's death at the Battle of Towton had left Margaret's youngest half-brother fatherless, just like her and the rest of her siblings. But, unlike them, because his father had been attainted, little John Welles would now have to rely entirely on their mother for financial support until he could overturn parliament's decision or win back the king's favour. Not much more than ten, John's future had been ruined by Lionel's Lancastrian allegiance.

In theory, women like Margaret and her mother were exempt from the effects of attainder. They were the legal possessions of their husbands and, as such, chivalry dictated that they should not be punished for actions in which they could not legally have participated. In reality, as Margaret herself had witnessed, women were often the partners of their husbands. Women's participation in the political actions of their families had been acknowledged in 1459 when, in an unprecedented move, York's sister-in-law, Alice, countess of Salisbury* was attainted for colluding with the family's treason.[17] Women might not don armour, but they could fight to protect their families through the law courts, and they often supported their husbands and sons financially. As such, the wives, widows and mothers of traitors were dangerous. Attainder law reserved to them certain slender pockets of inheritance – the dower they would usually get on a husband's death and whatever jointure had been arranged for them when they first married – and the women could, if they chose, use this money to fund the campaigns of the surviving rebels. To prevent them doing so, several noblewomen were effectively imprisoned by the new regime, among them Margaret's cousin Eleanor Beaufort, countess of Wiltshire. Eleanor had the double misfortune of being the widow of a despised Lancastrian commander and also the sister of the rebel Henry Beaufort, who was still at large in Europe. In March 1462, Edward appointed the grizzled veteran John, Lord Wenlock as 'governor' to Eleanor and two of her West Country neighbours, whose husbands had also fled into exile with the Lancastrian court:

---

* Alice was married to Richard Neville, earl of Salisbury, the brother of Cecily, duchess of York.

Anne Whalesborough, Lady Hampden and Eleanor Moleyns, Lady Hungerford. Wenlock was given control over the women, their young children, and their estates and servants.[18]

At least Lady Hampden and Lady Hungerford had the comfort of knowing that, for now, their kinsmen had escaped overseas. Less fortunate were some of Margaret's Stafford relations. Early in 1462, Sir Harry's young brother-in-law Aubrey de Vere and both his parents were suddenly arrested for collusion in a Lancastrian plot to murder Edward IV. Aubrey's wife, Anne Stafford, was spared captivity but Aubrey's aged mother was taken prisoner, then both Aubrey and his father, the earl of Oxford, were condemned to be beheaded as traitors. It was hoped that Aubrey might be offered a last-minute reprieve because of 'his goodly personage and youth'.[19] But, on a bitterly cold morning in February, Aubrey was dragged along the ground from Westminster to Tower Hill, where his head was cut off. A week later, his father was forced to walk to his own execution barefoot, but spared the 'drawing' on account of his 'great age'.[20]

The fate of the de Veres was a stark warning to Margaret, but one that her brother-in-law Jasper refused to heed. In the months after Towton, as family after family came to terms with the new regime, Jasper instead redoubled his efforts for the Lancastrian cause and mounted a defiant resistance in Wales. Since four-year-old Henry Tudor was still nominally in Jasper's care at Pembroke Castle, this must have given Margaret some cause for concern. Worse, when Jasper left Pembroke to rally the rebels in North Wales, a Yorkist force under Edward's Welsh lieutenant, Sir William Herbert, seized the castle and took custody of Henry. Although Jasper escaped into exile, he was attainted. Herbert was appointed senior authority in Wales in his place. It remained to be seen how Edward IV would deal with the fugitive rebel's nephew and heir.[21]

As Margaret and Sir Harry weighed up whether to submit to Edward, they must have considered the fate of their relatives and peers: the misery inflicted on those who continued to struggle for Lancaster, compared with the open-armed generosity meted out to those who submitted to York. Perhaps their most important influences at this time were their own mothers, who would both have argued for submitting to the new regime. The dowager duchesses of Buckingham and Somerset were in no position, in 1461, to resist Edward IV. As the widow of an attainted rebel, Margaret's mother badly needed Yorkist approval to regain her son's lost Welles inheritance. Meanwhile, Harry's mother, Anne, duchess of Buckingham, had been the effective head of their family since her husband's death in battle, as the new duke was her five-year-old grandson.* Anne had been no friend to the Yorkist cause when it stood in rebellion against an anointed king, but like all magnates she knew how to navigate the delicate line between honour and pragmatism. Her husband was dead, the Lancastrian royal family had fled and the fate of her children and grandchildren was in her hands. Within a fortnight of Towton, she submitted to Edward, probably appealing to him through the intercession of her sister Cecily, Edward's mother. Thus, on 9 April 1461, 'without any fine or fee' Anne was granted her dower lands and over the following years 'the king's kinswoman' was showered with gifts, the most valuable of which were a parliamentary promise not to confiscate her estates and the continued guardianship of her grandson.[22]

Despite their lifetime of Lancastrian service, neither Harry nor Margaret could see an alternative now to Yorkist rule. Following in their mothers' wake, they, too, chose submission. On 25 June 1461, in return for his capitulation to Edward IV, Sir Harry was granted a royal pardon. The financial underpinning of the couple's fortune – Margaret's inheritance and dower – was protected in the first parliament of King Edward's reign.[23] A few lines higher on the parliament roll, Margaret's mother and Stourton relatives were similarly rewarded. Almost Margaret's entire family had thrown in its lot with York.

However, far to the west in Pembrokeshire, Margaret's five-year-old son Henry remained in the hands of William Herbert, the man arguably responsible for the death of his father. As a long-term Yorkist, Herbert was rewarded handsomely by Edward IV.

---

* The eldest son of the duke and duchess of Buckingham, Humphrey, earl Stafford, had died of plague in 1458.

Among the many grants he received was, in February 1462, the legal wardship of Henry Tudor. But, like Margaret, Henry was too rich for his own good. Everyone wanted a piece of his estate. The following April, Henry's paternal inheritance, the lordship of Richmond, was gifted to Edward's ten-year-old brother Richard, duke of Gloucester, and soon the rest of the boy's patrimony was parcelled out to other Yorkist supporters.[24] Since Edward IV could not get his hands on Jasper Tudor, Henry would suffer in his place.

There is no record that Margaret resisted Edward's treatment of her son, although, as her personal correspondence and household accounts do not survive from this period, it is possible she tried. Throughout her life, Margaret was sensitive to, and strongly opposed, any impingement on her family's honour, so it is doubtful she would have suffered the vindictive stripping of her only child's inheritance without complaint. But, perhaps she realised it was too dangerous to publicly resist the Yorkists at this difficult time. Moreover, when Margaret considered the changed circumstances, she may have reasoned that her son was better off as a ward of William Herbert than anywhere else. Herbert was, after all, one of the closest advisers of the new king. In 1461, he was named a baron – the first ever Welsh-born peer – and in 1468 created earl of Pembroke. Like Margaret's half-brother John, Henry had a lot of ground to recover. His entire estate was in the control of other lords, and if he was to have any hope of regaining his inheritance in adulthood, he needed to forge bonds with the new regime as swiftly as possible. Although Herbert had offended the Tudors deeply, Margaret was learning the politic art of burying private resentments for the good of her kin. She would not follow Jasper Tudor's example and alienate Yorkist good will.

In the longer term, the best provision that Margaret could make for her son was the protection of his inheritance as earl of Richmond. If she had any doubts about the wisdom of this course, her own mother's example must have provided reinforcement. Having made her peace with Edward IV, the dowager duchess of Somerset channelled her energies into protecting John Welles, who was utterly reliant on his mother for his financial security. The dowager duchess had to keep assiduous watch to assert their rights, for not only was John suffering from the effects of his father's attainder, but he also had to go toe-to-toe with his Welles half-siblings from his father's earlier marriage to claw back pieces of his father's estate. The eldest of these, Richard, Lord Welles and Willoughby, soon regained Edward IV's favour and was a particular challenge. Contrary to attainder law, Richard took possession of the duchess's dower lands and Margaret's mother had to appeal through the law courts against him. By the late 1460s, she in turn was attempting to divert the remaining Welles inheritance to John, usurping Richard's superior claim. Several royal grants and explications during the years after Towton are testament to the dowager duchess's close surveillance of any attempts to deprive her or her son of their rights.[25]

It was becoming clear that under Edward IV, if one nobleman fell from favour, his whole family could suffer by association. In late 1463, Margaret's cousin Henry Beaufort, duke of Somerset raised the north of England for Henry VI. It was not long since the young Duke Henry had reconciled himself to the Yorkist regime and received considerable demonstrations of royal magnanimity, publicly hunting with the king and even sleeping in the same bed. But, while King Edward had apparently forgiven Duke Henry, many of his supporters had not and at Northampton, in July 1463, a mob attempted to assassinate him. This may have been what tipped Margaret's cousin into open rebellion. But he learned that Edward IV would not forgive twice. A Yorkist army hounded Duke Henry and his rebels across Northumberland, crushing them in one battle after another. He was captured while fleeing battle at Hexham and beheaded in the town marketplace. For his family, the failure of this rebellion was disastrous. Duke Henry was attainted, his entire estate forfeited, his brothers forced into exile on the Continent and his mother, Eleanor, imprisoned under such harsh conditions that 'she was like to have perished for lack of sustenance…[and] bodily infirmities'. In desperation, Eleanor pleaded with King Edward to provide her with an annuity of over £200 that was owed to her. She received only £50.[26]

While Margaret's immediate family were ever ready to support each other – her St John half-siblings were frequent visitors at Bourne – they were not willing to associate themselves with such politically toxic relations. She and Harry distanced themselves from Somerset's Beaufort line and, perhaps out of gratitude for their loyalty during this testing time, Edward IV rewarded them. In December 1464, they received a share of the confiscated Beaufort estates in Kendal and Bassingbourne and in 1466 the manor of Woking in Surrey, an ancestral property of Margaret's Holland ancestors.[27] For once Margaret found herself in a position to materially benefit from crown patronage, rather than bearing the brunt of it.

This grant proved momentous. For five years Margaret and her husband had remained on the periphery of political life. The grant of Woking offered them the opportunity to move south, close to the political heartland of the royal court and parliament. They could mix in circles close to the king, perhaps build a real position of trust within the new regime. They might be able to regain Henry Tudor's lost inheritance. The opportunity for further reward and power opened out before them. They seized it with both hands.

In December 1466, Margaret and Harry spent their last Christmas in Lincolnshire. In a final extended farewell, they stayed with Margaret's mother and half-sister Elizabeth St John at Maxey for six weeks. Already plans were underway for their move to Woking. Their expensive velvet and silk clothes were carefully folded into trunks, their furniture loaded onto carts and their horses bridled. There was so much to transport south that they had to call on the assistance of the abbot of Bourne to help them move it all. But, by March 1467, they had entered their new home, and a whole new phase of their lives.[28]

5

'The way of life of the wise princess'[1]

✳

Margaret's new home was only a mile away from Woking, screened from the town by a copse of trees. She would have entered the manor house over a drawbridge, her horse's hooves clattering as she passed under the shade of the gatehouse and into the outer courtyard. Then, having handed her horse over to a groom, she would have walked on, through a second gateway to the great hall, then on again, towards the chapel, perhaps for a momentary prayer of thanksgiving, and at last into the private chambers of the lord and lady of the manor.

This fine residence brought fresh responsibilities and the move placed many demands on the new mistress of Woking. Although Margaret and Harry arrived in Surrey as important figures in their own right – a countess and the son of the duke of Buckingham – they had to forge entirely new relationships there. Reliable merchants needed sourcing to stockpile their home, local tenants met so they could address concerns and establish their authority. Their modest household swelled to almost fifty servants, a new hierarchy represented by the different fabrics and colours worn by these retainers, from the vivid blue livery of its lower attendants to the russet and black of its officers. Only a handful of female staff worked in this entourage, the most important of them Margaret's personal servant Elizabeth Jackson.[2]

A number of these new servants were recommended by Harry's mother, Anne, dowager duchess of Buckingham, who was close at hand and provided considerable assistance to Margaret while she transitioned to Surrey life. Among the Stafford transplants was the late duke of Buckingham's treasurer, William Wisetowe, who became Margaret's steward. Most importantly, Anne kept a close watch on political affairs in London, and alerted Margaret and Harry to any 'great matter' that might be of material advantage. When such missives arrived from 'my Lady of Buckingham', Margaret and Harry could respond swiftly, for the capital was now only a short journey away. Their meticulously maintained household accounts recorded much hiring of boats and chairs to ferry them back and forth to court, and payments for bread and ale in taverns where they broke their journey.[3]

Ordinarily, when a lord went up to London, his wife would stay home to watch over their manor, but Margaret and Harry preferred to remain together. Even when Harry attended parliament, Margaret accompanied him, staying in her mother's residence of Le Ryall or with Anne. At home, the pair worked together to maintain their household finances and foster the loyalty of their new neighbours and servants. Each New Year they presented gifts of money to their officers, and when members of their household left or 'went to be wedded' they paid their expenses. 'Christopher of the Chamber' received more than thirteen shillings for his marriage, while John Day and his wife both had their wedding clothing provided at their masters' cost. The Woking household became a unit bound tightly together by bonds of more than money – they were united by loyalty, trust and mutual respect.[4]

The servant who best personified this bond was the capable and dogged Reynald Bray. Both his father and brother, John, were also in Harry's service but neither gained the esteem enjoyed by Reynald. Despite being 'plain and rough in speech' and with little interest in cultured chivalric pursuits, the Worcestershire-born Bray was a regular guest at his master and mistress's table. Like Margaret, he had a meticulous eye for detail and a firm sense of reciprocal duty ('where he took,' wrote one later commentator, 'the giver was sure of a friend' in future).[5] As receiver-general, Bray was trusted to take receipt of the considerable tolls, rents and other monies due to Margaret and Harry, riding across their estates from Cumbria to the West Country with his slim leather account book safely tucked in his saddlebag.⁶ Every penny received and expended needed accounting for, and Bray's neat, scrupulous notes ensured that it was. He was to prove one of the most enduring supports to Margaret in the years to come, his interests bound inextricably to those of his mistress.

PEACE HAD FINALLY BEEN ESTABLISHED IN ENGLAND, AND AS they settled into their new home, Margaret and Harry's lives took on a steady rhythm. Together, they oversaw their estate, keeping the scullery and the bakehouse, the spicery and the pantry well stocked, but never over-saturated (for wastage was a terrible thing). In summer, when they were not enjoying cherries and strawberries in London, they hunted in the parklands of Surrey. One year they progressed all the way to the West Country to assert Margaret's lordship there. During the winter months, they nested at Woking. At Christmas, Harry indulged his minor vice of gambling at dice and cards and local actors were brought into the hall to perform. His brother John often visited and joined Harry at the card table. Margaret and Harry enjoyed music and maintained a chapel of well-dressed choristers to sing the religious offices. Both also loved to ride, even in winter, and Margaret took pleasure in maintaining a good stable. At New Year, Harry showered his wife with gifts of expensive fabrics – gold of Venice, fine lace, crimson ribbon and sarcenet – and once presented her with five pounds of gold farthings. In short, they were content. Their lives were uneventful and perhaps, after all that she had experienced, that was exactly what Margaret wanted.⁷

There was one dark shadow that fell over Margaret at Woking, however. Despite their close, affectionate relationship, Margaret and Harry never had a child of their own. The birth of Henry Tudor probably scarred Margaret physically and psychologically. As well as any anatomical damage resulting from the difficult birth, Margaret may have suffered from the lingering mental impact of her experience, causing heightened levels of anxiety around pregnancy and sex, which could only be compounded if she actively sought to bear another child. We now know that the stress hormone cortisol can impede fertility, which could have prevented Margaret from conceiving and carrying another child. Or is it possible that, to quell these anxieties, Margaret took steps to prevent another pregnancy? Morally, contraception was only condoned where pregnancy would endanger life, but the appearance of abortifacients and contraceptives in widely available medical texts suggests people made use of this knowledge in other circumstances as well. The absence of detailed records of her kitchen supplies means we cannot be sure if Margaret used such means. However, the change in Margaret's attitude to her son a decade into her marriage suggests she had not chosen this path. Rather, there is a strong sense that she had hoped for children with Harry, and was saddened by their absence.

In the mid-1460s, as Henry neared his tenth birthday, Margaret started to take a greater interest in her son. Margaret was now in her twenties and perhaps realised that Henry was likely to be her only child. As such, she wanted to get to know him better. Messages were dispatched to 'my lord Richmond' in the keeping of Margaret's servants, making the twelve-day round trip to Raglan Castle in South Wales where Henry was being brought up.[8] In 1465–6, in a sign of their renewed relationship, Henry was included with Margaret and Harry in documents admitting them to the confraternities of religious orders in Leicestershire and Yorkshire.[9] Finally, in autumn 1467, Margaret made her first recorded visit to her son, braving the 130-mile journey with Sir Harry and twenty-two attendants.[10]

After a steady progress through Surrey and Wiltshire, on Saturday 12 September 1467, Margaret returned to Wales for the first time in almost a decade. As she crossed the broad expanse of the River Severn by ferry, the sensation of re-entering a country that had been the scene of so much turmoil must have been intensely challenging. She might well have clung closer to Harry as Bristol faded from view and their boat neared Chepstow, whose fortress loomed over the river from its craggy cliff edge. They rested at this border castle on the Sunday, then rode onwards, finally trotting through Raglan Castle's magnificently turreted gatehouse in time for supper on Monday 14 September. They were to remain as the guests of Lord Herbert of Raglan, his wife, Lady Anne, and their brood of nine children for the next week.[11]

The little baby that Margaret remembered was now a growing boy. Almost eleven, Henry was well advanced in his schooling and starting to grow tall and serious. Under the attentive supervision of Lady Anne Herbert he was proving an able student, impressing his tutors with the same quick capacity for learning that Margaret herself had possessed as a child. While reacquainting himself with a mother who was virtually a stranger to him, young Henry also bonded with his stepfather. When Harry wrote his will, his stepson was one of only three to receive a personal bequest: a horse and four new harnesses of blue velvet.[12]

During this visit, Margaret and Harry may have discussed Henry's future with Lord and Lady Herbert. Henry's guardians hoped to unite the promising young earl of Richmond with their daughter, Maud. Such a union would bind Henry closer to the inner circle of the Yorkist regime, improving the chances of the restoration of his inheritance, and by extension of Margaret and Harry's status at court, so Margaret is likely to have approved of this match.

Although Margaret's stay was brief, she appears to have been impressed by her son. Perhaps she saw glimpses in his appearance, his bearing, his character, of herself or her half-siblings – perhaps, less comfortably, of his late father. After this visit, Margaret was more invested in her son's fortunes than hitherto. He was no longer the stranger-child who had inflicted such harm on her. He was her son, the rightful heir to Richmond. From then onwards, Henry was to find his mother was his greatest champion. And Margaret, despite all her other commitments – to her husband, mother, siblings, cousins, retainers and in-laws – would gradually come to place Henry's interests above everything else. The visit to Raglan marked the beginning of Margaret's self-identity as Henry's mother. It did not, however, mean that she became more physically present in his life. On 19 September, Margaret and Sir Harry bade Henry and the Herberts farewell and returned to Woking. Margaret would not see her son again for three years.[13]

★

BY 1468, MARGARET AND HARRY'S EFFORTS TO INGRATIATE themselves with King Edward were finally paying off. That December, they were given the surest indication yet of royal favour – Edward paid them a personal visit. The first hint of the possibility of an audience with the monarch appears in the couple's household accounts, with the urgent dispatch to London of Reynald Bray, who was 'sent for in haste to my lady of Buckingham for a great matter touching my lord and my lady'.[14] It was indeed a 'great matter', for the king's visit raised the enticing prospect of further royal patronage. Margaret and Harry were having difficulty establishing their authority over some of their territories, such as Kendal in far-off Westmorland. Perhaps these could be settled in their favour? Now that Henry was nearing his twelfth birthday, many of Margaret's hopes must have been for him and for the restoration of the Richmond inheritance. The good grace of the king could make all the difference.

Edward's visit would be brief – a meal in their hunting lodge at Brookwood, two miles from Woking manor – yet Margaret was consumed by preparations for several weeks. Servants were dispatched to Guildford and London, returning laden with pewter plate and bolts of expensive cloth. The kitchen worked tirelessly to prepare a feast fit for a king. Over the open hearth the cooks roasted 'all manner of wildfowl' and the table groaned with fish and seafood: lamprey, pike and tench, 700 oysters and 'half a great conger [eel] for the king's dinner'. King Edward was known to enjoy indulging himself, which might explain the two gallons of wine readied for his arrival.[15]

On 20 December 1468, Harry rode out with his grooms – resplendent in their new blue livery – to wait on King Edward at Guildford and escort him to Brookwood. There, beneath a specially commissioned purple sarcenet canopy, Margaret finally had her first personal meeting with the Yorkist king. She found herself in the presence of a tall, auburn-haired man in his mid-twenties whose form was, according to one contemporary, 'as well turned for love intrigues as any man I ever saw in my life'. The handsome young king was a notorious flirt: 'His thoughts were wholly employed upon the ladies (and far more than was reasonable).'[16] Margaret had ensured that, diminutive though she was, she met the king looking as magnificent as possible, wearing layers of expensive Holland and Brabant cloth, and a velvet gown made for the occasion.[17] The dinner passed off without a hitch, to the strains of royal minstrels. Margaret could feel justly proud of her team at Woking, of her husband and – perhaps she would permit, although she hated vainglory – of herself. The king's undivided attention enhanced the possibility of future enrichment.

But the preparations for the visit may have demanded too great an exertion on Harry's part. For around the time of the Staffords' audience with King Edward, the account book of Reynald Bray begins to be peppered with ominous entries relating to Harry's health. Payments appear with increasing regularity to the physician 'Mayster Wolford' of London and for medicines including 'a pound of treacle'* – that famous cure-all of the Middle Ages concocted of, among other ingredients, roasted snake flesh. In the New Year of 1469, Harry was so ill that Margaret had to step in to oversee the giving of seasonal rewards to their servants, the payment of recent purchases and the fee of Mayster Wolford.[18] Although he recovered a little in the spring, a journey up to London struck Harry down again, forcing him to 'lay abed' at his mother's house, so 'feeble' that a second physician was summoned to attend him.[19] Reynald Bray took over conducting business from his master in the fortnight before Easter, personally meeting with an auditor in London when Harry could not. Margaret never forgot Bray's loyal service in a time of need.

It is possible that Harry was suffering from 'St Anthony's fire', known today as erysipelas, a bacterial skin complaint regarded as a mild form of leprosy. This disease can particularly affect the legs, which may explain the frequent purchase of lined hose for Harry. He and Margaret both joined the religious confraternity of Burton Lazars, a site with a sulphurous hot spring that had cared for lepers for centuries, and in 1470 Harry's chaplain John Bush

---

* Also known as *theriac* or *theriacle*, this medical compound was reputed to be an antidote to poison and malignant diseases.

gave alms at several 'places of the lepers' on the road north to York. If he did suffer from this disfiguring skin condition, it may explain Margaret's particular devotion to St Anthony, who offered protection to lepers.[20] Soon, however, Margaret's concerns about her husband's health paled into insignificance in the face of wider troubles. For, after years of courting the favour of King Edward, Margaret's efforts were finally yielding fruit at the worst possible moment.

6

'Brittle fortune'[1]

✳

In July 1469, Reynald Bray rode home to Woking with troubling news from the capital. He found his mistress receiving the ministrations of 'Mayster William Surgeon', who had been summoned to provide 'medicines for my lady's mouth'.[2] A month past her twenty-sixth birthday, Margaret was embroiled in a contentious legal dispute over the fee* of Kendal in Cumbria, which was part of her dower from Edmund Tudor. Anxieties around the case may have caused grinding of teeth or stress-related ulcers. What Bray had to report would do little to allay her concerns. Throughout spring and summer, a wave of rebellions had swept the northern counties under the aegis of 'Robin of Redesdale', an enigmatic leader whose pseudonym was a conscious echo of the legendary English outlaw Robin Hood. Margaret may have feared that her own northern properties would be affected. Already, she faced a challenge in Kendal from a local rival, Sir William Parr, who had the support of Edward IV's cousin Richard Neville, earl of Warwick. Warwick's Neville clan was the dominant power in the north and Margaret had found it impossible to assert herself against his interests. Bray had been sent to London to pursue the Kendal dispute in the law courts, with little success. Even worse, while in the capital Bray had learned that Robin of Redesdale's rising was slowly assuming the form of a wider revolt to remove Edward IV.

---

* A 'fee' was land with certain feudal obligations.

English loyalty to Edward had soured in recent years. The furthest corners of his realm were never entirely reconciled to the Yorkist regime and Edward's taxes and debasement of the coinage were highly unpopular. Late in 1468, Edward had to condemn Richard Steris, 'one of the cunningest players at the tennis in England', when this ex-Lancastrian was found to have committed treason. Steris's renowned athletic abilities, which included leaping in and out of a breast-high bath tub, could not save him from the executioner's block and he was beheaded at Tower Hill.[3] Steris represented a groundswell of dissatisfaction with Edward's regime. Now that enough time had passed for them to have forgotten the previous king's worst failings, the English had begun to hark back to the days of Henry VI with something resembling nostalgia.[4]

More serious for Edward was his progressive estrangement from Warwick 'the Kingmaker'. The earl of Warwick was a man of fascinating contradictions: he enjoyed an enviable common touch, and the rhetorical genius to tailor his arguments perfectly to the emotional touchstones of his audience, but he was as ruthless and self-serving as any of his noble peers. For his Yorkist relatives he had whipped the English commons into a rebellious frenzy that drove Henry VI from his throne. He courted, and won, the admiration of papal legates, European princes and ambassadors, and convinced them of his moral rectitude even as he was assassinating his rivals. As captain of Calais – a post he held for over a decade – he actively harmed English coastal security by plundering foreign ships, yet he was considered by many Englishmen to be the 'most courageous and manliest knight living'.[5] He was, in short, a very dangerous man to alienate. But that was precisely what Edward IV had done.

The root of their division lay in Edward's marriage, in May 1464, to an English gentlewoman by the name of Elizabeth Woodville. Elizabeth had little to recommend her as queen: she was older than her husband, widowed and English.[6] The marriage thus brought almost no economic or diplomatic advantages to the realm. Elizabeth Woodville had only one international card to play, and it was a weak one: her mother was Jacquetta of Luxembourg, the daughter of a cultured, European royal line and widow of the Lancastrian prince John, duke of Bedford.* But Elizabeth's father was one of Jacquetta's servants, and Elizabeth herself had married a lowly Lancastrian knight called Sir John Grey. He died in battle at St Albans in 1461, leaving her with two young sons, Thomas and Richard Grey. Although lacking in patronage and consequence, Elizabeth was pragmatic, assertive and, crucially for her future relations with Edward, sexually alluring. According to legend, when the king met this beautiful young widow beneath a tree in a forest close to May Day 1464, it was lust at first sight. Edward attempted a ploy that had worked with other beautiful young women: he promised Elizabeth marriage, intending to abandon her after the 'wedding night' on the grounds their union wasn't legally binding. But Elizabeth was no fool. She and her family ensured that whatever 'marriage' she and Edward shared had sufficient legitimacy for the king to be unable to slip its snare.[7]

Unfortunately, while Edward was cavorting with Elizabeth, the earl of Warwick had been negotiating a diplomatic union between the king and a French princess – a marriage that would cement an international alliance and establish the Yorkist dynasty on the European stage. The fact that Edward had thrown over such an opportunity for the widow of a Lancastrian knight with two children and ten unmarried siblings was baffling, and it did Edward little credit that the marriage was born more of sexual frustration than political reasoning. Even worse, Edward concealed his marriage from Warwick, only eventually revealing the truth to his council in September 1464.

Margaret may have encountered the queen and her myriad kinfolk at court. She certainly would have known them by reputation. By the end of the 1460s, the promotion of Elizabeth's family had become notorious. The Woodvilles and Greys monopolised the slim pickings of royal patronage available, taking the choicest marriages, from dukes to heiresses. Contemporary morals were scandalised when the queen arranged for her twenty-year-old brother John to marry the sexagenarian Katherine Neville, duchess

---

* The duke of Bedford was Henry V's brother.

of Norfolk – 'a diabolical marriage' that could only be explained by bare-faced greed.[8] Only scraps were left for longer-term Yorkists like the earl of Warwick and his Neville relations. Warwick was painfully conscious that his two adolescent daughters, Anne and Isabel Neville, were still unmarried and that the few remaining high-ranking potential bridegrooms were disappearing into the Woodville fold. What little royal patronage remained was funnelled towards Edward's Welsh comrade-in-arms William Herbert, who had not only gained control of the lucrative wardships of Henry Tudor and the young earl of Northumberland, but was also made Knight of the Garter and, in 1468, granted Jasper Tudor's old title of earl of Pembroke.

By the late 1460s, the court had fractured into a Warwick faction and a Woodville faction, with foreign policy the latest battlefield. Warwick still harped on about the benefits of a French alliance, while Edward and his in-laws, led by his mother-in-law, Jacquetta of Luxembourg, preferred to treat with her relatives in Burgundy.[*] The Woodville will prevailed, and, in 1468, Edward allied with the cultured and handsome Charles 'the Bold' of Burgundy, sealing the union by offering his sister Margaret of York in marriage. Enraged at this latest countermanding of his will, Warwick retreated to his northern estates to brood on his disappointments.

For Margaret and Harry, Warwick's fall from grace represented an opportunity. The earl's protection had been Sir William Parr's trump card in the Kendal dispute, and his diminished influence gave Margaret the chance to press her case against him to the king. To this end, Margaret sent Reynald Bray to Windsor in June 1469 to appeal to William Herbert to discuss the dispute and 'divers matters of my lord and my lady'.[9] Margaret probably also continued negotiations for her son's marriage to Herbert's daughter. But soon William Herbert had far greater concerns than Margaret's affairs. Early in July, betrayal within the Yorkist regime came to light: the northern rebellions of Robin of Redesdale were not, as King Edward had complacently imagined, a rising of disorganised

---

[*] Charles the Bold was duke of Burgundy, in what is now eastern France, and also held territories in Luxembourg and the 'Low Countries': what are now the Netherlands and Belgium.

commoners, easily snuffed out, but a coup devised by none other than Warwick the Kingmaker.

The first open demonstration of Warwick's defiance occurred on 11 July 1469. Safe in his military heartland at Calais, Warwick married off his eldest daughter Isabel to Edward's ambitious brother George, duke of Clarence – even though Edward had expressly forbidden the match. Demonstrating the seriousness of the Neville clan's defection, many members of Warwick's family attended the wedding: the ceremony was conducted by Warwick's brother the archbishop of York, in the presence of their powerful brother-in-law John de Vere, earl of Oxford.* Within days the newly expanded Neville clan returned to England loudly proclaiming the rebel manifesto of Robin of Redesdale. Disillusioned Englishmen flocked to Warwick's and Clarence's banner as they marched towards London from Kent, calling for the removal and punishment of 'seditious persons' around the king who were concerned only with 'enriching of themselves and their blood' (i.e. relatives).[10] To ensure the intended targets of their ire were crystal clear, Warwick and Clarence then listed these wrongdoers, who included the queen's parents and siblings, and William Herbert. King Edward, who had been on pilgrimage in East Anglia, was caught completely off-guard. Panicked royal summons flew from his hand. Among the first to respond was Herbert.

At Woking, Margaret dispatched a steady stream of retainers to London and Wales as she attempted to stay informed amid the escalating turmoil.[11] Any hope she had that Warwick and Edward's alienation could work to her advantage had been dashed. If Edward was deposed, she would lose a vital, and long-cultivated, patron. But if William Herbert faced Warwick's mob justice, Henry Tudor could lose much more. Margaret's son was twelve years old now; old enough to potentially represent a target for the rebels, and to ride to war. For when William Herbert marched his army out of Raglan to answer the king's call to arms, he took Henry with him.

* The earl of Oxford was married to Warwick's sister Margaret Neville.

★

WORD OF THE CONFRONTATION BETWEEN HERBERT'S ARMY AND the rebels reached Margaret in snatches, each new detail more disquieting than the last. Henry Tudor was with Herbert when he and his ally the earl of Devon caught up with the rebels near Banbury on 25 July. That night, while they should have been preparing for battle, Herbert and Devon quarrelled over their lodgings and their forces were split. The next morning, the divided royal army engaged the rebels at a plain called Edgecote and Herbert's Welshmen endured terrible losses. The battle lasted for hours, eventually turning in the rebels' favour when northern reinforcements arrived. Among their captains was Margaret's rival Sir William Parr. The earl of Devon fled the field, and Herbert was captured. Between two to five thousand of his countrymen were slain, a toll so high that it incited the laments of Welsh bards.[12]

At a war council after battle, Warwick condemned Herbert and his brother Richard to death. Herbert spent his last hours making careful alterations to the will he had drafted ten days earlier, when death had seemed a more remote prospect. He charged his wife Anne, 'as I love and trust you', to obey his dying wishes, including his intention for Henry Tudor to marry their daughter Maud. Towards the end of his will, as Herbert requested that priests pray 'for all their souls slain in the field' at Edgecote, he began to break down, his pleas growing more desperate: 'Wife, pray for me... as ye had in my life, my heart and love. God have mercy upon me and save you and our children... Amen.'[13]

The following morning, 27 July, William Herbert, his brother and ten other Welsh captains were marched into the marketplace of Northampton and beheaded. Two days later, still unaware of the massacre at Edgecote, King Edward rode into a trap at Olney on the road to London, and was captured by Warwick's brother George Neville, archbishop of York.

But where was Henry Tudor throughout all this? For, after the Battle of Edgecote, he disappeared. Margaret sent riders crisscrossing the country in search of him. Twice, she dispatched her servant William Baily to London to gain 'tidings of my lord' Herbert and his ward.[14] Another retainer was sent to Worcester, and yet another – Reynald Bray's brother John – to Raglan. Finally, it was Harry's mother, the duchess of Buckingham, who provided the longed-for information. Henry had been plucked from danger by Lady Anne Herbert's nephew, and carried to her brother's border fortress at Weobley. There, Anne and her children also fled to escape rebel reprisals. It took five days for John Bray to pin down Henry's location and check the boy was unharmed before he could return to Woking and reassure Margaret that her son was safe.[15]

Meanwhile, more heads rolled as Warwick eliminated his enemies one by one. Shortly after the Battle of Edgecote, Herbert's brother Thomas was captured and killed at Bristol. Queen Elizabeth's father and brother John were captured at Chepstow and taken to Kenilworth, where they were executed on 12 August. Five days later, Herbert's erstwhile ally the earl of Devon was lynched by the commons of Bridgwater. As the political landscape continued to shift, Margaret focused her energies on protecting Henry at all costs. With Reynald Bray at their head, a band of eight Stafford retainers rode to Weobley 'by my lady['s] commandment' to discuss Henry's future with Anne Herbert.[16] The death of Henry's guardian meant his wardship was once again prey to fortune-hunters, and Edward, Warwick, Clarence or any of their allies might use the boy as a pawn in their deadly game. Since Margaret could not come to Henry in person, on her behalf Bray presented twenty shillings to Henry's attendant at Weobley and gave the boy a bow and arrow 'for his disports'.[17] More envoys from Margaret followed throughout the summer and into the autumn as she tried to establish the legal parameters of Henry's status and, if possible, regain his wardship for herself.

Margaret also desperately sought clarity on Edward IV's position, sending riders north to Warwick Castle, where he was first imprisoned. She also sought the advice of Harry's family about how to proceed. Harry's stepfather Walter Blount, Lord Mountjoy was in communication with Margaret, and his younger brother John Stafford visited Woking in person. Lord Mountjoy had married Harry's mother, the dowager duchess of Buckingham, in 1467, and was a long-time associate of the Yorkists, having served as their treasurer in both Calais and England. His guidance was valuable, but probably concerning. Warwick showed no sign of submitting to Woodville domination. Ugly rumours were circulating that Edward was not his father's son, but the illegitimate product of his mother's affair with an archer. It was an unfounded slander but it hinted at the true motivation for Warwick and Clarence's rising. If Edward was not the rightful king then his younger brother Clarence must be. Warwick and Clarence did not just want to eliminate their rivals to control Edward. They sought the crown for themselves.

The Staffords held strong for King Edward, but Margaret's situation was more complicated. Since 1464, the earldom of Richmond had been under Clarence's control, so if Henry regained his estate the duke would be materially disadvantaged. Thus, Margaret needed Clarence's support to have any hope of regaining her son's wardship, especially if Clarence succeeded in deposing Edward and became king himself. But to negotiate with Edward's captor could invite reprisals from Edward if he regained control. By the end of August, Margaret had decided she must take the risk. On St Bartholomew's Day (24 August) 1469, she and Harry travelled to London and moved into her mother's residence. As her servants unpacked their belongings, Margaret travelled by boat, alone, to 'Lord Clarence place' at Fleet Street, where she dispatched messages to Clarence in the north, seeking his support for the recovery of Henry Tudor's wardship. Despite the years she had spent courting Edward IV, Margaret was willing to abandon him if it would help her regain control of her son.[18]

However, Margaret's approaches to Clarence proved woefully ill-timed. He and Warwick were struggling to control the chaos they had unleashed. Lawlessness engulfed the realm, with private feuds flaring from east to west and a fresh Lancastrian rising in Country Durham. Lacking the king's authority, Warwick and Clarence found it impossible to suppress this unrest, and reluctantly they released Edward from captivity. In the second week of September 1469, the king was free and issuing royal commands at York. By mid-October, he was approaching London as undoubted ruler once more.

Now Margaret had cause to regret her rash communications with Clarence. By treating with him, she had opened herself up to royal suspicion. It was imperative that she and Harry greet the returning king with every possible indication of their continued fealty. On 10 October, Harry rode to Edward's side with a retinue of armed men, black spurs at his horse's flanks, a newly bought hat on his head and fresh arrows bristling in his retainers' quivers.[19] But this demonstration of military readiness did not convince Edward and nor did the professions of – undoubtedly genuine – loyalty by Harry's stepfather, Lord Mountjoy, who escorted the king into the capital. Edward rewarded Harry's younger brother Sir John Stafford along with others who had stood firm during the rebellions: John was created earl of Wiltshire, and Edward's fifteen-year-old brother Richard, duke of Gloucester was granted offices that gave him the same Welsh pre-eminence that the late William Herbert had enjoyed. Margaret and Harry, however, were pointedly ignored. Margaret's attempts to gain Edward's favour in the past decade had been fatally undermined by her opportunism during the rebellion.[20]

For now, an uneasy truce settled over public affairs. Warwick and Clarence were not punished for their treachery, but nor were they forgiven. One London-based correspondent hinted at tensions in the court when he wrote that 'the king himself hath good language of the lords of Clarence [and] of Warwick, saying they be his best friends. But his household men have other language'.[21] The country's schisms were far from resolved and Margaret had good reason to worry. She had gambled on the rebels' victory, and badly miscalculated. Hoping she could still secure Henry's wardship even without royal support, she scrambled to make use of the means at her disposal. Her retainers combed the records of the Exchequer and Chancery in London and pored over documents in South Wales to find legal support for her claim. A parliamentary clerk was paid to copy a deed regarding 'my lord of Richmond's matter'.[22]

On 21 October, Margaret's lawyers held a conference with Lady Anne Herbert's council at the Bell Inn on Fleet Street, London, where they discussed the terms of the 'wardship of my lord of Richmond' over bread, ale, mutton and autumn fruits.[23] The meeting was amicable, and for the rest of her life Margaret would remain grateful to Anne for protecting her son during this awful time.[24] But, without a royal seal of approval, any resolution Margaret and Lady Herbert reached about Henry could only be provisional.

IT WAS SEVERAL MONTHS BEFORE MARGARET AND HARRY HAD an opportunity to prove themselves to Edward and, when it came, the circumstances were far from what Margaret would have wished. Around Candlemas Day (2 February) 1470, violence broke out in Lincolnshire. The home of one of Edward's household knights, Sir Thomas Burgh, was pillaged and destroyed, and the king announced he would ride in person to deal with the perpetrators. The Burgh incident was just one of many recent occasions when local enmities spilled over into bloodshed, but in this case the violence touched Margaret directly. For the rabble-rousers who had attacked Burgh's home and invoked the king's wrath were her stepbrother Richard, Lord Welles and Willoughby, and his son Sir Robert Welles.[25]

Among those summoned to join the king's forces as he marched on Lincolnshire was Harry Stafford. He and Margaret thus faced an uncomfortable choice. They needed to prove their loyalty to Edward, but marching against Margaret's stepbrother and nephew went against the grain of familial loyalty. Relations within their family had been strained in recent years as Margaret's mother fought Richard for control of their Lincolnshire estates, but the Welleses remained kin nonetheless. Margaret's anxieties may have been slightly allayed when Edward granted a pardon to Lord Richard and his brother-in-law Sir Thomas Dimmock, who had been summoned to Westminster to answer for their offences. It seemed there was to be no sanguinary display of royal vengeance. So, trusting to Edward's promise of grace, and hoping to regain their previous standing, Margaret and Harry made their choice. On 6 March 1470, Harry bade farewell to Margaret and left Woking with an armed retinue of thirty servants, including Reynald Bray.[26]

As Harry rode past London and followed the road north through St Albans towards Lincolnshire, his anxieties could only have increased. Far from pacifying the shires, the king's advance seemed to be fanning the flames of unrest. The commons of Lincolnshire feared he was coming to avenge himself on the county for rising with Robin of Redesdale the previous summer. To protect his tenants and apply pressure to the king, Sir Robert Welles proclaimed himself captain of the commons and tens of thousands flocked to his raised banner. Robert even invited the earl of Warwick and duke of Clarence to join his cause. This local quarrel began to take on the appearance of a serious rebellion.[27]

As they neared Stamford, Harry and his retinue were overtaken by royal guards, galloping up that same road to escort prisoners to the king: Lord Richard Welles and Thomas Dimmock. Despite his promised pardon, Edward proclaimed that if the Lincolnshire commons did not disperse, he would behead the rebel lords. By the time Harry caught up with the royal army at Stamford on 12 March, events had reached a crisis. Sir Robert Welles refused to stand down and his army had assembled at Empingham, five miles away. Robert assumed that Edward would not really reverse his pardon – but he was mistaken. The same day Harry joined the king, Lord Richard Welles and Thomas Dimmock were marched out of Stamford and, within sight of the rebel army, beheaded. Battle now seemed inevitable.

As the king's encampment echoed with the readying of armour and sharpening of weapons, Harry slipped away with a single servant and rode to Maxey to break the news of Richard's death to Margaret's mother. Despite the bad blood between them over the Welles inheritance, the dowager duchess could hardly be expected to rejoice in her stepson's violent demise.[28] Indeed, Edward's brutal suppression of the Lincolnshire rebels overrode his original pledge to be merciful, which was deeply unnerving for both the dowager duchess and Margaret. As the Tudor chronicler Edward Hall wrote, the execution of Lord Welles was a 'terrible example [to] others which shall put their confidence in the promise of a prince'.[29] It suggested that Edward's promises and pardons could not be trusted.

But, although their lords were dead, the Lincolnshire rebels refused to surrender. The following day, 13 March 1470, Edward's army advanced on them and the battle swiftly disintegrated into a rout. As they struggled desperately with the king's forces, the rebels were heard to cry out 'A Clarence! A Clarence! A Warwick!' and among the corpses were found 'divers persons in the Duke of Clarence livery'.[30] This confirmed Edward's suspicions that his brother was once again plotting against him. Sir Robert Welles was captured and forced to confess that Warwick and Clarence had conspired in the rising. Perhaps he hoped this confession would save his life. But Edward was no longer inclined to be merciful. At Doncaster, Harry was present for another act of royal vengeance as Sir Robert followed his father to the block.[31]

But the true targets of Edward's vengeance were still at large: the perfidious Clarence and Warwick. Over the course of the next month, Harry was forced to march with Edward's army as it pursued his fleeing kinsmen. First north towards the Peak District and Yorkshire, where Harry re-provisioned and readied his armour in case of further violence, buying spurs, horse harness and gilt 'vests'. To be on the safe side, Harry also donated to lepers' houses at the roadside, in return for prayers for his safe return. Then the king's army marched south at increasing speed, through the Midlands and Cotswolds, Somerset and Devon, covering almost three hundred miles in three weeks, until finally, on 14 April, they reached Exeter – only to come to the infuriating realisation that Warwick and Clarence had slipped the leash. Just in time, the rebels and their wives had taken ship to Calais. But they would return. For now, King Edward disbanded his army, and Harry led his exhausted men home to Woking. This protracted period in the saddle did little to improve his precarious health, nor to allay Margaret's anxieties for the future.[32]

7

'Rule the king'[1]

＊

On 2 October 1470, Margaret and Harry rode through the gates of London and into a city on the brink of revolution.[2] Across the country, armies mustered and panicked Yorkist loyalists fled. The changes that had taken place over a politically volatile summer had required all Margaret and Harry's vigilance, and constant recourse to their network of friends and informers, as they tried to stay apprised of events. Secret emissaries had repeatedly crossed the Channel while Margaret and Harry circled the hunting lodges of Surrey. Now, as they entered the capital, they came committed to a new regime.

It was only three weeks since Warwick and Clarence had returned to England, on 13 September, bolstered by an international alliance. That summer Louis XI of France had promised them an army to depose Edward IV and restore Henry VI, in exchange for their support in his wars against Burgundy. With the incentive of French funds and a puppet king through whom they could rule, the rebel Yorkists had accomplished their purpose with remarkable speed. The very day that Margaret arrived in London, Edward IV fled the country aboard a boat from East Anglia, and sought asylum with his brother-in-law Charles the Bold. Edward left behind his heavily pregnant queen, Elizabeth Woodville, who sought sanctuary along with her children in Westminster Abbey. On 3 October, in an extraordinary reversal, the doors of Henry VI's prison in the Tower of London were thrown open and the ageing, melancholic king shuffled out of captivity and back onto the throne. The Lancastrian 'Readeption'* was complete, and events that only a year ago would have seemed impossible were now stark reality.

Margaret was suspiciously well prepared for these events. So much so that it seems certain that she and Harry had spent the summer in secret communication with the rebels. Margaret's main contact in the rebel camp was probably Jasper Tudor, who had witnessed Louis's agreement with Warwick and Clarence at Angers in July. Jasper's true aim, of course, was not the success of his old Yorkist adversaries, but the restoration of Henry VI, Queen Marguerite of Anjou and their now teenage son, with whom Jasper had been living in exile. Under Lancastrian patronage, the Tudors could be re-established, and Jasper hoped that through his ambitions for Henry he could enlist Margaret's support. It is likely, however, that Margaret had another confidante who was involved in the Readeption coup – someone with rather more complex motivations: Cecily, duchess of York.

Cecily had been in an impossible situation for the past eighteen months. Torn between her loyalties to her eldest son, Edward IV, and her younger son, the rebel duke of Clarence, Cecily had desperately striven to reconcile her warring boys and had maintained contact with both, even as Edward and Clarence raised armies against each other. Cecily hoped that, if Clarence could be detached from Warwick, he might resolve his issues with Edward. She had engaged the support of her daughters in this endeavour, especially the youngest, Margaret of York.[3] When the Wars of the Roses first ripped through her family, Cecily's three youngest children, Margaret and the dukes of Clarence and Gloucester, had been living under her care. Her desire to protect them had become instinctive, so even as Clarence was forging his alliance with Louis, Cecily still tried to lure him home. She was thus well placed to know the rebels' movements that summer, and probably shared her anxieties with her sister Anne, duchess of Buckingham. Anne, of course, was Harry Stafford's mother and it was presumably through her that Margaret gained access to Cecily

---

* As Henry VI's restoration to the throne was called.

and her intelligence. While their interactions during the summer were necessarily secretive, by the autumn Margaret was regularly visiting Cecily at her London home, Baynards Castle.[4]

Margaret and Cecily had history. Like many noblewomen, they shared common ancestry: Cecily's mother was Joan Beaufort, daughter of John of Gaunt, making her and Margaret distant cousins. They may have first met in 1459, when Margaret was newly married to Harry and Cecily was a hostage in Anne's custody at Maxstoke Castle. Although their husbands served in opposing armies during the wars, Anne and Cecily's shared experiences outweighed their political differences and they remained close until their deaths. They had grown up together in the rambling nursery of Raby Castle in County Durham as two of the twenty-three legitimate children born to the earl of Westmorland. Both identified themselves closely with their beloved husbands, remaining proud 'duchesses' long after violent death had robbed them of their ducal spouses. In an age when noblewomen often resided apart from their husbands on their home estate, both Anne and Cecily had travelled with their husbands whenever they could. They oversaw the running of their households, assembled libraries of religious and classical works, and patronised monastic orders – all interests they shared with Margaret. In the peaceful years of Edward IV's rule, before factional chaos returned, Cecily had been a near constant presence at court, standing at her son's side, a resplendent figure adorned with exquisite religious jewellery. Nicholas O'Flanagan, bishop of Elphin, witnessed Edward's accession and believed that Cecily's influence over her son was such that she 'can rule the king as she pleases'.[5] By 1470, Cecily would have viewed that suggestion rather ruefully.

But while the Readeption divided Cecily's family, it brought Margaret's back together. After landing in Wales, Jasper Tudor rode on to the Welsh borders and finally removed Henry from the care of Lady Anne Herbert. Henry was conveyed all the way to London in Jasper's keeping, and there Margaret saw her son for the first time in three years. Henry was now nearly fourteen – almost exactly the same age Margaret had been when she gave birth to him. With the Readeption of Henry's uncle and namesake,

Margaret hoped to finally restore him to the earldom of Richmond, with all the status and comfort that would convey.

Since 1464, Henry's earldom had been held by George, duke of Clarence. Now, with the duke's return to political authority, Margaret must have hoped that Clarence could be satisfied with his other gains, and persuaded to surrender Henry's estate. Of course, if the king – or, perhaps more accurately, the king's effective controller, the earl of Warwick – granted Henry the earldom, there would be little Clarence could do to prevent it. With this in mind, Margaret moved swiftly to offer her fealty to the restored King Henry VI. Proudly united, on 28 October 1470, Margaret, Harry, Henry and Jasper entered the palace of Westminster to greet their returning king.

It was fifteen years since Margaret had seen Henry VI, and she must have found him profoundly changed. The experience of exile, imprisonment and constant anxiety had reduced him to a shadow of his former self; a man grown bearded and shabby during his captivity, whose choice of blue velvet mourning robes for his public processions was an outward sign of deep inner sadness. According to his confessor and earliest biographer, John Blacman, the pious King Henry had been blessed with prophetic visons and messages from God. He saw Jesus appear to him in the Mass and, as he attempted to evade the clutches of Edward IV in 1464–5, had received a mystical warning from Saints Anselm and Duncan that he would be betrayed and captured. The meeting with Margaret's family on 28 October 1470 was to be the source of another prophecy – or so it was later claimed by the Tudor writer Polydore Vergil, who wrote a description of the scene:

> It is said that the king, seeing the boy [Henry Tudor], held his silence for a while, studying his character, and then said to the nobles who were present, "This indeed is the one to whom we and our adversaries must yield our power." Thus this pious man predicted that someday Henry [Tudor] would obtain the crown.[6]

A similar tale was related by Margaret's confessor John Fisher and the blind court historian Bernard André, who probably heard the story directly from Margaret and her son. The prophecy un-doubtedly served their interests, but it is also possible that Henry VI made some such intimation – or at least that Margaret and her son thought he had. Margaret genuinely believed in the king's otherworldly piety. He was the architect of the marriage that gave Margaret her son and, despite the misfortune that had flowed from it, for that simple fact Margaret was grateful. It was surely not lost on any member of the Tudor party at Westminster that day that Henry was now the king's closest blood relative after his own son. Given the vicissitudes of royal fortunes in the past decade, it was not absurd to imagine he might one day claim a crown for himself. But Margaret's ambitions for Henry at this point are unlikely to have stretched that far. Queen Marguerite and her Lancastrian prince were still in France, held hostage by King Louis until Warwick delivered on his promise to send an English army against Burgundy. With so much still unsettled, Margaret's price for supporting the Readeption government was simple: she wanted Henry's earldom restored, and to regain control of her own long-contested territories in Kendal.

How much King Henry VI absorbed the details of these re-quests during his audience with Margaret is questionable. She probably had to repeat her wishes after the king retired, fatigued, and her party dined instead with his chamberlain and compan-ion in exile, Sir Richard Tunstall. She repeated them, too, in the numerous visits she made to Baynards Castle that autumn, when she probably met with both Clarence and Cecily.[7] She enjoyed some success, winning the right to hold an additional third of the Kendal lands for seven years. But Margaret's gain was another's loss. Her newly acquired portion was seized from Jacquetta of Luxembourg, Elizabeth Woodville's mother. Grieving the loss of a son and husband during Warwick's coup of 1469, Jacquetta spent the Readeption hiding in sanctuary with her daughter and grand-children at Westminster Abbey, so was in little position to contest her rights. Warwick had an animus against the duchess as head of the despised Woodville clan, and had even brought charges of witchcraft against her – unsuccessfully – the year before.[8] Perhaps the proudly aristocratic Margaret privately shared Warwick's distaste for the upstart Woodvilles. At the very least, she was content to profit from their downfall. She and her son had endured a great deal in the past decade. The enjoyment of her current success probably silenced any qualms she might have felt about the means used to acquire it.[9]

Or perhaps Margaret held firm to this victory because she was more desperate than she let on. In the division of spoils by the Readeption regime, Margaret did not regain the Richmond earldom for her son. Instead, as a reward for his role in the Readeption coup, Clarence was regranted Henry's Richmond earldom, for life, on 24 February 1471. The duke was a more important ally to the earl of Warwick than Margaret and her adolescent son and whatever the king might have said on the matter was immaterial. This grant meant that Henry would have to wait for Clarence to die or fall from power before he could regain his inheritance. Nor did Margaret succeed in regaining custody of her son. On 14 November 1470, Jasper was restored to all the powers and titles he had lost to William Herbert under Edward IV, and with them his rights as guardian of both Wales and Henry.[10] The Readeption had not brought Margaret what she had hoped.

Margaret was able to sink her frustrations, for a time at least, in the pleasure of her son's company. She and Henry spent the weeks after their audience with the king touring the hunting lodges and parklands of Surrey, riding, hunting and hawking in the crisp autumn air. In these leisurely hours on horseback, Margaret may have finally developed a close relationship with her son. It was perhaps with some reluctance that, on 11 November, she bade farewell to Henry once more and watched him ride away with his uncle. They were bound for Jasper's Welsh estates. Margaret and Harry, meanwhile, returned to London to continue their negotiations with the Readeption regime.[11]

ON 14 MARCH 1471, A FLEET OF SHIPS WAS TOSSED ABOUT BY storms as it made its way from Flushing to the East Yorkshire coast. Aboard one of these vessels could be seen the tall, golden-haired figure of Edward IV. Separated from the rest of his fleet, that morning his ship was driven ashore at Ravenspur, where seventy years earlier another claimant to the throne – Henry Bolingbroke, the future Henry IV – had landed and begun his successful campaign to gain his rights. With this auspicious omen, Edward IV turned his army south and marched on London to seize the crown of Henry VI.[12]

Good fortune seemed to shine on Edward IV that spring. The tempests in the Channel that blew his fleet over the waves to England roared so fiercely to the south, at Harfleur, that the vessels of his Lancastrian rivals in the command of Marguerite of Anjou and her son could not leave harbour. Although Edward's queen and children were still locked away in Westminster Abbey, their number had expanded in one crucial way: in November, Elizabeth Woodville had finally given birth to a son, named Edward for his father. The baby, and with him hope for the Yorkist future, was growing in strength with every passing day. Even the divisions that had riven Edward's family for two years were resolved swiftly on his return. On 3 April 1471, the constant entreaties of his mother and sisters – and the inadequate rewards of Warwick the Kingmaker – finally convinced Clarence to reconcile with his brother, and the duke's considerable army joined Edward IV on the Banbury road as he headed south. Meanwhile, the supporters of the Readeption regime seemed hopelessly divided, lacking common cause. Lancastrian loyalists who had spent years in exile with Marguerite of Anjou, like Margaret's Beaufort cousins, had no interest in serving the earl of Warwick. Nor did they show any obvious zeal for the bumbling and gloomy Henry VI, although his more soldierly son, the Prince of Lancaster, might have been a unifying force if only he could get to England in time to lead his army.

The unhappy state of the Lancastrian regime must have been brought home to Margaret that spring as she hosted her cousin Edmund Beaufort at her Woking home. Edmund had originally lived in Marguerite's court-in-exile, but he had spent much of the past few years in the entourage of Charles of Burgundy. It had been Edmund's great hope that Charles could be enticed to support the Lancastrians, a prospect dashed by the earl of Warwick

in February when he fulfilled his promise to King Louis and declared war on the Burgundians. In retaliation, Charles bankrolled
Edward IV's invading army.

During two visits to Woking that March, over Lenten feasts of
roast eel, whelks and 'great raisins', Margaret sounded out Edmund
and his retinue of forty men about the future of the Lancastrian
faction.[13] She was worried. If Edward IV regained his throne, and
it was looking increasingly likely he would, then she and Harry
needed to welcome him back with open arms. Otherwise, political
isolation was the least of their worries – for supporting his enemies, they might face forfeiture of their lands, banishment or even
death. Thus, when Margaret bade her cousin farewell and watched
him march away to meet Marguerite of Anjou's eagerly anticipated
fleet in the West Country, she and Harry gave him no tangible assurance of support. The Lancastrians had largely deserted Henry
VI, who was left marooned in London by his supporters. Harry
and Margaret continued to communicate with Edmund as he rode
for Dorset, but the advancing threat of Edward IV's army, its ranks
swelling as it approached London, cautioned them against committing to the Lancastrian regime.[14]

On 2 April, Margaret and Harry made their choice. Accompanied
by a small retinue of men, Harry left Margaret at Woking and
rode, not west to join the Lancastrian forces, but north to London,
to welcome Edward IV.[15] A week later, with Edward only a day's
ride away, the few remaining supporters of Henry VI and Warwick
attempted to inspire the Londoners with a ceremonial procession
of the Lancastrian king within the city walls. Perhaps Harry witnessed this pathetic spectacle, in which the fragile king was led
around on horseback, hand in hand with an archbishop, preceded
by a swordbearer in his seventies. The sight weakened rather than
bolstered the city's desire to resist Edward. On 11 April, Edward
IV entered the city unopposed and took Henry prisoner. On Good
Friday, 12 April, Edward and his reunited family heard Mass with
his mother at Baynards Castle. The following morning, all those
loyal to Edward IV were commanded to march for St Albans,
where the earl of Warwick had massed his forces. Harry Stafford
and his retinue were among them.[16]

They found the earl of Warwick's army encamped a mile beyond Barnet on a green next to the St Albans high road. Edward gave the command to pitch camp for the night. As darkness settled over the marshy hollow where Harry and the rest of Edward's forces lay, they prepared for the battle to come.[17] Owing to the speed of their departure from the capital, Harry found himself ill-equipped. Vital parts of his armour were missing. There was a last-minute scramble to secure mail tassets, the plate metal kilt that protected his upper legs. These were delivered to him by a servant at Barnet that night, only hours before the anticipated battle. Perhaps mindful of William Herbert's fate after Edgecote, Harry dispatched a dozen of his men to wait at Kingston, to assist his escape if events turned against Edward IV. It had become unnervingly common for noblemen captured in battle to be executed, and to survive and fight another day Harry might need to flee the field on horseback. Through the night, as Warwick's cannon pounded the area around Edward's camp, Harry wrote his will. Then, on Easter morning, before the sun was fully up, he rode out to battle.

AT WOKING, THE FIRST MARGARET KNEW OF THE BATTLE AT Barnet was probably the arrival of Harry's servant, John Day, who rode posthaste to deliver her Harry's last testament. Remarkably, this document survives today, a stained and creased flap of parchment that testifies to Harry's abiding trust in Margaret, his 'most entire beloved wife'. He named her his sole executor, and entrusted her 'to do for my soul according most after her discretion and wisdom'.[18] The will expressed a pious concern for his soul and a debt he owed Reynald Bray, which he suggested settling by selling some land around Windsor. It also suggests Harry's anxiety at what might follow, for in places he appears to have pressed too heavily on his pen, leaving splodges of ink.[19]

Perhaps John Day also told Margaret that, the night before battle, as Harry was scrawling his will, Edward IV ordered complete silence so that the earl of Warwick would not realise that his artillery was overshooting the Yorkist camp, uselessly pounding the earth beyond them. From Harry's other servants, and from the reports of soldiers limping back from the battlefield, Margaret gained further snatched impressions of what ensued at Barnet that day. She heard how the armies lined up against one another before dawn, in a mist so thick that men could scarcely make out the battle standards above their heads. In this eerie half-light, the opposing forces stood out of alignment, so that the Yorkist left flank – under Edward's friend William, Lord Hastings – bore the brunt of the assault, pressing forward and causing the armies to wheel around the field.

The first news to reach London was that Edward IV was defeated, as Hastings's men fell back, crying that the day was lost. Within hours, however, this intelligence was reversed: Edward's army had regrouped, and now it was Warwick who had been defeated, betrayed by his own side. In the fog, the livery of Warwick's ally the earl of Oxford, emblazoned with a shooting star, was mistaken for Edward IV's emblem of the sun in splendour. The confusion caused Warwick's soldiers to attack their own allies, inciting chaos. Like Harry, Warwick had readied a horse to flee and he now leaped into the saddle, making for nearby woodland in the hope of escape. But, as he fled, he was overtaken and cut down by Edward's men. After six hours of hard fighting, the battle was won. Edward IV was victorious.

In London, more and more survivors made their way through the city gates, bandaged, bleeding, in some cases missing noses. Edward IV's battle standards were processed to St Paul's Cathedral, shot through by missiles and torn, to be presented in thanksgiving on the altar. A more grisly demonstration of Edward's victory trailed in their wake: a cart bearing the battered bodies of the earl of Warwick and his brother John Neville, naked except for cloths covering their genitalia. Edward had ordered that his enemies' corpses be publicly displayed at St Paul's.

But no news of Harry's fate reached Woking. He had not, in the end, fled the field and ridden for Surrey. Hours passed, then days, and Margaret waited in vain for information. Growing increasingly anxious, she travelled to London and on 17 April sent out riders, who returned with the news that Harry had been wounded in battle. His injuries were severe enough to keep him out of Edward's ongoing campaign as the Yorkists pressed west to crush Marguerite of Anjou. He thus managed to avoid fighting against Margaret's cousin Edmund Beaufort, and escaped the bloodshed that ensued.[20]

On 4 May 1471, as Harry recuperated with Margaret, Edward dealt a death blow to the Lancastrian cause in battle at Tewkesbury. Harassed and harried all the way through the West Country, the Lancastrian forces under Marguerite of Anjou, Prince Edward and Edmund Beaufort failed to rendezvous with Jasper Tudor's approaching Welsh army in time. Forced to fight without their full forces, and with dissension in their ranks, the Lancastrians were butchered in the water meadows and hedgerows surrounding Tewkesbury Abbey. Marguerite's son, Prince Edward, only seventeen years old, was killed attempting to flee, and Marguerite of Anjou captured hiding in a 'poor religious place' a few days later.

Death in battle and capture of the vanquished were regarded as tragic but inevitable outcomes of warfare. What Edward and his brother Richard did next, however, offended contemporary sensibilities and gave Margaret an abiding distrust of the king. As Edmund Beaufort and a handful of other Lancastrian captains escaped into the sanctuary of the abbey, Edward IV pursued them, marching into the church with the mud and blood of the battlefield still clinging to his boots, sword drawn. He was only prevented from dragging Edmund out to be murdered by the swift intervention of a priest, who rushed from Mass with the consecrated wafer still in his hands. Edward IV begrudgingly agreed to pardon the soldiers who had taken sanctuary – then, two days later, he changed his mind.[21]

On 6 May, Edmund Beaufort and over a dozen of his comrades were hauled from the abbey to Tewkesbury marketplace, where Edward IV's seventeen-year-old brother Richard, duke of Gloucester, served as judge in his capacity as constable of England. All were condemned to death and summarily beheaded beneath the market cross. Their dismembered corpses were then laid to rest in Tewkesbury Abbey.

In a further month of campaigning, Edward demonstrated that opposition to his rule would no longer be tolerated. He was unwilling to let even the most pathetic of his Lancastrian rivals survive. On 21 May, the same day that Edward returned to London as a conquering hero, Henry VI died in the Tower. The official Yorkist line was that he died 'of pure displeasure and melancholy', but his body was seen to bleed as it travelled open-faced through London for burial.[22] For Margaret, who believed wholeheartedly in Henry's piety, and who had seen for herself how feeble King Henry had become, this was an act of brutality. It was also a dire warning. By sheer good fortune, Henry Tudor and his uncle Jasper had escaped the bloodbath of Tewkesbury. As word of Edward's implacable action spread, Henry and Jasper fled into Wales, pursued by Yorkist agents, first to Chepstow and then on to Pembroke and Tenby.[23] With Henry VI dead, there was little to gain from fighting, but the Tudors were uncertain whether to risk surrender to Edward IV. Margaret urgently advised against it. According to Bernard André, she 'appealed in private to' Jasper to take Henry out of the country to protect him. In André's retelling Margaret addresses Jasper directly, although she in fact communicated with him via messenger, but the tenor of her feelings – and her efforts to persuade Jasper to share her opinion – are probably accurate: 'Go abroad,' Margaret exhorted Jasper:

> ... Unless my imagination or maternal instinct deceives me, the great distance of the sea will help us avoid all perils. I know that the hazards of the sea will be great; yet [Henry's] life will be safer on the ocean's waves than in this tempest on land.[24]

Thus, in September 1471, Jasper and Henry took ship from Tenby, intending to seek refuge with Jasper's cousin King Louis XI in France. However, storms in the Channel drove them off course and their ship eventually limped ashore in Brittany, where they appealed instead for the mercy of Duke Francis II. While Margaret must have hoped that circumstances would eventually allow Henry to return and take up his rights as earl of Richmond, there was little sign of any such restoration in 1471. In the wake of his actions in those fateful months, Margaret, more than most, had grown to mistrust King Edward IV's promises for clemency. She had seen that the Yorkist king was no longer the magnanimous ruler of ten years earlier and she knew that she and Harry had forfeited his good opinion by their open support of the Readeption. It was not in their power to win Henry's wardship nor protect him from Edward's vindictive attentions. By urging Henry to be taken overseas, she may have saved his life.

THAT AUTUMN, MARGARET FACED THE PAINFUL REALISATION THAT she had not only lost her son to exile, but she was also losing her husband. Harry had never recovered from the injuries received at Barnet. On 2 October 1471, sensing his death was close, he rewrote his will, taking the time to provide for the details of his burial and leave bequests for his faithful servants and relatives. Though he was 'whole in mind and in [his] good memory', he was too infirm to write himself, and his testament is penned in the neat, steady hand of a professional. Harry asked Margaret, as chief executor, to oversee his burial in the College of Pleshey in Essex, the ancestral burial place of the Staffords. Their local church in Woking also received offerings to pray for his soul.

Harry's chief concern was to ensure Margaret's material security after he was gone, and apart from a few horses – left to the priory of Martock, to his stepson Henry Tudor, to Harry's brother John and Reynald Bray – he left all his goods to 'mine entirely beloved wife Margaret'. He appealed to his mother and other trustees to ensure that Margaret was able to hold the lands they had been jointly granted by his father for the rest of her life. Unlike William Herbert, whose will insisted his wife remain unmarried, Harry placed no restrictions on Margaret. Perhaps he realised that she might need a high-ranking ally in his absence, and that marriage provided one of the surest means of securing such. Two days after writing his new will, on 4 October 1471, Harry died.[25]

Margaret was still only twenty-eight when she buried her third husband. Unlike her early marriages, this had been a long, contented match with a man who was clearly her partner. In her grief, she withdrew to her mother's residence of Le Ryall in London with a small retinue of sixteen attendants. In the following months, she relied on her servants and her family for personal comfort, and also for the pressing tasks of fulfilling Harry's last wishes and establishing her control over the lands they had jointly held.[26] Harry's death and the exile of her son and brother-in-law left Margaret vulnerable. In the absence of a close support network to protect herself from royal mistrust and, potentially, privation, she faced an uncertain future.

8

'Live and die with him'[1]

✳

Shortly after her twenty-ninth birthday, in June 1472, Margaret dipped her pen into a pot of ink and neatly inscribed her name at the bottom of a piece of parchment: 'M. Rychemonde'. A slice of the parchment was carefully cut off to make a tab onto which a blood-red globule of wax was poured and allowed to pool into a disc, before Margaret pressed her seal into it. As usual, while she undertook this business, Margaret was surrounded by men: witnesses, clerks, family and friends. Unusually, most of the men were from Lancashire and Cheshire, or from North Wales. Once Margaret was finished, one of them stepped forward, a man ten years Margaret's senior, and inscribed his own name – rather less assuredly, Margaret may have noticed: the pen scratched un-evenly and he had to take a second pass at the letter 'y'. Then he too set his seal: the crest of an eagle. The symbol was apt. For this lord joining his name to Margaret's, and in this document merging their interests, had the watchful serenity of a bird of prey. His name was Thomas Stanley, lord of the north-west and King of Man. And six months after the death of Sir Harry Stafford, Margaret had just married him.[2]

As Harry's corpse slowly progressed along the roads to Pleshey in Essex, behind it trailed the scattered wreckage of inten-tions left unfulfilled. Servants' wages unpaid, debts to merchants still owing, a horse bought in the hope that he might recover enough to ride it. Then there was the business of his afterlife: his body must be buried, his tomb constructed, a priest found to sing for his soul. Little wonder that, in the midst of all this death, Margaret's thoughts turned morbidly to her own demise. Entrusting Reynald Bray to attend to her late husband's business affairs, Margaret drew up her own will. It was the first time in her adult life that she had been able to assert her wishes in this way – married women, as the property of their husbands, had few personal possessions, and required the permission of their husband even to bequeath those. Now, Margaret exercised her independence in a manner that showed, despite more than a decade of marriage to Harry Stafford, that her self-identity was still exactly as it had been when they wed in 1457: she was descended from a noble line of Holland and Beaufort ancestors stretching back into the past, she was the countess of Richmond in the present, and she was the mother of Henry Tudor, who she hoped would rise to greatness in the future.[3]

As such, Margaret chose not to be buried with Harry beneath the cold stones of his family's foundation* in Essex, but at Bourne Abbey in Lincolnshire, a place closely associated with her own paternal ancestors.† She directed that a tomb should be constructed at Bourne for herself and for Edmund Tudor, the father of her only child. She wished Edmund's body to be removed from Carmarthen to this grander location where, in the fullness of time, she would join him. Even though Henry Tudor was currently an exile in Brittany with no certainty of return or restoration to his title, Margaret optimistically made provision for him to inherit her estates. Her mother's West Country relatives, the Stourtons, and Harry's Stafford relatives served as witnesses and trustees for Henry Tudor's future inheritance.[4]

As a widow with Lancastrian blood in her veins and a brother-in-law and son who had conspired against the House of York,

---

* Pleshey was founded by Thomas of Woodstock, Harry's paternal great-grandfather.
† Her grandmother Margaret Holland, duchess of Somerset had been a patron of the abbey during the late fourteenth century.

Margaret's position was extremely precarious. Without highly placed patrons in the Yorkist court, Margaret could have no certainty that the wishes she was taking such pains to commit to paper would be fulfilled. The Yorkist regime was not kind to one-time Lancastrians like her. Ordinarily, her wealth would have been an advantage but in 1471 it was just another liability, making her all too appealing prey to the predatory attentions of Edward's family. The Yorkist dynasty were young men and women on the make. They had suffered more than their fair share in the early years of the Wars of the Roses, enduring the violent loss of a father and brother, the political exiling of their mother and European exile themselves. Now that the Yorkists were firmly replanted in English soil, they were determined to capitalise on every opportunity for self-enrichment, often at others' expense.

The most notorious instance of their mercenary behaviour was the treatment of Anne, countess of Warwick by Edward's brothers. Like Margaret, the countess was a considerable heiress in her own right, and possessed the rich estates of both the Despenser and Warwick dynasties. In combination, these were worth almost six thousand pounds. But Countess Anne was also the mother-in-law of the capricious duke of Clarence and the late Lancastrian Prince Edward,* and – worse still – the widow of the rebel earl of Warwick. So, as soon as she learned of her husband's death at the Battle of Barnet, the countess fled into sanctuary at Beaulieu Abbey. Initially, it seemed the Yorkists would be merciful to their unfortunate kinswoman. In 1472, her daughter Anne Neville remarried Edward's brother Richard, duke of Gloucester, and the Warwick estates were safeguarded, rather surprisingly, from attainder. But these good omens were misleading. For the next two years, Edward's brothers vied for control of their wives' inheritances, causing Edward considerable vexation. In 1474, he finally resolved their dispute by dividing the Warwick inheritance between Anne and Isabel Neville (in effect, between the dukes) and, to ensure their control was compete, Edward declared the

---

* Her daughter Anne Neville had been married to Prince Edward of Lancaster as part of the Treaty of Angers, and was widowed by Prince Edward's death at Tewkesbury in May 1471.

true heir, Countess Anne, to be legally dead. Despite repeated appeals to her sons-in-law, the king and to Edward's mother, the countess of Warwick remained a corpse in legal fiction for the rest of the dukes' lives.[5]

Richard, duke of Gloucester did not stop at defrauding his own mother-in-law. In December 1472, he interrupted the Christmas festivities of the sexagenarian countess of Oxford at Stratford Priory in Essex and took her into his custody.[6] Countess Elizabeth's Lancastrian son John de Vere, earl of Oxford was fomenting trouble off the mainland of England, and Richard had been sent by the king to ensure that Elizabeth was not abetting her son's rebellion. Richard's true intentions, however, may have been more self-serving. According to testimony given by her servants and trustees twenty years later, after Richard had placed Elizabeth under house arrest, he intimidated the aged countess into granting over her estates to him. When she tearfully attempted to resist, he threatened to transport her to his Yorkshire seat of Middleham Castle, notwithstanding that the winter roads were icy and snow-bound. Afraid for her health, Elizabeth felt she had no alternative but to surrender her estates to Richard. Any of her trustees who tried to oppose the grant, protesting that it was obtained under duress, were bullied into submission. Elizabeth died almost exactly two years later, having never enjoyed the 500-mark annuity Richard had promised her in compensation for her lost estates.[7]

Even before Elizabeth's death, Richard had seized control of the inheritance of her son John, which King Edward had confiscated and granted to him, leaving John's wife Margaret Neville, countess of Oxford without support for herself and her children. Margaret Neville had the double misfortune of being the wife of an active Lancastrian traitor and sister of the late earl of Warwick. However, Yorkist suspicion that the countess might use John's estates to finance his conspiracies was not entirely unfounded. After the Battle of Barnet, John sent his wife a letter bidding her 'send [him] in all haste all the ready money that you can make and as many of my men as can come well horsed'.[8] After the failure of the Readeption, she was forced to rely on the charity of her relatives and, according to one London chronicler, 'what [little] she might get with her needle'.[9]

The Yorkist men were not alone in subverting the law to their own ends – their sister Anne, duchess of Exeter was similarly successful, illegally procuring the estates of her estranged husband, the Lancastrian rebel duke of Exeter, even after she divorced him and remarried her lover, Thomas St Leger.[10] Thus, Margaret was rightly anxious in 1472 to secure a powerful Yorkist ally. But what Margaret really needed was a sponsor within government. And, by good fortune, the steward of King Edward's household had recently been widowed, and was looking for a high-born wife.

EXACTLY WHEN AFTER HARRY STAFFORD'S DEATH THE PROSPECT of remarriage entered Margaret's mind is unclear. Even when and how she met her prospective bridegroom is an enigma, as is much of her fourth, and final, marriage. While there are records for Margaret's marriage to Harry, only scattered fragments survive for Margaret's daily life in the decade after his death. What is clear is that, despite the undue haste of the union – widowhood was ordinarily expected to last for at least a year – this was a far from romantic affair. Instead, it represented a melding of interests between two pragmatic pessimists with a shared verve for political self-preservation.

Thomas, Lord Stanley was a lord of Cheshire and Lancashire who exulted in the title 'King of Man' thanks to his family's lordship over the island just across the Irish Sea from their estates. If fifteenth-century politics was a game of chance that Margaret had been losing badly at in recent years, Thomas Stanley was expert in the art of hedging his bets and emerging on top. Throughout his career, which began when he inherited his estates at the age of twenty-six in February 1459, Thomas had put his responsibility to his family and locality ahead of loyalty to any political faction, standing apart from conflict wherever possible and playing both sides so effectively that each believed they enjoyed his support. This dishonourable – but highly effective – strategy was born of necessity, since, although the Stanleys had long-term Lancastrian loyalties, Thomas had married into the Neville dynasty just as they emerged as the Yorkist powerhouse. His first wife, Eleanor Neville, was the sister of Warwick the Kingmaker. Infamously, at the Battle of Blore Heath in September 1459, where his father-in-law the earl of Salisbury dealt a crushing blow to Queen Marguerite of Anjou's forces, Thomas refused to engage his force of 2,000 men for either side. More recently, during Warwick's rebellions of 1469–71, Thomas had again refused to commit his army, thus escaping the bloodshed of Barnet and Tewkesbury, where his brothers-in-law were either butchered or forced into exile. (By contrast, Thomas's brother Sir William Stanley of Holt fought for the Yorkists at virtually every battle that counted in the Wars of the Roses.) Yet, despite Thomas's stark betrayals, both Yorkists and Lancastrians forgave him. They had little alternative.

For Thomas Stanley was virtually an independent prince of the north-west, where he and his family enjoyed extraordinary authority. The Stanleys had embedded themselves so firmly in Lancashire and Cheshire that they could not be uprooted; Thomas was even confident enough to defy the king's brother. In October 1469, while trying to subdue his rebellious northern territories, Edward IV had installed his brother Richard, duke of Gloucester in various Stanley offices in the north-west and the duchy of Lancaster. But the Stanleys and their supporters would have none of it. Gloucester's men were forcibly prevented from taking office, and his local clients, the Harringtons, were violently assaulted. Despite Gloucester's protests, Edward eventually had to admit defeat and let the Stanleys rule as they wished. Eager for powerful allies after his restoration in 1471, Edward appointed Thomas steward of the royal household, and allowed him to retain his post as receiver of the county of Lancashire. Gloucester was quietly removed from his more sensitive offices, and thenceforward exercised his lordship solely in territories east of the Pennines, away from Stanley influence.[11] Thus, Thomas was safely absorbed into the Yorkist regime and the considerable retinue at his command returned peacefully home.

A husband like Thomas Stanley was precisely what Margaret needed in 1472. An experienced politician, integrated with the Yorkists but with a protective buffer of independent authority. Yet, although Margaret recognised her political inferiority to Thomas, she was still keenly aware of her social superiority. After all, she was a countess and heiress in her own right, and by merging their estates Thomas gained a valuable stake in the south. So, throughout May and June the pair engaged in fierce bargaining before drawing up their marriage agreement. Thomas would control Margaret's considerable estates during their marriage, but on his death she – and ultimately Henry – would regain control of her inheritance. To sweeten the deal, Thomas guaranteed her a yearly income of 500 marks from his estates in Cheshire and North Wales, with the agreement that her own steward, Gilbert Gilpyn, would secure these properties for her. Indeed, Thomas permitted Margaret to bring many of her trusted advisers and servants with her to the marriage.

As a symbol of their merging interests, and to safeguard Margaret as she joined an entirely new family, the arrangements for her future were witnessed not only by Stanley confederates and kin, but also by Margaret's trusted Stourton and Stafford relations.[12] Evidently, there was no bad blood with Harry's family over Margaret's hasty remarriage. Almost a decade later, when Harry's mother, Anne, wrote her will she left bequests for 'my daughter Richmond', listing Margaret alongside her blood daughter. Margaret was the only person to receive a bequest of books from Anne – an expression of their shared bibliophilia.[13] As an experienced political operator who had made her own astute second marriage, Anne understood that Margaret needed what Stanley could offer as husband.

The practicalities of this most pragmatic of unions having been satisfactorily agreed and committed to paper, Margaret packed up her household in Surrey and undertook the 200-mile journey to Cheshire. She exchanged a precarious life as a lonely widow for one as stepmother and kinswoman to a large north-western clan of men, women and children.[14]

MARGARET HAD PLENTY OF TIME TO CONTEMPLATE HER changed circumstances as she journeyed north. Travelling with long-term servants like Reynald Bray, William Hody and Elizabeth Jackson, she watched the Surrey Downs fade into the distance and the craggy Cumbrian hills rise to greet her. The difference between Margaret's home at Woking and the Stanley stronghold of Lathom Castle in Lancashire was stark: Woking manor was the sort of genteel fortification that had become popular in recent years, a simulacrum of military might. Lathom was the real thing. Nine towers pierced the thick stone wall of the central keep. A moat, carved wide and deep into the marshy turf, encircled the castle, which was itself surrounded by imposing hills. It was either here, or at neighbouring Knowsley Hall, that Margaret and Thomas Stanley wed early in June.

When she married Thomas, Margaret became not only a leading lady of the north-west and a subsidiary of the wider Yorkist household, but also a stepmother. By 1472, four of Thomas and Eleanor's ten children were still alive, of whom the eldest, George, was an adolescent old enough to enjoy a flutter on a game of cards, and the youngest, another Margaret, was perhaps only a toddler.[15] Between George and little Margaret came Edward and James Stanley, one destined for a life of soldiery, the other for the Church. And Margaret's new family extended far beyond Lathom: Thomas had six surviving siblings, and extensive kinship ties to families all over the north-east.[16] The scale of the Stanley dynasty might have been one of the factors in its favour, for Margaret had grown up in just such a household, among half-siblings who could provide omnipresent emotional and political support.

For the next few years, Margaret would live principally between Lathom, Knowsley, and Hawarden in North Wales, but she had not entirely exchanged southern England for the north. Thomas's business as receiver-general of the duchy of Lancaster meant he moved around a great deal, and his stewardship of the royal household necessitated regular journeys back to the south-east, for which Margaret's manor at Woking provided an ideal base. Having always travelled with Harry, Margaret was accustomed to accompanying her husband – so where Thomas went, she tended to follow. In September 1472, the couple progressed from Lathom to Chester and then on to Hawarden with Thomas's three younger brothers.[17] Margaret travelled so regularly, and across such considerable distances, that on at least one occasion her hard-worn horse harness had to be repaired.[18]

Fifteenth-century noble marriage was a business partnership but it was also a personal relationship. In the Beaufort–Stanley merger it is difficult to decipher how much importance Margaret and Thomas attached to the romantic aspect of their relationship. The personal items that might indicate the couple's feelings for one another – letters, gifts, even household accounts – are almost entirely lacking for this period. When Thomas wrote his will thirty years after their marriage, in 1504, he left Margaret no bequests and used no terms of affection in describing her, unlike Harry who had re-peatedly called Margaret his 'best beloved wife'. Yet Margaret had rejected burial with Harry, whereas Thomas Stanley left provision for her to be buried with him and Eleanor. Was this affection, or merely an expression of Thomas's dynastic completism? The same site was also designed to hold his parents and siblings.

Their inner emotional lives are difficult to discern, but Margaret and Thomas's joint marital venture was visibly carved in the stonework and earth of their homes. Alterations were made to the great hall at Knowsley to accommodate the new Lady Stanley, where a magnificent fireback was installed, resplendent with her Beaufort arms. Woking manor, too, was improved for the couple, its parkland ditched and paled, the house itself overhauled.

The clues about their joint life in this decade suggest Thomas and Margaret worked well together. The year after their mar-riage, Thomas used his political clout to Margaret's advantage and intervened in a case of illegal hunting on her West Country estates.[19] Margaret, meanwhile, stepped into the vacated position of Lady Stanley, arbitrating local disputes as Thomas's first wife had done.[20] The pair also had religious interests in common – no small matter when the Church was the dominant force in daily life. In 1478, Margaret and Thomas both joined the confratern-ity* of the Carthusian order, a popular religious movement whose

---

* Members of the confraternity promoted the order's teaching and in return received the prayers of the Carthusian monks.

early supporters had included Margaret's powerful Lancastrian great-uncle Cardinal Henry Beaufort. Beaufort interest in the order found its way down the generations not only to Margaret but also, through a shared ancestor, to her mother-in-law Anne, duchess of Buckingham and Anne's sister Cecily, duchess of York, and from those noblewomen into the royal court. By the 1470s, Edward IV, too, was a prominent supporter, lavishing gifts of wine on the Carthusian brothers. Thus, Margaret's Beaufort and Stafford influences aligned with Thomas's courtly connections. It was telling that in return for Thomas and Margaret's support, the Carthusians promised to pray not only for the couple but also for Thomas's first wife and parents. By 1478, Thomas clearly considered Margaret an integrated part of his family unit.[21]

But it was possible in the fifteenth century for a noblewoman to be both of a family and slightly apart from it, and Margaret's dual status as Stanley and Beaufort – one somewhat independent of the other – is writ large in a beautifully illuminated prayer book that Margaret commissioned for her husband, which survives in the collection of Westminster Abbey.[22] It reveals the couple's shared piety and anxiety about the dangers of contemporary life, but also Margaret's self-image as heiress in her own right. Across multiple beautiful illuminations, the Stanley badge of an eagle's foot is inked inside letters or at the margins of religious images. But the appearances of her husband's crest are considerably outnumbered by instances of Margaret's Beaufort arms – the portcullis – and by flowers that played on her name in French – *Marguerite* means daisy, and daisies appear across several pages, as well as red roses associated with the Virgin Mary. The symbols connected to Margaret proliferate on pages relating to holy women, including an image of the Annunciation to the Virgin Mary. Only three illuminations in the 125-page work feature Margaret and Thomas's symbols alongside one another. In the midst of the Latin prayers of the Passion of Christ and the Virgin Mary are repeated invocations to save the reader from battle, to protect them from the plague or during pregnancy. Were the prayers for pregnant women simply included as a matter of form, or was there still some hope that Margaret might fall pregnant? Was this, in fact, a true marriage as well as a business agreement?[23] It is a tantalising possibility.

There is no doubt that Margaret benefited from her marriage to Thomas Stanley. When they wed, she was the widow of a nobleman under royal suspicion, but marriage to the emollient Thomas helped ease her back into court circles. Within the carefully maintained pages of Reynald Bray's daily account book – one of the very few surviving sources for the Stanley marriage – there are subtle indications of how association with the steward of Edward IV improved Margaret's circumstances. Fine fabrics had always been bought to adorn Margaret's person but now violet velvet – the richest hue, associated with royalty – edged its way into her wardrobe beside her usual staid black damask. In winter, money was paid to a London skinner to fur a gown for her, to be sent to the freezing north. Her elevated status was also visible in the attendants who surrounded her. At Lathom, Thomas's children were clothed in expensive sarcenet and his senior servants in cloth of silver. Margaret could now afford to have a golden livery collar made for a harp player in her service and to reward her ladies-in-waiting at New Year with finely wrought golden spoons. When she retired to her chambers at night, she laid her head on a purple velvet pillow. These were the trappings of a noblewoman whose family was no longer on the outer limits of politics but instead closely associated with the royal court.[24]

THE YEAR 1474 BROKE OVER ENGLAND WITH A BLAST OF trumpets and unfurling of battle standards. Twenty years after Henry VI had lost Gascony, and almost exactly thirty since Margaret's father had died in disgrace for his own military efforts, Edward IV announced the resumption of the long war with France. In alliance with his brother-in-law Charles the Bold, duke of Burgundy, and with England's old comrades in arms, the Bretons,*

---

* Brittany was an independent duchy within the land mass of France. Its dukes were vassals of the king of France but often preferred alliance with England.

Edward planned the largest military campaign across the Channel since the days of King Henry V. Indeed, if contemporary reports of the size of the English army were accurate, Edward's forces would exceed even those of that famed warrior king.[25] As Edward inspected his artillery and personally toured the realm to persuade his subjects to fund the war, Margaret and Thomas made their own preparations for campaign. Bray's account book shows payments to saddlers and armourers to ready Lord Stanley for battle. New spurs were bought and gleaming crimson and blue sarcenet banners sewn to flutter above the heads of the 40 men-at-arms and 300 archers Thomas had indentured to serve under him in France. To ensure that Lord Stanley himself was fit for war, he made improvements to his 'white harness' and had his sallet helmet garnished.[26]

Of course, even in the midst of an international military campaign, Thomas still put his family interests first. Before he left for France, he insisted that Edward IV officially recognise his right to bear arms as the 'King of Man', in opposition to a rival lord who asserted his own claim to the title. Sure enough, when Thomas bade farewell to Margaret and rode out of London to join the king at the muster near Canterbury, he did so with the arms of Man proudly flying above him.[27]

Thomas may have won his rights as payment for certain clandestine services he undertook for the crown – services that required Stanley's ability to conceal dishonourable deeds beneath a veneer of propriety. In English financial accounts, Thomas is simply listed as one among over a hundred noblemen providing retinues of soldiers for the king, but the chronicle of Philippe de Commines (an adviser to Louis XI of France) suggests Thomas played a rather more discreet part in the operation. For, even before Edward IV and his vast army had sailed for France in their 500 flat-bottomed Burgundian boats, the king was already plotting a truce. War was costly and dangerous, and Edward's purported ally Charles the Bold was proving to be frustratingly fair weather, preferring to pursue a siege on the Rhine for his own ends rather than send his men to assault France ahead of the English arrival. As his ships rocked on their moorings at Dover, Edward sent one of his heralds to King Louis with a public message of defiance but a private admission that, once he reached France, he would be willing to swiftly come to terms to prevent bloodshed. According to Commines, the herald advised Louis that, to enter negotiations for peace, the French king should address himself to either the herald or to two noblemen; one of them was Thomas Stanley.[28]

Sure enough, within weeks of the English army disgorging itself across the flatlands of Calais and engaging in little more than a minor skirmish, Louis dispatched a servant to the English camp, with 'orders to address himself to the Lord... Stanley'.[29] Thomas's secret mediation between the French and English kings had the desired effect. On 29 August, Edward IV met Louis XI on a bridge over the River Somme at Picquigny to conclude terms for peace.

Thomas's role as mediator was not considered positively by all. Edward's brother Richard, duke of Gloucester thought it dishonourable to raise an army then come to terms before a blow had even been struck, and refused to attend the summit with Louis. He was not alone. Many Englishmen shared his hostility, including Margaret's kinsman, the young head of the Stafford clan, Edward, duke of Buckingham.[30] Even as King Edward was meeting Louis, there was anxiety that this could all be some French ruse. Decades earlier, a similar 'peace conference' on a French bridge had been a façade to allow the Dauphin of France to get close enough to his enemy to slaughter him. Taking no chances, when Edward met Louis, he did so behind a 'strong wooden lattice, such as lions' cages are made of'.[31] Louis approached Edward and extended his arms through the barriers to embrace his fellow king. A seven-year truce was promptly concluded, with a marriage to follow between Louis's eldest son and Edward's eldest daughter, Princess Elizabeth. Edward agreed to leave France peacefully, and to refuse any future alliances in opposition to Louis's interests, in return for a payment of a substantial 75,000-crown pension. As if to prove divine sanction for the treaty, English soldiers reported that a white pigeon sat on the king of England's tent throughout the meeting on the bridge, and could not be frightened away – proof, it was claimed, that 'the Holy Ghost had made that peace'. Thus, 'the most numerous, the best disciplined, the best mounted, and the best armed' English army ever to invade France trotted back home before summer was out, thanks in no small part to the diplomatic subterfuge of Margaret's husband.[32]

THE SAFE RETURN OF LORD STANLEY IN HIS GLEAMING WHITE harness would not bring Margaret peace of mind. Not only had her husband solidified his reputation for untrustworthy dealing, but Edward's treaty with the French threatened the safety of her son. Since 1471, Henry and his uncle Jasper had been living as hostages in Brittany, under the largely benign guardianship of Duke Francis II. But Edward never quite suppressed his concern about this Lancastrian with bastard royal blood, especially as Henry matured into manhood. In 1475, Henry reached his eighteenth birthday – old enough to oppose the Yorkists by force of arms if he chose. For years, King Edward had been urging Duke Francis to surrender the Tudors into his custody and, eager not to displease his chief ally, Francis duly straitened their conditions – early in 1474 he separated Jasper and Henry and replaced their English servants with Breton guards. But he refused to release them.

Throughout Edward's campaign of intimidation, Francis had always been able to rely on King Louis of France to support his defence of the Tudors. For Louis, this was a matter of family pride. Jasper Tudor was his cousin (Jasper's mother, Catherine of Valois, was Louis's aunt) and had been personally granted a French pension, guaranteeing Louis's protection. As far as Louis was concerned, if the Tudors were going to be surrendered to anyone, it ought to be to him, not to Edward of England. But the Anglo-French treaty changed everything. With Louis and Edward now officially allies, Margaret faced the very real danger that Louis might finally permit Edward to claim the Tudors for himself. If confronted with the combined coercion of the kings of France and England, Francis II of Brittany would crumble. And so it proved.

Since 1474, Henry had been held captive in the Château of Largoët, lodged on the top floor of an immense octagonal tower surrounded by woodland. But, suddenly, late in autumn 1476, he was transferred under armed guard to the port of Saint-Malo and handed over to the custody of an English embassy led by Robert Stillington, bishop of Bath and Wells. As the price of renewing an expired Anglo-Breton treaty, Edward demanded the extradition of the Tudors. The Breton admiral Jean de Quelenhec was the Tudors' foremost supporter, but the English embassy took advantage of his absence from court to increase their pressure. As well as promising Francis 'a great weight of gold' in exchange for the Tudors, the English insisted that Henry would be treated respectfully by King Edward, perhaps even given a high-ranking bride. Unable to parry Edward IV's ceaseless 'presents, promises and prayers' without Quelenhec to bolster him, Duke Francis finally capitulated. Any day, it seemed, Henry would be bundled aboard a ship bound for England. Presumably he was given the same assurances as Francis about his fate in Edward's hands. But Henry had grown cautious, verging on mistrustful, during his time in Brittany. Hoping to buy time until Quelenhec returned, Henry told his English captors he was too unwell to travel. The delay saved him.[33]

Margaret's misgivings about Edward IV had grown the longer he ruled. Where once Edward had been a merciful young prince, age and experience had warped him into an unforgiving king. Her stepfather, uncle and cousins had all died at Edward's hands as a result of battle.[*] That could be accepted under the rules of warfare but no such rules governed Edward's treatment of the rest of her kinsmen. Only a year ago, as the king travelled home from his French 'war' in 1475, one of the last remaining rivals for his throne met his end in the frothing waters of the English Channel. The duke of Exeter, who had been a thorn in Edward's side for twenty years, was pitched into the sea at royal command – or so the embittered Charles of Burgundy reported.[34] With the deaths of Henry VI and his son, Margaret's Beaufort kinsmen and now Exeter, Henry Tudor was one of the last surviving Lancastrians who had not either surrendered to Edward IV or been killed for his defiance. Bernard André claimed that Margaret did not trust

---

[*] Edmund Beaufort at the Battle of St Albans in 1455, his sons Henry and Edmund Beaufort after the Battles of Hexham (1464) and Tewksbury (1471), and Lionel, Lord Welles at Towton (1461).

Edward's 'fine promises, bribes and entreaties', and that 'through secret addresses by messengers and in letters she continually forbade [Henry] to return' to England.[35]

Heeding his mother's warnings, Henry remained on his sickbed at Saint-Malo just long enough for his ally Quelenhec to return to court. Finding Henry in English hands, Quelenhec remonstrated with Duke Francis:

> You have handed over Earl Henry of Richmond, a most innocent young man, to butchers for the rending, the tormenting, and finally the killing... Trust me, most illustrious duke, Henry is all but dead. For if you once allow him to set foot outside your borders, no man alive can rescue him from death.[36]

Belatedly remorseful, Duke Francis sent his treasurer Pierre Landais to Saint-Malo to distract the English envoys and allow Henry enough time to slip away into sanctuary at the neighbouring cathedral. The English attempted to remonstrate, and even to drag Henry out of sanctuary, but the local townspeople resisted. By Christmas 1476, Henry and Jasper were safely reunited at Château de l'Hermine in Vannes.[37]

For now, Margaret could rest easy in the knowledge that her son was safe. Publicly, as the wife of the royal steward, she maintained every appearance of loyalty and trust in King Edward. While he ruled, she had to work through him to protect Henry, and attempt his restoration. Perhaps there might even come a time when she had gained enough reassurance to advise Henry he could trust Edward's promises of pardon. But, until that day, she would attempt to manoeuvre herself as close to the heart of power as she could. For only by entering that lion's den could she hope to protect her son.

9

'Now fell there mischiefs thick'[1]

✳

The yard of Westminster Palace was rimed with ice but, inside St Stephen's Chapel, a warm crowd gathered in velvet and cloth of gold. Somewhere amid the press of Yorkist royals – the king and queen, their seven-year-old heir Prince Edward, the king's mother, his brother Gloucester, his two stepsons and three daughters – was Margaret Beaufort. She was short enough to be entirely overlooked beside the famously tall Plantagenets, but proudly present nonetheless for this royal event: the marriage of the king's younger son, Prince Richard. At four years old, on 15 January 1478, the prince married Anne Mowbray, six-year-old heiress to the duchy of Norfolk. As the crowd bustled from the chapel to king's great chamber for the wedding banquet, showers of gold and silver coins rained down on them from the hands of the duke of Gloucester.[2]

Margaret's presence at this marriage was the latest public display of her incorporation into the Yorkist establishment. Eighteen months earlier, she had attended the reburial of the king's father and brother: Richard, duke of York and Edmund, earl of Rutland. They had lain in lowly graves within a Pontefract priory since their deaths at the Battle of Wakefield in 1460 and in July 1476 they were transferred over the course of eight days to princely interment in their ancestral mausoleum at the College of Fotheringhay. At the funeral ceremony, Thomas Stanley was one of only six noblemen permitted to stand with the chief mourner, Richard, duke of Gloucester, inside the barriers beside the late duke of York's candle-smothered hearse.* After the queen and her daughters had laid offerings on the altar, Margaret was invited to join them. By 1480, Margaret's position was so assured that she played a leading role in the ceremonial, personally carrying the latest Yorkist princess, Bridget, to the font at Eltham Palace during her christening.[3]

Margaret's presence at these rituals of Yorkist authority was testament to the wisdom of her marriage with Thomas Stanley, as it was through his connections as steward of the royal household that she achieved such public rehabilitation. But these bombastic expressions of the unity and power of the House of York were a veneer to conceal a rotting canker at the heart of their family. For, while the rest of Edward IV's relatives enjoyed the spiced sweetmeats and wine in Westminster in January 1478, his brother George, duke of Clarence was imprisoned in the Tower of London.

Clarence's troubles had begun a year earlier, in December 1476, when his duchess, Isabel, died in childbirth. Perhaps Isabel had been a calming influence, for in the wake of her death Clarence unravelled, indulging in reckless acts of authoritarian lordship and defiance of the king. In April 1477, he intimidated a jury into executing three of his servants on charges of poisoning his wife and child. A month later, one of Clarence's squires, Thomas Burdet, was executed by the crown for colluding in treasonable necromancy. Before his execution, Burdet made an unrepentant scaffold speech in which he protested his innocence and Clarence had the protest read aloud in the council chamber at Westminster – a tacit criticism of the injustice of Burdet's death, and of his own irritation at Edward's interference. Clarence was also spreading rumours about Edward's illegitimacy again, presenting himself as the rightful heir.

Despite being sexually slandered by her son, Duchess Cecily continued to mediate between her warring children. There was something pitiable about Clarence that the women in his family had more patience with than the men: while Cecily and her

---

* Not a hearse as we understand it, but a super-sized candelabra bedecked with heraldic and religious symbols.

daughters Elizabeth, duchess of Suffolk and Margaret, duchess of Burgundy tried to appease Clarence, Edward grew increasingly severe. After Isabel's death, Margaret of Burgundy hoped to arrange Clarence's remarriage to her stepdaughter, Marie, heiress to the duchy of Burgundy, but Edward refused to countenance such a union. Rumours about Edward's illegitimacy had reached the Burgundian court and if his disaffected brother went there as duke-apparent it would only stoke his ambitions.[4] Clarence had sufficient charisma to win support for himself – perhaps even enough to claim the throne. In 1475, a Milanese ambassador to the Burgundian court had claimed that Edward hastened back to England after concluding the Treaty of Picquigny for fear that, if Clarence got home first, he would incite another uprising.[5]

Clarence's frustration with his brother was not ill-founded. He had repeatedly been subjected to humiliations since his thwarted rebellion. When Edward repealed royal grants in his first post-Readeption parliament, he refused to safeguard Clarence's lands, and even removed him from his post as lieutenant of Ireland in order to deprive him of a crucial area of potential military support. Edward's fear of Clarence can only have been encouraged by Queen Elizabeth Woodville, who bitterly remembered Clarence's role in the assassinations of her father and brother in 1469. By June 1477, Edward had had enough. Clarence was arrested and, even as the marriage feast of Prince Richard and Anne Mowbray was ongoing, in January 1478, parliament assembled to condemn him for treason.

The eclipse of the duke of Clarence shocked contemporaries. Margaret may have shared the feeling expressed in the anonymous Crowland Chronicle continuation, whose author was a royal councillor and witness to events. The Crowland Chronicler reported that in parliament 'no one argued against the duke except the king; no one answered the king except the duke' and that those called to appear as witnesses in the case actually played the part of accusers.[6] With such concerted royal pressure, the outcome of Clarence's 'trial' in parliament was never in question. On 7 February, Harry Stafford's nephew Henry Stafford, duke of Buckingham was appointed steward of England to pass judgement and, sure enough, Clarence was attainted as a traitor.* Yet, as the court historian Polydore Vergil noted: 'I have interrogated many men who were members of the Privy Council at that time, [and] I have nothing certain to report about the reason for his death.'[7] Clarence had simply become too dangerous to survive. In February 1478, Clarence died in the Tower. The rumour swiftly developed that he had been drowned in a vat of wine.[8]

Disquieting as Clarence's sudden downfall must have been, it held promise for Henry. Clarence had tenaciously clung onto the Richmond earldom, and at his attainder the estate was forfeited to the crown. Years passed and the earldom remained in King Edward's hands. Was he simply awaiting a worthy recipient of this valuable grant, or did he consider the possibility of using it to lure Henry back to England? After all, during his years in exile, Henry had fostered no foreign wars, encouraged no English rebels. Compared with his fellow Lancastrian partisan John de Vere, earl of Oxford – whose recent career included conspiracy, siege, prison breaks and piracy – Henry was a model citizen. An undated pardon now in the archives of Westminster Abbey suggests that Edward may have been prepared to restore Henry to the earldom of Richmond.[9]

By 1482, Edward's willingness to pardon, or even restore, Henry if he returned peaceably to England had become so marked that Margaret was prepared to work with the king to entice her son home. Various witnesses at court would later report to a papal investigator that around this time Edward and Margaret 'held themselves as kinsmen', 'related in the fourth... degrees of kindred'. Subtle though this conversation sounds, it had enormous significance, as it suggests that Edward was willing to let Henry marry into his family. Since Margaret and Edward were kinsmen, the union would demand a papal dispensation. The likeliest candidate to be Henry's bride was Edward's eldest daughter Elizabeth, who was sixteen in 1482 and whose betrothal to the Dauphin of France had dissolved as Anglo-French relations soured. Edward

---

* This was not the same stewardship that Thomas Stanley held as 'steward of the royal household'. The Steward of England was an officer of state with exceptional legal powers to try peers.

and Margaret's discussion of the match was sufficiently well known that 'many grave nobles and persons worthy of belief' were heard to discuss it, from Margaret's mother-in-law Anne, duchess of Buckingham to the dean of Cecily of York's chapel, Richard Lessy, and John Morton, bishop of Ely. Indeed, the match may have been considered for some time, since among those heard to discuss the matter was George Neville, archbishop of York, who died in 1476.[10] By marrying Princess Elizabeth, Henry would be absorbed into the royal family, which gave him and Margaret a far more compelling reason to trust Edward's intentions than the nebulous discussions Edward had used when trying to extradite Henry from Brittany by force.

By 1482, Margaret was sufficiently convinced that Henry would be safe if he returned to England that she worked with Edward to provide a further inducement for her son. In May of that year, Margaret's mother, the dowager duchess of Somerset, died, leaving her daughter a considerable inheritance in the West Country. The duchess had lived into her seventies[11] and was laid to rest beside Margaret's father at Wimborne Minster in Dorset. Margaret proposed to Edward that she use her mother's inheritance as a lure for Henry. If he returned 'in the grace and favour of the king's highness', he could succeed to an estate from his grandmother worth 600 marks a year.[*] If, however, he failed to reconcile with Edward, the inheritance would be divided instead between Margaret and Thomas, with no reversion to Henry.[12]

As a married woman, Margaret needed her husband's permission to divert the inheritance during his lifetime, but, when asked for his approval, Thomas proved reluctant to give it. The provision for Henry would materially disadvantage him, depriving him of 300 marks annually. So, to enforce her deal with Edward, Margaret asked the king to personally witness the drawing up of an agreement for the disposal of the inheritance, which he duly did on 3 June 1482 at Westminster. Thomas's reluctance is apparent in this document, which explicitly forbade his 'interruption and contradiction' of the plans. This was a relatively standard

---

[*] £400, or in modern terms around £276,500.

expression – more pointed was the demand that Thomas must observe the settlement '[as] the said Lord Stanley before the said marriage promised [he would] *upon his honour*'. This sounds like a jibe at Thomas for failing to respect his agreements with Margaret. After a decade of marriage, the union of Margaret and Thomas Stanley may no longer have been quite as functional as in its early years.[13]

However, Margaret and Edward's scheme was soon overtaken by events beyond their control. The international situation was evolving, and since Henry relied on the support of Francis of Brittany to remain on the Continent, this was bound to impact him. The Treaty of Picquigny was due to expire at sundown on 29 August 1482, and King Louis of France was already manoeuvring against English interests, inciting both the Scots and Burgundians to join him. Edward's ally Charles the Bold had died in 1477, succeeded by his daughter, Marie of Burgundy. She followed her father to the grave in March 1482, leaving Burgundian territories in the hands of her widower, Maximilian, the Holy Roman Emperor,* who was readier than Marie to broker an alliance with Louis. Death already stalked the northern borders of England, which had been disturbed for two years by Scottish incursions encouraged by Louis and English reprisals under Richard, duke of Gloucester. All-out war with Scotland seemed inevitable, and Edward IV aggressively announced his intention to lead an army north to check 'the fickle movements of the Scots'.[14]

At Lathom in Lancashire, Margaret was far enough south to be out of immediate danger from a Scottish invasion, but as northern lords were expected to defend the borders of England, Thomas could not pursue his preferred policy and simply sit out Edward's Scottish wars. When the Stanleys raised their banners, they could muster a formidable army, and Edward insisted these forces be deployed in the coming conflict. On 12 June 1482, Edward appointed his brother Richard to lead the English army into Scotland to drive King James III from the throne and replace him with his more biddable brother Alexander, duke of Albany. A month later,

---

* The Holy Roman Empire covered most of central and eastern Europe.

Thomas and his twenty-two-year-old son Edward joined the 20,000-strong, largely northern army to besiege Berwick.

This crucial border town was the scene of a confrontation between the Stanleys and Richard. When the Scottish garrison in Berwick Castle refused to surrender, Richard directed Thomas to command a siege with a small force while he led the bulk of the English army over the border. According to a sixteenth-century Stanley chronicle, the risk-averse Thomas was not happy with this arrangement, which he felt left him 'in great danger'. Perhaps partly to assuage Thomas's irritation, Richard knighted Edward Stanley at Berwick on 24 July.[15] But Thomas still felt abandoned when Richard led his army north.

As the Stanleys maintained their siege with 'slaughter and bloodshed', Richard pressed on into Scotland, 'wasting and burning its fields far and wide' until he reached Edinburgh, where he found the city gates open and James III already a captive of his own noblemen.[16] Unable to gain access to the king, or to force the Scots to accept the duke of Albany as an alternative ruler, Richard was forced to retreat and broker terms of peace. Berwick was finally suppressed and, in the Anglo-Scottish truce of August 1482, restored to the English for the first time in twenty years. Edward wrote proudly to the Pope of his brother's victory, and both Richard and Thomas were singled out for praise by the Commons in the next parliament. Opinion was divided, however, about how successful the Scottish campaign had really been. The possession of Berwick was criticised by the Crowland Chronicler as 'a trifling gain, or perhaps more accurately loss (for the maintenance of Berwick costs 10,000 marks a year)'.[17] Thomas may have agreed that the danger he ran had not been worth the ultimate reward.

While her husband and stepson were at Berwick, Margaret had been attempting to appeal to Henry to return, using the promised agreement with Edward. Unfortunately, she had hit an insurmountable challenge. Henry's character had been shaped by his experience of long-term imprisonment and he had started to display the same unfortunate traits that John Beaufort had developed in captivity in France half a century earlier. Eleven years of political exile and tension had left Henry paranoid, with an instinct to keep his own counsel. When the paperwork was finalised and Margaret finally entered her late mother's dower lands that November, there was still no indication that Henry would risk coming to England to claim the inheritance. Margaret awaited his return in vain.[18]

And then, on 9 April 1483, suddenly and unexpectedly, Edward IV died. In an instant, Margaret's hopes for the future were dashed. The kingdom now passed to Edward's twelve-year-old son, who was immediately acclaimed King Edward V. As Margaret knew all too well, the last reign of a child-king had ended in civil war, international catastrophe and bloody usurpation. Suddenly everything was uncertain again.

10

'Woe is that realm that hath a child to their king'[1]

✳

A round the corpse of the king, the black-clad courtiers gathered. Edward IV had cut an impressive figure in life, and even in death the immensity of him as he lay 'all naked saving he was covered from the navel to the knees' was overwhelming. His size may well have been the cause of his death. The Crowland Chronicler took a certain righteous pleasure in attributing Edward's demise to 'conviviality, vanity, drunkenness, extravagance and passion'. Another source claimed that Edward fell sick after catching cold on a fishing boat shortly before Easter and 'being a tall man and very fat', the illness proved fatal. How ironic it must have seemed to Thomas Stanley, attending his dead master in the mourning robes of a royal steward, that having survived rebellion, usurpation and bloody civil war to secure his throne, what finally killed the champion of York was a fishing trip.[2]

Or perhaps Thomas blamed the stresses of kingship for his master's early death. Still only forty, Edward had been ground down by endless internecine feuds, which had grown so severe that even on his deathbed he had to force his chamberlain William Hastings and his stepson Thomas Grey, marquess of Dorset to take one another by the hand and swear to be friends. But, despite Edward's best efforts, Dorset's and Hastings's 'hearts' remained 'far asunder' and, with their master dead, the two men and their factions scrambled to gain mastery.[3] The handsome young Dorset, son of Queen Elizabeth, was firmly entrenched in the Woodville faction, who hoped that their blood relation to the twelve-year-old heir, Prince Edward, would enable them to rule through the child-king. Hastings, on the other hand, wanted to exclude the parvenu Woodvilles from power altogether until the prince came of age, and instead entrust government to a capable protector, ideally Edward's last surviving brother Richard, duke of Gloucester. But the suddenness of Edward's death meant that both Prince Edward and Duke Richard were hundreds of miles away: Richard in Yorkshire and Prince Edward in Ludlow on the Welsh borders.

True to form, Thomas Stanley avoided allying himself with either faction until political uncertainty transformed into tangible reality, and Margaret – who was probably in London with her husband when Edward died – followed his example, at least for the time being. She did not join the grim parade of counsellors staring at the royal corpse, and nor was she invited to Edward IV's funeral procession, since noblewomen did not customarily attend the funerals of kings. But Thomas followed behind his late master's coffin as it was interred at the chapel of St George in Windsor. With him was his younger son Sir Edward Stanley and Margaret's half-brother John, Lord Welles, who was now in his twenties and serving in the royal household. After Edward's body was lowered into his tomb, Lord Hastings and Thomas threw their staffs of office into the grave, symbolising the end of their master's rule. The heralds followed suit, laying aside their coats of arms before donning fresh ones as a public demonstration of loyalty to the new king, Edward V. Then they cried out, their voices echoing around the stone vaulting of the chapel: 'Le roy est vif! Le roy est vif!' The king is alive.[4]

While her husband performed his last duties for his king, Margaret was contemplating how to approach his successor. Edward IV's death had ruined her carefully cultivated plan to rehabilitate Henry and bring him back to England, but the accession of Edward V might provide an even better opportunity. A child with no personal experience of the wars between Lancaster and York might be more willing to set aside old enmities and restore Henry, especially if Margaret's long-cherished match between her son and Elizabeth of York could be resurrected. If absorbed into the young king's family, Henry could not only regain his lost inheritance but perhaps even take up a central role in the new regime. To bring this hope to fruition, however, Margaret needed to choose her allies wisely.

Through her Stanley in-laws and her own observations at court, Margaret had come to know the key players in this dispute well. The Stanleys had not enjoyed an entirely harmonious relationship with either faction: the long-standing grudge between Thomas and Richard had reignited during the Scottish wars, and the Stanleys had tussled with the queen's family in the early 1470s when the Woodville-dominated household of Prince Edward was established in the Marches. The prince's new powerbase threatened Stanley dominance, which led to an acrimonious process of arbitration between the parties. However, in recent years, the Stanleys and the Woodvilles had developed a mutually beneficial working relationship. Margaret's brother-in-law Sir William Stanley had become steward of Prince Edward's household, where he worked alongside the queen's family.[5] The prince's guardian was Queen Elizabeth's brother Anthony Woodville, Earl Rivers, and her adult son Sir Richard Grey served on the prince's council, giving both men unfettered access to the future king.[*] Anthony was internationally renowned as a model knight: brutally effective yet chivalrous on the tournament field, a poet and pilgrim off it, and a successful soldier who had campaigned across Europe.

From Sir William's accounts, Margaret must have formed some impression of the twelve-year-old now acclaimed Edward V. The handsome young prince was charming and precocious, and fiercely protective of his relatives. With the advent of adolescence, he had grown wilful, occasionally chafing against the restrictions placed on him by his elders. These flashes of assertiveness recalled his father and suggested that, even if he was placed in the power of a protector until adulthood, he was likely to retain his Woodville

---

[*] Richard and Thomas Grey were Queen Elizabeth's sons from her first marriage.

loyalties. And, in April 1483, the possibility of a protectorate seemed remote.

For no sooner was Edward IV entombed at Windsor than his hope for compromise and conciliation was swept away. The decision was taken by the royal council, dominated by the supporters of Queen Elizabeth, to proceed immediately to crown Edward V. There would be no protectorate, no power share between child-king and Richard, duke of Gloucester. Instead, the boy king's rule would begin at once and the dominance of the Woodvilles would be assured. The marquess of Dorset peacocked around court, proclaiming his family's triumph over their enemies: 'we are so important [now] that even without the king's uncle [Richard] we can make and enforce [our] decisions'.[6] The matter seemed clear, then. Margaret must court Elizabeth and the Woodvilles.

Edward V's arrival in London was expected within a fortnight of his father's funeral, allowing time to prepare for his coronation on 4 May. To quell her rivals' concerns, Queen Elizabeth agreed to appeals from Lord Hastings and his allies that her son's escort should not exceed two thousand.[7] With all the cards in their hands, the Woodvilles could afford to be conciliatory. Little did they realise they had already been outmanoeuvred.

Lord Hastings – appalled at the royal council's pronouncement and fearing for his prospects under this Woodville regime – had secretly contacted Richard, duke of Gloucester and urged him to speed south to London with a strong military escort.[8] Given his customary circumspection and long association with Hastings, it is possible that Thomas knew of the missives to Richard. But what happened next seems to have taken even Hastings by surprise.

On the last day of April, like the rest of London, Margaret awaited word of the approach of the new king. When messengers arrived at the city gates, however, they brought tidings that inspired panic and uncertainty. For on the road near Stony Stratford that morning, Edward V's attendants, including his half-brother Richard Grey and uncle Anthony Woodville, had been arrested. Their captors had then galloped to Stony Stratford before word of the arrests could spread, and taken possession of Edward V. Edward's new keepers were Richard, duke of Gloucester and Henry Stafford, duke of Buckingham. This news shocked the capital – and, presumably, Margaret. There had been no previous indication of animosity between Richard and the Woodvilles. In the past few weeks, Richard had written to both Queen Elizabeth and Edward V assuring them of his loyalty.[9] Buckingham's disgruntlement was less surprising, perhaps, as the young duke had already built a reputation for political disaffection.

Margaret knew Buckingham of old. He was the nephew of her late husband Harry Stafford, and had spent some of his childhood in the care of her mother-in-law Anne, duchess of Buckingham.[10] Buckingham's earliest quarrel with Edward IV arose when Queen Elizabeth arranged his marriage to her sister Katherine Woodville, 'whom he scorned to wed on account of her humble origin', according to the Italian Dominic Mancini.[*][11] During the French war of 1475, Buckingham's opposition to Edward IV's peace treaty had been so bitter that he stormed back to England ahead of the army without royal permission. Perhaps this was what initially drew him and Richard together, for Richard, too, had been dissatisfied with the inglorious conclusion to that campaign. For the past decade, Buckingham had moodily exiled himself to his Breconshire stronghold, ruminating on his misfortunes and tormenting his tenants with overzealous rent collection. Not least of his irritations was the encroachment of the Woodvilles into traditional areas of Stafford authority in Wales and the Marches. Buckingham therefore saw common cause with the sidelined Richard – and an opportunity to turn these inauspicious circumstances to his benefit.

Shocked as Margaret may have been by this unexpected reversal of the Woodville fortunes, she must have considered the potential advantage to herself of Buckingham's sudden restoration to national politics. A kinsman who held the king of England in his power was an asset that she could exploit. Less heartening was the

---

[*] Mancini was an Italian visiting London in summer 1483, who wrote a report of his observations later that year.

prospect of the elevation of Richard, duke of Gloucester. Thomas and Richard had clashed several times in their careers. Richard had emerged on the scene as a teenage lord with a keen eye for personal aggrandisement and a cool certainty as to the justness of his own actions. This self-assurance was a family trait, but in all other ways Richard was wholly unlike the late king. Where Edward IV was tall, broad and magnetically handsome, Richard was short, slender-limbed and apparently plain, although we should be cautious of giving too much credence to Thomas More's assertion that Richard was 'hard favoured of visage'.[12] Richard's scoliosis, or curvature of the spine, confirmed by the skeletal remains discovered in a Leicester car park in 2012, was sufficiently marked that a number of his near contemporaries described him having one shoulder higher than the other. This condition did not impede his martial abilities, however, and even his staunchest critics praised his courage in battle. But where Edward IV paired military prowess with liberality and charm, Richard kept his own counsel, trusting largely in a coterie of northern associates who had proved their loyalty to him. He had the same instinct to be 'close and secret' as Thomas Stanley.[13]

For Margaret, Richard's ascendancy did not necessarily dash her hopes for Henry but his actions introduced a worrying degree of uncertainty into politics. There was no assurance either that Thomas would retain his position in the heart of the royal court, nor that Richard would agree to his late brother's agreement regarding Henry. Thomas, of course, would try to achieve his ambitions by dancing between two masters as usual, but that was becoming a harder task with every passing day.

For Queen Elizabeth, reports of the capture of Prince Edward and her kinsmen's arrest had inspired terrible memories of 1469–71, when another coup had ended in her relatives' murder. Refusing to trust to Richard and Buckingham's good faith, she first attempted to rouse London against them; then, when that proved impossible, she fled to sanctuary at Westminster Abbey with her youngest son Prince Richard, her daughters and – the most likely target of her enemies – her eldest son the marquess of Dorset. The rival supporters of Woodville and Richard began clustering between Westminster and the City of London, braced to defend their leaders – if necessary, by violence.[14]

Edward V had been expected to reach London on May Day, ahead of his planned coronation on 4 May, but it was only on 4 May that the outriders of Richard and Buckingham were finally seen approaching the city gates. Since it was impossible to crown Edward V with the necessary ceremony at such short notice, his coronation was delayed until 22 June. In accordance with royal custom, on 9 May Edward moved into the Tower of London.[15]

The safe deliverance of Prince Edward reassured the citizens, who listened attentively to the accusations that Richard and Buckingham now levelled against the Woodvilles. The dukes had arrived accompanied by four carts laden with weapons bearing the devices of Queen Elizabeth's brothers and sons. Richard claimed that the Woodvilles had assembled this arsenal to murder him and his allies. Some suggested that the arms had actually been assembled for the recent Scottish war, but surely Richard, his head bowed before the king in his coarse black mourning gown, would not have indulged in such subterfuge?

Trusting Richard's accusations, the public mood turned against the Woodvilles. On 8 May, the council's decision to fast-track Prince Edward straight onto the throne was overturned and Richard was named Protector. In a restoration of the old status quo, Lord Hastings was confirmed as chamberlain for Edward V, and Thomas Stanley as steward. For his part in the coup, the duke of Buckingham was given near vice-regal authority over Wales and its Marches. Hastings rejoiced at the overthrow of his rivals. 'Bursting with joy over this new world,' he was heard to observe that the transfer of power from the Woodvilles to Richard 'had been accomplished without any killing and with only so much bloodshed in the affair as might have come from a cut finger.'[16]

Margaret and Thomas did not share Hastings's sentiments. Perhaps Margaret, who was always braced for a blow to fall, feared to express any opinion at all. As weeks passed, tensions between Queen Elizabeth and Richard worsened. The refusal of the king's mother to leave sanctuary or deliver her children from it was becoming a public embarrassment. More Woodville followers flocked into the abbey, including Elizabeth's brother Lionel Woodville, bishop of Salisbury. Meanwhile, her son the marquess of Dorset had fled, not even trusting the stone walls of the abbey to protect him from his enemies.[17]

But Richard's power as Protector was still not absolute. His control of affairs would end as soon as Edward V was crowned, and the king could then remove him from office, leaving him at the mercy of his enemies. There were already rumours of Edward's resistance to the dukes' schemes. Dominic Mancini reported that at Stony Stratford Edward had protested the arrest of his kinsmen and attendants, insisting they were 'good and faithful' men and that his mother was acting in his best interests. Having 'seen nothing evil in them… he had complete confidence in the peers of the realm and the queen'. To this, the duke of Buckingham, 'who loathed' Elizabeth and her relatives, 'answered [that] it was not the business of women but of men to govern kingdoms, and so if [Edward] cherished any confidence in her he had better relinquish it'.[18] Evidently, although Richard and Buckingham controlled access to Edward V, they had not yet succeeded in asserting their influence over him.

Thomas was present at council meetings throughout this period and witnessed Richard's forceful attempts to condemn to death Anthony Woodville, Richard Grey and the other men arrested at Stony Stratford. Richard claimed that the alleged Woodville conspiracy against him was treason since it attacked his position as Protector. His real intention, however, was to destroy Woodville and Grey so that they could not supplant him once Edward was crowned, and potentially exact their vengeance. But the council refused to bow to Richard's wishes. The queen's kinsmen might be resented, even disliked, but there were no grounds to kill them. No concrete plot had been uncovered and, even if it had, Richard was not Protector when he arrested Anthony and Richard Grey at Stony Stratford, so any planned ambush could not constitute treason.[19]

Unable to force his will on the council, and with Queen Elizabeth still refusing to release her children from sanctuary, on 10 June Richard summoned an army from York. He alleged this was to defend himself 'against the queen, her blood, adherents and affinity, which have intended and daily doth intend to murder and utterly destroy us and our cousin, the duke of Buckingham, and the old royal blood of this realm... by their subtle and damnable ways'.[20] His true motivation may have been to enforce his rule on a less than compliant council. The approach of Richard's army gave credence to worrying rumours that had begun circulating that he sought to continue his protectorate after Edward's coronation – even that he sought the throne for himself. Some of the councillors were growing uneasy at his high-handed behaviour. If Richard sought to control or remove the king, his intentions could impact Thomas Stanley, for in concert with Hastings, as chamberlain and steward of the royal household, they controlled access to Edward V. It was starting to appear that resistance to Richard's will was dangerous.

IN THE WITCHING HOUR OF 13 JUNE, A MESSENGER SLIPPED OUT of Thomas Stanley's London residence.[21] He wove through the city streets until he reached the home of Thomas's colleague Lord Hastings. Hastings had been busy of late. Not many days prior, he had held a secret meeting with two men who once stood on opposing sides of the York–Lancaster divide: Thomas Rotherham, archbishop of York and John Morton, bishop of Ely.[22] Rotherham, a Yorkshireman of humble origins, had risen through the ranks by dint of loyal service to Edward IV, much like Hastings himself. Morton, however, had spent most of the 1460s at war with them. He was a Dorset-born lawyer and dedicated Lancastrian rebel who had lived in exile with Queen Marguerite and Jasper Tudor, only reluctantly bowing to Yorkist rule once Henry VI and his son had been killed in 1471. Although he had hoped for a Lancastrian succession, Morton later claimed with characteristic fifteenth-century pragmatism that he submitted to Edward IV because, 'I was never so mad that I would with a dead man strive against the quick.'[23]

In the last years of Edward IV, Morton, Rotherham and

Hastings had become his unimpeachable servants, and it was their dedication to Edward's family that brought them to a meeting with Hastings. It may also have brought Thomas Stanley. By early June 1483, Hastings's concerns about Richard and Buckingham's intentions had become impossible to ignore. The precise details of his meeting with Morton and Rotherham are unclear, but Hastings probably shared his anxieties for the safety of Edward V, secure in the knowledge that the bishops, too, wanted to protect their late master's heir. Rotherham had already provided evidence of his sympathy with the Woodvilles by giving Queen Elizabeth the Great Seal* when she fled into sanctuary. For this he had been stripped of the chancellorship and replaced by a Ricardian nominee. Whatever Hastings said, he made it clear to his allies that, if Richard intended to move against Edward V or usurp the crown, Hastings would oppose him.[24]

Unfortunately for Hastings, he held a similar conversation with his legal adviser, William Catesby, not realising that Catesby was a spy for Richard and Buckingham. Catesby relayed Hastings's defiance to his new masters. If the dukes' informants were investigating Hastings, they must also have been surveilling Thomas Stanley in the home he shared with Margaret and somehow the usually wary Stanley also aroused Richard's suspicions. Had he participated in Hastings's conspiracy? Or had his behaviour at royal councils caused Richard and Buckingham concern? Perhaps, acting in the interest of his brother Sir William Stanley, who had a long-term association with the prince's household, Thomas had been among the councillors who refused to execute Anthony Woodville and his alleged accomplices. If so, his resistance almost spelled his undoing.[25]

On Friday 13 June, Margaret's husband was scheduled to join Richard, Buckingham, Lord Hastings, Archbishop Rotherham, Bishop Morton and other members of the council at the Tower of London. But, the night before, Thomas had a 'fearful dream', 'in which him thought that a boar with his tusks' attacked both him and Hastings. It slashed them so terribly 'by the heads that

---

* The Great Seal was used to authenticate government documents.

the blood ran about both their shoulders'.[26] The boar was the heraldic symbol of Richard, duke of Gloucester and, disturbed by this vision, Thomas dispatched a messenger to Hastings to share his unease and suggest they avoid the council meeting, and instead 'ride away'. Hastings, however, insisted all would be well, trusting in his allies on the council. This, at least, was the tale told by the London lawyer and humanist Thomas More, writing around 1513. More grew up in the household of Bishop John Morton, and may have heard the story from Morton himself.[27]

Only half of the royal council joined Thomas as he was rowed downriver to the Tower that day. Richard had instructed the other half, including the new chancellor, John Russell, bishop of Lincoln, to assemble at Westminster. Edward V, in whose name the council was still nominally ruling, was also absent. It was shortly after ten o'clock when the lords settled into the council chamber deep within the Tower. Suddenly, cries of 'Treason!' erupted outside the door. Armed men stormed in with the duke of Buckingham and seized Lord Hastings. To the astonishment of the councillors, Richard accused his erstwhile ally of treason. Later, more fanciful, accounts reported that Richard also accused Hastings of colluding with his mistress Elizabeth Shore and Queen Elizabeth to bewitch the Protector, causing one of his arms to wither and waste away.[28] Close contemporaries record no such supernatural charges. Dominic Mancini claimed only that Richard 'cried out that an ambush had been prepared for him' by Hastings – 'a false pretext of treason' that was a brutally efficient repetition of the ploy by which he had arrested Edward V's attendants outside Stony Stratford.[29] Allowing the accused neither a trial nor time to prepare for death, Richard condemned Hastings to immediate execution. He was dragged out to a green near the chapel 'and there upon an end of a squared piece of timber... [they] struck off his head'.[30]

Rotherham, Morton and Edward IV's secretary, Oliver King, were immediately arrested. So too, according to early sixteenth-century writers, was Thomas Stanley; the life of Margaret's husband hanging in the balance as Richard considered whether to kill him too. Thomas More provides the fullest narrative of

Thomas's arrest. As one of Richard's men seized Hastings: 'another let fly at the Lord Stanley, which shrank at the stroke and fell under the table, or else his head had been cleft to the teeth, for as shortly as he shrank, yet ran the blood about his ears'.[31]

The blow to Thomas's head, and Hastings's summary execution, fulfilled Thomas's prophetic dream that a boar would inflict bloodshed on them that day.[32] The neatness of this metaphorical vision might render it suspect but less literary sources agreed with More. The *Great Chronicle of London*, written by a citizen of London before 1512, and the history of the northerner John Rous, written by 1492, both agreed that 'Lord Stanley was also wounded, seized and imprisoned.'[33] Polydore Vergil and the author of the *Great Chronicle* went further, suggesting that Margaret's husband only survived the day because Richard feared that Thomas's son George, Lord Strange would raise a formidable Lancashire army against the Protector if Thomas was executed.

Yet contemporaries writing their accounts closer to events do not mention Thomas in relation to Hastings's execution at all. Dominic Mancini, the Crowland Chronicler and letter writers living in London in June 1483 all neglect to mention Thomas Stanley's arrest, or even his presence at this council meeting. The reason for this omission is almost certainly that, as John Rous wrote, Thomas 'shortly [afterwards] regained [Richard's] favour and his liberty'.[34] Only a fortnight after these ugly proceedings in the Tower, Thomas attended a council meeting on 27 June. A week after that, he and Margaret were given Richard's support in a financial dispute that she had inherited from her mother, suggesting any issues between them had been resolved.[35]

For Thomas to wheedle his way back into Richard's good graces so swiftly gives the lie to the notion that the Protector seriously intended to kill him. Richard's actions in June 1483 were ruthlessly efficient, taking both his enemies and allies completely by surprise. Had he really wanted Thomas dead, Thomas would have ended the day in his grave. The later suggestion that Richard was worried about resistance from Thomas's north-western supporters if he killed him is probably correct – Richard had experienced Stanley's military might at first hand and would not underestimate it. It is likely, therefore, that Thomas's life was never really in danger, even if he was arrested. But, if that is the case, how did the story of Thomas's arrest and threatened assassination take root?

It is entirely plausible that Thomas and Margaret felt themselves to be in considerable danger in the summer of 1483, but given Thomas's track record for flexible political affiliation it is also easy to believe that he transformed a moment of potential peril into an opportunity to prove his usefulness to Richard, and thus quickly achieve his restoration. Considering the later prevalence of the story about Thomas's presence at this council meeting, it seems impossible that his attendance was a complete fabrication, but it is likely that Thomas's role in proceedings – and particularly the violence he endured – were exaggerated after the fact, to fit the circumstances of Thomas's later life. It suited Thomas in future years to appear to have opposed Richard's accession because, if he had not, then he was implicated in the murkiest chapters of Richard's coup. In the decades after Richard's death, as the dark legend of the Yorkist king developed, Thomas's role in Hastings's arrest grew in the retelling, and his place in Richard's regime was retrospectively downplayed. When the Stanleys came to write their own family history in the late sixteenth century, Thomas was presented as a lifelong enemy of the tyrannical Richard.[36]

ON 16 JUNE, THREE DAYS AFTER HASTINGS'S BLEEDING CORPSE was hauled from the chapel green to a swiftly dug grave in the Tower, a ring of soldiers encircled Westminster Abbey. Richard's patience had worn thin. In the star-studded chamber in Westminster Palace where council met, only metres from Elizabeth Woodville's refuge, the Protector announced his intention to remove her younger son from sanctuary, if necessary by force.[37] Richard's kinsman Thomas Bourchier, cardinal archbishop of Canterbury was appalled, less by Richard's defiance of the queen's wishes than by the prospect that he might violate sanctuary. The cardinal insisted on making one last attempt to bring out the prince peaceably, giving the queen his personal assurance that the child would be safe in Richard's custody. When confronted by the head of the Church in England and the very real threat of her sanctuary being violated, Elizabeth had little alternative. She surrendered her youngest son. The prince was bundled from his mother's arms into a waiting boat, and rowed upriver to the Tower. That very day, Edward V's coronation was again postponed – this time until November. Elizabeth's trust in the cardinal's assurances for her son had been woefully misplaced.[38]

Within a week, the uneasy stasis in London was rocked by the words of a preacher at St Paul's Cross. On Sunday 22 June, Ralph Shaa, the priest brother of the mayor of London, denounced the princes now dwelling in the Tower as bastards with no right to the crown. Their parents, Shaa claimed, had never truly been married, for at the time Edward IV secretly wed Elizabeth Woodville, he had already been contracted to another woman. Exactly who this other woman was took a little while to emerge – contemporaries named her variously as a princess of Spain, a continental lady promised by Warwick the Kingmaker or an English noblewoman, either Elizabeth Lucy or Eleanor Butler, daughter of the earl of Shrewsbury. In France, a garbled version of the story reached the ears of the Norman chronicler Thomas Basin, who believed that Elizabeth Woodville's first husband had still been alive when she married Edward. The late king's reputation for lechery and luxurious living lent credence to Shaa's words and planted a seed of doubt in his listeners' minds. If the princes were illegitimate, they could not rule. And, since the entire line of George, duke of Clarence had been attainted for his treason, his children were likewise debarred from inheriting the crown. This meant that the true king of England was Richard, duke of Gloucester.[39]

The story of the princes' bastardy took root. On 25 June, Buckingham made a rousing speech before the leading citizens of London at the Guildhall, expanding on the themes of Shaa's sermon and insisting that Richard must be named king.[40] The next day, Buckingham led the citizens and nobility to Baynards Castle, where Richard was staying with his mother. There, within the walls of a palace Margaret had visited many times during previous periods of political unrest, Buckingham presented Richard with a piece of parchment that recited the illegitimacy of his rivals and called on the Protector to accept the crown. After a customary display of reluctance, Richard accepted. He was immediately rowed upriver, still surrounded by variously bemused, bewildered and enthusiastic citizens, to Westminster Hall. Richard took his seat on the marble throne at the upper end of the hall, as a visual symbol of his accession to the crown of England. Within the abbot's house in the sanctuary of Westminster Abbey close by, Elizabeth Woodville might have heard the shouts of acclamation.[41]

By then, her brother Anthony and her son Richard Grey were dead. On 25 June, on Richard's orders, they were beheaded at Pontefract Castle alongside the other attendants of Edward V who had been arrested at Stony Stratford.[42] Richard had deemed them too dangerous to survive. As the blood-soaked straw around their corpses was cleared away, Richard's ally Sir Richard Ratcliffe gathered together his northern army and marched towards London. The reign of Richard III had begun.

II

'The Head of that Conspiracy'[1]

*

A s she paced the ray cloth walkway in the nave of Westminster Abbey, Margaret had to measure her stride to match the queen's. It was 6 July 1483 and Margaret had been appointed to carry the crimson velvet train of Anne Neville, Richard's queen, in their joint coronation – the first in almost two centuries. As her fingers caressed the pure white squirrel fur (miniver) that fringed the queen's magnificent gown, Margaret had plenty of time to contemplate her status. She had been accorded this role as a mark of respect and reconciliation. It acknowledged Margaret's importance as a countess in her own right and the rehabilitation of Thomas Stanley after the ugly events surrounding Lord Hastings's execution.[2]

Somewhere ahead of them – for queens must trail behind kings even in joint celebrations – Margaret's husband Thomas bore the 'mace of constableship' before King Richard. The day had been masterminded by the duke of Buckingham, who enjoyed 'chief rule and devising' of the coronation. He, like Margaret, held a royal train in his hands during this procession, like a pair of reins leashing himself to the uneven shoulders of King Richard, who was resplendent in purple satin.

When Margaret reached the shrine of King Edward the Confessor, around which royal forebears were clustered in a protective ring, she paused as Richard and Anne stepped forward for their anointing. During the Mass that followed, Margaret was one of only two ladies permitted to sit at the queen's side. The other was King Richard's sister Elizabeth, duchess of Suffolk. Finally, the royal party processed in state into Westminster Hall for the coronation banquet, where Margaret sat with the duchesses and countesses on one side of the room, while Thomas bore a white staff of office near the king. As was customary, the feast of fifty dishes was interrupted by the arrival into the hall of the royal champion, Sir Robert Dimmock, on horseback and fully armoured in plate harness.* His horse's trappings of red and white silk trailing along the ground, Dimmock rode up the hall to King Richard's table and bowed before him. A herald proclaimed that if any man should defy Richard and attempt to take his crown, Dimmock would fight him. What was usually a theatrical piece of coronation ritual must have had uncomfortable resonance that day. Across Westminster Yard, one deposed queen and her daughters sat miserably in the abbot's house contemplating an uncertain future, while upriver in the Tower, the boy king that Richard had deposed was still, apparently, alive. Did any eyes cast themselves unconsciously out of the windows towards these ghosts at the feast? If so, no one publicly mentioned these discarded remnants of the Yorkist family, so Dimmock trotted back down the hall and the nobility returned to their feasting.

Yet the Princes in the Tower had not been forgotten. Not by the citizens of London, nor the faithful servants of King Edward IV – and especially not by Margaret Beaufort. For even as she had paced in the footsteps of her new queen, Margaret may already have been plotting to bring down Richard III and restore King Edward V in his place.

MANY PLOTS WERE HATCHING IN THE SUMMER AFTER Richard III's coronation. The country had been stunned into submission by the ruthless efficiency with which Richard's coup was achieved. But, as his subjects recovered from their shock

---

* The Dimmocks had a family duty as royal 'champion', ceremonially challenging to a duel any who would challenge the king's right to the throne.

and adapted to the new reality of Ricardian rule, many were discontented. It went against nature, some felt, for an uncle to usurp the prince he had promised to protect. Others, long-term servants of the late Edward IV and his children, felt their own oaths of fealty had been compromised. Surely they could not just abandon Edward V to the cold embrace of the Tower of London? It was not what the dead king would have wanted. The few friends and retainers whom Queen Elizabeth and her family had managed to cling onto – many of them related to her – were fearful of what would befall them in this new regime.

The details of one conspiracy survive only in the *Annals* written by the sixteenth-century London antiquarian John Stow, published in 1615. Stow had access to an ancient indictment file that is now missing, although his information is supported by references in the closely contemporary chronicles of Crowland Abbey and the Norman bishop Thomas Basin. Stow reported that old servants of Edward IV's household, led by John Smith, the groom of King Edward IV's stirrup, and Stephen Ireland of the Great Wardrobe at the Tower, planned to free Edward V and his brother. Their scheme was to set fires across London as a diversion while they stole the princes away so they could restore Edward V to the crown. Another plot, its membership less clear, sought to rescue Elizabeth of York and her sisters from sanctuary and send them overseas in disguise.[3]

While Margaret had sympathy for the children of Edward IV, she did not immediately leap to their defence as did the rebellious Smith and Ireland. Instead, she adopted the Stanley position, and sought to play both sides. When Richard departed London for a triumphal progress in July, Thomas went with him, and Margaret probably followed. There are no surviving household accounts for Margaret during this period, and contemporary sources provide few clues as to her location, but it would have served her cause to pursue the royal court as it progressed north towards York, where Richard planned to celebrate the ceremonial investiture of his son as Prince of Wales.[4] Margaret hoped that her Stafford connections would enable her to appeal to Richard through Buckingham, so that he would honour Edward IV's promise for the marriage of his daughter to Henry. But while she and Thomas publicly demonstrated their obedience to Richard, in private Margaret must have wished that Edward V still ruled. A boy king with unmarried sisters was a far more appealing entice-ment to draw Henry home than a jealous uncle and illegitimate bride hiding in sanctuary. Thus, throughout that summer, as Thomas enjoyed his place of honour in Richard's court, Margaret continued to cultivate her Woodville connections and communi-cate with the faithful adherents of the late Edward IV. Should one of the plots to restore Edward V succeed, Margaret would thus be able to ingratiate herself with that regime too.

Of course, Margaret could not be seen to be conspiring against Richard when her husband was so newly integrated into his court, so she sent secret intermediaries to sound out Queen Elizabeth and the late king's supporters: her trusted retainer Reynald Bray; her physician, Lewis of Caerleon; her Stanley associates; and her one-time attendant Humphrey Cheyne, whose brother John had worked in the royal stables alongside the rebel John Smith. It was almost certainly by Margaret's urging that the rebels Smith and Ireland were persuaded to recruit Henry and Jasper Tudor to their conspiracy that summer.[5]

But even as Margaret's confederates were at work, sinister news started to trickle out of London. All these plots depended on Edward V being alive and, as the weeks ebbed by, there was less and less certainty of the survival of the Princes in the Tower. Edward V and his younger brother, Prince Richard, had not been seen publicly since the latter was enticed away from Queen Elizabeth and escorted into the Tower on 16 June. One Londoner, whose chronicle was compiled in c.1512, could recall sightings of the boys shooting arrows and playing in the gardens of the Tower at some point that summer.[6] Even this liberty was soon denied them, however, as Dominic Mancini reported: '[They] were with-drawn into the inner apartments of the Tower proper, and day by day began to be seen more rarely behind the bars and windows, until at length they ceased to appear altogether'.[7]

Mancini's source was Edward V's physician, John Argentine, a Cambridgeshire cleric and astrologer in his fifties who had studied medicine in Italy and could thus converse with Mancini in his own language. Argentine had spent his early career at Eton and King's College, Cambridge, both founded by, and closely venerating the memory of, Margaret's kinsman Henry VI of Lancaster. Henry VI was the last monarch to be imprisoned in the Tower and his incarceration had ended with his murder. It is possible that Margaret was also in communication with Argentine, who was a friend of her imprisoned ally Bishop John Morton – himself an old companion in exile of Jasper Tudor – for Argentine went on to enjoy a lucrative career in the service of Margaret's son.[8] Moreover, Sir William Stanley's attendance on Edward V as Prince of Wales meant it was possible that Margaret and Argentine had existing connections to one another. If Margaret did communicate with Argentine, she would have learned, as did Mancini, that Edward V was all too cognisant of the precedent of the Lancastrian King Henry. A scholarly youth with a keen interest in literature, Edward V must have heard the legends of Henry VI's assassination, and he had come to believe that he would meet the same end. Argentine told Mancini that Edward 'believed that death was facing him' and 'like a victim prepared for sacrifice, sought remission of his sins by daily confession and penance'.[9]

By July, Dr Argentine was 'the last of his attendants whose services the king [Edward V] enjoyed' and Mancini seems to have learned no more from him about the fate of the princes. Mancini left England at some point between Richard's coronation on 6 July and December 1483, when he wrote his report on English events for Angelo Cato, archbishop of Vienne and councillor of King Louis XI of France. Since Mancini's narrative ends shortly after Richard's coronation and contains no reference to any of the attempted risings that ensued that summer, he had probably departed by the time they occurred. Yet, even at that early stage, it was suspected that Edward V was dead: 'I have seen many men burst forth into tears and lamentations when mention was made of [Edward V] after his removal from men's sight; and already there was a suspicion that he had been done away with.'[10]

If Edward V and his brother were still alive that July, they would not remain so for long. While Richard was making his way north with the duke of Buckingham and Stanleys in tow, the conspiracy to free the Princes in the Tower was uncovered. Richard's retribution was swift and bloody. Fifty plotters were rounded up in the streets of London and the leading four, including the royal servants Smith and Ireland, were dragged to Tower Hill and beheaded. Meanwhile, the guard at Westminster Abbey was increased, under the vigilant eye of a newly appointed captain, John Nesfield. No one was to enter or leave without permission. The wife and children of Edward IV would not be permitted to escape.[11]

Margaret's collusion in the July plots, however far it went, remained mercifully concealed. At Worcester that August, she made one last attempt to gain royal support for her son's restoration, appealing to the duke of Buckingham as he departed the court and headed home to his estates in the Welsh Marches. In the early sixteenth-century chronicle of lawyer Edward Hall, Margaret and Buckingham's conversation was described as if by the duke himself:

> [Margaret] prayed me first for kindred sake, secondly for the love that I bear to my grandfather Duke Humphrey [of Buckingham] which was sworn brother to her father, to move the king [Richard] to be good to her son Henry… and to him with his favour to return again into England, and if it were his pleasure so to do, she promised that the earl her son should marry one of King Edward [IV]'s daughters at the appointment of the king, without anything to be taken or demanded for the said espousals, but only the king's favour.[12]

But, although Thomas remained in Richard's good graces, Margaret received no assurances for Henry from either Buckingham or the king. With little to show for her Ricardian allegiance, she may already have been regretting it. She and Thomas had escaped the terrible fate of the rebels whose heads were skewered atop London Bridge, but they had not gained all they had hoped from their alliance with the king. It was also becoming clear that, by uniting behind Richard, they risked being tainted by association with the darkest aspects of his regime.

By August, the whispers about the fate of the Princes in the Tower had grown much louder. In the wake of the attempted uprisings that summer, it was widely reported that Richard had deemed it too dangerous to let his nephews live. No one knew by what 'manner of violent destruction' the boys met their ends, but few were in doubt of their fate.[13] Whether he was responsible for the murder of his nephews or not, 'Richard allowed the rumour of their death to be spread about,' according to Polydore Vergil, 'so that people would know that no issue male of King Edward [IV] was left alive and therefore might be more willing to put up with [Richard's] government.'[14]

But if Richard had promoted this story – still more, if he was responsible for the princes' death – he would soon come to regret it. The presumed murder of the Princes in the Tower radically altered his subjects' feelings towards him. Disaffection was not quelled, but magnified. The murder of children was no less horrifying in the fifteenth century than it is today and stories of slaughtered innocents loomed large in medieval popular consciousness. The biblical tale of Herod's murder of the 'holy innocents' was commemorated every year on 28 December during the Twelve Days of Christmas and it formed one of the most moving pieces of theatre in the ritual cycle of civic pageants throughout the country. As harvests were brought in and communities gathered around bonfires to drink and gripe that summer, many hearts hardened against King Richard. Pockets of rebellion began to swell across the south, snaking through the Weald of Kent towards the City of London, across the Downs to Wiltshire, up into the Marches of Wales and south-west through Devon into Cornwall.

By mid-August, Margaret seems to have returned to London.[15] She may have diverted her eastward journey from Worcester to visit her half-brother John Welles, who had taken up residence in their late mother's home at Maxey Castle in Northamptonshire. There, they would surely have discussed the latest, troubling rumours swirling around the king, and what it would mean for their family. They had, after all, lost kin little more than a decade before, in another attempted rebellion against a king denounced as a tyrant: the 1470 Lincolnshire rising. If Edward V really were dead, and his brother with him, there seemed little hope that Richard would legitimise his nieces, nor allow Henry to unite his own blood claim with a Yorkist princess. Richard might even begin to view Henry himself as a threat. John Welles was sufficiently disturbed by reports of the princes' deaths that he committed himself to the growing ranks of dissidents. Richard discovered this nascent conspiracy by 13 August, when he ordered his northern supporter Lord Scrope of Bolton to seize the lands of 'our rebel John Welles'.[16] John evaded Richard's men and fled to the West Country, joining a rebel army massing at Exeter.[17] By then, if not before, Margaret too was committed to rebellion.

Ever since Richard's coup, Margaret had been sounding out the lands in which she had followers, friends and relatives to ascertain the level of loyalty of her tenants to the new king. Her patchwork of territories extended across most of the kingdom and beyond – traversing the Channel into Brittany to the exiled Tudors and Lancastrians. For, while Margaret was undoubtedly concerned to right the wrongs done to the Princes in the Tower, the resistance to Richard III also offered her and her son an unlooked-for opportunity.

It must have been apparent to Margaret that these opponents of Richard were a disparate band, with little uniting them except disdain for the manner of Richard's accession. They included Woodville adherents of Queen Elizabeth's family, faithful servants of Edward IV who hated the Woodvilles, attendants of Edward V who mistrusted Buckingham or Richard, and even some old Lancastrian stalwarts who wanted rid of the Yorkist line altogether. Their very heterogeneity offered an opening to Margaret. If the princes were dead, and by August it seemed they must be, then the opponents of Richard needed a new figurehead for rebellion, a rival for the crown who could unite the factions that threatened to tear England asunder. This figurehead would need to be an adult with royal blood and no loyalty to Richard – and since they might have to fight for the crown militarily, it would need to be a man. There were few noblemen left who could fulfil these criteria without offending one or other rebel faction. Edward, earl of Warwick, the eight-year-old son of George, duke of Clarence, was Richard's prisoner at Sheriff Hutton. John de la Pole, earl of Lincoln, the twenty-five-year-old son of Richard's sister Elizabeth, remained loyal to his uncle. Attrition and the ruthless suppression of Lancastrian revolt under Edward IV had wiped out almost all of Margaret's Beaufort cousins, who like her were descended from Edward III. Only one legitimate Beaufort male had escaped: Henry Tudor.[18] The illegitimacy of the Beauforts and the 1407 parliamentary act that barred their right to the throne had not dispelled a lingering recognition that royal blood flowed in their veins. Margaret and Edward IV had openly acknowledged one another as kinsmen, and further evidence that Margaret's potential royal claim was taken seriously can be seen in the fact that the duke of Suffolk's marrying of her to his son was a factor in the duke's murder in 1450.

Henry's relation to the popular saint Henry VI made him a highly desirable claimant to Lancastrians, and the fact he had been abroad for most of the period of Woodville ascendancy rendered him acceptable to those who would refuse to follow a Woodville claimant. Best of all, Henry was single and the negotiations that Margaret had started with Edward IV had laid the foundations for his marriage to Elizabeth of York. That made him acceptable to the Woodvilles. The unprecedented circumstances of summer 1483 made it possible for Margaret to hope not merely for the return of her son to England but, for the first time, to contemplate the extraordinary prospect of his accession as king.

A LONE FIGURE WEARING THE DISTINCTIVE BLACK ROBES OF A physician departed Lord Stanley's London residence and made the short journey upriver to Westminster. Disembarking at the busy wharf, he wove through the customary crowds of market hawkers, law students and sanctuary seekers, now so swollen with royal guards under Richard's command that the abbey resembled a fortress.[19] Every entrance and exit was being watched, including a small side gateway near the cloisters to the north, for which the physician was headed. At sight of him, the guards parted and nodded the physician through, into a cool flagstone passageway. He ascended to the sanctuary quarters within Cheneygate, the humble residence where the one-time Queen of England and her daughters still dwelt, months after the death of King Edward IV. That Queen Elizabeth should require the services of a doctor, given all her recent griefs and anxieties, was entirely plausible. But, in fact, the physician did not come to provide medical aid – he arrived as an envoy from Margaret Beaufort.

To have any hope of presenting Henry as a serious rival to Richard III, Margaret knew it was vital to secure the support of Elizabeth Woodville and, through her, the wider Woodville cabal. Since it would be impossible for Margaret or her well-known retainers like Reynald Bray to enter Westminster Abbey undetected, she sent an emissary insignificant enough not to arouse the guards' suspicions, but sufficiently trustworthy that Elizabeth would give credence to their message. For this dangerous task, Margaret chose her physician, Lewis of Caerleon. Lewis was a Welsh graduate of Cambridge with the fifteenth-century penchant of combining medicine with astronomy, and a roster of noble patients, including Elizabeth Woodville. 'Since he was a grave man,' Polydore Vergil later reported, Margaret '…was often accustomed to speak freely with him' about political matters.[20] Margaret directed Lewis that he should raise delicately the possibility of an alliance between her and Elizabeth, as if it were his own idea. He must learn whether Elizabeth would be willing to depose Richard and, if so, if she would marry her daughter to Henry to achieve it. Margaret's own complicity in the plot was to be concealed until Lewis ascertained whether Elizabeth was willing to support it.

Margaret awaited Lewis's return at Thomas Stanley's London residence. She hoped that with Elizabeth's backing she could convince Thomas to muster his substantial Lancashire forces to her aid, but she knew enough of her husband's character to be aware that she could not rely on him. He would choose whichever party looked strongest – and he would doubtless hope not to have to choose at all. Her stepsons George and Edward Stanley were vigorous, war-making young men, more willing to risk themselves for potential reward than their aged father, but they, too, tended to toe the Stanley line. The one family member of whom Margaret had greater expectations was her brother-in-law Sir William. A loyal servant of both Edwards IV and V, Sir William had always been readier to march to war than his cautious older brother. Through Sir William, Margaret had made contact with other rebels now committing themselves to her son's cause, including Hugh Conway, a dependable servant from a prominent Flintshire family within Stanley territory who, like William, was an old servant of Edward IV. But these distant, middling-status associates would not compensate for the lack of Thomas Stanley's support if Margaret could not secure it.

Fortunately, Lewis was able to inform Margaret that Elizabeth wholeheartedly agreed with their plan, and promised to galvanise Edward IV's supporters and her own kinsmen in their endeavour. Elizabeth even made the pragmatic suggestion that, if her eldest daughter died, Henry should marry her second daughter, Cecily, to ensure the alliance was maintained.[21] With the backing of the Woodville clan, Margaret proceeded to recruit other disaffected noblemen to her son's cause. In this, she trusted to Reynald Bray, who had served her ever since the early years of her marriage to Harry Stafford.

That summer Bray rode untiringly around the south of England for his mistress, assembling a network of dissidents that included Richard Guildford, a knight with long-term connections to Bray's family who would spearhead a rising in Kent,* and Giles Daubeney, who led a West Country cell and was Margaret's distant relative through her mother's Stourton cousins. Giles was recruited by 20 August, when he took the precaution of settling his estates jointly on his wife, Elizabeth, in the hope that his inheritance could be saved for their children in the event of his attainder. In Wiltshire, Bray gained the support of John Cheyne, master of Edward IV's horse and the brother of Humphrey Cheyne, who had grown up in Margaret's household.† John Cheyne, who at 6'8" was famed for his remarkable height, may have been involved with Margaret

---

* Guildford had brokered Reynald Bray's marriage to Katherine Hussey by 1475, and was also related to Bray's sister, Joan, by marriage.
† The Cheynes were also distant relatives of Margaret's, through her mother.

in the July plot to rescue the Princes in the Tower, since he had worked with John Smith in the royal stables. Thus, in covert meetings and hushed conversations, Bray infiltrated and forged alliances with one bloc of rebels after another.[22]

While Bray galloped through the green lanes and downlands of England, Margaret's mind turned to Brittany. It was vital that she prepare Henry Tudor to coordinate an invasion with international support to coincide with the English risings. To convey a message and 'a good great sum of money' to Henry, she employed the thirty-five-year-old Lancashireman Christopher Urswicke, who had entered Margaret's service as chaplain and confessor. Urswicke was discreet but tenacious, and had got to know Henry slightly during the Readeption, possibly because, as Polydore Vergil suggested, Urswicke 'had always been a follower of Henry VI.'[23] Margaret was to depend on him as a messenger in the years ahead. But, just as Urswicke was on the point of leaving for Brittany, Margaret received intelligence that utterly transformed her plans. Through Bray, she learned that among the rebels seeking to unite with Henry and the Woodvilles against Richard was the king's right-hand man, the duke of Buckingham.

HOW BUCKINGHAM CAME TO JOIN A REBELLION AGAINST THE friend whose reign had brought him unprecedented reward, with one woman whose hopes for her son he had so recently dashed, and another whom he openly detested, is an enduring mystery. The story spun by writers long after the leading players were dead was that the instigator was John Morton, the wily one-time Lancastrian bishop and, in summer 1483, Buckingham's prisoner at Brecon Castle in Wales.[24] In private conversations between these unlikely confidants, so this version of events goes, Morton teased out of Buckingham that, despite his many rewards in Richard's service, the duke still burned with unfulfilled ambition and envy.[25] Morton stoked the embers of Buckingham's discontent until the duke was ready to depose Richard. Meanwhile, Reynald Bray used his Stafford connections to infiltrate Buckingham's plot, and encouraged the duke to join Margaret's rebellion to supplant Richard with a Woodville–Tudor alliance.

But this narrative does not entirely add up. That a man as ambitious as Buckingham should have been willing to risk all his new-gained power in the cause of a Welsh exile and illegitimate princess is scarcely credible, even presuming, as London chroniclers claimed, that Buckingham was shocked into rebellion when he learned that Richard had murdered the Princes in the Tower.[26] It is far more likely that Morton and Bray, acting on the guidance of Margaret and Elizabeth, enticed Buckingham to rebel on the false promise that, when Richard was dead, he would be king. Such active duplicity on the part of the matriarchs of the new regime was not a narrative that either they or their descendants would have sought to promote. Thus, in later retellings of events, their go-betweens were elevated to the status of ringleaders, and the participation of Margaret and Elizabeth was downplayed.

Whatever tale they spun to lure Buckingham, by September, the duke was in contact with Elizabeth Woodville's brother Lionel Woodville, bishop of Salisbury, who had fled sanctuary to hide at Buckingham's Gloucestershire castle of Thornbury.[27] With Buckingham's complicity confirmed, it was vital that Margaret updated Henry, advising him to invade through Wales in the hope that he could unite his forces with the West Country rising and Buckingham's Welsh retinues. To convince her son of the seriousness of this plot, she recalled her relatively lowly envoy, Christopher Urswicke, and entrusted the Breton mission to the higher-ranking Hugh Conway. Meanwhile, to ensure that this vital intelligence reached Henry safely, the ringleader of the Kentish rebels, Richard Guildford, also dispatched his own servant Thomas Romney to Brittany. After an anxious wait, Romney and Conway returned with the message that not only had Henry agreed to lead a Breton invasion force, but that his appeals to Duke Francis of Brittany for material support had succeeded: Francis promised to provide a flotilla of five vessels and more than three hundred soldiers, and had granted Henry 10,000 gold coins with which to assemble and arm his men. With such international

backing for the rebellion, it seemed that Margaret's hopes for her
son might at last be realised.[28]

THROUGH MUDDY FIELDS SWOLLEN BY RAIN, SKIRTING
overflowing riverbanks, the Welsh soldiers trudged their way
north. At their head the duke of Buckingham urged them onwards,
his orders carried away on a fierce wind that whipped their banners and drove stinging raindrops into their faces. Buckingham
was an unpopular landlord and few of the soldiers marching in his
wake had joined him of their own volition.[29] They were receiving
precious little recompense for their service. From the outset, the
weather on the march had been appalling. Torrential downpours
and fierce wind battered Buckingham's soldiers and deluged the
countryside. The River Severn burst its banks and 200 drowned
in the Bristol area as merchants' cellars were flooded and ships
damaged in the Bristol Channel.[30] Unable to cross from Chepstow
to Bristol to unite his Welshmen with the West Country rebels,
Buckingham was forced to turn his dwindling forces back north
and rendezvous with the Stanleys and Talbots in Lancashire. But
desertion was eating away at his army and the further he marched
the clearer it became that his calls to arms were being ignored. It
was not only his own tenants who resented him. His sudden elevation to almost vice-regal authority in Wales under Richard III
threatened the interests of the very lords whose support he now
demanded. These misfortunes set the tone for Margaret's rebellion.

In the last week of September, a flurry of dismissals, arrests and
seizures suggested, for the first time, that Richard's suspicions had
been roused. John Morton's nephew Robert was replaced as keeper
of the rolls of chancery and the possessions of Lionel Woodville,
bishop of Salisbury were seized. On 10 October, rumour blazed
through London that 'Kentishmen be up in the Weald'.[31] Richard's
ally the duke of Norfolk rode out of the capital at the head of
an army to resist the rising, but it was already spreading through
Berkshire, Wiltshire, Devonshire and Cornwall. When Richard
learned that even his friend the duke of Buckingham had joined

the rebels and assembled an army against him, his sense of betrayal was visceral. In a hand-written note he appended to an official missive to his chancellor, John Russell, Richard railed against 'the malice of him that had best cause to be true, the Duke of Buckingham, the most untrue creature living'.[32]

As Richard rallied his subjects to bring down the perfidious Buckingham, Thomas was still entrenched at the king's side in the Angel Inn in Grantham. Richard would not permit the fickle Lord Stanley out of his sight. On 18 October, Thomas's Lancashire stronghold received simultaneous commands from Richard and from the duke of Buckingham, summoning the local men to rise in each of their causes. Margaret's stepson George, Lord Strange rode out of Lathom at the head of a force reported to be 10,000 strong, but it was still unclear if he marched for the rebellion or the king.[33]

Ultimately, Stanley self-interest won out. Thomas could not escape Richard, and the Buckingham campaign was mired in failure. Abandoned by his own soldiers and his hoped-for allies, the duke made it as far as the Herefordshire manor of his old steward Walter Devereux, Lord Ferrers at Weobley before the truth became painfully apparent. The Stanleys refused to join the rebellion. They had chosen to remain loyal to Richard III.

When Buckingham learned of his allies' betrayal he fled in disguise, leaving his wife and children to face Richard's rage alone. The king's men sacked Buckingham's principal seat at Brecon Castle and seized control of Buckingham's duchess, Katherine Woodville, and their daughters. They could not, however, secure his heir, five-year-old Edward Stafford, who was smuggled into hiding by a servant called Elizabeth Delabeare, who twice evaded search parties by disguising the young lord as a girl.[34]

For Margaret, it can hardly have been a surprise that the Stanleys chose to prioritise their own family interests over hers, but it was nonetheless a bitter disappointment. For the rebellion, it was disastrous. The hoped-for national rising did not materialise. The duke of Buckingham was betrayed by the servant who was hiding him, and dragged to Salisbury, where Richard's army had assembled to suppress the West Country rising. Buckingham appealed to Richard to meet him one final time so that he could plead his case – or, so the duke's son later claimed, so he could assassinate the king with a concealed dagger – but Richard no longer had any patience for his former ally. On Sunday 2 November, the feast of All Souls, Buckingham was marched to the marketplace of Salisbury and beheaded.[35]

All this time, Margaret had been waiting to receive word of Henry's landing with his Breton fleet. The same blistering winds that had roared up the Bristol Channel had blasted Henry's fleet as he waited in port at the little harbour of Paimpol in Brittany. He could only eventually set sail on 30 October, when the rebellion in England was already extinguished. His fifteen ships were blown apart, some driven back to the coast of Brittany, while others were thrust over the waves towards Normandy. Henry's was one of the few vessels that managed to reach the coast of England, arriving at the harbour mouth of Plymouth early one November morning.

From the deck of his ship as it rocked at anchor offshore, Henry could make out the shapes of men, dotted along the green sward coastline of Devon: soldiers, a considerable number of them. When Henry sent a boat to inquire if these were friends or foe, the soldiers insisted that they were allies of the duke of Buckingham. But Henry had inherited the Beaufort instinct for caution. Choosing not to trust to the soldiers' assurances, he weighed anchor and let the winds blow his ship all the way back across the Channel, making landfall in Normandy. Henry was right to be suspicious. The armed men surrounding Plymouth were in the service of Richard III, and by fleeing Henry probably saved his own life.[36]

Henry's escape unharmed was one of the only pieces of good news that Margaret received that autumn, for after Buckingham's death the rebellion was mercilessly crushed. Any of Margaret's allies who did not manage to flee the country were rounded up and condemned as traitors. An act of parliament, passed in February 1484, attainted them all, confiscating their goods to the crown and condemning them to imprisonment or execution. Lewis of Caerleon was arrested and thrown in the Tower of London. Thomas Romney, whom the Kentish rebels had dispatched as a messenger to Henry, was captured and beheaded. Margaret's half-brother

John Welles at least managed to escape into exile, with Richard Guildford and John Cheyne. Queen Elizabeth, still languishing in sanctuary at Westminster, was left to contemplate her failure in the same miserable conditions she had endured since Edward V was seized months earlier. Now that Henry had been proven a rebel and she a traitor, any hopes Margaret had for her son's restoration and marriage to Elizabeth of York were dashed. If Henry set foot in England again, he was likely to be imprisoned or even executed.

With her co-conspirators dead or captive, Margaret could hardly expect to escape justice. As a noblewoman, she could be reasonably confident that she would not be executed for her collusion in treason, but she could be attainted and so endure the form of living death that was aristocratic disinheritance. Now Thomas's decision not to join the rebellion proved Margaret's salvation. For remaining loyal to Richard, Thomas received the king's gratitude and reward. On the very day that Buckingham was executed, Thomas was granted the duke's manor of Kimbolton in Huntingdonshire. Shortly afterwards, he was appointed constable of England and gained further estates that had been forfeited by rebels, including the manors of Thomas St Leger, Richard's brother-in-law and another executed rebel. Thus, for 'the good and faithful service which Thomas, lord Stanley, has given and… the sincere love and trust which the king has in him', Margaret was saved from the rigours of attainder.[37] But she did not escape with her freedom, nor her independence. Margaret was understood to be 'the head of that conspiracy', reported Polydore Vergil, and as such she faced harsh punishment.[38]

Condemned in parliament as 'mother of the king's great rebel and traitor, Henry, earl of Richmond', Margaret's estates and dower lands were held forfeit.[39] Thomas was allowed to hold these estates for the remainder of his life, but on his death they would revert to the crown. Since Margaret was ten years younger than her husband it was likely he would predecease her, and she would face abject poverty or whatever minimal allowance Richard would be willing to grant her. Richard wasted no time in granting the reversion of Margaret's estates to his chosen recipients, including his squire Rauf Willoughby, who was given a Norfolk manor 'late of Margaret, countess of Richmond, to him and his heirs forever'.[40] Even Margaret's precious silver and gilt cups, which clearly Richard suspected might be sent overseas to aid her traitor son, were seized by Richard's enforcer Robert Brackenbury.[41]

Worse, far worse, for an independent noblewoman like Margaret, she was placed in the custody of her husband, as if she were a prisoner. All her servants were removed and Thomas was ordered to: 'keep her in custody in his household, stripped of all her servants... She should henceforth send no messenger to her son or to her friends, so she could contrive nothing against the king'.[42]

For a woman who had striven since childhood to enforce her own will, it was a humiliation. Decades of effort on Margaret's part to ensure Henry's inheritance were thus wiped out. All her carefully negotiated arrangements were cancelled. The lands of her mother, her father and her late husbands were dispersed. Her plans for the future lay in tatters. Once again, she had gambled on rebellion to ensure her son's future, and once again she had lost.

12

'Unnatural subjects'[1]

✳

In the gloom of the cathedral, the exiles gathered. It was Christmas Day 1483, just past the darkest point of the year. Grateful to escape the bitter cold outside, they flocked towards the candlelight and gilded images surrounding the altar of Rennes Cathedral. There, falling to their knees, the assembled English- and Welshmen bowed their heads before the tall young man in their midst: Henry Tudor. Margaret's son and heir, the crucible of all her hopes and ambitions, and according to those gathered the true king. At the altar, Henry swore a sacred oath that when he had deposed the tyrant Richard III and secured the crown, he would marry Elizabeth of York. The dynasties of Lancaster and York would be united, and his own distant right to the throne would be strengthened by her royal birth. On this condition, his followers gave him a mutually binding oath, swearing in turn that 'they would, with God's help, strengthen him to be king of England, and aid him in such manner that he – and also she [i.e. Elizabeth] – were... possessed of their rightful inheritance'.[2]

Just as Margaret had hoped, Henry had united the factions that opposed Richard. His court of exiles in Brittany was now 500 strong, swollen with Woodvilles, Yorkists and Lancastrians – Henry's closest kinsmen side by side with those who had opposed his rights under the Yorkist regime. Among those kneeling before Henry, swearing to uphold his claim to the throne, were his uncle Jasper Tudor, now in his fifties but with energy undiminished, and Margaret's half-brother John Welles. The disgruntled servants of Edward IV – like West Country knight Sir Giles Daubeney and John Cheyne, one-time standard bearer to King Edward – formed a network with close ties to the south-west or East Anglia. Princess Elizabeth's half-brother Thomas Grey, marquess of Dorset led a sizeable Woodville presence at Henry's court-in-exile, which also included Princess Elizabeth's uncles Sir Edward Woodville and Lionel, bishop of Salisbury. But Margaret was still hundreds of miles from her son. And, as 1484 dawned, hopes of Henry's return to England seemed destined to proceed no further than that promise in Rennes Cathedral.

THE BLOW, WHEN IT CAME, WAS DELIVERED BY THE WOMAN WHO had spent the last year rousing opposition against Richard III. On 1 March 1484, Margaret's chief ally, Elizabeth Woodville, came to terms with Richard and agreed to discharge her daughters, including the precious Princess Elizabeth, into his care. Margaret was bitterly disappointed, and her sense of betrayal found its way into Polydore Vergil's account of these events: he accused Elizabeth Woodville of being 'forgetful of the wrongs she had suffered, [and] heedless of her pledge to Henry's mother Margaret'.[3]

But Elizabeth Woodville, like so many fifteenth-century noblewomen – like Margaret herself – had learned to put pragmatism before promises to her allies. Whatever Elizabeth's private feelings towards the man widely suspected of murdering her infant sons and known to be responsible for the deaths of her brother and elder son, in spring 1484 she accepted the unpalatable fact of Richard's victory. If she was to have any hope of protecting her surviving children, she had to come to terms with him. But Elizabeth did so with extreme caution, insisting on a royal oath in front of the lords and aldermen of London that Richard would treat her daughters 'as [his] kinswomen', providing dowries for their honourable marriage and disbelieving 'any surmise or evil report to be made... of them'. Elizabeth hoped that this public assurance would prevent her daughters being confined as her sons had been. In the process of negotiation, Elizabeth also secured herself a pension of 700 marks. After all, maternal pride would not keep her clothed and fed.[4]

That spring and summer, Richard maintained a state of readiness against potential Tudor invasion, but as the months passed it became clear that the continental promises of support for Henry were as empty as those made by Elizabeth Woodville. Although Francis II had offered Henry a flotilla and several hundred soldiers, Henry could not safely land in England without knowing the followers of Elizabeth Woodville and her children would support him. The planned invasion could not proceed.[5]

Devoid of military support, Margaret and Henry turned to subtler devices, plotting for their future through a covert intelligence network that relayed information and funds between mother, son and their supporters. Their agents operated west as far as her son's patrimony in Wales and east to her estates in Surrey and Lincolnshire; south to the Beaufort heartland of Dorset and north to the Stanley dominions in Lancashire and Cheshire. They also infiltrated the East Anglian back country and London warehouses where disaffected supporters of Edward IV and his children lurked. They crossed the Channel concealed in merchants' ships and slipped past Richard's soldiers into the garrison town of Calais. From there, they radiated along the coastline of France, west towards the Breton court-in-exile of Henry and Jasper Tudor, south into the French royal heartland of the Île de France, where old associates of Marguerite of Anjou might still linger, and east into Flanders, where they found their way to the hiding place of the long-practised conspirator Bishop John Morton.

It was through this cross-Channel network that John Morton learned, in summer 1484, that Henry was no longer safe in Brittany. A churchman by appointment, but a lawyer by training, Morton had a talent for subtlety. He sensed danger in the reports from Brittany that Duke Francis languished sick in his chambers, surrendering authority to his unpopular treasurer, Pierre Landais. He saw it too in the furtive arrivals of Englishmen from Richard's court, who crossed the duchy's contested frontier with France to deal secretly with Landais. By June, he was certain. Landais had concluded an alliance with Richard. In return for 1,000 archers to bolster Breton forces against the French, Landais had promised to hand over Henry Tudor to his enemy.[6]

Immediately, Morton called for Margaret's confessor Christopher Urswicke, his fellow exile and conspirator, and sent him to warn Henry. Urswicke found Henry at the port city of Vannes, where he and Jasper were living with around five hundred of their English followers, and delivered Morton's warning: Henry must flee east, to the lands of the kingdom of France. There, he could claim sanctuary at the court of the teenage Charles VIII. Henry hesitated, unwilling to abandon his supporters. But he could not move them all without arousing Landais's suspicions. He would have to trust that the protection of Duke Francis would preserve them in his absence. His warning delivered, Urswicke turned his horse and galloped to the court of King Charles, seeking the necessary permission for Henry to cross the border into France. Meanwhile, Henry covertly warned his uncle Jasper and a handful of close advisers of his plans. It was imperative that they left Brittany before Pierre Landais could arrest them.

By the end of summer, everything was in place. Charles had granted Henry and Jasper permission to join his court, and the Tudors rode, separately, towards the border. Jasper's party claimed to be visiting the ailing Duke Francis, who was staying conveniently close to France. But at the last moment he galloped instead for the neighbouring territory of Anjou, within Charles's realm. Henry's alleged destination, meanwhile, was a local manor belonging to a Breton friend. Since he travelled with a small riding household and left the mass of his supporters behind in Vannes, Landais sensed no danger. Indeed, Landais intended to seize the opportunity of Henry's separation from his court to arrest him and place him under armed guard. But five miles into his journey, Henry suddenly turned his horse off the road and into the forest. Stripping off his expensive clothes, he exchanged them for the plainer apparel of one of his servants, then mounted his servant's horse and let one of his henchmen, clad as if he were the earl himself, lead the way back onto the road and to Anjou. As soon as Landais learned of Henry's escape, he sent horsemen galloping in his tracks. The Bretons knew the roads better than Henry and gained quickly on him. By the time Margaret's son crossed the border into France, Landais's men were only an hour behind. But Henry reached Angers safely, and threw himself on the mercy of Charles VIII.

News of Henry's escape from Brittany would have been a great relief to Margaret, but she could take little solace in his latest refuge. For France, too, was riven with faction, as nobles vied for dominance around fourteen-year-old Charles VIII. Ascendancy was currently held by the circle of Charles's twenty-two-year-old sister Anne de Beaujeu, but Anne was opposed by her kinsman Louis, duke of Orléans. Anne was accused by contemporary chroniclers of the same female vices that allegedly bedevilled most powerful medieval women – her pride, duplicity and imperiousness were so infamous that they earned her the nickname 'Madame la Grande'. She was said to have inherited her father's vindictiveness as well as his penetrating intelligence. Men, it was claimed, found it hard to hold her piercing gaze. Anne's ultimate ambition was to subjugate Brittany to French overlordship and by 1484 the opportunity was ripe: Francis II was elderly and ailing, his only heir his seven-year-old daughter. Henry's flight to France provided Anne with just the ammunition she needed for her campaign. Pierre Landais's alliance with Richard III had threatened Anne's schemes, but with Henry in her clutches she could intimidate Richard into abandoning the Anglo-Breton alliance – or, at the very least, distract Richard from any military efforts in Brittany with domestic rebellion. Thus, despite evading Landais's attentions by fleeing to France, Henry remained a fugitive – and a pawn of foreign powers.[7]

In October 1484, the rest of Henry's supporters followed him to the French court, now headed towards Paris. There, his numbers were bolstered still further by the arrival of some unexpected allies. Late that month, two of Richard's senior commanders in the Calais Pale defied royal orders, deserted their posts and defected to Henry's cause. Margaret would have known the defectors by name, if not personally: one was the custodian of Hammes Castle, James Blount, stepson of her late mother-in-law Anne, duchess of

Buckingham. With him travelled John Fortescue, porter of Calais.* The defection of such prominent commanders was hugely advantageous to Henry, especially as they had chosen to escape in the company of the man who had been, for over a decade, their prisoner: the arch-Lancastrian John de Vere, 13th earl of Oxford. Daredevil escapades had been the hallmark of Oxford's career ever since he seized St Michael's Mount and withstood a four-month siege by vastly superior forces in 1473–4. In 1478, he had attempted to escape Hammes Castle by leaping from one of its great round towers, landing in the moat below and becoming mired up to his chin before he was dragged back into prison. Now he offered his sword, and considerable military expertise, to Henry's service – a welcome addition, considering Henry's inexperience. Even better, by January 1485 the earl of Oxford added more than seventy members of the Hammes garrison to Henry's army. They trooped out en masse to join Tudor's forces rather than stay and fight for Richard.[8]

Lancastrians, Yorkists, soldiers, diplomats – all were welcome in Henry's retinue. While Henry and the French court were in Paris, English scholars at the city university joined his ranks, among them a thirty-something cleric and lawyer from Lincolnshire called Richard Fox. Fox's capacity for hard work and compelling rhetorical flourishes impressed Henry to such an extent that he employed Fox as his secretary. It was the start of a career in Tudor service that was to endure into the next century.[9] Paying for the upkeep of this ever-growing Tudor faction was to be an ongoing struggle for Henry, however, as the French government refused to foot the bill.

In November 1484, Henry felt confident enough in his position that he set Richard Fox's 'great intellect and learning' to the task of pronouncing his right to the English throne in a rallying cry that was disseminated on both sides of the Channel.[10] Henry's message was circulated widely throughout England but survives now only in an undated seventeenth-century copy. In it, Henry called on his 'right trusty, worshipful and honourable good friends' to rise up against 'that homicide and unnatural tyrant [Richard,]

---

* Namesake nephew of the John Fortescue who had been, with John Morton and Jasper Tudor, a pillar of the Lancastrian court-in-exile during the 1460s.

which now unjustly bears dominion' over England. They must unite to depose Richard in favour of Henry, who had the 'rightful claim, due and lineal inheritance of that crown'. Although Henry acknowledged that he was merely 'your poor exiled friend' at present, he signed the missive as if he were already king, with a flourished 'H' rather than a more customary use of his comital title, 'Richmond'. Margaret, who had witnessed the Yorkist uprisings and heard tales of Henry IV's usurpation of Richard II, would have recognised that Henry Tudor's pronouncement was astonishingly bold. Public assertions of a pretender's intention to usurp the throne were unprecedented. Previous claimants to the English crown had veiled their designs behind a veneer of disinterest: the Lancastrian Henry IV, and Yorkists Edward IV and his father Richard, duke of York had all returned to England from overseas exile claiming no further aspiration than the restoration of their good names and noble estates. Only once safely landed did they announce their real intentions. But Henry was resolved to stake everything on seizing the throne.[11]

Richard did not allow Henry's bill to go unchallenged. Soon papers were flying from the hands of royal envoys and pinned at the church doors and market crosses of English towns. Richard railed against Henry in his own proclamation, denouncing Tudor and his followers as 'rebels and traitors', and undermining his rival's claim to the throne by insisting he was 'descended of bastard blood both of the father's side and mother's side'.[12] Margaret might accept the disparagement of her Beaufort claim on the old grounds of illegitimacy, but the assertion against the Tudors was entirely false, resting on the misapprehension that Henry's paternal grandfather Owen Tudor was also bastard born.

Yet distant though Henry's claim on the English throne was, it caused Richard considerable alarm, for it came at a period when his own dynasty was insecure. Earlier in 1484 – close to the anniversary of Edward IV's death, as the Crowland Chronicler noted with ghoulish insinuation – Richard's only legitimate child, Edward of Middleham, died after a short illness. For Richard and Queen Anne, this was a deeply felt personal tragedy; the Crowland Chronicler said they were 'almost out of their minds for a long time when faced with this sudden grief'.[13] Richard had already begun paving the way for his son's accession, investing the boy as Prince of Wales, and opening negotiations for his marriage to a princess of Spain.[14] Without an heir, Richard's dynasty might end with him, which made Henry Tudor considerably more appealing to English malcontents.

But at Christmas 1484, just as Margaret could begin to feel optimistic about Henry's prospects, scandalous rumours trickled from the royal court. The alliance on which so much of Henry's support depended, and which Margaret herself had devoted years to advancing – his marriage to Elizabeth of York – was endangered. Richard was determined to prevent Henry marrying his niece. If necessary, by marrying her himself.[15]

IN 1484, RICHARD WAS STILL ONLY THIRTY-TWO, BUT HIS apparently contented marriage to Anne Neville had produced just one child in twelve years. Now approaching thirty – middle age for fifteenth-century women – Anne had grown sickly and was probably suspected of infertility, since Richard had managed to sire at least two illegitimate children outside his marriage. Their union was also prey to the same accusations of invalidity that Richard had used to smear Edward and Elizabeth Woodville, as they were related multiple times within the forbidden degrees of consanguinity and affinity and may not have had all the papal dispensations necessary.[16] During his son's lifetime Richard ignored these claims of illegality since, if they were upheld, they would render his heir illegitimate. After his son's death, however, Richard could consider a divorce with more equanimity and, according to both Polydore Vergil and the Crowland Chronicler, that is exactly what he did.[17]

The Crowland Chronicler* was a civil servant who probably attended Richard's court at Westminster Palace at Christmas 1484

---

* Or 'anonymous author of the second continuation of the Crowland Chronicle' to give him his more accurate moniker.

and reported the scandalous scenes he witnessed with sanctimonious relish. Richard allowed 'too much attention [to be] paid to singing and dancing and to vain exchanges of clothing', wrote the chronicler, and insisted that Queen Anne and Princess Elizabeth appear at court in the same ensembles. The pair were very 'alike in complexion and figure'[18] – albeit with the cruel distinction that Elizabeth was almost half Queen Anne's age. Now eighteen, the golden-haired princess had inherited her parents' good looks and, robed in the finery of a queen, she made a more alluring sight than her ageing and ailing aunt. Richard had already been censured by his courtiers for his sexual dalliances. His ally Thomas Langton, bishop of St Davids regretted in autumn 1483 that 'sensual pleasure [held] sway to an increasing extent' in the king's activities.[19] 'It was said by many,' reported the Crowland Chronicler, 'that the king was applying his mind in every way to contracting a marriage with Elizabeth, either after the death of [Queen Anne] or by means of a divorce, for which he believed he had sufficient grounds.'[20]

Leaving aside any personal unease she may have felt at the incestuous nature of this connection, for Margaret these reports had troubling implications. If Richard married Princess Elizabeth, he would deprive Henry of the chief pillar on which he had established his popularity, for Henry had united disparate interests with his oath in Rennes Cathedral to wed her – and only on this condition had his claim been accepted in some quarters. Richard's marriage to Princess Elizabeth could thus secure his 'crown and dispel the hopes of his rival'.[21]

On 16 March 1485, Queen Anne died, probably from tuberculosis. Rumours soon circulated, however, that her death had been hastened by her husband's abandonment – or even by poison.[22] To counter these accusations of uxoricide and incest, Richard summoned the mayor and citizens of London to St John's Hospital of Jerusalem in Clerkenwell. He declared that 'it never came into his thought or mind to marry [Princess Elizabeth…] nor was he pleased or glad at the death of his queen but as sorry and as heavy in heart as a man could be'.[23] Further proclamations were issued as far north as York. Anyone repeating the rumours would be arrested and seditious bills against him were to be torn down and brought to the city council for destruction.[24] However, once again the eyewitness Crowland Chronicler was sceptical. Despite Richard's insistence that he never intended to marry Elizabeth of York, some of his councillors 'knew well enough that the contrary was true'.[25] He had, after all, made similar pronouncements about his intentions in the past – of loyalty to Elizabeth Woodville and her sons, for instance – and then reneged on them at his pleasure. The Crowland Chronicler suggested that Richard only hesitated to marry Princess Elizabeth because the marriage would alienate his northern powerbase, many of whom had long-term affinities with Queen Anne's Neville family. If the rumours of Richard's lascivious interest in his niece were confirmed they might 'assume he had indeed killed [his wife] in order to complete his incestuous association with his near kinswoman, to the offence of God'.[26]

The Crowland Chronicler was a former councillor of Edward IV with links to Richard's court and, if he was cynical about the king's intentions, it is likely that Margaret was too. In any case, Richard did not have to marry Elizabeth himself to deprive Henry of his putative bride. Richard could simply marry her off to a member of the royal household. Thus, Elizabeth's sister Cecily was married to Richard's esquire of the body, Ralph Scrope of Upsall. Ralph was not quite 'some unworthy no-account' as Polydore Vergil claimed, but he was certainly nowhere near as high-born as Cecily's previous betrothed, King James II of Scotland.[27] Richard's protestations about Princess Elizabeth were unlikely to have allayed Margaret's fears.

The timing for these developments could hardly have been worse, for in that spring of 1485 Henry finally gained the concrete support of the French court. At a meeting of the estates of the kingdom at Rouen, on 4 May, Charles VIII formally committed himself to Henry's cause: he promised a fleet of ships, 2,000 soldiers and tens of thousands of *livres tournois*.[28] Charles matched his financial aid with public assertions of Henry's right to the throne of England. Henry had entered Rouen in April at the heart of Charles's entourage, and during the glittering procession for the feast of Ascension on 12 May, he was accorded a place of honour behind the French princes of the royal blood, styled 'Prince of England' (*Princeps Anglie*). By late June, Henry's stock rose still higher: he made offerings to the Rouen cathedral chapter as 'Lord of the Realm of England' (*Dominum regem Anglie*).[29] Everything seemed ideally arranged, then, for Henry to launch his long-awaited invasion of England in summer 1485. If Richard now divided the Tudor supporters by marrying Elizabeth before Henry could reach her, it could fatally undermine the unity of Henry's cause, and potentially destroy consensus in England for him. 'This was a matter of no small importance,' wrote Polydore Vergil, '... and it began to gnaw Henry greatly' for 'fear lest his friends desert him.'[30] Henry hastily dispatched Margaret's old ally John Morton to Rome, to secure a papal dispensation that would enable him to marry Elizabeth as soon as he reached England and to lodge objections against Richard's putative remarriage.[31]

Ever the pragmatist, however, Henry also took steps to arrange an alternative English match. He knew that marriage was one of the few bargaining chips available to him and, if necessary, he would use it to cement whatever alliance would enable his invasion to succeed. After fourteen years in exile, Henry had few personal links to the English nobility, and Margaret was hardly well placed to assist him during her banishment from court. So Henry relied instead on the childhood connections he had forged at Raglan Castle, hoping that his old guardian's son William Herbert, now second earl of Pembroke, or his fellow playmate and Herbert's brother-in-law Henry Percy, earl of Northumberland would find him an alternative wife. Once again, Margaret's confessor Christopher Urswicke was dispatched as envoy. This time, however, his mission was unsuccessful. 'The highways were so blocked that nobody was able to reach' Northumberland.[32] Henry and Margaret both had to hope that Elizabeth of York would remain free until Henry could get to her.

AS DUSK SETTLED LATE OVER THE CITY OF PARIS, THE GATES of the Château de Vincennes opened to allow a rider to gallop north along the road to Flanders and the court of the duchess of Burgundy. Later – late enough for the well-dressed horseman's disappearance to be noted, alarm to be raised, horses bridled and saddled – the gate released two more riders in pursuit. They moved with the speed of huntsmen, their quarry the last surviving son of Elizabeth Woodville: Thomas Grey, marquess of Dorset.[33]

Since fleeing sanctuary two years earlier, Dorset had been buffeted by the same tides of fortune as Henry, but he withstood his reversals less stoically. Perhaps encouraged by his doting mother, Dorset esteemed himself more highly than his contemporaries did. It was a letter from Elizabeth Woodville that sent Dorset racing from Henry's court-in-exile. She had arranged his reconciliation with King Richard. All he had to do was come home and he would be pardoned and restored.

When Henry learned of Dorset's flight, wrote Polydore Vergil, he was 'deeply disturbed'.[34] Dorset knew too much about Henry's plans and resources to be allowed to join Richard, and his supporters in England were essential to Henry's plan for invasion. Immediately, Henry tasked two of his most trusted supporters with running Dorset to ground: his Welsh servant Matthew Baker and distant kinsman Humphrey Cheyne. Humphrey had a long history with Henry's family, having spent his youth in Margaret's household and even ridden to war with Harry Stafford.[35] It was Humphrey who overtook Dorset just beyond Compiègne, fifty miles from Paris. Henry had instructed his ally only to use 'persuading' words, not force, to win Dorset back to their cause, but presumably threats were intermingled with persuasion, as the next time Henry saw Humphrey, he was shepherding the marquess reluctantly back to Paris.[36]

The betrayal of Elizabeth Woodville and her son was never forgotten by Margaret and Henry. Neither fully trusted the queen or Dorset again.[37] Henry particularly resented Dorset's abandonment, because it endangered the lives of the 500 fellow exiles for whom he was responsible. Henry was a young man who felt his obligations keenly – a trait he had inherited from his mother, whose memory for kindness and favour was renowned. But the corollary to that strong sense of duty was contempt for disloyalty in others. Once crossed, Henry might outwardly forgive a transgression – but he never forgot it.

Dorset's attempted desertion was a symptom of wider troubles confronting Henry as he prepared for invasion that summer.[38] The Franco-Breton war ended in June with French triumph when a Breton force in the pay of Anne de Beaujeu seized control of the government of Brittany, overthrowing and executing the perfidious Pierre Landais. With nothing now to fear from Brittany and its ally King Richard, the French court no longer needed to support Henry's invasion. As a result, Henry only received the first quarter of the promised French funds. As the summer campaigning season ebbed away, he was left to supply his army, coordinate the fleet at Rouen and maintain the eye-watering daily sustenance of his court-in-exile from his own increasingly empty pockets. Weighed down by mounting debts and with little prospect of further international support, Henry turned in desperation to private loans from French local dignitaries, pawning his personal possessions as surety.[39]

As Henry prepared to move up the River Seine to assemble his navy at Honfleur, his financial straits had begun to have serious consequences for his strategy. It had long been his intention to capitalise on a West Country cell of supporters by invading there. Among his connections were many members of Margaret's family: the St Johns, Stourtons, old Beaufort loyalists and those like William Berkeley of Gloucestershire, who was connected by marriage to Margaret's kin and had joined Henry in exile in October 1484.[40] The Berkeleys were also associated with John Blount, the lieutenant of Hammes who had defected with his troops to Henry's cause the previous autumn, and who was the stepbrother of Margaret's late husband Sir Harry Stafford.[41] Most importantly for Henry's invasion plan, however, the marquess of Dorset had substantial regional retinues that could be summoned to the Tudor banner. But, in July 1485, as surety for a much-needed French loan, Henry was forced to leave the marquess of Dorset in Paris as a hostage, with another leading Yorkist, John Bourchier.[42] Without Dorset in his army, Henry could no longer rely on a substantial bloc of potential English followers to join his force. It was at this moment of near desperation that an emissary arrived with news that would save Henry's invasion: an alternative invasion route had opened up for him, and to fund it Margaret had managed to assemble 'no mean sum of money for the payment of soldiers'.[43]

Margaret had probably been sending her son money since at least the nascent risings of summer 1483. In the parliamentary indictment against her, Richard condemned Margaret for abetting Henry by taking '*chevissances* [i.e. loans] of great sums of money as well within the city of London as in other places of this realm'.[44] It had been to prevent further funds being funnelled into Henry's purse that Richard seized Margaret's estate and placed her, and her servants, in Thomas Stanley's custody. But Margaret knew that a reliable cash flow was essential to a successful campaign and, try as Richard might to physically and financially constrain her, she had decades of experience, resources and contacts across vast sweeps of England, Wales and even France whom she could cajole for money to support her son.

Margaret's family was linked by blood and marriage to most of the leading figures of the realm, and by extension to the working men and women who owed them service. St John, Welles, Stafford, Stourton, Stanley, Savage, Tudor, Cheyne – these were only the beginnings of her network. And it was not just princely blood that made Margaret such a vital contributor to the Tudor cause. The connections she had forged over a long lifetime to all walks of society were mobilised now for Henry. They can be read in her membership of religious guilds, the friendships with neighbours rewarded with gifts or letters, in little favours recorded in her household accounts, the relationships with merchants and crafts-men who had provided for her husbands and parents, and in so many more ways, scarcely tangible then and almost entirely lost now. The loyalty of these associates to Margaret was far longer-standing, and almost certainly more immediately beneficial, than their allegiance to the new king. Subterfuge and obfuscation neces-sarily concealed the details of the loans that Margaret negotiated for her son, but the scant glimpses we gain of Margaret's associ-ations before, during and after this pivotal period of her life suggest how widely her web extended.

We can follow some of these networks through generations and across regional borders. For instance, in Margaret's childhood, she and her mother had built a relationship with the wool-trading Stokes-Browne dynasty of Stamford. The Stokes women were neighbours, visitors and co-godparents with Margaret's family at Maxey Castle, and it was presumably through this lifelong connection that one of their sons, Christopher Browne, took up Henry Tudor's cause and ultimately followed him into exile. Browne had a further likely entry point into the Tudor conspiracy because he was a Merchant of the Staple, operating out of Calais.[45] This mercantile network straddled the Channel and was probably a vital communication route for Margaret and her son after 1483. The Merchants of the Staple tended to also have bases in London, their business relationships with the capital's leading citizens strengthened by intermarriage and shared guild membership. Many such merchants had served Margaret's household for decades, forging friendships with her servants. The alderman and mercer Henry Colet, who was later rewarded for helping the Tudor rebellion (probably with cash), had provided Margaret with rich cloth since at least 1468 and became such a close friend of Reynald Bray that he executed Bray's will in 1503.[46] Bray, too, developed a personal relationship with the international merchant community, marrying Katherine Hussey, daughter of the victualler of Calais.*

As well as using her extensive networks to gather money for Henry, Margaret and her co-conspirators also destabilised the Ricardian regime through subversive acts that undermined confidence in his rule and materially disadvantaged him. This activity was even more covert, but equally crucial, alienating potential supporters from the king and disrupting Richard's campaign to thwart Henry's invasion. War was always expensive and the costs of English military preparations were spiralling as Richard maintained a state of readiness across vast sweeps of the coast, uncertain from which direction Henry's force would invade, or even when. The king's constant vigilance was bleeding the royal

---

* The victualler was responsible for supplying 'victuals' (i.e. food) and other provisions to the Calais garrison.

treasury dry. By February 1485, Richard even had to resort to drawing up demands for a forced loan to cover his expenses – a dangerous move, given that his last parliament had condemned similar extractions made by Edward IV.[47]

Margaret and her allies took advantage of Richard's financial insecurity, maintaining a clandestine campaign of economic espionage to drain his coffers of much-needed cash. They suborned his regional financial officers – particularly sheriffs and escheators[*] – and fraudulently underestimated local duties and fines. Since the products of these fines and customs were major sources of royal revenue, they thus stopped money from reaching Richard at a time when he badly needed it. If the king could not pay his followers, they might abandon him at a vital moment in his campaign – as, indeed, Sir John Saville, the underpaid captain of the Isle of Wight, was to do. By creating fraudulent sureties for rebel local officers, Margaret's allies not only prevented money being collected from real sureties but also disrupted normal government business, causing delay, disorder and confusion. Shortly before disappearing overseas, Henry's collaborator Thomas Lovell sent an imposter to the exchequer to stand surety for a bond of £40, which was supposed to ensure a Devon escheator fulfilled his job. In reality, the escheator was also a rebel, and having failed to present his accounts to Richard, he too fled into exile. When Richard's men tried to reclaim the bond of good behaviour, they found only fraud and empty coffers. Precious time and limited resources were wasted as the Ricardian regime struggled to unravel this knot of deceit. And this was only one example of the chaos that Margaret's co-conspirators unleashed on Richard. In her home county of Lincolnshire, the sheriff Thomas Meres similarly failed to make his account for 1484–5, likely because he was working to further Henry's cause.[48]

Henry was depending on such regional networks to back his conquest and indeed had built his plan to invade via the West Country on the sizeable local cell of supporters. With that scheme in tatters by summer 1485, the arrival at his court of an emissary

---

[*] Escheators were local officers, like sheriffs appointed annually, who monitored 'escheats' – cases where land lapsed to the crown on the death of an owner without heirs, an important source of royal funds.

with money and fresh intelligence could not have been more welcome. Polydore Vergil reported that the message came from the Welsh lawyer John Morgan, who was evidently acting as a middle man for highly placed contacts throughout Wales and the north-west of England. Morgan assured Henry that Reynald Bray 'had scraped together' a substantial treasure chest to fund his army, and that Henry could now rely on the support of the leading regional lords Rhys ap Thomas of Carmarthenshire and Sir John Savage of Cheshire.[49] Although Vergil gave credit for this financial backing to Bray, Margaret's long-term servant must surely have been operating under instruction from her, and it is likely that she too had been helping pull the strings of these associates. She had some connection to both: Thomas had been tutored by Margaret's physician and accomplice Lewis of Caerleon, and Savage was Thomas Stanley's nephew and had been a knight of the body to Edward IV.[50]

When he received word of this patronage, Henry was able to plot a new invasion strategy: he could land in the old Tudor heartland of Pembrokeshire, proceed through Rhys ap Thomas's Carmarthenshire territory and thence through north-western Wales and Cheshire towards the Midlands. Although the quicker route would have taken him through the duke of Buckingham's lands in Brecon and across the River Severn, that was blocked by Richard's followers.

There was only one problem with Henry's new strategy. It depended on an element that ought to have been in Margaret's power to control, but over which she felt frustratingly little influence. North-west Wales and Cheshire were Stanley lands, and Henry could not traverse them if the family opposed his passage. For Henry's invasion through Wales to succeed, Margaret needed the support of the Stanleys.

LATE IN JULY 1485, THE GATES OF LATHOM CASTLE OPENED TO welcome its prodigal sons. Thomas had summoned his heir George, Lord Strange, his younger son Sir Edward Stanley and their retainers to discuss how to proceed when war reached English shores. They may also have been joined by Margaret's brother-in-law Sir William and his kinsmen, using the cover of some minor business of lordship – a contract releasing some land – to convene a family council of war. As Margaret was still in her husband's custody, and had the greatest vested interest in the Stanley decision, she was surely also in attendance.[51]

Ninety miles to the south-east, soldiers summoned to the standard of Richard III were assembling at Nottingham Castle. Richard had based himself right at the centre of the kingdom so he could face Henry's invasion wherever it landed. He expected the Stanleys to bring their armies to the muster any day but, as ever, Thomas was prevaricating. On this occasion, it was not merely Thomas's propensity for caution that held Stanley forces at Lathom. As must have become clear at their family council, the clan was divided over who to support in the coming war. Margaret had gained an unexpected ally in her stepson George, Lord Strange, now in his twenties and willing to risk life and liberty to put Henry on the throne. George's eyes were filled with visions of the bright future that could beckon if the Stanleys won his stepbrother a crown. Margaret's brother-in-law Sir William also inclined towards Henry, less for his own sake than for reasons of honour. Having personally served both Edward IV and his son, William wished to avenge the deposed Princes in the Tower. Similarly motivated was Thomas's nephew Sir John Savage, son of his sister Katherine and a leading Cheshireman in his own right – and the man whom John Morgan had assured Henry was ready to fight at his side. But, as head of the family, Thomas held the casting vote and he refused to commit until the endless possibilities crystallised into certainty.

However, delay was growing perilous. Already, Richard's suspicions about the Stanleys had been aroused. Margaret had proven her allegiance to her son once and, according to the Crowland Chronicler, Richard feared that she 'might induce her husband to support her son's party' again.[52] Since the chronicler was serving as a cleric in or near Richard's forces, he was well positioned to know. Thomas had excused himself from an earlier royal summons pleading sickness, but by late July Richard had grown impatient.

If Thomas could not come, Richard commanded, then George should bring their soldiers instead – and then the Stanley heir must remain as hostage for Stanley loyalty.[53] Thomas could not refuse. On 1 August 1485, George rode into the custody of Richard III at Nottingham Castle.

The same day, Henry weighed anchor and set sail from Honfleur with a fair southerly wind and around 2,000 men in his fleet. They were a ragtag bunch: 1,000 Scots in French service, 500 English exiles and perhaps 1,500 French pikemen, unruly veterans whom Philippe de Commines considered 'the loosest and most profligate persons in all that country'.[54] Within a week, Henry would set foot on the sandy cove of Mill Bay, Pembrokeshire, arriving shortly before sunset on Sunday 7 August. Margaret and her son would finally be on the soil of the same realm once more. But, with so much riding on the support of the Stanleys, could Margaret really hope that her husband would prioritise Henry's life over that of his heir?[55]

13

'Die as a king or win'[1]

*

M argaret was probably at Lathom when she received news of Henry's arrival in Wales. The early sixteenth-century chronicle attributed to the Londoner Robert Fabyan reported Henry's landing at Milford with all the dramatic flourish of a returning hero of chivalric romance. When he made landfall, Henry:

> knelt down upon the earth, and with meek countenance and pure devotion began this psalm: "*Iudicame Deus, et decerne causam meam.*" [Judge me, God, and settle my cause.][2] The which when he had finished to the end, and kissed the ground meekly and reverently, made the sign of the cross upon him, he recommended such as were about him boldly in the name of God and St George to set forward.[3]

If such pious displays on her son's part were genuine, they would surely have pleased Margaret, but they were not motivated solely by religion. The declaration of belief in divine justice, and the knighting of followers like John Welles, provided a smokescreen of ceremony to distract from more immediate dangers.[4] A Scottish chronicler, who may have received his information from his compatriots in Henry's army, claimed that some had so little faith in him that they tried to turn back the moment they landed, and Henry had to burn their ship to prevent them.[5] Whether Henry resorted to such measures or not, his ability to bend thousands of men to his will – to motivate, cajole and inspire them through mountainous terrain, at speed – would be vital in the days ahead. Both he and Richard wanted to come to battle swiftly, before the enemy could bolster its ranks with fresh recruits.

At daybreak on the morning after his landing in Wales, Henry assembled his forces and marched north. Margaret was informed by Henry's 'most faithful supporters' that he intended to pass through Shropshire on the way to London.[6] Henry's messages to Margaret, and any response that she gave him, have not survived. Clandestine acts of treason by those as cautious as Margaret and her son leave little paper trail. Indeed, very few of Henry's many letters from this crucial period have been discovered, but one survives in a copy of the late sixteenth or early seventeenth century. It called on a prominent Caernarfonshire family to come to his aid, and Henry wrote as if already 'the king', commanding his 'loving friends and true subjects' to join him, 'defensibly arrayed for the war... as ye will avoid our grievous displeasure'.[7]

As his messengers traversed the country, Henry slowly drove his troops and trundling artillery through the bare and rugged Preseli Hills, over coastal streams and into the rolling valleys towards Welshpool. There, he turned onto the 'wild and twisting tracks in the north', which were, according to the Crowland Chronicler, 'in sole command' of Sir William Stanley.[8] Every day Henry awaited some reassurance from Sir William or Thomas that their troops were ready to join him. Instead, he learned that disaster had befallen the Stanleys.

At some point in August, George, Lord Strange attempted to escape Richard and was captured in flight. Worse, on being dragged back to Nottingham, under interrogation George had revealed the conspiracy between himself, Sir William and their kinsman Sir John Savage to support Henry's invasion. On King Richard's command, George wrote to his father, pleading with Thomas to bring his army to Richard's aid. George feared that, if Thomas did not obey Richard's command now, his life was in danger. To demonstrate his deadly seriousness, Richard pronounced Sir William Stanley and Sir John Savage traitors.

By 15 August, Thomas was forced to act. He marched his forces, numbering into the low thousands, out of Lathom and south towards Lichfield.[9] Margaret's location is not recorded by contemporary documents, but she probably remained behind at Lathom with the few attendants that Richard permitted her. There, she would have to make do with reports from envoys of her son and husband to follow events. At first, the news she received was good: Sir William Stanley and Sir John Savage did indeed join up with Henry's forces.[10] On 18 August, Sir William enabled Henry to gain control of the vital border town of Shrewsbury, despite a bellicose oath by one of its bailiffs, Thomas Mitton, that 'before [Henry] should enter there, he should go over [Mitton's] belly' – meaning that Mitton 'would be slain to the ground' before he allowed Henry through the gates. Within a matter of hours, Mitton was made to regret his hasty words. One of Sir William's retainers persuaded the town's citizens to allow Henry to pass through peacefully and, according to the town chronicle, Mitton 'lay along the ground and his belly upward' as Henry passed by, 'so the said earl stepped over him and saved [Mitton's] oath', while leaving him unharmed.[11]

As Chief Justice of North Wales, Sir William Stanley could provide Henry with the local influence, provisions, manpower and intelligence about Richard's movements that he badly needed. By 20 August, Henry probably had around 5,000 men in his army, including 500 brought by Gilbert Talbot the night before, and a Shropshire host led by Sir William Stanley's stepson Sir Richard Corbet.[12] Corbet had a longer history with Henry: he was the nephew of Lady Anne Herbert, and had saved the adolescent earl of Richmond from the slaughter of the Battle of Edgecote, ultimately delivering Henry into Margaret's care, in 1469.[13]

There were now clear signs that Henry was gaining ground. At Lichfield the city gates were thrown wide to welcome him as guns fired in celebration. But, although Thomas was in communication with Henry and Sir William, he still would not commit his forces. He pointedly stayed ahead of Henry's advancing army, maintaining the impression that he remained the king's man. It was unclear if this was a double bluff or a classic Stanley triple bluff, but it left Henry ill at ease: he was 'in no small anxiety', explained Polydore Vergil, 'because he could assure himself of nothing concerning Thomas

Stanley'.[14] Even a reported meeting on the banks of the River Anker on 20 August, when Henry shook hands with both William and Thomas Stanley, did little to reassure him. He must have learned enough from Margaret about Stanley deception to remain unconfident of his stepfather's intentions.[15] Thomas's reluctance to commit himself was understandable: his eldest son George remained in Richard's power and, if Thomas defected, his son's life would be forfeit. But such reasoning was cold comfort to Henry and Margaret. By the evening of 21 August, Henry's and Richard's armies were just over twenty miles apart, the king's forces at Leicester and Henry's camped at Merevale Abbey in northern Warwickshire. It was the Sunday before the feast day of St Bartholomew the Apostle, and the following morning the armies would face one another not far from the market town of Bosworth. The fate of Margaret's son – and of all England – hung in the balance.

WOMEN – ESPECIALLY NOBLEWOMEN – DID NOT ATTEND battlefields. Even the warrior queen Marguerite of Anjou, who led Lancastrian armies in the name of her husband and son, absented herself when blows were traded. And so, at the event that would prove most pivotal in her son's life, Margaret was absent. Nonetheless, the events of that fateful day at Bosworth Field would have been reported to her by numerous eyewitnesses in the days and years that followed. Many of her closest allies rose with Henry at dawn, quarter past five, on the morning of Monday 22 August. With him in Merevale Abbey were a number of Margaret's most loyal servants, including Reynald Bray, who had once delivered the infant Henry a gift of bow and arrows from his mother.[16] Her half-brother John Welles was among those preparing to advance on the royal camp, leading their troops west along Fen Lane with the sun rising at their backs. Associates from Margaret's youth – Jasper Tudor and Philip ap Howel, the husband of Henry's childhood nursemaid Jane[17] – rode alongside friends who had proven their loyalties in recent years: her confessor Christopher Urswicke, the scholar Richard Fox and her Stanley kinsman Sir John Savage, who had defected from the royal force to Henry's army only the night before. Margaret even had a link to Rhys ap Thomas, whose fiercely bargained support of her son was pivotal to his safe passage through Wales. Rhys's childhood tutor was Lewis of Caerleon, the astronomer-physician who had served as Margaret's go-between during Buckingham's Rebellion. These sources would have told Margaret that her son rose refreshed, after a good night's sleep, and led his forces towards the lowland meadows and marsh where King Richard was already deploying his troops.

Richard was far less well rested. The Crowland Chronicler reported that the king suffered terrible dreams the night before battle, 'with a multitude of demons surrounding him', and in the morning appeared before his household 'drawn, pale and deathly'.[18] The disorganisation Richard discovered in his camp that morning, which prevented him taking Mass or breakfast, was witnessed by his attendant Sir Ralph Bigod and, from his report written down in the 1550s by Henry Parker, Lord Morley. It also made its way into Polydore Vergil's official account. The connection between Bigod, Vergil and Parker was Margaret: Parker grew up in her household, where he often heard one 'Bygoff' relate the story of Bosworth Field. But the words of soldiers were not Margaret's only sources for events that day.[19] She had one further, unusually intimate window into Richard's soul, for she later acquired the Book of Hours that Richard took with him to battle. Both Margaret and Richard inscribed the book: on one of the pages of calendars, Margaret could trace Richard's jagged handwriting, recording in Latin the date of his birth. She added her own message, in English, in the flyleaf, requesting prayers from a later owner. Amid the vibrantly illuminated initials and religious scenes was a devotion composed for Richard's personal use. 'Lord Jesus Christ,' it appealed, '…free me, thy servant King Richard from every tribulation, sorrow and trouble in which I am placed, and from all the plots of my enemies… Save me from all perils of body and soul.'[20] It was easy to imagine the man who spoke such words suffering from mental torment before battle.[21]

Yet, despite Richard's unease, Margaret must have known

that the king had the advantage over her son. He arrived at the clay-rich plains beyond Bosworth first, allowing ample time to deploy his men and artillery to his best advantage. Richard was also a skilled veteran, and had commanded men on the battle-field since he was a teenager, whereas Henry was fighting for the first time. His only experience of warfare was observing the carnage at Edgecote from a distance, sixteen years earlier. Moreover, Richard's army outnumbered Henry's forces – an obvious tactical and psychological benefit. Richard lined up his soldiers to capitalise on their numerical superiority, positioning them all the way along a ridge overlooking the plains near Stoke Golding. This was the sight that confronted Margaret's son when he arrived at about ten o'clock that morning: a daunting bank of bows, billhooks and artillery stretching across the high ground almost as far as the eye could see.

Between these opposing forces, close enough to Richard's army to imply allegiance to the king, were the Stanleys. As Henry approached, both Sir William and Lord Thomas maintained their distance. Probably not even Margaret herself could have been sure which way her husband's loyalties would lean in the battle to come. Henry was disturbed by their aloofness. As he moved his men from the line of march into battle array, he sent an urgent message to his stepfather, 'asking that he would come with his forces and place his soldiers in battle order'.[22] According to the sixteenth-century *Song of Lady Bessy*, Henry personally presented his appeal for military support to Lord Stanley:

> Down [Henry] falleth upon his knee;
> Said, "Father Stanley, full of might,
> The vanguard I pray you give to me,
> For I am come to claim my right,
> And fain revenged would I be."
> "Stand up," [Thomas] said, "my son quickly,
> Thou hast thy mother's blessing truly."[23]

But this boastful ballad originating in the Stanley family's oral tradition minimised any divided loyalties, so must be read sceptically. More creditable is the assertion of Polydore Vergil that Henry was disturbed to discover the Stanley forces 'midway between the two armies', and that the only response Thomas gave him before battle was that Henry should organise his forces as he saw fit, and the Stanley soldiers would do the same. 'This response was not what Henry had expected, and was contrary to what the opportunity and importance of the thing demanded. So Henry was filled with no little anxiety.'[24]

Lacking the reinforcement of Stanley men, Henry had to create a single slender vanguard, which was placed in the command of his veteran commander, the earl of Oxford. Gilbert Talbot and his soldiers, the 'Talbot dogs', took the right wing, Sir John Savage and his men in striking white hoods the left. Henry, like Richard, positioned himself at the rear of his troops with a bodyguard including his standard bearer, Sir William Brandon, and his distant kinsman through Margaret, the giant John Cheyne.[25]

With Richard already controlling the high ground, and his artillery primed to blast lead roundshot as wide as 9 cm into Henry's men, Henry had to make what tactical preparations he could. Local knowledge gleaned from a Leicestershire guide may have persuaded Henry to arrange his men to the side of 'a marsh, so it would serve to protect his men'.[26] 'When the king saw the enemy pass by the marsh,' Vergil related, 'he commanded his men to attack. They raised a sudden shout', which almost drowned out the whistling of arrows flying through the air, before they fell upon each other, fighting hand-to-hand with blades.[27] The generally reliable Burgundian chronicler Jean Molinet, who wrote around five years after the battle, believed that the 'great number of cannons' in Richard's army played an important role. 'The king had the artillery of his army fire' on Henry, reported Molinet, 'and so the French [soldiers in Henry's army], knowing by the king's shot the lie of the land and the order of his battle, resolved, in order to avoid the fire, to mass their troops against the flank rather than the front of the king's battle.'[28]

The military experience of the earl of Oxford proved pivotal during this mêlée. 'Fearing lest his men be outflanked [... Oxford] passed an order through the ranks that no man was to stray more than ten feet from the standards.'[29] At one point, this caused a peculiar cessation to fighting as Oxford called the soldiers back towards their standards. Richard's men were confused, and fearing a feint or treason, briefly also halted their advance. But, within a few moments, combat resumed with even greater savagery.

By now it was clear that the Stanley forces would not engage for Richard. Infuriated by their treachery, Richard ordered that his hostage, Thomas's son George, be beheaded. Once again, the *Song of Lady Bessy* romanticises events, giving George a parting speech in which he takes a gold ring from his finger and asks a gentleman from Lathom to carry it to his wife, Joan, with the advice to flee overseas with their child if Richard won the day. Stanley legend told that the man given the task of killing George, their old rival Sir William Harrington, 'felt things were at a critical stage' and failed to complete his task.[30] The more reliable Crowland Chronicler agrees, claiming George's life was saved because Harrington did not wish to kill Henry's stepbrother when it looked increasingly likely Henry would win.

For, by the second hour of battle, events were turning against Richard. His ally the earl of Northumberland, who commanded a substantial force of northerners, hung back, awaiting an enemy attack that never materialised. Richard's faith in his superior numbers and firepower had probably led him to engage his men too quickly in hand-to-hand combat and he was paying the price. The vanguard led by the duke of Norfolk was disintegrating in front of him.

It was as he witnessed the destruction of his army that Richard made a fateful decision. Diego de Valera, a Castilian courtier who wrote an account of the battle based on reports he gleaned from merchants in England at the time, claimed that Richard was advised to flee and 'put [his] person in safety'. But he refused. 'God forbid I yield one step,' he said. 'This day I will die as a king or win.'[31] Then, the crown on his great helm glinting, he spurred his horse not against the rebel vanguard but directly towards Henry and the slim force of bodyguards encircling him.

In his first charge, Richard killed Henry's standard bearer Sir William Brandon. The Tudor dragon standard tumbled from his hands. In most battles, the fall of a commander's standard would signal defeat, but the dragon was swiftly raised aloft once more, by a Welshman called Rhys Fawr ap Maredudd.[32] In the same assault, Richard's lance unhorsed the 6'8" frame of John Cheyne. Henry stoutly resisted, and 'withstood this attack longer than even his own soldiers expected', reported Vergil, 'for they had almost despaired of victory'.[33] As Henry fought back, his men gained the advantage. Richard's standard bearer, Sir Percival Thirwall, was unhorsed and his legs cut from under him.

Perhaps the sight of Margaret's son spiritedly defending himself inspired the Stanleys at last, for at this crucial moment they finally committed themselves to Henry. The hart's head standard of Sir William Stanley surged into the field, outflanking Richard and pushing him back towards the marsh on Henry's right side. Jean Molinet reported that Richard's horse became mired in the marsh and could not free itself. Unhorsed and isolated, Richard was hammered with blows. 'They beat his bassinet [in]to his head,' related the *Song of Lady Bessy*, 'until the brain came out with blood.'[34] The skeletal remains discovered in Leicestershire in 2012, identified as those of King Richard, confirm his brutal death: his bones bear the marks of eleven pre- or post-mortem injuries, from glancing blows that clipped the skull and jawline to potentially fatal wounds that penetrated deep and drove flaps of bone inwards into the brain.[35] One of these penetrating injuries could have been dealt by a Welsh halberd, as Jean Molinet reports. Whoever dealt the fatal blow, Richard fought until the bitter end. Even his most vituperative critics acknowledged his bravery in his last moments. His courage was 'fierce', wrote Polydore Vergil, 'and did not fail him even in death', for he 'was killed, fighting in the thick of the fray'.[36]

Seeing their king butchered, the royal army threw down their weapons and fled. Thomas Stanley played an inglorious part in the rout that ensued, picking off Richard's soldiers as they tried to escape the field.[37] Nonetheless, the Stanley forces had turned the battle in Henry's favour and Henry never forgot the debt he owed them. Around midday, the sun now high in the sky above him, Henry made his way to the top of Crown Hill, near Stoke

Golding, to survey the aftermath of battle and proclaim his victory. He thanked his soldiers, giving 'immortal thanks' to the noble commanders who had supported him, and ordered his men to help the wounded and bury the dead. All around him, cries reverberated of 'God save King Henry! God save King Henry!' The golden crown from Richard's helmet was brought up to Henry and placed on his head. Later narratives would insist that the man who made this informal coronation was Margaret's husband Thomas.[38]

Margaret would give thanks for her son's victory for the rest of her life. In the Book of Hours that Margaret inherited from her mother, she carefully reported the date of the battle. 'This day,' reads the margin of the calendar for 22 August, 'King Henry VII won the field, where was slain King Richard III.'[39]

In the hours that followed, the ugly aftermath of battle ensued. Richard's baggage train was raided, his royal furnishings and possessions dispersed among Henry's supporters. A fine set of hangings from his tent went to adorn the walls of Sir William Stanley's home. His prayer book ended up in Margaret's possession, and after her in the hands of Elizabeth Neville, Lady Scrope, Richard's cousin and Margaret's friend in later life. Richard's corpse was despoiled. Stripped of its expensive armour and the tabard emblazoned with the royal coat of arms, his slight body was thrown over the back of a horse with his long hair tied mockingly under his chin. Limbs dangling either side of the horse's flanks 'as one would bear a sheep' to market, he was paraded back to Leicester, a rebel soldier piercing his buttocks with a taunting blade.[40] For two days, Richard's body was displayed openly at Greyfriars Church in Leicester, 'covered from the waist downward with a black rag of poor quality'.[41] The purpose of such apparently callous disregard was the same as the post-mortem displays of Warwick 'the Kingmaker' and Henry VI of Lancaster by Edward IV – to demonstrate publicly that a dangerous enemy had been defeated and killed. Now, with Richard's mortal remains entombed 'without royal solemnity' in Greyfriars Church and public proclamations of Henry's victory cried the length and breadth of his kingdom, the son of Margaret Beaufort – the heir to the most unlikely of royal inheritances – was king. The Tudor dynasty had dawned.[42]

II

'HIGH AND MIGHTY PRINCESS'

14

'High and mighty princess the mother
of the king'[1]

✳

As Richard III's half-naked body was borne on horseback to
Greyfriars Church, news of the accession of King Henry VII
spread through the shires. From Bosworth it was carried to York in
the care of the civic emissary John Spooner, who had spent August
riding back and forth between the city and King Richard's army. It
travelled the hundred miles to London in a matter of days, inspir-
ing a flurry of panicked preparations by the aldermen, who dusted
off their violet gowns to greet a king who was, to most of them,
a complete stranger. The prevailing response to the news was astonishment. Few had expected that this French-sponsored Welsh
exile fighting his first ever campaign would seize the crown from
a battle-seasoned Englishman. Henry himself was unprepared for
the speed of his transition from pretender to monarch. As they
progressed south, Margaret's right-hand man, Reynald Bray, and
Henry's servant John English hurried to assemble the necessary
accoutrements of kingship for Henry. They had to beg and borrow
everything from cloth of gold to fine linen shirts – rose-shaped
ornaments to crimson velvet for horse harness. Like Margaret,
Henry's personal preference was for expensive but unshowy black
– long black velvet gowns, black satin doublets and 'fine straight
black' hose for his legs – but as king he had to look the part.
Within days of his victory, he swathed himself in vibrant purple

cloth of gold and glistening violet satin, the costume of kingship that had previously been far beyond his social status, never mind his means. Henry VII's claim to the English throne could easily be queried, and it was vital that his first procession inspired awe in his subjects. Kingship could be as much about pageantry as birthright. From the first, Henry – like Margaret – understood the importance of appearances.[2]

In London, Henry's arrival was greeted with thundering cheers and an eager press of citizens reaching out to touch or kiss his hands, but not everyone shared this public delight at the pretender's accession.[3] It was almost harvest time and the careless movements of armies and artillery as they gathered for battle had destroyed long-tended crops and pastureland.[4] Communities which had rallied to the banner of King Richard fretted about how to win the favour of their new monarch, appealing to local lords for guidance and protection. Already, people turned to the Stanleys for help: the citizens of York pleaded not only with their customary 'good lord' the earl of Northumberland but also with Lord Thomas Stanley to intercede on their behalf for grace from the new king.[5] Henry did what he could to allay anxieties. He dispatched emissaries to reassure his new subjects of his desire for justice and good order, and issued a proclamation that anyone found robbing those returning from battle would be hanged.[6]

But Henry could do nothing about the sickness that trailed in the dusty footfall of his soldiers, a previously unknown epidemic that afflicted the cities through which he passed, marked first by a blaze of all-consuming heat that gave the illness its name: 'the sweating sickness'. This plague was so virulent that within a few days of its appearance it killed 'two mayors and four or five aldermen in the city of London',[7] as well as 'many worshipful commoners'.[8] The coincidence of Henry's arrival with an outbreak of plague must have been a double concern to Margaret, who had feared that pestilence would rob her of her child since before he was even born.

The details of Margaret's reunion with her son are lost. She may have joined Henry and her husband from Lathom as they rode at the head of their army on the journey south. Or perhaps she had already travelled to London, awaiting the first sighting of Henry's dragon banner on the horizon at the end of August? Did she loiter at her manor in Surrey, where Henry quickly retreated from the plague after summoning parliament to confirm his sovereignty? Undoubtedly, by the end of September, Henry was at Guildford, an easy ride from Margaret's manor of Woking, and mother and son had the luxury of almost three weeks together to revive a relationship that had never lain dormant, despite the years they had spent apart. Together, they could hunt through the autumn grasses then retire to the privacy of their manor to converse.[9]

What must Margaret have made of him, the son whom she had bade farewell as a teenager? Henry returned to her a fully moulded adult, fluent in French and with an unmistakably continental bearing and attitude. And what must he have made of her? In her forties, Margaret was still slight and small as ever, and Henry towered over her. Despite that difference, in other ways Margaret and Henry were very similar: they had the same long, thin faces and fine fingers; the same instinct for caution and closeness. Writing of Henry in middle age, Polydore Vergil described him as 'slender but strong and solid, a little above average in height. His appearance was handsome, particularly when his expression was happy in conversation.'[10] There is little sense of this in surviving portraits of Henry, where his wiry hair frames gaunt cheekbones and eyes that squint from deep-set sockets. But static images cannot convey the energy of personality, and clearly Henry had inherited Margaret's dynamism. From the very start of his reign, he impressed with his charisma. He enjoyed that ineffable ability to magnetise and inspire confidence that Edward IV had possessed – although Margaret was probably relieved that Henry lacked Edward's impulse for high living.

Henry had many Beaufort family traits too: schooled by his past misfortunes, he had an instinct for suspicion, the same long memory as Margaret and a matching agility of mind.[11] He also shared his mother's pessimism. As the early Tudor chronicler Edward Hall expressed it, Henry feared 'the burning fire [of danger] like an infant that [has been] a little singed with a small flame' and having been 'made wise and expert with troubles and mischiefs before past, remembered that it was wisdom to fear'.[12] This accords closely with Margaret's character. As her confessor John Fisher described, she 'never yet was in that prosperity but... she was in dread of the adversity for to come'.[13]

This conviction – that hardship must follow joy – produced behaviour that became a defining characteristic of Margaret's. At Henry's coronation, she 'wept marvellously', which was to be her customary response to great dynastic occasions.[14] She would weep later, too, at the marriage of her firstborn grandchild and the successful accession of her last surviving grandson. These were not tears of joy, or even an involuntary response to the release of pressure after years of anxiety and heartache. Rather, Margaret wept because she knew that such heights of happiness could not endure. A lifetime of trauma had not hardened her. Even when 'she had full great joy', John Fisher continued, 'she let not to say that some adversity would follow'.[15] The only uncertainty was what form that adversity would take.

THE RITUALS OF HENRY'S CORONATION IN THE LAST DAYS OF October gave little indication that this king was as much a usurper as he insisted that Richard III had been. Trumpets blared in the streets of London to herald King Henry VII, their pipes adorned with fringed banners of blue sarcenet, painted in oil with gold. The images adorning the banners and trappers* of horses that accompanied Henry from the Tower of London to Westminster Abbey asserted his just right to the throne. As tradition dictated, the arms of Saints Edmund and Edward – two holy Saxon monarchs – were interspersed with the cross of St George. But everywhere there were subtle clues, understood by Margaret and many in attendance, that this day marked the dawn of a new dynasty. Instead of the white roses and suns in splendour that had emblazoned Yorkist state occasions, now velvet *red* roses studded the skyline, affecting to mirror the Lancastrian heraldry of the early fifteenth century.

---

* A covering draped over a horse, sometimes highly ornamented.

Emphasising Henry's Welsh antecedents, gold of Venice embroidery wound around the feet of a vast crimson dragon banner, and the arms of the legendary ancient Briton Cadwaladr were embroidered on the horse trappings of the royal champion, Sir Robert Dimmock. Both Polydore Vergil and Bernard André referred in their works to Henry's mythical descent from Cadwaladr, who 'had forecast that his stock would reign once more'.[16] Perhaps most gratifying for Margaret – a noblewoman whose prayer books and lodgings were richly adorned with her family's coat of arms – 500 Beaufort portcullises of silver and gilt glinted amongst the decorations for the coronation.[17]

Being a woman, Margaret played no official role in her son's coronation. Only a queen, jointly crowned as Anne Neville had been, was accorded a leading part in such occasions. But, despite her public inactivity, Margaret's influence and long-term allegiances were evident in the roles Henry gave others in the pageant of accession, and in the rewards he lavished on them in the early months of his reign. Few kings of England have come to the throne with so little close family: besides Margaret, the only immediate relation Henry had was Jasper Tudor. But, in the absence of blood relatives, Henry chose in the early days of his kingship to elevate the family he was connected to through Margaret, including John Welles, who was created a viscount. The chief victors were the Stanleys. Henry never forgot the debt he owed them. A grant to Thomas Stanley on 26 September 1485 recognised, 'the good and praiseworthy services performed by him before now with great personal exertions and costs… [especially] lately in the king's conflict within the realm of England'.[18]

Thomas was referred to as Henry's 'right entirely beloved father' and his eldest son, George, Lord Strange, as 'our right trusty and entirely beloved brother'.[19] Rights to forest, fishing and farming were granted to both in their home territories north of the Trent, while Thomas's brother Sir William Stanley received promotion in North Wales and was created chamberlain of the royal household, controlling access to the king within the upper chambers of the court. A grant to Sir William Stanley of Hunsdon Manor in Hertfordshire was made in return for him 'rendering yearly a red rose'.[20] Thomas's younger sons James and Sir Edward Stanley also received royal patronage in their respective careers as churchman and aristocrat: James was named dean of St Martin the Great, London, while Sir Edward was made a knight of the king's body and sheriff of Lancashire.[21]

On the feast day of Saints Simon and Jude (Friday 28 October), in the presence chamber of the Tower of London, Henry elevated his stepfather Thomas to the earldom of Derby. Margaret would henceforth proudly declare herself 'Countess of Richmond and of Derby'. Henry would prove notably reticent to promote his nobility to high rank, and on this rare occasion only his uncle Jasper and Edward Courtenay – heir to the Lancastrian earls of Devon – were granted similar honours. Courtenay was restored to his family's West Country earldom and Henry's 'dearest uncle'[22] Jasper was created duke of Bedford. The following day, Jasper and Thomas personally laced spurs to the heels of Reynald Bray, as Henry created him one of five new Knights of the Bath – a testament to his decades of diligent service in Margaret's household as well as to his role in the last two years of political intrigue for her son. Margaret herself, of course, was also rewarded: in his first parliament that autumn, Henry overturned the restrictions placed on Margaret by Richard III and returned her confiscated estates. This parliament also reenacted the 1397 legitimisation of the Beaufort family, omitting the awkward 1407 statute that denied them the dignity of the crown.[23]

But Henry's accession did not represent the triumph of the Lancastrian cause at the cost of the Yorkist. Among those attending Henry's coronation and parliament were surviving members of Richard III's family and affinity: Richard's twenty-five-year-old nephew John de la Pole, earl of Lincoln,[*] who had fought against Henry at Bosworth; his kinsman Cardinal Thomas Bourchier, archbishop of Canterbury, who now had the distinction of having crowned three kings and two queens.[†] Henry's most prominent Yorkist supporters, Thomas Grey, marquess of Dorset and John

---

[*] Son of the John de la Pole who had once been married to Margaret.
[†] Edward IV, Richard III, Henry VII, Elizabeth Woodville and Anne Neville.

Bourchier, Lord Fitzwarin, were not in attendance but Henry had already made arrangements for their return to England from French exile, and in November they would be back at court.[24] Although Elizabeth of York was absent, Henry had not neglected his promise to marry the daughter of Edward IV and thus unite their dynasties. While preparations were made for this union, Elizabeth lived in the care of her future mother-in-law. Both she and Margaret were about to embark on a wholly new life together.

HENRY'S TRANSITION TO KINGSHIP WAS HERALDED WITH trumpet blasts and echoing shouts of acclaim, but the change in Margaret's circumstances, though equally discernible to her, was quieter. It could be felt when she travelled to London in September 1485 and docked not at the steps of her mother's manor on the western limits of the city, but at a palace close to the seat of power beside the Tower. Her new London home was called Coldharbour: a huddle of buildings, fragrant gardens and smoking chimneys that extended 150 feet alongside the river, and 300 feet north to Thames Street.[25] Impressive as it was, Margaret already had plans for improvements. She had left a trail of Beaufort portcullis heraldry through Lincolnshire, Surrey and Cheshire as she moved from home to home, and now Coldharbour too would be emblazoned with her coat of arms. The windows of the great hall would soon be re-glazed with Margaret's heraldry by the finest Dutch artisans. Margaret's own suite of chambers – a bedroom, private closet, little dining hall and 'close chair' (portable toilet) – would also be branded with the crests, and a few of Thomas Stanley's eagle-foot emblem for good measure. Everything must proclaim the authority of Margaret's family. Even the kitchen windows would be reset with costly Venetian glass, should any visitors she sought to impress wander into the service wing. And the stables would be so well stocked with horses that the labourer John Johnson would need two boats to bear their dung away by water.[26]

In another change, when Margaret alighted at Coldharbour's water gate – that, too, she would renovate – she was not alone. The weeks immediately after Henry's accession transformed Margaret's home into something between a prison and a crèche: almost every politically sensitive, under-age dynastic rival to her son was placed in her care. As well as the Yorkist princesses, whom Richard III had held in custody at Sheriff Hutton, Margaret took guardianship of Ralph Neville, the Yorkist earl of Westmorland and Edward, earl of Warwick, the ten-year-old son of George, duke of Clarence. The two earls were maintained comfortably enough that Margaret received £200 for three months of her expenses providing them with clothing and food.[27] By the year's end, however, Warwick was moved into the Tower of London, to grow to adolescence in obscurity and seclusion. Taking his place in Margaret's home were two Stafford lords: seven-year-old Edward, duke of Buckingham, who had escaped capture in 1483 by disguising himself as a girl, and his younger brother Henry.

The most important guest in Coldharbour, however, was un-doubtedly nineteen-year-old Princess Elizabeth, who moved in with her sister Cecily. All the children were treated well, those of the highest status like Elizabeth and the duke of Buckingham being given their own private suites, which Margaret took care to renovate appropriately for their rank. 'Lady Elizabeth's Chamber' had its own 'wardrobe' and windows that caught the last of the evening sun. As a mark of how essential he had become to her family, Reynald Bray was also accorded his own chamber within the manor, along with Margaret's most important female attend-ants Edith Fowler and Elizabeth Denton. Although most of these young noblemen and women would ultimately demonstrate their allegiance and leave Margaret's care, Princess Elizabeth – soon to be queen – would continue to live close to her mother-in-law for the next fourteen years.

The older generation of Yorkist women chose at Henry's ac-cession to retire from the political sphere. Cecily, duchess of York was already living in ostentatious piety at Berkhamsted Castle and Elizabeth Woodville later moved to Bermondsey Abbey. But Margaret was not ready in 1485 to act as Cecily and Elizabeth chose to do. She did not want to retire into pious obscurity; she wanted to help Henry establish his regime. He, in turn, deeply valued Margaret's counsel, since she was one of the few unbiased and experienced English advisers he had. Henry himself had never lived in the royal court, and had not visited England in the past fourteen years.

After decades of estrangement from her son, it was little wonder that Margaret now sought to live close to him, but her constant presence within the royal court presented a difficulty. When Elizabeth became queen, what would Margaret's status be? And how could she reconcile her identity as the mother of a king but not a queen dowager – not even a widow? Her situation as married royal mother was unprecedented, and potentially troubling. Henry and Margaret must have discussed her status as royal matriarch and married woman. They did not want to alienate the Stanleys, but it would not do for the king's mother to be legally in the power of a husband when that could contradict her loyalty to the crown. Yet, despite all her years at court, Margaret was in uncharted territory. There had been surviving dowager queens before, like Elizabeth Woodville – even surviving princesses who were mothers of kings, like Richard II's mother, the dowager Princess of Wales, Joan of Kent* – but there had never been a king's mother who did not herself have a royal title.

Perhaps Margaret discussed the issue with her old friend and closest antecedent, Cecily, duchess of York. Like Margaret, the septuagenarian mother of Edward IV and Richard III had not been a queen or Princess of Wales before she became the king's mother, but her family insisted that her late husband, Richard, duke of York, was the rightful king of England, so she had a quasi-regal claim that Margaret lacked. Nonetheless, Cecily had found it hard to settle on a clear role for herself. At the head of her letters, she pronounced herself verbosely as 'Cecily, the king's mother and late wife unto Richard [of York], in right king of England and of France and lord of Ireland'. More commonly, she simply signed herself 'Cecily', assuming the same style as a crowned queen.[28] Similarly, in the early years of Henry VII's reign, Margaret's title

---

* Joan's husband, the Black Prince, predeceased both his father, Edward III, and his son Richard II.

oscillated. In September 1485, she was described in a royal grant as Henry's 'most dearest mother', later 'our most dear and best beloved lady and mother' and, as early as December 1485, 'the most dear and most excellent princess and lady his mother'.[29] At New Year 1487, Henry's heralds addressed Margaret as 'high and mighty princess the mother of the king, countess of Richmond and Derby'.[30] Her clothing, too, suggested some ambiguity in her position. At Christmas 1487 Margaret processed behind Henry wearing 'a rich coronel' [coronet] and at the Epiphany festivities that followed she appeared in a luxurious surcoat and mantle fit for a queen.[31] Eventually, like Cecily, Margaret too would shorten her name, using 'Margaret R' in her missives.* More commonly, she came to be known simply as 'my lady the King's Mother'.

Margaret's unique status was matched by exceptional independence. Thus, in Henry's first parliament, he created Margaret 'femme sole', giving her the power at law to hold her lands 'as any other single unmarried person may do, without interruption or contradiction'.[32] The crucial word here is 'person' – Margaret was no longer to be treated as a woman, legally 'covered' or controlled by her male relatives. Instead, she was free to make her own will in her husband's lifetime, to hold estates independently and to pursue any legal concerns she chose, for the rest of her life. When she died, her estate would descend to Henry, which was exactly as she would have wanted it.

To placate Thomas, who was materially disadvantaged by Margaret's newfound independence, Henry split his mother's estate into pieces: her inheritance from her mother, the dowager duchess of Somerset, was divided between Margaret and Thomas, while those possessions that had been held as jointure or heritage were divided as they had been before the dowager duchess's death in 1482: Margaret received one third, and Thomas two thirds. But Margaret was given sole power to administer these estates, under her own officers. Thomas merely received profits, delivered to him by Margaret's retainers. Crucially, anything granted to Margaret after 1485 was to be held entirely by her – and, within

---

* See Chapter 20 for the debate surrounding Margaret's title.

two years, Henry gifted her an extensive sweep of lands and properties in the 'Great Grant'.[33] Thus, Margaret gained control over
estates from Lincolnshire in the east of England to Devon and
Dorset in the west; from Derbyshire and Westmorland in the
north to Hertfordshire and Essex in the south. The annual income
Margaret received from this vast sweep of territory was over a
thousand pounds – and that was before Margaret's other properties, their incomes shared for now with Thomas, were taken into
account. With this grant, Margaret's income became comparable
to the leading noblemen of her day. Lands that she had struggled to
retain for most of her life – which even her parents had been unable to control – she now possessed unquestionably. Among them
were Holland patrimonies, including the rich manor of Ware
in Hertfordshire, which Margaret claimed as granddaughter of
Margaret Holland, duchess of Somerset and Clarence. Her strug-
gles to secure the Kendal part of the Richmond earldom, which
stretched back to the lifetime of Edmund Tudor, were finally rewarded, and her possession of the castle and liberties of Corfe in
Dorset reasserted her connection to her paternal Beaufort estate.
By 1488, she was undertaking substantial repairs to Corfe Castle
so that she could welcome her son to stay.

Of course, for Margaret to gain these lands others must lose
out. Margaret's control of the Holland estates in Devonshire,
Derbyshire, Northamptonshire and North Wales dispossessed
Ralph, earl of Westmorland, who was the heir general. The young
earl of Warwick was also deprived of his rights as heir of the earls
of Kent and Salisbury, with his inheritance diverted to the king's
mother.[34] Neither Margaret nor Henry publicly acknowledged
the morally dubious nature of these acquisitions. Perhaps, like the
Yorkists before them, they felt they were owed for their suffering
under the previous regime. Richard III had dispossessed Margaret
when he was in the ascendant and, now her family ruled, she
meted out the same treatment to her rivals.

Margaret's new autonomy changed her relationship with
Thomas Stanley, but did not end it. Thomas had, however,
come to represent her frustration with the limitations imposed
on her in recent years. Even before Edward IV's death, in the

agreement Margaret and Thomas drew up in 1482, there were hints of irritation at her husband's interference in her business.[35] Under Richard III, things had been even worse, with Margaret essentially Thomas's prisoner. She had never been a 'hands off' administrator of her estates – few, if any, noblewomen were – and this depredation must have been profoundly challenging. It is also possible that Margaret felt some residual resentment at Thomas's lack of support for her son in 1483 and his wavering commitment in August 1485.

But if Margaret and Thomas's relationship was faltering after thirteen years of marriage, contemporary documents do not reflect it. The couple continued to spend time in each other's company, and even when they were not living together their household staff and the architecture of their homes represented the enduring fusion of their lives. Margaret still visited the Stanley seats of Knowsley and Lathom, where her coat of arms and the inscription 'our lady the King's mother' were proudly displayed. Her new home at Coldharbour regularly welcomed Lord Stanley; multiple visits are documented in his book of accounts for 1491–2, and his servants continued to attend to 'my lady's matters' in the city.[36] Even the additions that Margaret made to Coldharbour recognised her ongoing status as Thomas's wife: when she upgraded her chamber there in autumn 1485, she installed a set of stained glass bearing the 'arms of my Lord [Stanley] and my Lady'.[37] Being 'Countess of Derby' – Thomas's wife and stepmother of his children – remained as publicly important to her as her position as 'Countess of Richmond'. In turn, the association with Margaret and thus the crown reflected prestige and honour on the Stanleys.

Having established Henry's rule, the next challenge for the king and his mother was to ensure its survival. The dynasty would need heirs, which meant the king needed a queen. After years of thwarted hopes, by the dawn of 1486, Margaret would finally see her long-cherished wish come to fruition: the roses of York and Lancaster would be united.

15

'Rejoice for both roses'[1]

✳

As Margaret watched her son at Christmas 1485, processing through the corridors of Westminster Palace in 'a rich gown of purple velvet furred with sables', she might well have considered how starkly their circumstances had changed in the past year. Last Christmas, Margaret had been in the custody of her husband, and Henry an impoverished exile. Now the 'crown of gold set with pearls and precious stones' that had so recently adorned Richard III's brow weighed heavy instead on Henry.[2] Some things, though, had not changed. For the eyes of the court and the king were drawn to the same demure, beautiful young woman who had been at the heart of court scandal for two years: Princess Elizabeth of York, Margaret's daughter-in-law.

Although still awaiting the papal dispensation permitting their marriage, which would arrive in January, Elizabeth and Henry had started to get to know one another. For propriety's sake, they probably met under Margaret's eye and perhaps with Elizabeth's sister Cecily in attendance. But, during the winter of 1485, it appears that Henry and Elizabeth exchanged private vows and consummated their union. Although the details of this secret ceremony of commitment are scarce, royal documents begin referring to the king's 'wife' from late 1485 and their first child was born a slightly suspicious eight months after their official wedding on 18 January 1486.[3] On 6 December 1485, the papal collector Giovanni de' Gigli heard it 'positively asserted that the King is about to marry [Elizabeth], which everybody considers advantageous for the kingdom', and later that month fifteen parcels were delivered to Henry, including the queen's gold wedding ring, which cost twenty-three shillings and four pence.[4] Whether Henry and Elizabeth wed in December or January, Margaret would have rejoiced to see the marriage for which she had hoped and planned for almost twenty years finally come to pass.

When Henry had made his fateful promise to marry Elizabeth of York, in Rennes Cathedral at Christmas 1483, he had probably never even laid eyes on her. During his only recorded visit to the royal court, in the Readeption of 1470, Elizabeth had been hiding in sanctuary at Westminster Abbey. But, although Henry and Elizabeth were strangers, Margaret knew the princess well, and her choice of bride was proof of not only her political but also personal judgement. Henry and Elizabeth would enjoy a remarkably contented married life. Bride and groom were older than most royal couples: Henry was just shy of twenty-nine, and Elizabeth about to turn twenty. A good age, however, to safely begin building their family, and cementing the Tudor dynasty by providing for its next generation.

There had always been much to recommend Elizabeth as Henry's queen. As eldest-born child of King Edward IV, Elizabeth had received the benefits of a royal education: she was schooled in English and French (like Margaret, her parents discouraged Latin) and owned several books, in which she assiduously signed her name. The French prose *Romance of St Graal*, which was evidently passed around Elizabeth's family, contains the signatures of *Elysabeth, the kyngys dowther*, her sister Cecily, 'E Wydevyll' (possibly their mother), their cousin *Alyanor Haute* and aunt *Jane Grey*. Elizabeth's family had long been associated with the literary arts. Both her mother and uncle Anthony Woodville patronised the earliest English printer, William Caxton, and Anthony translated a number of philosophical and religious texts in his lifetime. Perhaps because of this family association, Princess Elizabeth was later remembered for her own, quite possibly exaggerated, literary abilities. The *Song of Lady Bessy*, a sixteenth-century work by a Stanley associate, makes Elizabeth its heroine and imagines her penning secret messages for Thomas Stanley to dispatch to allies in the cause of Henry Tudor.[5] Yet, like Margaret herself, Elizabeth combined intellectual interests with other cultural pursuits. Throughout her life, she enjoyed music and dance, later patronising the court composers William Cornish and Robert Fayrfax, and even in infancy possessing a flair for performance. When the Burgundian nobleman Louis de Gruuthuse visited the English court in 1472, he observed the six-year-old princess dancing for the court, once with her handsome father. Elizabeth also rode. She sewed. She played the clavichord.* Perhaps she did not share Margaret and Henry's zeal for hunting, but she was interested enough to maintain a pack of greyhounds and a goshawk.[6] Also like Margaret, the princess had been schooled from her earliest years in the vagaries of fortune. Born in 1466, Elizabeth had been old enough to experience, and doubtless recall, the tribulations her family endured in 1469–71 and 1483–5. Some of Elizabeth's earliest memories must have been of the winter she spent in sanctuary at Westminster Abbey with her pregnant mother and younger siblings.[7]

The only potential blot on Elizabeth's character occurred in Richard's reign. Henry knew that Richard III considered marriage to Elizabeth, but a more troubling uncertainty hovered around Elizabeth's own feelings on the matter: had she ever welcomed the late king's intentions? If so, would that have given Margaret pause in promoting Elizabeth as Henry's bride? Sixteenth-century commentators like Polydore Vergil insisted that Elizabeth strongly rejected Richard. *The Song of Lady Bessy* cites Elizabeth's alleged loathing for the king in the most violent terms:

My uncle Richard sent after me
... And bade that I should to his chamber go;
His love and his *leman* [lover] that I should be...
Yet had I rather burn... on the Tower Hill that is so high,
[Before] I would to his chamber come.
His love and his *leman* will I not be,
I had rather be drawn with wild horses five
Through every street of that city.[8]

---

* A keyboard-like instrument.

Since these commentators wrote under the Tudor regime such hyperbole fitted a dynastic representation of the pious, chaste queen. But Elizabeth's true inner feelings are more difficult to discern. Two manuscripts survive that may cast doubt on the idea that Elizabeth rejected Richard. Both contain inscriptions written by Elizabeth, almost certainly dating from Richard's reign, as she signed the works simply 'Elizabeth', rather than with her customary inscriptions of either 'king's daughter' (pre-1483) or 'queen' (post-1485). One of the manuscripts, a French verse of the Arthurian romance *Tristan*, had previously been owned by Richard himself and Elizabeth wrote a cryptic subscript to her name: '*sans re[mo]vyr*' (without changing). The other was the hugely popular translation of Boethius's *Consolations of Philosophy*, in which Elizabeth adopted Richard's own royal motto: '*loyaltie me lie*' (loyalty binds me). In neither instance do we know how the books came into her possession nor – most crucially – what intention lay behind her enigmatic subscripts. Was she expressing loyalty to her family, or to Richard, or was it an ironic statement about the king's acts of 'loyalty' towards Elizabeth's family? As with most facets of Elizabeth's interior life, the precise emotional truth is hard to discern.[9]

Most infamously – and, at first sight, damningly – Elizabeth is alleged to have written a letter expressing her love for Richard during the anxious period of Queen Anne's illness. This letter only survives in Sir George Buck's 1619 *History of King Richard III*, where he summarised Elizabeth's writing. Buck alleged that the letter was written in February 1485 to Richard's ally the duke of Norfolk. In it, Elizabeth:

> prayed [the duke]... to be a mediator for her in the cause of the marriage to the king, who... was her only joy and her maker in the world and that she was his in heart, in thoughts, in body and in all... [for] she feared the queen would never die.[10]

If genuine, this letter would be compelling evidence of Elizabeth having reciprocated Richard's desire. However, we cannot accept this source at face value. Such callous and indiscreet words are wholly out of character with what we know of Elizabeth and, even if she was the author of this letter, fifteenth-century syntax and hyperbolic expressions of loyalty to a sovereign make it very difficult to unpick its meaning. Damning as Elizabeth's last words appear, there was another reason for her to associate the queen's death with her own marital prospects – albeit one of which Buck knew nothing. For, as Queen Anne lay mortally ill in early 1485, Richard had begun secret negotiations with the Portuguese royal family for an alliance to be cemented by a double marriage: Richard would wed King João's sister Joana and Elizabeth would marry João's cousin Manuel, duke of Beja. Elizabeth's potential union, then, was dependent on the death of the queen and her uncle's remarriage.[11] A more recent historian who looked at a damaged copy of the alleged letter in the hand of Buck's scribe suggested a more innocent interpretation:

I pray you now to be a mediator for me (in the cause of my marriage) to the king, who is my only joy and maker in this world. I am the king's true subject in heart, in thought, in body and in all, Elizabeth. P.S. The better part of February is past, and I fear the queen will never die.[12]

In all events, even if Elizabeth welcomed the intentions of her uncle in spring 1485, it need not have altered her willingness to marry Henry that autumn. Noblewomen were just as capable as their male counterparts of adapting to new political realities for their own self-preservation. Elizabeth had witnessed at first hand how her mother had adjusted to constantly evolving circumstances over the past two years.

As for Elizabeth's feelings for Henry, contemporary report was of genuine affection. In January 1486, when questioned by a papal ambassador, Thomas Stanley claimed to have seen 'great and intimate love and cordial affection' in Elizabeth towards Henry, and Henry's co-exile William Berkeley, earl of Nottingham agreed that Henry felt 'singular love' towards the princess in return.[13] There is no indication that either Henry or Margaret resented Elizabeth, nor she them, regardless of the lingering scandal about her putative relationship with her uncle.

The benefits of marrying Elizabeth in any case outweighed any potential qualms. Uniting the warring dynasties – entwining the roses of Lancaster and York – had enormous symbolic value. But Henry was cautious lest it appear that the marriage was the means by which he gained his throne. When Henry accepted an appeal from parliament in December 1485 to marry Elizabeth swiftly, he ensured that his acceptance was put on the record after an extensive explanation of his own royal claims. In March 1486, Henry reiterated this point by printing the papal bull that pronounced excommunication against anyone challenging Henry's right to marry Elizabeth – or his right to the throne, which it emphasised was not dependent on that marriage.[14]

Whatever private exchange of vows Henry and Elizabeth held late in 1485, they delayed their public wedding until 18 January 1486, after the necessary papal dispensation had been granted. The wedding that proved so vital to establishing Margaret's family on the throne has left frustratingly little mark on the historical record. Henry's official court historian, Bernard André, described the event with calculated vagueness, and asserted only that 'wedding torches, marriage bed and other suitable decorations were prepared... Great magnificence [was] displayed to everyone's satisfaction at the royal nuptials'.[15] He then, as he was wont to do when he lacked first-hand information, left half a page in his manuscript blank to fill in the details later – and never returned to do so. Surviving Exchequer accounts suggest the splendour of the occasion but, perhaps most importantly, multiple sources emphasise how popular the marriage was with Henry's subjects, who burst into a celebratory frenzy of bonfires and dances when the union was announced.[16]

Shortly after their wedding, Henry left his new wife in Margaret's company and embarked on a progress towards the north of England to assert his authority there.[17] By Easter 1486, he was in his maternal heartland of Lincolnshire, accompanied by Jasper Tudor, the earl of Oxford, Thomas Stanley and George, Lord Strange. Margaret would have been glad of the presence of so many leading supporters of her son, for that spring was not an easy time. Plague was once again rife – Henry had to avoid Newark 'because they died' there[18] – and, while Henry was riding north, two prominent Yorkist survivors, Francis Lovell and Humphrey Stafford,* broke out of sanctuary at Colchester, where they had been hiding since the Battle of Bosworth. Their intention was to raise rebellion in the West Midlands and Yorkshire, but when Jasper led a royal army against them, Lovell and Stafford's rising swiftly collapsed. Stafford attempted to claim sanctuary again, this time at Culham Abbey near Abingdon, but after a debate in King's Bench about whether the abbey's sanctuary status extended to accepting traitors – it did not – Stafford was dragged out and executed.[19] Lovell escaped overseas and sought refuge with the duchess of Burgundy.[20] Brief though this rebellion proved, Henry continued his progress into the early summer, insistent that he must display himself to his subjects and assert his rule. From York he turned south-west to traverse the restive lands around Worcester, then rode on to Gloucester and Bristol. He did not return to London until Monday 5 June, when his royal barge was greeted at Putney by the citizens.[21]

During Henry's absence, Margaret and Elizabeth lived together within the court and, when he returned, they all moved together to the clean air of Surrey. It was now clear that Elizabeth was well advanced in her first pregnancy. High summer was an uncomfortable time to be pregnant, and the queen suffered in the heat. On 19 August, Henry dispensed almost twelve pounds to the royal apothecary, John Pynkam, for medicines for 'our dearest wife the Queen'.[22] Alongside tending to the health of the queen, Henry made his own specific preparations for the imminent childbirth.

Although he could not be certain that the child would be male – and therefore an acceptable heir to his newly established dynasty – Henry did all in his power to capitalise on the dynastic symbolism of his first child's birth. In a break from recent royal practice, the court did not prepare for the birth in the Thames Valley, at the palaces of Westminster or Eltham, but instead at

* A distant relative of Margaret's Stafford in-laws through a cadet branch of the family.

Winchester. This capital of Anglo-Saxon England was believed to have been the home of King Arthur. Inside the great hall of Winchester Castle stood a round wooden table, where – according to legend – Arthur and his knights had gathered centuries ago. By associating himself and his child with the ancient history of England and Wales, Henry hoped to mollify those subjects who still viewed him as an outsider. It had been noted disparagingly that during his entry into London he proceeded in the manner of French kings rather than English.

With everything prepared, on 31 August Margaret and the royal court migrated en masse to Winchester. In the uncertain science of medieval maternity, they calculated that Elizabeth was in her eighth month of pregnancy. It was time for her to enter her confinement, a ritual withdrawal from the court and from the company of men. Elizabeth took her leave of the court with 'spices and sweet wine', bidding all the men in attendance to 'pray God to send her the good hour' – that is, a safe delivery.[23] Then, the queen's chamberlain, her uncle the earl of Ormond, drew back a screening curtain and Elizabeth led Margaret and her other female attendants into a suite of private rooms where she would remain 'confined' until four weeks after the birth. She stayed in St Swithun's Priory within the cathedral close, the prior's great hall serving as the queen's great chamber.

As Elizabeth neared her first childbirth, she probably welcomed the guidance of her female network, and the emotional support of her family and ladies-in-waiting. Among those attending her were her younger sisters Cecily and Anne, and her mother, Elizabeth Woodville. While awaiting the birth, Elizabeth may also have sought advice on the correct ceremony for royal childbirth from her more experienced female courtiers, but she did not – contrary to prevailing belief – submit to ordinances drawn up by her mother-in-law.

For centuries, it has erroneously been asserted that Margaret produced the ordinances that directed how Elizabeth's confinement chambers should be arranged: stipulations covering everything from the imagery permitted for the queen's wall hangings, to the number and type of coverlets for her bed and even how much light should be allowed in (only one window's worth). This false attribution played a key role in establishing Margaret's reputation as an overbearing matriarch who oppressed her daughter-in-law.[24] Like a number of her contemporaries, including Cecily, duchess of York, Margaret took a keen interest in her own household ordinances, insisting they were read before her servants several times a year. But she did not write any for the royal court until after Elizabeth's death.[25] The earliest attribution to her of the 'Articles ordained by King Henry the seventh for the regulation of his household' – which includes the ceremonial around royal birth – was made by an eighteenth-century antiquarian called Thomas Hearne, who published the articles and inserted the attribution to Margaret, without giving any reason for his assumption. Manuscript copies of the ordinances, which survive in the British Library, contain no reference to Margaret at all.[26]

Royal ordinances were not new – the practice of issuing them dated back to 1136 when the *Constitutio Domus Regis* gave instructions on dining arrangements, wages and livery for royal servants.[27] By the mid-thirteenth century, the first such ordinances were produced for a noble household – again, it was that of a woman: Margaret, countess of Lincoln. In the fifteenth century, ordinances were drawn up in an unavailing attempt to control the spending of Henry VI's royal household, and protocols prescribed for everything from the birth of a prince and reception of a foreign queen to conjugal relations between the royal couple. Although the Tudors (and, through Margaret, the Lancastrians) are traditionally associated with a pernickety insistence on these rules directing court behaviour, a number of contemporary ordinances survive connected to the House of York. As well as Edward IV, both his brother George, duke of Clarence and mother, Cecily, duchess of York, produced instructions for their own households. One royal ordinance that has traditionally been credited to Margaret has recently been re-dated to the time that Cecily was 'King's Mother' during Edward IV's reign.[28]

If Elizabeth sought advice on royal childbirth, she was far more likely to ask her mother than Margaret. Elizabeth Woodville had repeatedly given birth as a queen, and was a noted stickler for court protocol. Her churching* after the birth of Elizabeth in 1466 was recorded by a member of the entourage of the Bohemian nobleman Leo of Rozmital. This eyewitness was struck by the lavish ceremonial surrounding the English queen's emergence from confinement, and particularly by how Elizabeth Woodville dined that day: alone on an expensive golden chair in a crowded chamber, while her attendants (including her mother and royal sister-in-law) knelt before her for most of the meal. A woman so determined to demonstrate her rank that she kept her ladies-in-waiting kneeling for three hours while she ate dinner was surely the person Queen Elizabeth would seek advice from about correct court procedure.

Margaret and Elizabeth's relationship has also suffered historically from a misinterpretation of the descriptions given by Spanish ambassadors visiting the court in 1498. The ambassador to Scotland, Don Pedro de Ayala, passed through England in July that year and presented Margaret in his report home as actively oppressing her daughter-in-law: 'The King is much influenced by his mother and his followers,' he wrote, 'in affairs of personal interest and in others. The Queen, as is generally the case, does not like it.'[29] De Ayala went on to assert that Elizabeth was 'beloved' but 'powerless'. A week earlier, two other Spanish ambassadors, Fray Johannes de Matienson and Sancho de Londoño, used similar language in a letter to the Spanish monarchs: 'The Queen is a very noble woman, and much beloved. She is kept in subjection by the mother of the King.'[30] The source of Matienson and Londoño's intelligence was almost certainly De Ayala himself, and it is not clear if any of the trio ever met Margaret and Elizabeth in person. Indeed, Matienson and Londoño only paused in London for a matter of days.

Their reports present the same challenges as other diplomatic correspondence in this era: all native Spanish speakers, they were probably acting through translators, potentially in a third language such as Latin, and where they lacked first-hand evidence

---

* The churching ceremony marked a mother's re-entry into the world and first taking of communion after birth. Although largely discontinued in the Western Church, it still takes place in some Eastern churches.

of events they tended to pad their reports with rumour. As such, they provide compelling testimony about contemporary attitudes, but not necessarily subtle personal dynamics. Margaret's exalted status seemed an oddity to them, as they were accustomed to the considerable authority of Queen Regnant Isabella of Castile, and unfamiliar with the respected position held by earlier English royal mothers. Thus, they parsed Margaret's role through the misogynist trope of an over-mighty and resented mother-in-law. Even then, they did not accord Margaret wholly independent authority, and their suggestions of alternative influences over Henry display an ignorance of contemporary nuances. De Ayala claimed that the other leading royal advisers were 'the Lord Privy Seal, the bishop of Durham, the Chamberlain [Giles Daubeney], and many others'. He did not, apparently, realise that the Lord Privy Seal *was* the bishop of Durham, Richard Fox. Interestingly, Matienson and Londoño listed these 'many others' in more depth, adding the names of Cardinal Morton, Reynald Bray, Thomas Lovell and Thomas Savage, bishop of London.[31] Morton, Bray and Savage were all long-term allies of Margaret, and Lovell, Fox and Daubeney had shared Henry's exile. The impression is therefore more of a small coterie of proven, trusted courtiers around the king, not a single over-mighty mother.

These reports are also tainted by the internal jealousies of the Spanish representatives, as De Ayala, Matienson and Londoño all wrote with an agenda. They sought to undermine their rival Rodrigo González de la Puebla, who was then pre-eminent in English affairs and known to enjoy a close relationship with Elizabeth. She teased him about his endless visits to court to dine at royal expense, and tried to solve his financial troubles through the contrasting expedients of setting him up with either a church position or a wealthy English wife. By insinuating that the queen was powerless, De Puebla's adversaries made his carefully fostered relationship appear partisan, self-serving and futile.

It is noteworthy that De Puebla, who certainly observed Margaret and Elizabeth at first hand, never represents their relationship as problematic. Nor do other European agents in

England, who tend to minimise rather than criticise Margaret's authority. Raimundo de' Raimondi of Milan visited England several times between 1497 and 1499 and made no reference to Margaret – although he gave Elizabeth a letter of credence – and claimed that Henry did not need any special advisers. The Venetian Andrea Trevisano noted Margaret's presence, but not her influence, while Aldo Bramdine of Florence (in London in 1496) only identified Reynald Bray as holding sway over the king.[32]

All these sources, of course, were male and there is a powerful strand of misogyny running through them. At the very least, these observers seemed incapable of understanding that two powerful women could not only co-exist, but cooperate. The evidence of Margaret and of Elizabeth and Henry's own interactions and words – few though the surviving examples are – testify to profound mutual respect and affection. Margaret had never enjoyed a normal maternal relationship, having been deprived of Henry's company for most of his life and never having had any more children. Now, when she was offered a second chance to play the role of mother, she made considerable efforts to forge a bond not only with Henry but also with his wife and children. Elizabeth soon became almost a second child to her, and the Tudor grandchildren would be a source of profound solace to Margaret. This connection is clear in royal documents from the earliest moments of Henry's reign: time and again injunctions from Henry or his officers refer, virtually in one breath, to 'the Queen and King's Mother'. As early as February 1486, Elizabeth and Margaret acted together to found a chantry chapel at Guildford for two royal servants, Henry Norbrigge and Thomas Kyngeston.[33] A decade later, Margaret reported on Elizabeth's health with evident concern, in a letter to the queen's chamberlain: her daughter-in-law had been unwell after childbirth and her health was still not 'so good as I would, but I trust heartily it shall [be] with God's grace'.[34]

In any case, Elizabeth was quite capable of enforcing her own wishes and defying royal custom if she chose. During a later confinement, despite the convention that high-status mothers-to-be avoided the company of men, Elizabeth welcomed her kinsman

Margaret's larger-than-life-size portrait (hanging in St Johns College, Cambridge) shows her in later life, exactly as she wanted to appear: rich, pious and experienced.

(left) The patchwork families who raised Margaret and her son, Henry Tudor, had strong female influences. Cecily Neville, duchess of York and her sister Anne Neville, duchess of Buckingham, were Margaret's guiding lights.

(above) Anne Herbert (shown here with her husband William) raised Henry – and protected him as civil war broke out.

(left) The real victor of the Wars of the Roses was Margaret's fourth husband, Thomas Stanley, who survived by putting his own interests above dynastic loyalty. Here you can see his eagle claw heraldry in their shared Book of Hours.

(*above*) Edward IV and his queen, Elizabeth Woodville, led the House of York to triumph.

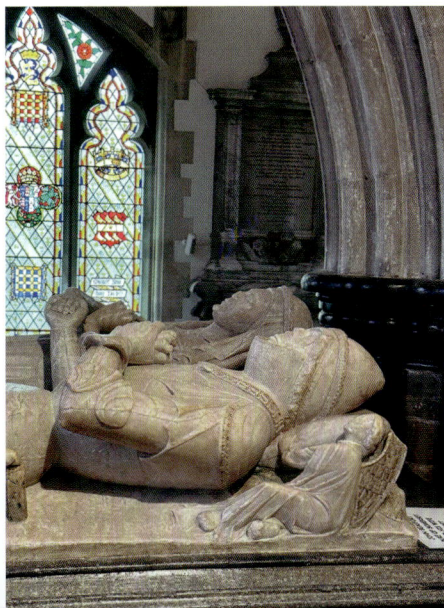

(*above*) Margaret's mother, the Dowager Duchess of Somerset, represented in the Book of Hours she bequeathed Margaret, and lying beside her husband John Beaufort in the tomb Margaret commissioned for them in Wimborne Minster (*left*).

(*above*) Margaret never knew her father, who died when she was a year old. Margaret's birth and her father's death are recorded only lines apart in their family calendar.

(*above*) The will of Margaret's third husband Sir Harry Stafford, written the night before the Battle of Barnet, and delivered to his 'best beloved wife' by one of their servants the next morning. Harry's fate took days to emerge.

After marrying Henry VII (*above left*) and uniting the warring roses, Elizabeth of York (*above right*) became almost a second child to Margaret. But her Yorkist relatives continued to threaten their family, none more than her aunt Duchess Margaret of Burgundy (*below left*) and the alleged 'Richard of York', Perkin Warbeck (*below right*).

(*left*) The Tudor Dynasty – Margaret's precious family. Clockwise from above: Henry sits on the throne while his children (Margaret, Mary and Prince Henry) grieve their mother.

The future Henry VIII as a toddler (*below*); Prince Arthur (*far right*), Katherine of Aragon (*middle*).

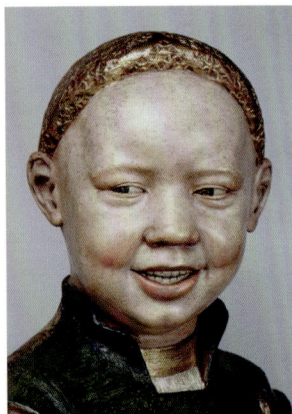

Margaret's evolving signature proclaimed her changing identity:
from 'M [Countess of] Richmond' to 'Margaret R' (for Regina?).
Although crippled by pain, she was still signing documents on
her deathbed (*bottom*).

The humanity of these extraordinary characters is expressed in the tombs of Margaret, Henry and Elizabeth at Westminster Abbey, by Pietro Torrigiano.

They were probably based on death masks, like the one that inspired Henry's funeral effigy (*right*).

Francis of Luxembourg into her great chamber. Francis was visiting England as part of a French embassy and was permitted to present his greetings in person to Elizabeth. In the record of this event, Margaret's attendance is noted, a tacit approval perhaps, but she played no role in proceedings.[35]

Margaret was undoubtedly influential at court, particularly in the later years of Henry's reign, but she was never a queen, nor – despite assuming the title once her son was king – was she really a princess. English court records suggest that Margaret was always careful to publicly subordinate herself to Elizabeth, giving the queen the position of honour beside the king, or on the right-hand side under a canopy of estate. In the presence of ambassadors, Elizabeth spoke, and Margaret was silent. On high occasions, when Margaret might dress in similar attire to the queen, she nonetheless followed in her daughter-in-law's wake. Everyone in this royal trinity knew their part.

ON THE NIGHT OF 19/20 SEPTEMBER, SOMEWHAT AHEAD OF schedule, a blaze of bonfires greeted the arrival of Elizabeth and Henry's child: a boy. Celebrations erupted throughout the kingdom. In Winchester, processions of thanksgiving wound through every church in the city and bonfires leapt in the streets. Royal messengers mounted their horses to bring the good news to the king's subjects. 'Let happy London celebrate festive games!' enjoined Bernard André in a celebratory poem. 'Let the multitude and the court shout hurrah! ... Let each one drink with his cup to the prince's name.'[36]

That name had never been in doubt. The child born in this city of ancient kings would take the name of his forebear, Arthur. The round table in Winchester Castle was repainted in Tudor green and white, with a red and white rose at its heart. A tapestry was commissioned for Winchester Cathedral decorated with the arms of King Arthur's ancestor Belinus, and pedigrees created to assert the direct descent of Henry and his son from legendary figures in British history, including Britain's eponymous founder, the Trojan

Brutus.* The humanist courtiers Giovanni de' Gigli and Pietro Carmeliano joined Bernard André in crafting poetry in praise of the little prince, claiming that the golden age of King Arthur would now return with a renewed period of peace.[37]

But Arthur's birth was not wholly auspicious. Driving rains delayed his christening, as the intended godfather, the earl of Oxford, struggled to reach Winchester from Suffolk. The prince might have been born prematurely, although it is possible he was the product of Henry and Elizabeth's informal marriage late in December 1485. The birth left Elizabeth suffering from an 'ague' that caused sufficient concern for the court to remain in Winchester longer than originally planned.[38] As they awaited her recovery, better weather and the arrival of the earl of Oxford, preparations got underway for the child to be christened with all the lavish pageantry possible. A font was built – for a princely five pounds eleven shillings – on a raised, carpeted platform hung with cloth of gold, so that everyone could see Prince Arthur being baptised.[39]

The Sunday after his birth, the weather still unfittingly 'cold' and 'foul', a great assembly of noblemen and – women processed to the queen's great chamber to collect Prince Arthur and carry him through the cloisters of Winchester Cathedral to a little door near the west end of the church. (The huge west door itself was too battered by inclement weather to be used.) Margaret is not named among those processing, and she probably remained behind in the queen's lodgings with Elizabeth and Henry, tending to her sickly daughter-in-law.† But Margaret's Stanley in-laws were in attendance, her stepson George, Lord Strange carrying a pair of gilt basins for the godmother to wash her hands in, and Thomas Stanley leading the barons. Reynald Bray, his wife Katherine and Margaret's illegitimate cousin, Charles Somerset, also played roles in the ceremony, but it was far from being a 'Lancastrian' affair. Henry was at pains to ensure that the christening of his son reflected the new age of two roses. Walking ahead of Henry's

---

* The myth that Brutus had founded 'Britannia' was 350 years old, recorded first in Geoffrey of Monmouth's *History of the Kings of Britain* (c.1136).
† As with funerals, it was the custom for a higher status royal not to attend baptisms, so royal parents did not participate.

companions in exile Richard Guildford and John Cheyne were a number of prominent Yorkist relatives of Queen Elizabeth: her sister Anne carried the baptismal robe, Princess Cecily bore Prince Arthur, assisted by their half-brother Thomas, marquess of Dorset and cousin John, earl of Lincoln. Another cousin, Margaret Plantagenet, daughter of George, duke of Clarence, walked with Lady Bray and Lady Strange in the procession, and Elizabeth's mother, Elizabeth Woodville, was honoured by being named godmother.[40]

As the noble procession crowded into the area surrounding the font, it was reported that the earl of Oxford was only a mile away. But, three hours later, he had still not appeared so orders came down from Henry, waiting impatiently in the queen's chambers, to proceed without him. In Oxford's place, Elizabeth's uncle Earl Maltravers and Margaret's husband Thomas stepped in to serve as godfathers. John Alcock, bishop of Worcester and once tutor to Edward V, took Prince Arthur from Cecily's arms and baptised him. When the child had been immersed three times, tapers held in the hands of the noble attendants were lit, surrounding the boy with a glow of light. At this celebratory moment, the earl of Oxford finally made his entrance, in time to tuck Prince Arthur in the crook of his right arm and carry him to the altar for his confirmation. Spices and sweet wines were passed around. Gifts were presented to cathedral altars. Then Princess Cecily reclaimed her nephew and the procession returned to the queen's chambers, this time with torches burning and trumpets blasting. Pipes of wine flowed in the churchyard below, while the king, queen and Margaret gave the prince their own private blessings.[41]

16

'A certain spurious lad'[1]

❋

On 19 February 1487, the Tower of London opened its gates to release Margaret's one-time prisoner Edward, earl of Warwick. Still a week shy of his twelfth birthday, the unfortunate heir of George, duke of Clarence had spent the past four years imprisoned and he emerged now to parade through the city streets and celebrate Mass at St Paul's Cathedral. Then, after a carefully monitored mingling among the nobility that demonstrated un-equivocally that the boy was still in Henry's keeping, Warwick was marched back to the Tower and the gates locked firmly behind him.

Warwick's brief taste of freedom was necessitated by persistent rumours of his escape. There had been reported sightings of him everywhere from Guernsey to Lincolnshire, and from Ireland to the Burgundian court in the Low Countries. One reason for these sightings was explained by an Oxfordshire priest called William Symonds, who appeared before a great council of lords at Sheen Palace two days before Warwick's day release. Symonds confessed to conspiring against Tudor rule, schooling a common-born son of an organ-maker called Lambert Simnel to assume the identity of the earl of Warwick, and use him as a figurehead to deprive Henry VII of his throne.[2] As a priest, Symonds could not be executed for his treason, so was instead condemned to imprisonment.[3] With Symonds and Warwick captive, it seemed that Henry's swift action had the desired effect: the country calmed.

As winter frosts gave way to spring, Henry bade his mother

and wife farewell and set out on progress through East Anglia in the company of its chief lord, John de Vere, earl of Oxford. They celebrated Easter in Norwich Cathedral, then Henry visited the famed shrine to the Virgin Mary at Walsingham, and prayed for protection 'against the deceits of his enemies, [so that he could] defend himself and his [family] from the impending peril'.[4] Margaret and Elizabeth, meanwhile, remained in the south-east, probably close to six-month-old Prince Arthur's nursery at Farnham. They were thus together when they received an urgent message from Henry in May.

Henry had abruptly broken his journey in Cambridge, and galloped full tilt for Warwickshire, covering eighty miles in just two days. At Kenilworth Castle, in the heartland of Lancastrian territory, he wrote to Elizabeth's chamberlain, Thomas Butler, earl of Ormond, on 13 May. He demanded that Ormond immediately escort 'our dearest wife and... dearest mother to come unto us'.[5]

Henry's actions were precipitated by whispers from his network of spies. On 4 May, his Irish agents reported a fleet of continental mercenaries numbering into the thousands approaching Dublin. On 24 May, a boy claiming to be the earl of Warwick – the same Oxford lad that the priest Symonds had schooled – was proclaimed 'King Edward VI' by a large body of Irish nobility and bishops, and crowned with a golden circlet filched from a nearby statue of the Virgin Mary.[6] With the pretender-king, too, were two prominent Yorkists: Richard's one-time right-hand man, Francis Lovell, and – more alarmingly – John de la Pole, earl of Lincoln. John's mother was Elizabeth, duchess of Suffolk, sister to Edward IV and Richard III, but despite this Yorkist connection there had been no warning that Lincoln would rebel. Like his parents and younger brothers, the earl of Lincoln had apparently made peace with the Tudor regime. He had been accorded prominent roles at Henry's coronation and the baptism of Prince Arthur and, as recently as February 1487, he had attended the great council Henry summoned to Sheen. But, shortly after the council broke up, he fled to Flanders to join forces with the traitor Francis Lovell. Even before his betrayal, Margaret may not have had particularly warm feelings for Lincoln. He had benefited from her fall from grace after Buckingham's Rebellion, having been granted the reversion of several Stanley estates by Richard III in April 1484.[7]

The next stage of this conspiracy was already becoming apparent: the boy king and an army of German mercenaries and Irish recruits would invade England, where they would be reinforced by men from Lovell and Lincoln's estates. Such a well-funded and coordinated operation was clearly not the work of a lone agent – especially not a lowly priest like William Symonds – and Henry's suspicions appear to have fallen on some within the royal family. Shortly after the earl of Warwick was paraded through London, in March 1487, the marquess of Dorset was suddenly escorted to the Tower of London by the earl of Oxford. Dorset had been Warwick's guardian in Edward IV's reign and his fickle allegiance in 1484 made it entirely plausible that he might turn his coat again, hoping to gain from a rebellion in favour of his old ward. Henry's cautious attitude towards Dorset was well expressed by Polydore Vergil: 'if he were a friend (as in truth he was) he would scarcely take amiss this small indignity for the sake of his own safety; or, if he were an enemy' swift action could prevent him 'work[ing] harm'.[8]

The decision to deprive Dorset's mother, Elizabeth Woodville, of her dower lands in February 1487 and transfer them wholesale to Queen Elizabeth may have been rooted in the same excess of caution.[9] Henry's mother-in-law had demonstrated more than once that she would materially aid Dorset's schemes for self-preservation. But, whatever her loyalty to her son – and whatever Henry's personal anxieties towards her at this time of reversal and suspicion – it is scarcely credible that Elizabeth Woodville would have supported a rebellion to depose her daughter and new-born grandson in favour of the child of the duke of Clarence. It is still less plausible that she would have been motivated to do so, as commentators since the seventeenth century have suggested, because she 'resented Margaret Beaufort's influence over Henry' and felt her daughter was being sidelined.[10] This is entirely unsupported by contemporary sources. Polydore Vergil interpreted Elizabeth Woodville's treatment as belated retribution by Henry for her defection to Richard III in spring 1484. Bitterness for that betrayal probably did linger, but it did not cause Elizabeth to be exiled in 1487.[11]

Until recently, the circumstances surrounding Elizabeth's death in June 1492 appeared to support the idea of her banishment from the Tudor court. Her will, written the previous April, contained no reference to Henry and bemoaned the fact that she had 'no worldly goods to do the Queen's grace, my dearest daughter, a pleasure with, neither to reward any of my children, according to my heart and mind'.[12] Elizabeth was also buried with an unusual lack of ceremony for a dowager queen. Her body was shipped to Windsor Castle by river, under cover of darkness with only five companions, among whom was an illegitimate daughter of Edward IV called Grace – presumably a sickbed attendant. No bells were tolled to announce the arrival of Elizabeth's corpse and, instead of receiving the usual royal funeral obsequies, Elizabeth Woodville was unceremoniously stuffed into her husband's tomb that same night.[13]

But new research has revealed that Elizabeth Woodville's funeral was not the result of royal neglect – it was an attempt to contain life-threatening illness. A Venetian ambassador writing during the reign of Elizabeth's grandson King Henry VIII first suggested that 'the Queen-Widow [Elizabeth]... had died of plague', and this has now been corroborated by previously unknown letters in Windsor College's archives.[14] Thus, Elizabeth Woodville's hurried and sparsely attended burial was most likely an attempt to prevent the spread of the sickness that killed her. Given Margaret's ingrained fear of plague, such treatment of the dowager queen must have appeared to her simple good sense.

After his initial panic about the marquess of Dorset had subsided, Henry treated Elizabeth Woodville with all due respect. In 1487, she followed the path taken by earlier queens dowager and retired to a monastic community: the Thameside abbey of Bermondsey. With its port, water access to the capital and position almost opposite the Tower, Bermondsey was still close enough to court to enable Elizabeth to see her family.[15] Indeed, a far more important rationale for Elizabeth's deprivation and retirement from 1487 was the financial necessity of securing her estates to support her daughter as queen. The challenge of maintaining both a dowager queen and queen consort was not unprecedented, but it was unusual. In late 1486, the additional financial pressure of maintaining a nursery for the Prince of Wales had thrown into unpleasant relief the monetary constraints on the queen's household. Traditionally, a queen was supported by income from the duchy of Lancaster, but that remained under the control of Elizabeth Woodville as dowager queen, forcing Henry to support his wife from his own funds. By 1487, this situation had become unsustainable. But, although Elizabeth Woodville lost her estates, she was granted an annuity of 400 marks, which was sufficient to cover her modest existence at Bermondsey Abbey.[16] She also continued to receive occasional royal gifts, including a tun of wine 'by way of reward' in 1488 and 100 marks 'in ready money' in December that year to help her celebrate Christmas in more lavish style.[17] The most compelling evidence that Henry and Margaret did not ostracise the dowager queen is the proposal Henry made in November 1487 that she marry James III of Scotland.[18] James's death the following year put paid to such schemes, but Henry's willingness to send his mother-in-law to a land renowned for its enmity towards England, where she could easily incite trouble if she so chose, is testament to his acceptance of her innocence.

It is interesting to note, however, that from 1487, Elizabeth of York appears to have made a conscious decision to insulate herself from her mother, and from the toxic legacy of the Woodvilles. She preferred instead to play the traditional role expected of queens of England by prominently associating herself with her husband's family. Whether or not she – like Henry and Margaret – felt any private resentment for her mother's actions in the reign of Richard III, Queen Elizabeth could hardly have been unaware of her mother's failures of judgement and subsequent unpopularity. Elizabeth Woodville's constant promotion of her own family at the expense of the wider nobility had carved deep rifts in the body politic and played their part in triggering the resulting family tragedies in 1469–71 and 1483–5. Having observed her mother's political ambition and missteps, Elizabeth of York may have purposefully adopted a more placid style of queenship. She was probably also more temperamentally inclined to such a role.

Elizabeth and Margaret must, in any case, have realised that in spring 1487 it was imperative that the Tudor royal family demonstrate their unity. For when Henry's agents warned him that a force of foreign mercenaries were sailing for England to champion the rights of 'Edward VI' of York, they also informed him that they came at the command of Margaret of York, duchess of Burgundy – the Yorkist princess who refused to accept Tudor rule, and who was a very dangerous enemy indeed.

THE YOUNGEST SISTER OF EDWARD IV AND RICHARD III, THE duchess of Burgundy was of a similar age to Margaret Beaufort, but would have been known to her largely by reputation. The tall, elegant princess had left England to marry Charles the Bold, duke of Burgundy in 1468, and since then had returned only once, in 1480, to negotiate an international alliance. Although the duchess of Burgundy and her husband spent little time in each other's company, she had become a respected and prominent political figure in his territories, proving herself capable at all levels of politics: she mediated in the endless disputes between Charles and his subjects, raised Charles's daughter and heir, the Duchess Marie, and played an active part in Burgundian culture by patronising manuscript-makers, printers and builders.

In his account of events, Polydore Vergil cast the duchess of Burgundy as an arch-villainess, motivated purely by a bloodthirsty hankering for revenge on the Lancastrian line. This certainly reflects Henry's own feelings towards the duchess. But Vergil's claim that the duchess of Burgundy always knew that the boy purporting to be the earl of Warwick was a fraud is probably overly simplistic. Even if the duchess did bear 'great malice' against Henry VII, as he and his mother came to believe, hatred of the House of Lancaster was insufficient motivation for her to incite a war that would deprive the duchess's (Yorkist) niece and her (half-Yorkist) new-born son of the English crown. It is likelier that the duchess thought it possible that 'Warwick' really was her own nephew – and a nephew, moreover, descended from her favourite brother, George, duke of Clarence. The duchess's efforts on Clarence's behalf had been noteworthy during his life. She may never have forgiven Edward IV for executing him. The prevailing belief that Elizabeth Woodville had used her malign influence to convince Edward to kill Clarence would have done little to endear the duchess to her half-Woodville niece Queen Elizabeth of York, perhaps further explaining her grudge against the Tudor regime. Warwick's descent, through Clarence, from Richard, duke of York, also elucidates the ready acceptance of 'Edward VI' in Ireland. York had once been lieutenant of Ireland, and had granted the Irish unprecedented liberties and privileges as he attempted to seize the English throne in 1460. The Irish lords retained a fierce Yorkist loyalty thereafter.

Thus, when confronted by the duchess's resources and long-established Yorkist sympathies, Henry found he could not bridle the pseudo-Warwick. As he brought Margaret and Elizabeth within the protective walls of Kenilworth that May, they could do little but await news of the landfall of the rebel army. Ever primed for misfortune, Margaret probably spent the days in grim contemplation and prayer. The precedent of the last pretender was cold comfort indeed. In just such a manner, Henry had arrived in the realm in 1485, and before a month was out had killed the king in battle and deprived his leading supporters of life or livelihood. At least Margaret knew that the might of the Stanleys was committed to Henry. Thomas was with the family at Kenilworth, while his eldest son, George, Lord Strange, mustered their forces in Lancashire. But the advantage of numbers was not always decisive. Henry's case had proven that at Bosworth. Margaret must wait once again for battle to decide her and her family's fate.

THE BLEAK HARBOUR AT FOULNEY ISLAND, DOMINATED by the dilapidated Piel Castle, was well known to Christopher Urswicke, Margaret's confessor – and Henry's most recently commissioned intelligence agent. Urswicke was born in Lancashire, a few miles inland of this shingle-strewn harbour – perhaps even inside the walls of the Cistercian abbey at Furness where his parents served as lay attendants. For days he had been watching for the coming of the pretender and his army. Furness Fells lay within Stanley territory – indeed it was through the Stanleys that Margaret had first become aware of Urswicke – and being across the Irish Sea from Dublin, the harbour at Foulney offered a natural safe haven for a fleet arriving from Ireland to drop anchor. But Urswicke, despite his local knowledge, could find no evidence of the imminent arrival of the rebel army, and by 4 June 1487 he was readying to return to court. It was then that he received word that ships had been sighted in the harbour. A chain of beacons was set ablaze, and Urswicke returned with all possible haste to Margaret and Henry. Behind him, on the windswept beachhead at Furness, cheers of acclamation greeted a pale child, hailed as King Edward VI of England by his ecstatic supporters.[19]

THE REBELS WERE A POLYGLOT ARMY: GERMAN AND SWISS mercenaries, justly feared across Europe for their discipline, training and deadly efficiency with weapons; and an Irish and English force renowned for its fierce courage. They marched from Furness to the eerie thud of drums and high-pitched shriek of fifes. Their advance was alarmingly rapid and their speed was matched with victories over the outlying royal armies moving across the north. In a twilight clash at Tadcaster, a force under Henry, Lord Clifford was bested, and on 12 June a rebel force attacked the gates of York, diverting a royal army from mustering to the king. Further skirmishes followed at Doncaster and Sherwood Forest.

To the south, Henry readied his forces to face the rebel army near Nottingham. His cause was greatly bolstered when his stepbrother George, Lord Strange brought up the Stanley host, which was reportedly 'great... enough to have beaten all the king's enemies' by itself.[20] But, as Henry's army marched on Newark, alarming reports trailed in its wake: rebel agents were spreading the falsehood that Henry had fled or been killed, causing desertions from the royal army and sending waves of panic across the country. Margaret's half-brother John Welles was unable to bring up his forces from the Home Counties, and at Westminster criminals took advantage of the distraction to break sanctuary, acclaiming the advancing 'King Edward' of York as they plundered the homes of their neighbours. To stem the flood of falsehoods, Henry subjected a band of rumour-mongering spies to a public display of royal retribution: the night before Corpus Christi, several captured Yorkist agents were hanged on an ash tree next to Nottingham Bridge.[21]

By the time Henry's army approached the Nottinghamshire village of East Stoke on the morning of Saturday 16 June, it was clear he still had the advantage of numbers and weaponry. The rebel forces assembled on a hill above Stoke – there were fewer than eight thousand of them and they lacked archers, heavy cavalry and cannon. Nonetheless, the sight of twelve-foot-long pikes glistening above the heads of the rebels was chastening for the king's forces. Unlike at Bosworth, Henry had enough men at Stoke to divide his forces into the traditional three battle divisions with two wings: the earl of Oxford led the vanguard, and Sir John Savage the left wing, just as they had when they won the day two years earlier. The right wing of cavalrymen was placed in the command of Queen Elizabeth's uncle Sir Edward Woodville, while George, Lord Strange brought up the rear. In total, Henry's forces probably outnumbered the rebels by almost two to one.[22]

On this occasion, Henry was determined to stand aloof from the fighting. He would not make the mistake that had cost Richard III his life. But, before battle commenced, according to Bernard André, Henry delivered a stirring speech to inspire his men, condemning the duchess of Burgundy as 'a trifling and shameless woman' and reiterating that his royal claim was divinely vindicated. 'Let a rightful inheritance now prevail over their wickedness,' he cried, 'for our help is from God.'[23] Whether the child masquerading as King Edward VI gave any sort of speech is not recorded, and he, like Henry, stood apart from the conflict, but the earl of Lincoln and Francis Lovell both fought among their men.

Battle opened with a hail of arrows from Henry's archers, which punched into the massed ranks of the rebel forces, inflicting large-scale slaughter on the largely unarmoured Irish soldiers. The

Burgundian chronicler Jean Molinet described them falling to the ground 'full of arrows like hedgehogs'.[24] The carnage devastated rebel morale. Return volleys of crossbow bolts could not inflict anything like such damage, and the rebels were forced to advance down the hill to engage hand-to-hand with the royal forces. The earl of Oxford's vanguard bore the brunt of the rebel assault, a 'sore and sharp fight' that Polydore Vergil claimed lasted more than three hours.[25] But the rebels came off far worse, pushed back up the hill as they attempted to regroup and eventually forced into desperate retreat towards the River Trent. The rebel captains were slaughtered in what became a vicious rout. Local tradition maintained that rebel soldiers were butchered by the royal army in a ravine running into the Trent, surrounded by scrub woodland, where so much blood was spilled that it earned the grisly name of 'Red Gutter'.[26] Polydore Vergil claimed that almost half the rebel army was killed, including the earl of Lincoln – much to Henry's irritation, as he had hoped to capture and question Lincoln about the extent of the conspiracy. Francis Lovell escaped the battlefield, allegedly by swimming his horse across the River Trent. His ultimate fate is unknown, although a skeleton discovered walled up inside his family seat at Minster Lovell, Oxfordshire in 1708 may suggest a gruesome end.[27] Thus, wrote André, 'God, the lord of vengeance, punished [the rebels'] unrighteous fury.'[28]

One of the rebel leaders was captured after battle: the boy pretender who had inspired all this trouble and bloodshed. The child initially said he was called 'John', but, when a parliamentary record of events was drawn up the following November, he bore the name Lambert Simnel. He was 'a child of ten years of age', the parliament roll reported, 'son of Thomas Simnel late of Oxford, joiner'. In a time when most English boys shared very few Christian names and the surname 'Simnel' was virtually unknown, Lambert's unusual name suggests a link to the Low Countries, where the relics of Saint Lambert had been presented to Liège Cathedral by Charles the Bold. If Simnel's father was not merely a joiner but an organ-maker, as the priest William Symonds had claimed, this scenario becomes more plausible, for the Netherlands were famed for the production of organs. Lambert's father may have been one of the myriad foreign-born itinerant craftsmen who settled in Oxford to ply their trade.[29] Whatever his heritage, Lambert was treated with remarkable compassion by Henry, installed first as a spit-turner in one of his palaces and allowed to work his way up through the ranks to the respectable position of royal falconer.[30] Doubtless the precedent of Richard III had demonstrated to Henry the potential danger of overzealously punishing child rivals.

As a marker of his victory, Henry's standard was planted atop the hill where his enemies had massed. Battle standards were dispatched, too, in Christopher Urswicke's keeping, to the shrine of Our Lady at Walsingham as an offering of thanksgiving, and Henry personally presented his standard of St George on the altar at Lincoln Cathedral. Margaret had the reassurance of seeing her son again at Kenilworth, but it was a necessarily brief reunion, before Henry was back on the road north, to chase down fleeing rebels and assert his kingship over any lingering doubters. At York, he paused to allow the citizens to parade their famed Corpus Christi pageants before him, then on he rode, over the rolling moorland, through Pontefract and Durham as far north as Newcastle. It was late October before he was reunited at Warwick with Elizabeth and, although sources do not specify her presence, presumably Margaret too. Margaret was certainly with Elizabeth on 3 November, when together they watched Henry make his triumphal return to London, mother and daughter-in-law peering down from the windows of a house beside the priory of St Mary Spital at Bishopsgate.[31]

The importance of the Battle of Stoke to the survival of the royal family was commemorated in Margaret's Book of Hours. There, twice on the same calendared page for 'June', the battle that might have claimed the life of her only child was memorialised. Once, beside the date in the text, in portentous, if simple, Latin: *Bellum de Stoke juxta Newark* [Battle of Stoke beside Newark] and again, more fulsomely, in Margaret's more comfortable English at the bottom of the page. There, she noted that, 'The xvj[th] day of June the year of our Lord 1487 King Harry the vij[th] had victory upon his rebels in battle at Stoke.'[32] The battle clearly held considerable significance for Margaret. Twice in so many years she had almost lost her son to the violence that had claimed the lives of so many of her male relatives.

To silence any lingering doubts about his rule, Henry embarked that autumn on a campaign of royal unity. His loyal subjects had already rallied to the military banners of their king; now they would unite around the pacific figure of its queen. On 23 November, the citizens of London thronged the riverbanks and boarded crowded rowing boats to join the first day of a carnival of celebration as Queen Elizabeth was finally crowned.[33] Throughout the festivities that followed, Margaret enjoyed a privileged view of the extraordinary pageant taking place on both land and water in honour of the queen's coronation. She coursed the Thames in Elizabeth's barge from Greenwich to the Tower as music echoed over the waters. In the heart of the river, she saw 'a great dragon spouting flames of fire into the Thames' – a physical manifestation of the power of the Tudor dynasty.[34] The following day, she watched the slight figure of her daughter-in-law emerge from the Tower to adoring cheers. Elizabeth was a golden vision that day, seated in a litter richly decorated with cloth of gold. She herself wore virginal white and an ermine-trimmed mantle, fastened at her breast with a great cord of golden silk and tassels. This glimmering gold matched her fair hair, which hung long down her back, her head framed with a jewel-encrusted circlet.

At Westminster Abbey, Margaret stood at Henry's side, high above the altar, within a specially constructed latticework stage.[35] From their position amid the soaring columns of the abbey, Margaret and Henry heard the shouts of celebration from spectators outside the building as the queen approached. Suddenly, the cheers mutated into screams. For a moment, perhaps, Margaret may have feared that her deepest fears were about to be realised. Was the queen in danger? Her son? But no. In their eagerness to secure a keepsake of the day, onlookers scrabbling to cut up the ray cloth pathway that the Queen walked had surged forwards, pushing into the procession of ladies following her and causing a deadly crush. Some in the crowd were killed. But Elizabeth and her attendants were swiftly ushered to safety inside the abbey, and the coronation proceeded as if nothing untoward had happened.

After the troubles of the past year, it must have been a profound relief for Margaret to see Henry and Elizabeth restored to
their full authority, in full view of their cheering subjects and loyal
nobility, kneeling now before them. Any who still doubted the
right of her son to the throne had ample proof of divine sanction
for Tudor rule. For, as Henry was careful to remind his subjects, for
the second time in two years, God had granted him victory over
his enemies in battle.[36]

17

'All our sweet children'[1]

✳

Cork harbour in Ireland was accustomed to welcoming merchant ships. Vessels from all over western Europe docked here,
carrying fish and raw materials for the cloth trade; disgorging car-
goes of wine, spices, iron, salt and liquorice. The magnificent tower
houses looming over the harbour's edge, their roofs in line
with the city walls, testified to the wealth of the local merchants.
But the cargo borne by one particular ship, which docked at Cork
in November 1491, was dangerous. It stepped ashore in the form
of a notably tall, handsome and well-built young man from the
Low Countries. Today he was using his God-given gifts to entice
customers towards his master's wares, modelling the fine silks
and expensive fripperies they had carried in the ship's hold from
Europe.

This handsome youth was called Perkin Warbeck, a Flemish
name that sounded strange in the ears of locals. Some insisted on
calling him by other names. He was so fair and tall, certain resi-
dents said, that Perkin might be taken for Edward, earl of Warwick.
Others suggested that, with his Yorkist looks and dazzling robes,
the lad could be a by-blow of King Richard III. One group went
further still: there was no mistaking it, they insisted. He must be
a Yorkist prince: surely he was none other than Richard, duke of
York, the younger brother of the late Edward V, who had somehow escaped from the Tower?[2]

The men voicing these wild – and, it hardly needed adding,
treasonous – opinions to young Perkin did not speak with idle

disinterest. They were led by an international conspiracy of
Yorkists, chief among them the former mayor John Atwater and
exiled English plotter John Taylor. Taylor, who had served as yeoman of the king's chamber for both Edward IV and Richard III,
had last been spied in the French court of Charles VIII, attempting
to drum up support for a Yorkist revolution. In Perkin Warbeck,
he found the perfect candidate to lead it.

After initially insisting that he was merely a merchant's son,
Warbeck was soon persuaded to join the conspiracy. He was taught
to use the plotters' secret signal, which entailed shaking his confederates by the thumb instead of the hand. By the end of the year,
the Warbeck conspiracy had gained the support of leading members of the Irish nobility and Perkin was proclaimed publicly to be
Richard, duke of York. It was insisted that he had escaped the Tower
of London with the aid of a servant, and thus – as the last surviving
direct male heir of Edward IV – he was the rightful king of England.
The spectre of the Princes in the Tower had been resurrected.[3]

In the years since Richard iii had allegedly done them
to death, the Princes in the Tower had disappeared from public
memory. No public declarations were made for them, beyond a
reference in Henry's first parliament to Richard 'shedding infants' blood'.[4] No plots had been mounted in their name. If
Henry, Elizabeth and Margaret had learned what had befallen
the princes – where they were buried, or if they were even still
captive – they never shared the intelligence. In the absence of evidence to the contrary, we must assume they knew as little as their
subjects. It was probably best that way. The last thing the Tudors
needed in the wake of the pretender Simnel was a cult of murdered children to develop in opposition to their own royal claim.
Indeed, to discourage alternatives, Margaret and Henry promoted the sanctity of another victim of the Tower: King Henry
VI, who was famed for his piety. The late Lancastrian king already had more than three hundred miracles attributed to him,
and his grave at Windsor was adorned with the walking sticks

of those whose disabilities had been healed, chains and nooses of wrongfully condemned and escaped prisoners, and wax effigies of almost every imaginable body part. Helpfully, everyone knew that Henry VI was dead because Edward IV had paraded his bleeding corpse through the streets of London and Richard III had reburied him publicly at Windsor in 1484.* Margaret's son appealed to three different popes to have Henry VI's sanctity confirmed, but in vain.† Meanwhile, the story of the holy king's prophecy that Henry Tudor would succeed to his throne was disseminated. The personal connection that Margaret shared with the late Lancastrian king extended even beyond that prophecy and the half-blood kinship he shared with her son. It was Henry VI, after all, who had been the architect of her marriage to Edmund Tudor, and thus the means by which Margaret bore her one and only child. The story of Margaret's childhood vision, in which the marriage with Edmund was promoted by St Nicholas (Henry VI's natal saint), probably developed from this connection. Now her traumatic past had transformed into a rosy present, she would repeat that tale as if Henry Tudor had always been divinely appointed to exist, and to rule. She and her son shared a flair for self-mythologising.

Before Perkin Warbeck stepped off the dock at Cork and resurrected the dead princes, Margaret might justly have felt that her family was finally safe from Yorkist threats. During the noisy pageantry of Elizabeth's coronation, Margaret had looked down upon a royal court whose body politic seemed mended after decades of bloodshed. Women and men whose relatives had once faced each other on the battlefield now supped peaceably together on feathered peacock and swan, united by new ties of kinship and marriage – ties that Margaret herself had bound. Years of experience in the Stanley clan had taught Margaret that loyalty to the interests of one's family easily outweighed loyalty to the crown. What better

---

* Henry VI was first interred at Chertsey Abbey, before Richard moved him into the Yorkist mausoleum at Windsor to attempt to quash or at least control his developing cult. See John W. McKenna, 'Piety and Propaganda: The Cult of King Henry VI' in Beryl Rowland (ed.), *Chaucer and Middle English Studies in Honour of Rossell Hope Robbins* (London: 1974).
† Innocent VIII, Alexander VI, Julius II.

way, then, to bind the nobility to her son than to make them part of her family?

For, although the fate of the Princes in the Tower was unknown, there were numerous princesses still walking the corridors of power: the sisters and daughters of York whose rival claim to the English throne could easily be used by their husbands or sons to justify future rebellion. It was vital that these noblewomen were married to trusted Tudor affiliates – but they had to be respectable ones. Margaret and Elizabeth had both witnessed the fallout of Elizabeth Woodville's self-interested arrangement of marriages for her family. They would not make the same mistake. When they were of age, all of Queen Elizabeth's sisters were united to men of good birth and breeding, but of unimpeachable loyalty to the Tudor dynasty. All except one: Bridget, whom Margaret had carried to the baptismal font in 1480, became a nun at Dartford Priory.[5]

The closest sister to Queen Elizabeth in age and affection was Princess Cecily, who was three years her junior. Like Elizabeth, Cecily was taken under Margaret's wing as soon as Henry seized the throne, living with the king's mother in Coldharbour during the first months of his reign. During the reign of Richard III, it had been arranged that Cecily, then aged sixteen, would marry Richard's ally Ralph Scrope of Upsall in Yorkshire. In 1486, that match was dissolved, apparently with Cecily's consent, and within two years she remarried Margaret's half-brother John, Viscount Welles.[6] Although John was almost twenty years Cecily's senior, the marriage seems to have been happy and when he made his will in 1499 John described Cecily as his 'dear beloved lady and wife... whom I trust above all other'.[7] Cecily's relationship with Margaret lasted even longer. In the years after John's death, as she remarried, lost royal favour and later fell sick, Cecily relied on Margaret's friendship and support – and Margaret readily offered it. Given their difference in ages, perhaps the king's mother assumed something of the role that her own late mother-in-law Anne, dowager duchess of Buckingham had played for her, providing political guidance and administrative advice to the young bride.

Margaret also developed a close bond with another potential Yorkist rival: Margaret Plantagenet, daughter of George, duke of Clarence, was fourteen in 1487 and, like the Tudors, painfully aware of her royal blood. In a later-life portrait she sports a bracelet with a barrel charm on it, as a ghoulish reminder of the fate of her father, who was allegedly drowned in a barrel of malmsey wine. Her brother, Edward, earl of Warwick, was still imprisoned in the Tower of London and, in the wake of Lambert Simnel's rising, their bloodline was once again a cause for Tudor concern. With Henry urging a prompt marriage to someone safe, Margaret chose to wed the girl to her nephew Sir Richard Pole, an affable, capable and (most importantly) loyal Cheshire gentleman in his twenties, who had recently proven his allegiance in the battle at Stoke. Richard's mother, Edith St John, was the half-sister with whom Margaret had spent a great deal of her youth. The Poles became a regular presence at court, and Margaret lavished attention on the couple and their children. As with Cecily, Margaret's patronage of Lady Pole endured beyond the death of her husband. After Richard died in 1504, his widow was left with five young children, and forced to reside in genteel poverty at Syon Abbey. She relied on regular gifts of money from Margaret to provide for their nurses and upkeep. When Margaret was staying near Syon, she would often visit Lady Pole and her children.[8]

Sometimes, Margaret worked in concert with Queen Elizabeth to settle the Yorkist princesses. The marriage of Princess Anne (fifth daughter of Edward IV) to Thomas Howard, eldest son of the restored earl of Surrey, in February 1495 took place 'at the special desire of the said queen', and Elizabeth handled the financial negotiations.[9] The Howards had been East Anglian stalwarts of Richard III, their loyalty to the Tudors so suspect that the head of the family and his heir were imprisoned during the early years of Henry's reign. Once rehabilitated, however, they proved their allegiance to the new regime. By contrast, when Princess Katherine (Edward's IV's sixth daughter) married William Courtenay, it had seemed the ideal marriage of York and Lancaster. Courtenay had lived in exile with Henry and fought for his cause at Bosworth. He was rewarded with his royal bride and restoration to the title of earl of Devon. Yet, despite Katherine's close relationship to her sister the queen, the marriage did not prevent Courtenay later defecting.[10]

Of course, not all the marriages Margaret brokered were strictly for royal benefit. In 1487, she arranged for her young protégé, Nicholas Vaux, to marry Elizabeth Parr, a widow with several young children. Elizabeth's late husband William Parr had contested control of the barony of Kendal in the north-west with the Beauforts since Margaret's father was alive. By contrast, Nicholas was from a family of unquestioned loyalty to the House of Lancaster and to Margaret herself. Thus, by uniting Elizabeth's family to Vaux, Margaret effectively neutralised a major threat to her authority in the area and trained Nicholas's Parr stepchildren in the same allegiances. They went on to become Margaret's clients, serving her interests in Kendal.[11]

Thus, Margaret moulded the next generation of loyal Tudor subjects. Many of the children born of the Yorkist–Lancastrian marriages would grow up at the royal court or in Margaret's own household. The two were, for now, almost synonymous. She consistently travelled with her son and daughter-in-law, even on their progresses to ride and hunt beyond the greater palaces near London. At the hunting palace of Woodstock, she shared a private withdrawing chamber with Henry, between their two suites of apartments.[12]

Of course, the most important fruits of a York–Lancaster match were the children born to Henry and Elizabeth themselves. Arthur was the pride of the family. Before he was three years old, his marriage had been arranged to the eldest daughter of Isabella and Ferdinand of Spain: the Infanta Catalina, better known as Katherine of Aragon. But the Treaty of Medina del Campo that settled the match in March 1489 was hard fought. The Spanish knew that Henry needed the alliance more than they did, to counter France's aggressively expansionist policy and the implacable intriguing of the duchess of Burgundy. The Spanish also had their concerns about sending their princess to a country that had seen an endless round of usurpations and depositions in the past half century. Both Margaret and Henry must have felt the sting of certain barbed comments made by the Spanish commissioners: 'Bearing in mind what happens every day to the kings of England,' they said in 1488, 'it is surprising that Ferdinand and Isabella should dare to give their daughter [in marriage to an Englishman] at all.'[13] But Arthur himself had impressed the commissioners, who visited him in his nursery at Farnham. The Spanish commissioners found 'such excellent qualities in the prince as are quite incredible… Whatever praise, commendation, or flattery any one might be capable of speaking or writing would only be truth in this case.'[14] Impressive work for a toddler.

The same year that Arthur's marriage was arranged, Margaret welcomed another grandchild. By coincidence, the princess arrived on the night of Arthur's investiture as Prince of Wales, on 28 November 1489, as the windows of Westminster Palace blazed through the darkness and the men of the court clustered in the great hall to watch the prince perform his chivalric duties before the king throughout dinner. Meanwhile, Margaret and her fellow ladies of court were gathered nearby in the queen's chamber as Elizabeth laboured to deliver her second child. All day long the king's chapel reverberated with the prayers of bishops and priests, pleading for the queen's safe delivery. Shortly after nine o'clock that night, as Margaret noted in her Book of Hours, her first granddaughter was born. The following morning, the baby was christened in Westminster Church, 'named Margaret after my lady the King's Mother'.[15] Margaret served as godmother to her new grandchild, sharing the duties with her friends Eleanor Talbot, duchess of Norfolk and John Morton, archbishop of Canterbury. Margaret's stepsons George, Lord Strange and Sir Edward Stanley played prominent roles at the baptism and John Welles presented the baby with 'a chest of silver and gilt, full of gold' on behalf of her grandmother.[16]

After the birth of her namesake, Princess Margaret, more royal grandchildren followed in rapid succession. Less than two years later, shortly after Midsummer 1491, Prince Henry joined the royal nursery. Less than a year after that, Princess Elizabeth was born on 2 July 1492. Then, at regular intervals of three to four years, three more children arrived: Mary, born on 18 March 1496;

Edmund, in February 1499; and finally Katherine, in February 1503. As an only child of an only child,[17] King Henry VII more than did his procreative duty in providing for the Tudor dynasty, and the always family-conscious Margaret rejoiced in the expanding branches of her family tree. Each of the children's births was carefully noted down in her Book of Hours – and, for the eldest prince and princess, so too was the hour of their arrival. Margaret's concern for her grandchildren is evident in a letter she wrote to the queen's chamberlain, the earl of Ormond, in 1497, when she assured him that 'the king, the queen and all our sweet children be in good health... God be thanked'.[18]

Margaret was a generous and affectionate grandmother, her account book dotted with regular payments for the princes, princesses and their attendants.[19] Even the midwives who attended Queen Elizabeth when these grandchildren first entered the world received Margaret's rewards in grateful thanks.[20] She gave brooches and clothes to Princess Margaret and Princes Henry and Arthur. She also involved herself in the interests of her grandchildren, being an early patron of Prince Henry's love of hunting and martial sports. Her eldest grandchild, Prince Arthur, was also the recipient of an educationally valuable and beautifully illuminated copy of Cicero's *De Officiis*, which is now in the keeping of Emmanuel College, Cambridge. Even once Princess Margaret grew up, married and moved away – as was the custom for royal women – her grandmother maintained contact. She sent regular gifts, including the customary New Year presents, and kept herself informed of her granddaughter's state of mind through mutual friends. In 1507, when she learned that Princess Margaret was unwell, she dispatched one of her own waiting women to attend to her.[21]

For Margaret, who was used to a lifetime on horseback or communicating with loved ones through servants, physical distance did not mean emotional detachment. The younger royal children lived close to their parents and grandmother, either within the court or downriver in the royal nursery at Eltham Palace, but Prince Arthur, as heir to the throne, was always slightly apart. Within weeks of his birth, he was given his own court at Farnham in Surrey, and before Arthur's sixth birthday his father established a princely household for him at Ludlow Castle. From here, Wales and its Marches were administered, nominally by the child-prince himself. Arthur's Farnham home was only about nine miles from Margaret's palace of Woking – an easy day trip for impromptu visits, even if Margaret chose the leisurely transportation of litter or carriage, rather than swift horseback riding. At Ludlow, Margaret's influence was felt even more powerfully. As the guardian of the young duke of Buckingham, she enjoyed considerable authority in the borderlands thereabouts, and her network of relatives and servants played a major role in the prince's household. Arthur's lord chamberlain, his leading attendant, was Margaret's nephew Sir Richard Pole, who had been so fortuitously married off to Margaret Plantagenet.[22] One of Arthur's councillors, and from 1494 his president of the Council of the Marches of Wales, was the Lancashire-born William Smith, bishop of Coventry and Lichfield, who had long been a neighbour of Margaret's and became a close enough friend that she lavishly celebrated his elevation to the bishopric of Lincoln in 1495.[23] Other associates of Margaret's in the prince's household included her counsellor Sir John Mordaunt and her ward John, Lord Grey of Powys.

The continued wellbeing of the growing royal family could not be a purely personal concern for Margaret, however. The fecundity, health and prosperity of the Tudors was also a public matter. It demonstrated divine favour for Henry's rule. It assured the realm that the dynasty would peacefully continue into future generations and that the Wars of the Roses were truly over. In a visually literate culture, lavish demonstrations of the family's magnificence were a political weapon and, just as much as marriage-brokering or gift-giving, this was an arena in which Margaret was an astute player.

In the years after Elizabeth's coronation, Margaret and her family took part in many further public manifestations of Tudor authority – now not merely for Henry's subjects, but for an increasingly interested international audience. On St George's Day (23 April) 1488, Margaret and Elizabeth donned scarlet robes and joined Henry and his Knights of the Garter as they processed through Windsor Castle in front of English notables and 'many ambassadors of divers countries'.[24] It was exceptionally unusual for women to participate in processions of the Order of the Garter. The last such occasion had been 1477 and the next would not take place until 1901. So noteworthy was Margaret's presence that a song addressed to Henry at the event referenced it:

> O knightly order, clothed in robes with garter:
> The Queen's grace [and] thy mother in the same.[25]

The intention in welcoming ladies to join the celebrations was surely to demonstrate to the international audience in attendance the lavish chivalry of the English, and the neutralisation of Henry's Yorkist rivals of both sexes. With Margaret marched Clarence's daughter, Lady Pole, and Elizabeth's sister Princess Anne, while the king was attended by the queen's cousins from the families of de la Pole and Bourchier. As the knights and ambassadors feasted, they were regaled with a song enjoining, 'England now rejoice... to see thy King so flowering in dignity'. The song commemorated the international embassy joining them to celebrate Henry's ascendant position after years of civil war: 'France, Spain, Scotland and Brittany, Flanders also', who appealed to King Henry as 'ambassadors seek[ing] for protection'.[26]

Further embassies followed, as curious international observers began to suspect that the Tudors might be here to stay. Representatives of Naples and Denmark came. So too envoys from the king of the Romans,* Maximilian, who with his son Philip 'the Fair' of Burgundy exercised lordship over most of the territory from the Low Countries in the north to Austria in the south. At Whitsun 1488, Margaret proudly watched her son being symbolically armed and crowned by the Pope's *Cubicular* (Chamberlain). Papal recognition marked the arrival of the Tudors on the international stage as a true European power – although the propaganda value of the occasion was marred by a fog so thick

---

* The King of the Romans was in fact the elected ruler of the Germanic states. He bore his title because traditionally he was crowned by the Pope. Maximilian later became 'Holy Roman Emperor' of the same territories.

that, as Henry and his courtiers traversed the Thames, they could scarcely be seen from the bankside.[27]

But, although Margaret did all she could for her family, danger always lurked close at hand. Most of the beloved grandchildren in whose births she rejoiced would not survive infancy. Sickness lurked even in the royal court. Weeks after the birth of Princess Margaret and the elevation of Prince Arthur, the royal family lingered at Westminster Palace as the court prepared to celebrate Christmas. Spanish ambassadors had been invited to feast on Twelfth Day (6 January), and an Abbot of Misrule appointed to entertain the assembled throngs. But the Christmas revels were suddenly interrupted when a deadly measles outbreak overran the court, 'so strong, and in especial amongst the ladies and the gentlewomen, that some died of that sickness'.[28] In the hot, stuffy chambers of the queen, where Margaret and Elizabeth's other attendants had been confined for weeks on end, the sickness spread with alarming speed. At least one lady died: a daughter of Margaret's cousin, Lady Mary Neville.[29] Elizabeth was hastily churched on 26 December, after which the whole court, including Margaret and Thomas, the king and queen, infant prince and new-born princess, fled by royal barge to the greater safety of the garden palace at Greenwich. There were few entertainments that anxious festive season: 'no disguisings and but right few plays', as one contemporary grumbled.[30] But perhaps Margaret might have considered, with her perpetual anxiety about infection, especially in infants, that the royal family had got off lightly.

ON 28 APRIL 1489, THE EARL OF NORTHUMBERLAND HURRIED from his castle at Topcliffe, under-attended and possibly unarmed, to confront an angry crowd of locals. Over the past week, he had grown increasingly disturbed by events in Yorkshire: the usual grumblings of disgruntlement at Henry's latest tax – the third heavy demand in two years – had started to assume the character of a local uprising. As warden for the East and Middle Marches towards Scotland, it was Northumberland's unhappy responsibility to put a stop to these gatherings.[31] Far to the south, Margaret was probably with Henry and Elizabeth at Hertford Castle when their leisurely post-Easter entertainments were brutally interrupted by a messenger arriving hotfoot from Topcliffe.[32] Northumberland's confrontation with the Yorkshiremen had disintegrated into violence. The earl was dead, murdered by his own tenants. The North had risen.

Henry's response was immediate. On 30 April 1489, only two days after Northumberland's fatal confrontation, Henry ordered his treasurer to send him gunpowder, ordnance and almost three thousand sheaves of arrows.[33] Messengers galloped from Hertford to mansions across the realm, summoning the nobility to muster their troops and proceed against the rebels. Henry could not be certain that the rising was not cover for a wider conspiracy, aided by his European enemies. Less than a year earlier, King James III of Scotland had been murdered by his own rebellious subjects, including his teenage son. That boy now ruled as James IV, and welcomed known Yorkist traitors like Francis Lovell to his court. Had treason infected the whole northern borderlands? Was the earl of Northumberland's assassination the first step in a plot to bring down the Tudors?

On 12 May, Henry marched out of Hertford Castle with a small force including Thomas Stanley and the recently rehabilitated Thomas Howard, earl of Surrey. Presumably watched vigilantly for any signs of sedition, the force also contained the leading Yorkists Edmund de la Pole (son of the duke of Suffolk and Edward IV's sister Elizabeth) and Henry Bourchier, earl of Essex (the nephew of Elizabeth Woodville). Henry met the bulk of his army at Leicester on 16 May, where he must have gained some comfort from the sheer weight of numbers that mustered to his standard, especially the multitude of Stanley soldiers. One herald who witnessed the muster believed that Sir William Stanley, Thomas Stanley and George, Lord Strange had assembled such mighty forces that they could have defeated the rebels all by themselves. Their support may have tipped the scales in Henry's favour.[34] While the king was still assembling his soldiers at Leicester, an advance force under the earl of Surrey marched north, where the seriousness of the king's response quenched vengeful spirits. The rebellion collapsed before Henry even rode into Yorkshire. On 20 May, the first handful of rebels were put to death, hanged in their armoured jacks* from prominent hills and bridge-heads as a warning to their comrades. In general, Henry was merciful, but he made a conspicuous display of his leniency. After a ceremonial entry into York, Henry presided over a series of mass pardons: 2,000 rebels came before him in the following days, nooses around their necks, and knelt on the hard earth to offer their submission.

The northern rising was snuffed out before it could truly catch light, but it had revealed alarmingly both the uneasy foundations on which Henry's rule still rested, four years into his reign, and his continued reliance on the Stanleys. Worse, the rising demonstrated the unequivocal dangers of embarking on foreign wars at a time when it seemed all too likely that England would be drawn into European conflict. For the tax that had precipitated the earl of Northumberland's murder was intended to pay for English military interventions in Brittany, which was in danger of being absorbed into France. Henry's one-time patron Charles VIII had grown from pubescent prince to posturing teenager just as the ageing Duke Francis of Brittany languished with a deadly illness. Determined to assert his manhood, Charles VIII invaded Brittany in 1488. The loss of Breton independence would have serious political and economic consequences for England, and Henry was highly sensible of the debt he owed Duke Francis for offering him sanctuary for so many years. But war was expensive, and in spring 1489 Henry's subjects had revealed just how hostile they could be to the taxes necessary to fund it. Family lore would not let Margaret forget that military campaigns had undone their Beaufort ancestors. Attempting to find a middle way, Henry secretly dispatched English forces to aid the Bretons under the command of Sir Edward Woodville, the uncle of the queen and a renowned 'courageous knight'. Publicly, however, he disavowed Woodville's activities. It was a ploy straight out of the Stanley playbook. But it failed. The English army was annihilated and Woodville slain.[35]

---

* A jack was a waistcoat of small iron plates sewed into fabric.

By the end of 1488, Brittany was overrun, Duke Francis was dead and his eleven-year-old daughter Anne of Brittany was duchess, her freedom of action severely curtailed by the terms of the treaty with France that had followed the Breton defeat. It seemed only a matter of time before England would be dragged into an expensive, unpopular but regrettably necessary war.[36]

The network of cross-Channel spies, or questmongers, that Henry and Margaret had built during their decade apart now became even more critical, a vital element in Tudor foreign policy. They helped to forge alliances, calculate the direction of European politics and unearth early rumours of further intrigues against the Tudors. Some of Margaret's informants were wholly respectable: high-born friends going overseas on business personal or political, bidden to share their observations with her. In March 1488, she requested news from Flanders in the conclusion of a letter to Bishop Richard Fox, and in 1497 she was in communication with the earl of Ormonde while he served on embassy to Burgundy.[37] Some of her informants may, however, have been less reputable – Henry's certainly were – but they were about to prove their worth. For it was through such informal, even illicit, channels that word first reached royal ears of the pretender who bore an unsettling resemblance to the dead Yorkist princes – the similarity so marked that even some within Henry's court were starting to wonder if this boy was the true King Richard. Treason had wormed its way into the very heart of Margaret's family.[38]

18

'A believable fiction'[1]

✳

At Epiphany 1494, the feast of kings, a pretender took the king's place at a banquet of Londoners in Whitehall. Margaret's brother-in-law and Henry's trusted chamberlain, Sir William Stanley, was given the honour – for one meal only – of enjoying the best seat in the house. Alone at the top table, 'served as the king should have been', William enjoyed 'all manner of dainties' and the salutes of his fellow diners.[2] Christmas was a time for playing at such inversions. Margaret, her son and even Queen Elizabeth and the royal children all sponsored lords of misrule, boy bishops and players, who asserted high status for a single day, fostering carnival and laughter, with order safely restored the following morning.

William's right to such a potentially sensitive role seemed unquestionable. Ever since he ordered his troops to engage for Henry on the field at Bosworth, William had proven his usefulness to the new regime. Time and again he had marched legions of retainers out of North Wales to strengthen Henry's cause. As chamberlain to King Henry, he enjoyed unrivalled access to the corridors of power, and protected the most private quarters of the king. He had grown rich on the rewards. By 1495, William was widely reported to be the wealthiest commoner in England, enjoying £3,000 annually from his land and office, and with a treasure concealed in his principal seat of Holt Castle worth 400,000 marks.[3]

Yet, despite his many rewards, in recent years Margaret's brother-in-law had privately muttered about his treatment by Henry, 'more mindful of the favor he had conferred than that

233

he received'.[4] It particularly rankled that, while his elder brother Thomas was made earl of Derby, William remained a knight.[5] He had hoped to win the earldom of Chester, whose lands were close to his territories and whose heraldic device of the wolf's head he displayed at the neighbouring St Winifred's shrine in Holywell, Flintshire.[6] As recently as January 1493, William had bridled when he was replaced as sheriff of Cheshire by his nephew Tom Stanley, the grandson and heir of Margaret's husband Thomas. As Tom was at most eleven years old, William had good reason for disgruntlement.[7] Margaret may have heard about William's gripes – noblemen were always complaining about some perceived offence – but she could not have foreseen how William would react.

Within a year, William's subversion of the natural order at Epiphany 1494 – his jovial collusion with pretend princes – would seem darkly prophetic. For even as he toasted the Londoners 'for the king' in 1494, Sir William Stanley was in secret communication with the young man who claimed to be the true king of England: Perkin Warbeck, now acclaimed throughout Europe as the lost Richard of York.

FROM THE MOMENT HE STEPPED ASHORE AT CORK IN 1491, Perkin Warbeck was a thorn in Tudor flesh. Henry's spy network had uncovered several traitorous conspiracies since his accession to the throne, and each ended with the plotters dangling from the end of a rope or kneeling in the dirt before their king begging for royal forgiveness.[8] But, for some reason, this 'feigned lad' (as Henry referred to Warbeck) snared the imagination of his contemporaries and could not be suppressed. It did not seem to matter that Henry's agents had traced the boy's origins to Tournai, in the Low Countries, a wealthy centre of the cloth trade and of tapestry weaving. It made no difference how many messages Henry disseminated informing his subjects, and the princes of Europe, that Warbeck was a con man rather than an escaped Yorkist prince.[9] Warbeck's story of imprisonment, escape and conspiracy was too enchanting, and the opportunity his counterclaim offered to England's rivals too enticing, to be ignored. Charles VIII promoted Warbeck's cause to divert the English from interfering in his Breton wars. James IV of Scotland used the pretender to woo France into a marriage alliance in the hope that together they could make war on his traditional enemy, England. The duchess of Burgundy championed Warbeck, depending on who you asked, either because she truly believed the lad was her nephew, or because of the 'old mortal hatred' she had conceived against Henry VII.[10] (Henry was inclined to believe the latter.)

By 1492, it was of little consequence why these princes supported Warbeck. What concerned Henry was that Warbeck's rival claim to the English throne was beginning to threaten the very pillar of Tudor diplomacy: the Anglo-Spanish alliance that promised Prince Arthur in marriage to Katherine of Aragon. In 1491, Charles VIII sealed a treaty with James IV, then married Anne of Brittany and absorbed her territory into his own. The following spring, Charles transported Warbeck, at his own expense and in some style, to join him in the French court as 'King Richard'. The Spanish were worried. Reluctantly, Henry acknowledged that his attempts to curb French expansion diplomatically had failed. It was time to go to war.[11]

Margaret would not have welcomed the news that her son was risking his throne, and potentially his life, to lead an army across the Channel. But there was cause for hope in the allies he won when he tentatively proposed an invasion of France: the steel-hearted king of the Romans Maximilian and his adolescent son Philip the Fair, who together exercised lordship over most of the territory from the Low Countries to Austria. Charles's marriage to Anne of Brittany had robbed Maximilian of a bride – he and Anne had been married by proxy in 1490. This dishonour had compounded Maximilian's lingering wrath at a degrading 1482 treaty that had forced him to surrender family territories to the French. The military-minded Maximilian was Henry's ideal ally. The plan was to trap Charles in a pincer movement, with English forces invading France from the west through Normandy, while Maximilian's armies advanced from the east, into areas of Burgundy and Champagne where his family traditionally had authority.[12] The alliance with Maximilian seemed to fulfil a contemporary prophecy that the 'Son of Man' (i.e. Henry) was destined to conquer France with the help of 'Esteurope' (Maximilian). It was alleged that this vision had been received in 1415 by the outlandishly named Alsons Frysauce, clerk to the astrologer of the Ottoman Sultan. In fact, the prophecy was written late in 1491 to encourage the ever-superstitious English that Henry's French war would end in glory, allaying the anxieties about tax and expense that had led to the northern rising of 1489.

In January 1492, a Milanese ambassador in England reported that, 'The king here attends to nothing but preparation for the war.'[13] Even in the depths of winter the south coast buzzed with activity. The dust of construction clung over Southampton, where a gunpowder factory was built, and at Portsmouth a new beer house to quench the soldiers' thirst. Pouring through the gates of these towns, which served as staging posts for the army, came sacks of wheat, flour, oats and beans, wheels of cheese, sides of bacon and beef, and barrels of beer and wine, purveyed nationally by royal commissioners. Among the supplies were considerable resources of grain, provided at Margaret's expense. Margaret was also the single greatest contributor of cash to the campaign, gifting Henry a thousand marks to pay his soldiers. The logistics were overseen by Henry's treasurer of war, Margaret's old servant Reynald Bray.[14]

On 2 October 1492, Margaret's son set sail for France, returning to a country he had left as a penniless hostage seven years earlier. Now he would arrive as king, at the head of the largest invasion army of the century, clad in bejewelled armour. Even his horse had blue velvet drapes and *fleur de lys* pendants dangling from its harness, as if Henry were a French prince.[15] Many of Margaret's kinsmen readied their harness and sailed with Henry: her half-brother John, Viscount Welles indentured to fight with 103 men, while her nephew Sir John St John, a knight of the king's body, could muster only 26. The Stanleys, as was customary, brought swathes of their followers from the north-west and North Wales. Margaret's stepson George, Lord Strange and brother-in-law Sir William Stanley promised over three hundred soldiers.[16]

Margaret herself stayed at home, probably maintaining greater than usual communication with her friends and family in Prince Arthur's household. Still not yet six, Arthur was named regent and lieutenant-governor, to rule England in Henry's absence. Since even Arthur's precocity was not yet a match for an adult ruler, he was assisted by Margaret's old ally John Morton, archbishop of Canterbury and the royal council.

October was very late in the season to begin a military campaign and Henry would need a swift victory. Unfortunately, when his army arrived before Boulogne, a frontier town whose capture was the essential first step on the road through France, Henry found it had been refortified, offering doughtier opposition than he had anticipated. To the east, Maximilian's forces were delayed, so Henry faced the prospect of a lengthy siege with dwindling supplies and worsening weather, without his ally. With such poor conditions, Henry chose – like Edward IV before him – to extract what benefit he could from his military posturing and swiftly end the war. Within a month of setting sail from Dover, he agreed a peace treaty with France and was back in England before Christmas. The war was over almost before it had begun.[17]

As had been the case in 1475, there were those who found this abrupt conclusion to a long-planned campaign dishonourable. The lucrative pension Henry won for himself of 50,000 French crowns only exacerbated the impression that he had been paid off, which may not have sat comfortably with Margaret. But Henry's war achieved one major objective: under the terms of the Anglo-French Treaty of Étaples, Perkin Warbeck was ejected from Charles VIII's lands, thus denying a vital sanctuary to the pretender. This ought to have been a substantial victory for Henry over his rival, but he badly miscalculated when he negotiated the treaty without including Maximilian and Philip. His erstwhile allies felt betrayed and humiliated. Until now, Maximilian and Philip had refused to engage with their kinswoman the duchess of Burgundy when she tried to promote Warbeck's cause. But, in the wake of the Anglo-French Treaty, they shared her vengeful spirit. So, when Perkin Warbeck fled from the French court, he ran straight into the arms of Maximilian and Philip.

★

AUTUMN 1494 SAW TWO DUKES OF YORK PARADING THROUGH the courts of Europe. In the Low Countries, Perkin Warbeck strutted at the Burgundian court with Maximilian and Philip the Fair, sporting the white rose of York, and impressing onlookers with his height, good looks and easy charm.[18] Meanwhile, under Margaret's watchful gaze, the English royal court travelled up the Thames to celebrate the creation of her grandson Prince Henry as duke of York – the *true* duke of York, as the family hoped to remind the princes of Europe. Looking taller than his three years, copper-haired and fair, Prince Henry impressed the assembled crowds of Londoners as he progressed from his nursery at Eltham through the city streets 'sitting alone upon a courser', a great horse. Little Henry was already a skilled rider and was probably delighted by the fortnight of 'goodly jousts' his father laid on at Westminster Palace to celebrate his investiture – and to flaunt Tudor affluence in front of invited foreign dignitaries. The tournaments were an ostentatious display of wealth, from the European armour of the knights and the African ostrich feathers bobbing on their helmets to the 'costeous' black velvet horse coverings pearled with local goldsmiths' work. For all their pageantry, these jousts were genuinely dangerous. A tournament at Sheen in May 1491 ended with the gruesome death of Sir James Parker, whose helmet crumpled when a spear struck him in the face. 'His tongue was borne into the hinder part of the head', choking him to death.[19]

Perhaps Margaret noticed, as the tournaments wore on and royal councils resumed at Westminster, that Henry was watching his courtiers more closely than usual. Did her son's gimlet eye fall coldly on certain men, seeking evidence of sedition? The past eighteen months had been an anxious time. The king had spent the whole summer of 1493, from May to September, braced for a Burgundian army to invade in Warbeck's name. As the king moved between the castles of Coventry and Kenilworth, his war armour was sent north from London, as were a dozen field gunners with light artillery ready for rapid deployment.[20] Tensions had escalated with Maximilian, and economic embargoes were imposed by both sides, ruining the trade of merchants in London and Antwerp who were usually economic partners. Riots had broken out around the Steelyard, the trading base of the Hanseatic League in London, and Flemish homes were ransacked by angry English youths.[21]

The jubilant unity of the court tournaments of autumn 1494 was little more than a painted mask. The very day after the tournaments closed, a wave of arrests swept through the court. A conspiracy had been uncovered, stretching between the two bases of the so-called duke of York: Englishmen of suspect loyalty had been slinking across to Perkin Warbeck's Burgundian sanctuary ever since the pretender moved in. Meanwhile, in the Thameside palaces of the English prince, some of the king's closest servants had been whispering behind their hands for the past two years about whether this Warbeck could really be the son of Edward IV. Messages between the conspirators had been carried back and forth since spring 1493 by a northern knight called Robert Clifford. Clifford's route into royal service was similar to his colleague Sir William Stanley's: both were sons of northern lords who gained status working and fighting for Edward IV. Clifford was a particularly adept combatant – in 1478, he had won the prize as best swordsman during celebrations for the wedding of Edward IV's son Richard, duke of York.[22] Perhaps this childhood connection to the boy is what drove Clifford early in 1493 to voice his anxieties about Warbeck's true identity to other veteran Yorkists who had transitioned into Tudor service. Clifford and his co-conspirators agreed that he ought to go to the Low Countries and meet Warbeck. If he was convinced that he was truly the duke of York and the son of Edward IV, the old Yorkists would commit to Warbeck and help him reclaim his throne. Clifford went, was convinced, and for almost two years fomented rebellion against Henry.[23]

But, by the close of 1494, Clifford had a crisis of conscience – or perhaps of belief. The physical similarity of Warbeck to Edward IV and to the duchess of Burgundy beside whom he so often stood was notable. The family of York were famously tall and handsome, a characteristic the diminutive Margaret was known to joke about. When Queen Elizabeth's chamberlain, the earl of Ormonde, sent

Margaret a gift of large gloves from the Low Countries, she replied teasingly:

> I thank you heartily that ye... remember me with my gloves, the which were right good, save they were too much for my hand. I think the ladies in that parts be great ladies all, and according to their great estate they have great personages.[24]

Increasingly, though, Clifford felt that the physical similarities between Warbeck and Edward IV were a smokescreen. There was something about the lad that roused his suspicions. Slowly, he grew convinced that Warbeck could not be a son of York after all. As Henry's spies uncovered more and more of Clifford's associates, and executions followed arrests, Clifford decided to jump ship before he was pushed. In a distinctly shady transaction, Clifford was promised a royal pardon – duly granted on 22 December 1494, when he was still living with Warbeck in Antwerp – and in return he was smuggled back to England to inform on his confederates. Some of Henry's most trusted men were put to the task of bringing Clifford home, and Henry's new paymaster Reynald Bray conveyed a sizeable bounty of £500 to the turncoat in January 1495.[25]

Under the cover of unusually lavish Christmas and New Year festivities in 1494–5 – feasts, plays, dances, even a dragon spitting fire in the great hall at Westminster – Henry extracted the details of Clifford's conspiracy and prepared to move against the plotters.[26] His spies had almost certainly been watching Clifford for some time. Two years earlier, a yeoman of the crown and long-standing Stanley client called Robert Bulkeley had been arrested but unexpectedly pardoned, probably because he turned informant.[27] Perhaps even then, Henry suspected that treason had infected Margaret's north-western network. But Henry had insisted on seeing hard evidence of treason before he took action, and Clifford the mole provided it. Only on 6 January 1495 was Henry ready. He moved into the Tower of London and ordered the arrests of the plotters that Clifford named as his accomplices. Chief among them were the two men who guarded both public and private quarters of the royal court: Henry's steward John Ratcliffe, Lord Fitzwalter and his chamberlain, Sir William Stanley.[28]

Precisely when Margaret learned that her brother-in-law had colluded in treasonable conspiracy against her son is unclear. Given Henry's reticence first to arrest and then to punish William, he may have sought to spare his mother his suspicions until there could be no doubt of William's guilt. Margaret had known that William felt dissatisfied with the rewards of his service, but could have little imagined it would drive him into treason with Clifford and Warbeck.[29] Although, as William saw it when called upon by Henry to explain his actions in the Tower, he had not really committed treason. True, he had told Clifford in March 1493 that 'he would never take up arms against the young man [Warbeck], if he knew for certain that he was indeed the son of Edward' IV.[30] But all he had done subsequently, he insisted, was attempt to discover if Warbeck was or was not the duke of York. His crime, as he saw it, was passivity, not collusion. But William was being woefully naïve. At the very least he ought to have informed Henry of Fitzwalter's and Clifford's more active support of Warbeck – not to have done so made him guilty of misprision of treason.[*] To state that he would refuse to fight with Henry against Warbeck if he discovered the boy was a son of York also made him a traitor. As had been demonstrated repeatedly, the Stanley forces were powerful enough to turn battles on their own. Henry could not allow one of their commanders to stand idle if Warbeck invaded, and certainly not risk the possibility that William's army would change sides as it had in 1485.

Henry did not wish to shed William's blood, but his confession in the Tower, and the seals and letters that Clifford brought with him from Warbeck's court as evidence, left him little choice. The day after the feast of the Purification of the Virgin Mary (3 February) 1495, William was put on trial in Westminster Hall. Among his judges were Margaret's ward the duke of Buckingham, who was celebrating his seventeenth birthday that day, and the

---

[*] Misprision of treason was the crime of deliberately concealing knowledge of a treasonable act.

queen's half-brother the marquess of Dorset. Thomas Stanley was spared the task of condemning his own brother to death, and instead presided over the trial of his nephew Humphrey Savage. The original reports of William's trial are missing, but a Latin manuscript copy in a sixteenth-century hand survives in the university library at Cambridge. This report recorded William's condemnation as guilty, and recited the proper punishment. From the Tower of London he was:

> to be dragged through the City of London to the gallows at Tyburn, and on the said gallows to be hanged, then cut down living, and his innards to be pulled out of his belly, then burnt while he lives, and his head cut off, then his body to be cut into four parts. And these head and quarters to be displayed where the King assigns.[31]

This gruesome punishment did indeed befall some of the lower-born supporters of Perkin Warbeck, but in deference to William's high birth and close relationship to the king, Henry granted his uncle the relative mercy of a quick beheading and private burial. On 16 February 1495, at about nine in the morning, Sir William left the Tower and walked up the long rise towards a scaffold on Tower Hill. Twelve days earlier, this had been the site of a public act of royal clemency, as two young men implicated in the conspiracy were pardoned and allowed to walk free, 'to the rejoicing of much people' in attendance – although only after they had watched their three co-conspirators decapitated.[32] William, however, did not escape. In a book of royal accounts, the financial exactions incurred by his death – debts owing to the servants who attended him in the Tower, payment for his burial in Syon Abbey, a ten-pound bonus delivered to his executioner to do the job well – sit incongruously alongside courtly payments for rhyming Welshmen, minstrels and pipers, Henry's losses at games of tennis and a purchase of seeds for a palace gardener. Ultimately, the downfall and destruction of the man who had been Margaret's brother-in-law for more than twenty years was just another line in the ledger of accounts.[33]

Margaret did not attend William's execution. Instead, she stayed close to Henry, who was reeling from the betrayal of some of his most intimate supporters. He had always had an impulse for the secretive, a tendency towards suspicion, but now he was beginning to exhibit the same darkly mistrustful nature that had been the self-destructive hallmark of Margaret's father. Margaret herself was renowned for her open-handed hospitality and liberal, but judicious, largesse. She would not have welcomed seeing such unpleasant family traits revived in her son, even if she could understand their justification. At first, Henry simply filled the roles vacated by William Stanley and his co-conspirators with trusted men. Margaret's nephew Richard Pole stepped into many of William's Welsh positions, bolstering a regional authority that Pole was building as part of Prince Arthur's Ludlow household. To replace William and Fitzwalter as chamberlain and steward, Henry chose men who had proven their loyalty in his hour of greatest need: Giles Daubeney and Robert Willoughby de Broke, both of whom had risked their lives and estates to join Henry's court-in-exile. But then Henry went further. He would no longer allow his servants – even long-trusted comrades like Daubeney and Willoughby – to get too close. Henry also created a new secret or privy chamber under the direction of an individual who was directly and solely accountable to him so that even chief officers no longer enjoyed indiscriminate access to the king. And, henceforward, Henry retreated more and more into this secret chamber, staffed by a very small number of trusted individuals, foremost among them Hugh Denys, the groom of the king's close stool.

As well as fearing for her son's emotional stability, Margaret must also have been concerned that William's guilt was shared by the wider Stanley family. There was no suggestion that Margaret's husband Thomas had allied with Perkin Warbeck, but as Robert Clifford eagerly revealed in return for the royal sweetener delivered by Reynald Bray, other Stanley confederates had certainly been implicated in the conspiracy: the Stanley client Robert Bulkeley; Sir Humphrey Savage, who was the son of Thomas's sister Catherine; and William's illegitimate son. That summer, Henry made two grand expressions of his authority to remind those who followed the Stanleys – indeed, who followed any of his nobility – that he alone was their supreme master.

First, on the south coast at Kent, he saw off the long-awaited invasion force of Perkin Warbeck, which weighed anchor near Deal on 3 July 1495. Warbeck's Flemish army was nowhere near the fearsome multitude that the duchess of Burgundy had threatened. When an advance force of 300 landed and raised their banners over the pebble beaches of Kent, the pretender received no hero's homecoming from locals. Henry's assertive action in rooting out treason within his court had deadened the appetite for rebellion. At sight of the foreign soldiers, the local commons drew bow and arrow, and inflicted devastating losses on Warbeck's men. As much as half of the advance rebel force was slaughtered and many of the rest were taken captive. From the deck of his ship, still out at sea, Warbeck watched the massacre of his men and, as the corpses of his soldiers bobbed in the water or lay studded with arrows on the beach, he weighed anchor and fled to Ireland.[34] Many of the captured soldiers were marched to London, lumbering on tattered feet or harnessed to carts, then dragged to the scaffold. The waters of the tidal Thames were soon lapping at the legs of executed rebels dangling from gibbets on the shoreline.[35]

But, according to the Tudor chronicler Edward Hall, such horrors were far from the minds of Margaret and her son, who took 'his progress into Lancashire... there to recreate his spirits and solace himself with his mother'.[36] Hall's Chronicle, perhaps deliberately, misrepresents Henry's northern progress as pure pleasure-seeking. In reality, it was as calculated to reassert Tudor authority as any of Henry's more sanguinary activities in the south for he trooped his magnificent court, and his considerable body-guard, through lands with traditional Stanley loyalties in a show of strength. The progress passed through Manchester, Derby, Sir William's seat at Holt Castle, and Thomas's manors of Lathom and Knowsley. It was a reminder to any restive elements in the north-west that their first loyalty was not to a Stanley lord, but to their king. It was not exactly a festive homecoming for Margaret, whose loyalties had been strained between the Stanleys and her son for over a decade.[37]

And it was while Margaret, Henry and Elizabeth were still in the Midlands, far from the southern nursery of the younger prince and princesses, that they received terrible news. On 14 September 1495, the three-year-old Princess Elizabeth had died. In an age of high infant mortality, when around a third of children died before their sixteenth birthday, the family had been fortunate – until now.[38] Margaret's first anxiety must have been for the queen. Elizabeth was four months pregnant with her fifth child, and her health was known to be delicate during pregnancy. The shock of losing her youngest child could have been dangerous to both Elizabeth and her unborn baby. Although the death of children was far from uncommon in the Tudor period, its sting was not lessened by its ubiquity. Love for your offspring was expected and natural, and expressions of affection survive in the writings of the royal family. In a note penned in a Book of Hours, Henry bade his eldest daughter, Princess Margaret, to 'remember your kind and loving father'.[39] She in turn wrote about her homesickness for her family when she eventually went away to marry. Even when her son was middle aged, Margaret Beaufort still referred to Henry in their letters as 'my dear heart', sending him 'most hearty loving blessings' and on one occasion calling him 'my only worldly joy'.[40] When they were apart on his birthday, she wrote to him remembering 'this day of St Agnes that I did bring into this world my good and gracious prince, king and only beloved son'.[41] It must therefore have been with sorrowful hearts that the family laid Princess Elizabeth to rest in Westminster Abbey in a coffin whose black shroud was fringed with red and white roses.[42]

Even excluding the shock of Sir William Stanley's betrayal and Princess Elizabeth's death, it had been a year of loss within the royal family. In March 1495, Cecily, duchess of York died at her Berkhamsted estate. Although she had lived away from court for some time, Cecily had been an exemplar for Margaret as king's mother. Testifying to their relationship, the dowager duchess remembered Margaret in her will, leaving her a fine breviary with golden clasps, covered with black cloth of gold. The pair shared a strong personal piety and perhaps an interest in books. Cecily's late sister, and Margaret's one-time mother-in-law, Anne, duchess of Buckingham had been another bibliophile who bequeathed Margaret precious manuscripts. Ever the politician, in Cecily's will she referred to herself as 'Cecily, wife unto the right noble Prince Richard late Duke of York... [and mother of] King Edward the fourth'. She made no mention whatsoever of Richard III. This omission, and her endowment to Henry of a lucrative right to customs debts, were probably made to ensure royal favour for the execution of her will. She needed his support, as one of her executors and close servants had unwisely involved himself with Perkin Warbeck.[43]

On 21 December 1495, Henry's uncle Jasper Tudor also died. He wrote his terse and largely religious will at Thornbury Manor in Gloucestershire a week before his death, and endowed priests to pray for the souls of himself, his parents, and Henry's father, Edmund, earl of Richmond. He made no provision for his wife beyond stipulating that Duchess Katherine should receive 'such dues as shall be thought to [his executors] appertaining by right law and conscience'. Perhaps he suspected her interests already lay elsewhere, as within two months the duchess remarried without royal licence a man twelve years her junior and substantially her social inferior. Duchess Katherine may not have overly grieved Jasper, but Henry and Margaret surely felt the loss of Henry's most zealous defender.[44]

The Wars of the Roses generation was dying away. Many of the once constant presences in Margaret's life were now gone. But – and perhaps Margaret contemplated this a little ruefully at Lathom that summer – the greatest survivor of them all showed no sign of dying. Now in his sixties, her husband Thomas was still thriving. Although probably unspoken, Margaret and Henry must have expected that by now death would have extricated her from her uneasy status as both king's mother and Stanley's wife. William Stanley's treachery had only made Margaret's situation more challenging. As she watched tumblers perform before her son's court in the territories of the kinsman who had betrayed them, was Margaret contemplating how to extract herself from her husband's family? For, undoubtedly, the time was coming when she could be a Stanley no longer.

19

'Wisdom to fear'[1]

✳

Spring 1496 found Margaret where she was probably happiest: at the heart of her beloved family. The past winter had been cruel, January bringing 'great snow, whereupon ensued mighty frosts' that endured until Candlemas in early February.[2] But, by the time 18 March arrived, the snow had melted away as a healthy daughter was born to Elizabeth and Henry. She was named Mary in honour of the Virgin Mary. Shortly afterwards, Margaret wrote to Elizabeth's chamberlain, the earl of Ormonde, and for once she did not dwell on the likelihood of future misfortune, instead focusing on present positives. 'The king, the queen and all our sweet [grand] children be in good health,' she wrote. Although Elizabeth had been 'a little crased* now she is well, God be thanked'.[3]

With the birth of a new grandchild, Margaret and her family attempted to move on from the grief and betrayals of the past year. Henry announced that, for this year's summer progress, instead of the usual Oxfordshire hunting lodges and Thames Valley palaces, the royal court would instead visit the ancestral territory of the Beauforts in the West Country. There would be a brief diversion to inspect the coastal defences around the Isle of Wight lest Perkin Warbeck or any of his allies plot another invasion, but the chief purpose of the progress would be to pay proper respect to the

---

* 'Crased' meant physical ill health, but in women often also suggested emotional or psychological distress. Deborah Thorpe, 'I Haue Ben Crised and Besy': Illness and Resilience in the Fifteenth-Century Stonor Letters', *The Mediaeval Journal*, 5, ii (2015).

lineage that he and Margaret shared, culminating in a stay at her castle of Corfe in Dorset. Thus it was something of a family party that approached Corfe that summer. On horseback and in litters, John Welles and his wife Princess Cecily, Thomas Stanley and other relatives skirted the chalk escarpments and coastal heathland to arrive at the castle on 27 July. Since Henry granted it to her in 1487, Margaret had stamped her mark on the fortress, installing new windows, enlarging the medieval keep and creating more comfortable residential quarters using locally mined lead.[4]

Pleasure and entertainment were the chief aims of the court that summer, as Henry's chamber books of accounts – still carefully maintained, even during this holiday season – make clear. Payments were dispensed for gambling at cards and to minstrels playing string and wind instruments, although the chief courtly diversion was hunting.[5] Henry had an ever-changing pack of hunting dogs who could travel with him, including the chivalrically named 'king's greyhound' Lancelot.[6] In her fifties, Margaret could no longer spend hours in the saddle, chasing deer across uneven terrain, but she could join Henry in the gentler sport of falconry. She was famed for her love of hawking, and every summer received gifts of hunting dogs and birds from friends, family and well-wishers.[7]

At Cirencester, the usually pious court indulged in a unique act of levity and paid a priest to wrestle for them.[8] He was rewarded six shillings and eight pence for the performance – precisely the amount also dispensed to two fools who performed for the court, which suggests he was playing out some sort of comic inversion.[9] Margaret and Henry both enjoyed joking with their households, sponsoring fools, actors, lords of misrule and boys to play the part of 'St Nicholas priest' on the saint's feast day (6 December).[10] Punning references to Margaret's name and patronage abounded, from the daisies (*marguerites*) in the margins of her prayer books, to the lofty arches of the passageways built into the Cambridge colleges she founded late in life, which were carved with a Beaufort motto, *Souvent me souviens*. This had myriad punning translations: 'often I remember' or 'forget me not' (another floral witticism) but also the literal 'often I pass underneath'. Henry also delighted in wordplay. He sometimes added the Latin motto '*altera securitas*' ('another defence') to Margaret's Beaufort portcullis heraldry: an allusion to his blood claim to the English throne, through Margaret, which bolstered his divinely endowed right as victor in battle. But the spiked portcullis and '*altera securitas*' was also a secondary defence within castle gateways: a 'two-door' (Tudor?) security system.

This levity within Margaret's household had a serious purpose too: it improved moral and physical wellbeing. 'Mirth is one of the chiefest things of Physick,' wrote the Tudor physician Andrew Boorde. 'Mirth and rejoicing doth lengthen a man's life and doth expel sickness.'[11] Providing 'honest mirth' was the chief task of court fools, who regularly appear in the books of accounts of Margaret and her family. Some were 'artificial' performers – tumblers, joke-tellers, wordsmiths – but others were 'natural fools' with a form of disability or additional need that, it was proposed, made them more attuned to the divine. They could therefore speak truth to power with a licence permitted to no other commentator, and gave their mistress a salutary counter to the general sycophancy of her subordinates. The connection between mirth and medicine was so established that, when Margaret was suffering from what would be her final illness, she sent for 'John Asshewell my lady's idiot' and 'Reginald my lady's idiot'.[12] Reginald was probably named as a private joke with Margaret's old servant Reynald Bray, also known as Reginald, and Henry VII similarly maintained a fool called 'Richmond'. As one of Margaret's attendants noted, when she dined with her household, she enjoyed 'joyous' conversation and honest 'tales... to make her merry', which could have been provided by her fools.[13] The great humanist Desiderius Erasmus wrote an entire book *In Praise of Folly*, noting that fools, 'are in so great request [i.e. favour] with princes that they can neither eat nor drink, go anywhere, or be an hour without them'.[14]

There were a number of fools attendant on the royal family: 'Diego the Spanish fool'; Queen Elizabeth's fool, William; John Goose, who attended Prince Henry and once delivered a carp to the queen. Margaret retained her own, including Skypp and John Asshewell. There was clearly great affection between the family and their fools. A court fool of Henry VII's called Lobe was eulogised in an epithet that praised him as 'a fool, without fraud... For our king and queen [he] was a treasure'.[15] Margaret, too, clearly felt considerable affection for her fools. When Skypp was terminally ill in February 1508, Margaret attempted to heal him with milk and ale, and even the expensive cure-all called aqua vita. When Skypp died, Margaret paid a not inconsiderable two shillings and ten pence for his burial.[16] Realising the depth of Margaret's attachment to Skypp, her kinswoman Lady Frideswide Cheyne* sent her own fool, Korse, to distract Margaret from her sorrows for a few weeks.[17]

The summer progress to the West Country did have some more sombre moments. Henry ensured the court made two important diversions, to the burial places of their lost relatives: at Keynsham, near Bristol, they paid their respects to Jasper Tudor; and at Wimborne Minster they made offerings before the tomb of Margaret's parents. In the chancel, life-like effigies of Margaret's beloved mother and entirely unknown father lay with their eyes turned towards the heavens, their hands eternally united.[18] The churchyard had been hastily cleaned ahead of the royal visit, and, when the court rode on, torches were left burning in commemoration at the Beaufort family tomb.[19]

Although no record survives of it, it is likely that while in the West Country Margaret called on her elder half-brother Oliver St John, whose principal seat at Lydiard Tregoze in Wiltshire was an easy diversion for Margaret as the progress made its way from Malmesbury to Woodstock.[20] Oliver was unwell at this time; he wrote his will in March 1496 and died in spring 1497. Margaret was not as close to the Wiltshire St Johns as her relatives through her eldest half-brother, John St John, but she had an abiding concern for her siblings and their families.

Henry's sudden desire to return to the homeland of his maternal ancestors may have been inspired by a creeping awareness of his own mortality, especially in the wake of his daughter's death. In January 1497, Henry entered his forties, which was considered old age by many early modern Europeans. Ageing was also an immediate concern for Margaret. Now in her mid-fifties, she had to wear

---

* Frideswide was the wife of Sir Thomas Cheyne, descended from Margaret's maternal Stourton cousins.

glasses: golden spectacles that were discreetly tucked away in their cases when she was not wearing them. Henry inherited Margaret's declining eyesight, an unfortunate by-product of their shared habit of poring painstakingly over household accounts. Writing his own letters became painful for Henry in later life, and he used his failing sight as an excuse for writing to his mother less often than he felt he should.* In one letter to Margaret he apologised:

> that it is so seldom that I do write, wherefore I beseech you to pardon me, for verily madam my sight is nothing so perfect as it has been; and I know well it may impair daily... for on my faith I have been three days or [before] I could make an end of this letter.[21]

Margaret's mind, meanwhile, was turning to the future. In 1496, she travelled in the heart of her son's court, with her husband at her side, but she was contemplating moving away from both. All the royal maternal figures she knew had ultimately retired from court and, although Margaret was not ready to withdraw altogether from her family, nor from the political sphere, she sought an escape from the endless bustle of life at the centre of power. A king's court must travel constantly from place to place for reasons both governmental and pragmatic: his subjects needed to see him, and his considerable entourage of attendants could not comfortably be housed in one place for more than a few weeks, or sometimes days. Henry's summer progress is a case in point, its movements revealed by his chamber accounts: over a week in early August Margaret and the court moved from Salisbury to Bristol, stopping every one or two days at a different Wiltshire residence.[22] Such constant travel was exhausting for a woman in her fifties. Moreover, with the suppression of the terrible plots of 1495, Margaret permitted herself, perhaps for the first time, to imagine an independent life. Against considerable odds, her son had proven himself more than

---

* It was not just Margaret who suffered as a result of Henry's faltering vision. In July 1507, the king had to pay eight pence compensation for a 'cock that the king's grace killed at Chesterford with his crossbow' by mistake while out hunting. TNA, E36/214, f. 88v.

capable of ruling the kingdom and of protecting himself and his family. He did not need the instantaneous counsel of his mother, and nor did Elizabeth – with her ever-expanding brood of children – require Margaret's constant presence. Margaret's mother, the dowager duchess of Somerset, had lived into her seventies at least, so if Margaret survived that long she potentially had another two decades of life before her. She sought to make something of it, to carve a legacy for herself more useful to wider society than the stonework of Corfe. At Wimborne, she planned to endow a priest and chantry chapel to pray for her parents' souls, and to provide education to local children. Perhaps she was also beginning to form more ambitious plans. Previous royal women had founded colleges at Oxford and Cambridge.* Might Margaret follow, even surpass, their example? Could she become one of the only noblewomen in English history to found her own college?

Whatever ambitions Margaret was contemplating that summer were shattered as autumn arrived. In late September, just as the court was settling back into the routine of life at Windsor, a message arrived from the north: war had broken out and the threat of Perkin Warbeck was revived.

ON 20 SEPTEMBER 1496, THE BORDERLANDS OF Northumberland were breached as King James IV and his Scottish army marched south 'with banner displayed, furnished with great people and all habiliments for the war'.[23] Heralds rode in advance of the forces, threatening to bring war like 'a raging fire or a ruinous storm' unless the English submitted to 'Richard of York' – Perkin Warbeck – who rode at James's side.[24] Warbeck had been living within James's court for almost a year, his marriage arranged to a young noble bride, Katherine Gordon. Riding four miles into England, the Scottish soldiers set fire to local houses and brought down two watchtowers. They occupied the area for five days

---

* Marguerite of Anjou and Elizabeth Woodville founded Queens' College, Cambridge, and Philippa of Hainault The Queen's College, Oxford.

before retreating ahead of a Northumbrian force. Although, as one London chronicler joked, the Scots 'did more harm with brag and boast than with dint of sword', Henry knew that, as long as King James supported Perkin Warbeck, there could be more raids.[25] And if – or when – the army of 'Richard of York' marched south, who knew how many disaffected Englishmen might join him?

Parliament was immediately summoned so that Henry could secure the necessary funds for an army to defend the northern borders. This was a dangerous move at a time of economic difficulty, when taxation – even for military defence in the face of a known threat – was unwelcome. Henry had to negotiate with the Commons for weeks before they would agree a grant, and even then it fell far short of the sum he had hoped for. Irked by his subjects' resistance, Henry failed to deliver the customary royal thanks.[26] Polydore Vergil disingenuously described the grant as 'a light head tax on all men',[27] but in reality this was the heaviest tax of the century. Areas that were traditionally exempt from taxation, like the borderlands of the extreme north, Wales and its Marches, were all expected to contribute. Moreover, the levy followed a national forced loan, and the clergy were assessed three times for taxation.[28] Under such circumstances, there were many quarters from which discontent with Henry might arise.

When resistance finally came, it was from the furthest corner of the realm. In mid-May 1497, in the small tin-mining parish of St Keverne in Cornwall, a local tax collector was assaulted. The incident lit a spark that burned bright in the brittle tinder of west Cornwall. Following a well-trodden path of insurrection, two local men incited their fellows to rebellion by condemning the king's advisers. The leaders of the Cornish revolt were a blacksmith called Michael Joseph, or *An Gof* in his native Cornish, and Thomas Flamank, the eldest son of a respected local gentleman. Worryingly for Margaret, the targets of the Cornish were her long-term associates, including Cardinal John Morton and Reynald Bray. It was these wicked counsellors, the Cornish rebels proclaimed, who were responsible for the latest extortions imposed on them.[29] It proved a popular war cry. The flames quickly spread as the Cornish marched east, demanding that the king remove his corrupt advisers. In Devon, the rebels seized control of the city of Exeter and threatened to behead the mayor. In Somerset, they gained the support of Lord James Audley, a crucial addition, as successful risings demanded noble leadership. But the rebellion dreamed of an even greater captain. In the first week of June, as the rebels entered Wells, they sent a messenger to Scotland asking Perkin Warbeck to join them. By then the rebel force had covered 160 miles in under two weeks and was already halfway to London.

Margaret was probably with Henry at Sheen Palace in Surrey when they learned of the rebel advance. Its sheer speed and momentum was terrifying. Henry urgently readied a royal force to block its path, recalling an army of 8,000 men led by his chamberlain Giles Daubeney that had originally been intended for service in Scotland. As Daubeney diverted his soldiers west, Henry summoned his loyal lords to confront the rebels near London. This force he would lead in person.[30]

Meanwhile, Margaret and Elizabeth's first concern was for the royal children. Ten-year-old Arthur should be safe at his court in Shropshire. A small retinue in the command of Margaret's nephew Sir Richard Pole mustered to serve in the prince's name, but the rest of Arthur's attendants stayed with him at Ludlow, prepared – if necessary – to carry him into exile. Heart-rending as such decisions were, it was only prudent that the heir to the throne remained at a geographical remove from the king and other royal children. Should they be killed, at least one Tudor son would survive. Elizabeth Woodville had known this when she tried, un-successfully, to keep her son and daughters out of their opponents' hands in 1483. The precedent of Richard III's coup must have been at the forefront of Margaret's mind. Those dark days had proven how dangerous rebellion could be to royal children. Young as the Tudors were – Mary barely fifteen months, and even the eldest daughter, Princess Margaret, just seven years old – they might still suffer for their royal blood if the Cornish rising turned into a full-blown rebellion in Perkin Warbeck's name.

On Tuesday 28 May, Prince Henry and Princesses Margaret and Mary were bundled from their nursery in Eltham to Margaret's palace of Coldharbour in London, where Margaret and Elizabeth awaited them.[31] Lying between London Bridge and the Tower within the city walls, it was hoped that the palace would protect them from rebel reprisals. But, less than a week later, on Monday 5 June, word reached London that Farnham in Surrey had fallen to the rebels, who were now reckoned to be 15,000 strong. 'Fear mounted hourly within the city,' wrote Polydore Vergil, 'the alarm was sounded in every ward, men came running to the gates, and likewise the watch and ward was wonderfully maintained.'[32] Margaret and Elizabeth did not hesitate. They fled with the children the short distance downriver to the Tower of London. The next day, the first blood of the rising was shed, as the Cornish 'bickered' with Lord Daubeney's spearmen near Guildford.

Within the crenellated walls of the Tower, Margaret, her daughter-in-law and grandchildren huddled, anxiously awaiting the outcome of battle between Henry and the rebels. For battle now seemed inevitable. On Thursday 15 June, they were joined by Cardinal Morton, one of the main targets of the rebels' ire, and Margaret must have hoped that Henry would follow. Anticipating the arrival of their king, on Friday 16 June, the mayor and leading craftsmen of London gathered their weapons and armour, and lined the streets from London Bridge to the Tower to attend him. But Henry knew that the morale of his men – not to mention the submission of the rebels – might depend on his presence. Late in the day, as the Cornish were seen pitching their tents on Blackheath to the east of London, Henry sent word that he would not be coming into the city. Instead, he camped with his army in the heathland of Lambeth on the south bank. One contemporary reported that he was 'seen in the field' that night 'comforting of his people', wandering among the 25,000-strong force clustered around campfires as they readied themselves for battle the next day. Daubeney's army lodged a little closer to the rebels, at St George's Field.[33]

At first it seemed that Henry's gamble had paid off, for throughout the night shadowy figures were seen slinking away from Blackheath. When the rebels heard that the king was close by, ready to raise his standards against them, many baulked at taking arms against their sovereign and preferred to sue for peace. 'In great fear and agony', some secretly stole away under cover of darkness.[34] Rebel cohesion was breaking down. But still An Gof refused to surrender.

The next morning, Saturday 17 June, royal forces in the command of Sir Humphrey Stanley* and the earl of Oxford mounted their horses early and advanced on Blackheath. It was almost the longest day of the year, and dawn had long since broken when the rebels on the heath found themselves surrounded. Stanley and his 'company of lusty spears' attacked one flank of the depleted rebel force, while Oxford ploughed into the other. The Cornishmen were barely standing their ground when Giles Daubeney's soldiers joined the fray, and the rebels broke and fled. An Gof attempted to reach sanctuary with the Franciscan Friary at Greenwich, but was overtaken by royal forces and captured. Two hundred rebels were seized, including Lord Audley and Flamank, who were taken unhurt. The battle was over so quickly that Henry was still riding towards the battlefield when news of their victory was brought to him. He immediately turned his horse back towards London, retracing his steps in a dizzying reversal of fortune.

At two o'clock, Margaret could have watched for herself, from the battlements of the Tower, as Henry crossed London Bridge in triumph. The mayor and leading citizens of London assembled to greet him, now dressed in triumphant scarlet instead of armed for war. At St Magnus Church next to London Bridge, Henry drew the sword from his belt – the self-same sword with which he had intended to subdue the rebels – and knighted three leading citizens of London: the mayor, the recorder of London and John Shaa, a local citizen who had repeatedly bankrolled Tudor endeavours. Then Henry rode on towards St Paul's Cathedral to make a thanksgiving offering, before finally reuniting with his family at the Tower.

By coincidence, it was almost exactly ten years since Henry's victory at Stoke over Lambert Simnel. Again, Margaret commemorated the event in her Book of Hours, setting pen to parchment just beneath the note of the Battle of Stoke. 'This day,' she wrote on the calendar beside 17 June, 'King Henry VII obtained battle

---

* From Staffordshire, Humphrey was not directly related to Thomas Stanley.

victory against the Cornishmen at Blackheath.'[35] Twelve days later, while the king and his family were still lodged within the Tower, Prince Henry turned six. Already the leaders of the rebellion had been arraigned, condemned and executed. Lord Audley was drawn to Tower Hill in a mocking paper coat of armour, 'all to torn and rent'. He received the relative mercy of a beheading. Flamank and An Gof, being low-born, were hanged, drawn and beheaded at Tyburn. As a final vengeance on these traitors, their dismembered corpses were pinned onto four of the city gates and at key points across the West Country. As Margaret and her precious family emerged from the Tower, they had escaped danger by what felt a very narrow margin.

WITH THE VICTORY AT BLACKHEATH, TUDOR LUCK SEEMED to turn. An English force in the command of the earl of Surrey led a spectacular defence of Norham Castle in Northumberland against King James and the Scots. Forcing the Scottish king into retreat, Surrey pursued him across the border in 'continual rain and cold weather' and destroyed several fortifications, including Hayton Castle, 'one of the strongest places betwixt Berwick and Edinburgh'.[36] To make this triumph all the sweeter, King James was only a mile away, within sight of the destruction, and despite 'many... boasting and *cracking* words,' fled the English rather than risk battle. By the end of the year, James abandoned Perkin Warbeck and came to terms with Henry instead, agreeing the first Anglo-Scottish peace treaty since 1328.[37]

Abandoned by his allies in Scotland, Warbeck attempted to capitalise on the groundswell of rebellion that had swept the West Country that summer, and on 7 September his ship moored near Land's End with his wife, Katherine, and a small force of 'rascally' and largely unarmed men.[38] According to Bernard André, Henry no longer feared the pretender. '"Well look," he said smiling,' when he learned of the invasion, '"we are being attacked again by that prince of rascals".'[39] But Henry was sufficiently anxious to capture Warbeck that he promised a thousand-pound reward and full pardon for 'whoso bringeth the said Perkin alive unto us'.[40]

As Warbeck's forces marched east, it became clear that the people of the West Country had been chastened by that summer's bloodshed. Contrary to Warbeck's blithe expectations, the people did not flock to his banner and every day Henry's superior army moved closer. Outside Taunton on 20 September, for the second time in two years, Warbeck chose to flee rather than fight. Under cover of darkness, Warbeck galloped for the sanctuary of Beaulieu Abbey in Hampshire, while his wife, Katherine, escaped to St Michael's Mount. Abandoned by their captain, Warbeck's army swiftly came to terms and Henry's soldiers ran the pretender to ground not long after. Henry did not violate Warbeck's sanctuary and drag him out. He did not need to. 'Now lacking in hope, lacking a home, lacking a fortune,' Warbeck's spirit was crushed.[41] He surrendered to Henry's forces on the mere promise of a pardon. Finally, Henry had the pretender in his power.

When Henry came face to face with his rival at Taunton Castle, on 5 October, he realised that Warbeck represented a far greater threat in the imagination of his followers than the reality of his person. The pretender's inadequacies are evident in a despairing letter he wrote to his mother, Kataryn, two days after meeting the king, full of self-pity and an almost adolescent inability to bear responsibility for his actions. He pleaded with her to send money to 'purchase his deliverance', or to bribe his warders into greater kindness, and fretted that Henry had given him 'no good answer' to his appeals for pardon. The blame for his actions he placed squarely on the shoulders of the Englishmen who had convinced him to invent the fraud in the first place.[42]

Henry agreed to pardon Warbeck on the condition that a public confession of his true identity would be printed and widely disseminated. So, as Perkin of Tournai, not Richard of York, Warbeck was permitted to join Henry's court when he returned to London. According to the Venetian ambassador Andrea Trevisano, Henry refused to celebrate Warbeck's defeat with a celebratory progress through the capital, 'saying that he had not gained a worthy victory, having been against such a base crew'.[43] But he still forced Warbeck to endure the hostile attentions of the Londoners when they entered the city together on Tuesday 23 November. Warbeck received 'much wondering and many a curse thrown at his head' by the citizens, but he escaped the punishment inflicted on the man riding behind him in that homecoming procession, his hands and feet bound fast to his horse. Sergeant Ferrour was a one-time servant of Henry who defected to Warbeck's cause then attempted to escape disguised as a religious hermit. For his betrayal, he was dragged from the Tower to Tyburn the following Monday and hanged and dismembered while still alive. With Ferrour, dangling on the hangman's rope that day, was a yeoman of the queen named Edwards, who had also defected to Warbeck. Henry would not permit treason to infect his court again. Perhaps he wanted, too, to ensure that Warbeck realised how fortunate he was to receive royal mercy.[44]

Margaret played a less sanguinary role in reasserting Tudor authority. While Henry was in the West Country, Margaret travelled with Elizabeth and six-year-old Prince Henry into East Anglia, purportedly on pilgrimage to the shrine of the Virgin Mary at Walsingham. On route, though, they took care to parade the prince – the *true* duke of York – before his public. This traditionally Yorkist area had produced two of the leading Warbeck supporters in Lord Fitzwalter and Sir Gilbert Debenham, so it was vital to rally the people to Margaret's family and reassure them that the dynasty was secure. What better promise of the future could there be than the golden-haired child riding so boldly through the country? On 17 October, Margaret returned with the queen and prince to London, where Elizabeth paused at Bishopsgate – so recently adorned with the dismembered flank of the Cornish rebel Flamank – to receive a loyal welcome from the citizens.[45]

In the end, Perkin Warbeck enjoyed the hospitality of Henry's court for only nine months. At midnight on Trinity Sunday (9 June) 1498, he slipped free of his captors and began to make his way south-west, probably intending to take ship to Burgundy. Warbeck's ability to escape from a locked room, directly above the king's apartments, within a royal palace complex and while guarded by two men, was sufficiently remarkable that many contemporaries believed that Henry had let him break free so he would have grounds to execute the pretender.[46] Nonetheless, the king took no chances that Warbeck might actually flee the realm, and dispatched urgent messages to every port and leading nobleman in the kingdom to be alert for Warbeck.

Warbeck made it less than ten miles along the river. 'Terrified by the shouts of his pursuers' and having found 'all the roads were blocked by the royal servants who had been his guardians', he threw himself on the mercy of the prior of the Charterhouse at Sheen.[47] The prior of Sheen, John Ingleby, was a friend of Margaret's and praised by Henry as his 'captain and envoy' – but, despite his loyalty to the Tudors, as a man of God Ingleby abhorred the shedding of blood.[48] He pleaded for Warbeck's life and, reluctantly, Henry agreed. Warbeck was condemned instead to imprisonment, but only after he had been subjected to public humiliation. On two occasions, outside Westminster Palace and at Cheapside in the City, Warbeck was locked for several hours in the stocks atop a scaffold of empty wine barrels to be 'jeered by the common folk, who spared him no insult'.[49] Having been informed that even his most zealous supporter, the duchess of Burgundy, had abandoned his cause and come to terms with Henry, Warbeck was finally locked in the Tower of London, so securely that 'he sees neither sun nor moon'.[50] There, it was hoped, he would be forgotten.

Warbeck's wife, Katherine Gordon, did not suffer by association. As a noblewoman, she was treated honourably by Henry from the moment she was captured in the West Country, provided with black velvet and satin clothing and a horse and saddle to make the journey to London to join the royal court.[51] After her husband's escape and imprisonment, she continued to reside there, serving in Elizabeth's household as a respected lady-in-waiting. Having been dragged the length of the British Isles in pursuit of her husband's ambition, she seemed content now to resume the more comfortable existence she had enjoyed before they met.

With the pretender suppressed, the Tudor dynasty finally seemed secure. Despite all the dangers Margaret's family had faced in the twelve years they held power, fate had one further trial in store for them. Two days before the year 1497 ended, another potential disaster was survived by what could only be considered a miracle.

As Margaret, Henry, Elizabeth and their younger children were celebrating Christmas at Sheen Palace, they were almost wiped out by a freak fire. It started in the king's lodgings on the night of 29 December, then tore through the royal apartments, burning to ash the wooden bedframes and silken tapestries. It was midnight before the conflagration could be contained, and by then 'much and great part of the old building was burnt' down.[52] Mercifully, no one was killed or injured – a sign, said contemporaries, that God truly blessed their family. True to form, however, the family did not linger on their misfortune. They immediately started rebuilding. The ashes of Sheen would transform phoenix-like into an opulent new Tudor palace for the world to admire.

Ever since her son had taken power in 1485, Margaret had been staunchly at her family's side, her own hopes and energies channelled into the collective endeavour of founding and protecting the new dynasty. But, as she entered her fifty-fifth year, in 1498, Margaret finally moved away from the Tudor court. She would continue to work for her son and his family – she scarcely knew how else to live – but she would do so from the comfort of her own home. And she would allow herself to divert some of her considerable reserves of knowledge, authority and wealth into her own endeavours. But, to do so, she must take an unprecedented step.

III

'ALTERA SECURITAS'

20

'According to her own design'[1]

*

T he summer of 1498 was unusually dry. As Margaret traversed East Anglia with Henry, the pounding of their horses' hooves sent plumes of dust into the air behind them. By the second week of September, they had crossed into Margaret's lands, where the appraising eye of the king's mother could discern that her tenants were uneasy. So little rain had fallen that 'great drought' ensued, 'by reason whereof grass increased not' and hay was selling at twice its usual price.[2] When the autumn rains came, this parched earth might flood. Most of Margaret's Lincolnshire estates were below sea level, in need of defences, embankments and drainage at the best of times. Margaret devised schemes to improve the local area with the help of Flemish engineers. The nearby port of Boston was so silted up it was becoming impassable, which impacted on Margaret financially, for she drew fees from the use of the harbour crane and leased properties along the quayside to traders. The merchants of Boston, like those of her neighbouring market town of Stamford, were also regular suppliers of her household. Improving the area thus made sound economic sense as well as being her moral duty as the local landlord.

Perhaps she ruminated on these possibilities as she and Henry entered her estates that autumn. They were making for Collyweston, the 'fair and pleasant' Northamptonshire manor that Margaret had received by royal grant in 1487.[3] For this, too, she had grand plans, but their precise nature depended on conversation with Henry. For Margaret was contemplating a major change for herself, and thus to her status within the Tudor regime. Collyweston would be at the heart of the next phase of her life – no longer as merely her home, but as her centre of operations. At Collyweston, or perhaps in another of the great houses at which they paused their travels that summer, Margaret discussed with Henry how she could detach herself from her husband and his Stanley kinsmen. Not by means of a divorce, for which she had little grounds and which – more importantly – risked humiliating Thomas and thus alienating Stanley followers from the king. Rather, Margaret sought the next most complete separation possible in her husband's lifetime. She wanted to become a vowess.

The vowess's status lay somewhere between nun and widow. The word derived from the 'vows' made by a woman in a religious ceremony where she promised 'never [to] use [her] body... after the common usage in matrimony'.[4] In other words, to end her sexual life, representing that change by taking on a widow's dark garb and nun-like black headdress. The chief attractions of becoming a vowess were that, unlike a nun, there was no necessity to renounce one's worldly goods and, unlike a widow, one's husband could still be alive. Indeed, retaining control over one's affairs was usually the chief motivation. The state of vowess was commonly entered into by widows of middling status – the wives of prominent citizens and urban merchants, eager to protect their children's interests and maintain control over their late husband's business. Women such as Alice Lynne of Mincing Lane in London, a mother of five young children whose merchant husband died in 1421. For the next fifty years, Alice continued to operate his profitable London Wool Wharf as a vowess.[5]

The market town of Stamford, less than four miles from Collyweston, was home to a lively network of educated, influential and devout women with long-term ties to Margaret's family, some of whom were vowesses.[6] Among them were the Stokes-Browne sisters, Margaret and Agnes, who had been friends of Margaret's family since her childhood at Maxey and who both became vowesses when widowed.[7] Margaret Stokes-Browne demonstrated an aptitude for money-lending in her years as a vowess, stamping documents with her own wax seal as a sign of her independent authority and living sumptuously in a large, tapestry-hung town-house in the parish of All Saints, Stamford. The Stokes-Browne network was part of a wider Lincolnshire affinity devoted to the cults of Corpus Christi and St Katherine, which included among its adherents Margaret and members of her household, her half-brother John Welles and Richard Fox, the Lincolnshire-born bishop who lived in exile with Henry and became his keeper of the privy seal. St Katherine was an exemplar to Margaret: a chaste, intelligent and independent holy woman, whose image adorned Margaret's home and whose feast day was marked with a special devotional fast.[8]

The status of vowess was relatively unusual for noblewomen, but not unknown. Henry's one-time guardian Lady Anne Herbert had promised 'to take the order of widowhood' on her husband William's death in 1469, so she could 'be the better master' of her estate 'and to help [their] children'.[9] Although Anne died in the early years of Henry VII's reign, Margaret and Henry fostered their links with the Herbert family long after. At Collyweston, rooms were set aside for Anne's daughter Anne, Lady Powys, who often stayed with her three servants.[10] When Lady Powys died, her daughter was also provided for by Margaret, and bequeathed 'a heart of gold with a fair sapphire'.[11] Henry's continued close-ness to the family was also marked with gifts and personal visits: every August when he did not visit Raglan Castle in person, his childhood companion Sir Walter Herbert would send the king a hunting hawk.[12]

Like Anne Herbert, Margaret wished to be master of her estate, but she was also concerned to avoid the slanders that had attached to her female royal predecessors. Marguerite of Anjou, Cecily, duchess of York and Elizabeth Woodville had all faced accusations of sexual misconduct – in Cecily's case, from her own sons. Insinuations about a woman's sexuality were the easiest way to undermine her authority. It is telling that when a yeoman of the crown called John Hewyk railed against the king's mother for blocking his access to Queen Elizabeth, he chose to call her 'that strong whore'.[13] The misogynist language of sexual defamation was as ubiquitous as it was potentially damaging to a powerful woman, and Margaret's unaccustomed status as both king's mother and wife to a man other than the king's father laid her open to allegations of divided loyalty tinged with sexual intrigue. Such insinuations against Margaret would also taint Henry's legitimacy, which could not be permitted.

How much Margaret discussed her plan to become a vowess with Thomas Stanley is as obscure as the rest of their relationship. Theirs had always been an ambiguous union of mutual political and economic benefit. Without Margaret, Thomas would not be an earl, nor the kinsman of a king, and without Thomas Margaret might not have escaped Ricardian retribution for her treasonable activities in 1483. Stanley armies had helped Henry gain and re-tain his crown, a service for which Henry remained profoundly grateful even after Sir William's betrayal. With so many ties to bind Margaret and Thomas, even after their marriage effectively ended in 1499, their relationship remained amicable. Although Margaret would never return to Lathom, Thomas regularly visited her at Collyweston and on at least one occasion Margaret gave her ex-husband stake money so he could gamble at cards with his grandson in her home.[14] When Margaret made her alterations at Collyweston, she ensured that Thomas continued to enjoy his own dedicated bedchamber, laid out in mirror image to Margaret's, just like any married noble couple.[15] Nor did Margaret sever ties with her Stanley kin, regularly hosting Thomas's relatives and remaining in close contact with them. But the couple had been moving apart since Henry's accession, with Margaret enjoying greater independence with every royal grant. So, however she framed her decision, whether to protect herself and her son, or to cement her independence, in 1499 Margaret followed the example of her friends and neighbours and vowed to live as if her husband was dead.

THE DETAILS OF MARGARET'S CEREMONY OF CREATION AS 'vowess' have not survived, but can be reconstructed from a later renewal of her vow and a closely contemporary pontifical* owned by the bishop of London in the 1520s.[16] She was professed by Henry's chaplain Richard Fitzjames, bishop of Rochester and on the day of the ceremony, she approached him at the altar wearing her usual clothing, carrying over her left arm a dark gown and headdress. These she laid with a ring before the bishop's feet. Kneeling, as if in prayer, she read her vow aloud from a piece of paper: 'In the presence of my Lord God Jesus Christ and his blessed mother the glorious Virgin Mary and all of the whole company of Heaven... I Margaret of Richmond... with all my heart promise from henceforth the chastity of my body.'[17]

Then she marked the paper with a cross and delivered it to the bishop. Her mantle, veil and ring were blessed and placed upon her. Prostrating herself on the floor of the church, Margaret listened to the rest of the Mass, then placed an offering on the altar. The ceremony ended when she kissed the bishop's ring, and departed the church, now dressed as she would be for the rest of her life, with wimple and black veil covering her head, leaving only the small angular features of her face visible.

It is in such attire that Margaret is presented in all her surviving portraits. But, less evident in these images than it would have been in person, Margaret continued to use her clothing to express her exalted status. She was still the king's mother, so her black clothes were made from costly velvet, satin and damask, and furred with luxurious sable.[18] In an inventory of Margaret's wardrobe, a black velvet gown edged with sable and marten furs vastly outstrips every other item of clothing in expense. At over eleven pounds (£11 1s 4d), it is almost fourteen times more expensive than the scarlet gown Margaret wore as a member of the Order of the Garter.[19]

Margaret's vow of chastity was part of a wider scheme to assert her authority. It is surely no coincidence that, around the same time she professed herself a vowess, Margaret abandoned her signature of 'M Richmond' in favour of signing herself 'Margaret R'.[20] 'R' customarily meant *Rex* (King) or *Regina* (Queen), so

---

* A book of church rites to be performed by bishops or the Pope.

Margaret's new signature recalled her son's: *Henricus Rex* or HR. But Margaret permitted herself some plausible deniability, for the 'R' could also signify 'Richmond', and the ambiguity was no doubt intentional. One of the earliest recorded uses of this signature was a letter that Margaret wrote to Henry from Collyweston in 1499, signing off 'your faithful true bedewoman,* and humble mother, Margaret R'.[21]

There was, however, little that was 'humble' about Margaret by 1499. Her household at Collyweston was comparable in size to a royal one. During her marriage to Sir Harry Stafford, Margaret had overseen a household of thirty-two, but by the time she became a vowess it numbered almost two hundred. Indeed, her cupbearer Henry Parker suggested that on occasion she employed 440, which would put her on a level with the king, and beyond the precedent of previous princesses.[22] Not all of these servants were in attendance at all times, and Margaret had an inner circle that was scarcely larger than her Stafford household: around thirty-eight trusted counsellors, grooms, chaplains and officers, of which thirteen were women. Her most important female attendants were Edith Fowler, who had responsibility for her purse, jewels and the 'almsfolk' who lived at Collyweston at Margaret's expense, and her great-niece Alice St John-Parker.[†] Alice, her husband Henry and young children, Margaret and Jane, all lived with Margaret, and the girls were lavished with attention. Margaret provided not just their fine matching black clothes but also their servants, nurses, ribbons, combs and poppets.[23] When little Jane fell ill during the plague season of June 1508, Margaret paid for her to receive treacle, candied sugar and extra rations of milk and butter.[24]

To ensure her household ran smoothly, Margaret relied on a team of clerks, accountants and auditors to keep the books balanced. Entries into her book of accounts were made by financial officers including the treasurer[‡] and cofferer[§] throughout the year, and Margaret would personally scrutinise and sign each batch

---

* *Bedewoman* was a woman praying for someone else – here, for Henry.
† Alice was the granddaughter of Margaret's half-brother John St John of Bletsoe.
‡ The treasurer was responsible for comestibles and stock.
§ The cofferer paid out and received money as dictated by the treasurer.

– sometimes several days of accounts in one sitting. She also maintained her own independent book of accounts, which was cross-referenced against her accountants' sums at the end of the financial year, early in January.[25]

Margaret's move away from the royal court and the nature of her life and expenditure at Collyweston is clear in these accounts. The peripatetic style of lordship that had defined her life since her marriage to Sir Harry Stafford thirty years earlier gave way to a more stable existence. When Margaret was regularly on the move, she had to keep track of both the location and dates of her payments and receipts. Thus, as James Clarell, her cofferer – the officer responsible for the money going into and out of her coffers – rode alongside his mistress throughout 1498–9, he made marginal notes in his accounts book about where they stopped to disburse money: '*Schene. Xxiiio de Junii anno xiiio. Sondaye... Wyndsore. Xxvo die. Mondaye... Estamstede. Xxvio die. Tewysdaye...*'* The accounts of Margaret's cofferer between 1499 and 1502 are lost, but, when they resume, their style has noticeably changed. Now the presumption was that Margaret stayed in one place for weeks, even months, at a time so there was no need to regularly mark her location in the accounts. Progresses between different towns had become an anomaly.

A practical reason for Margaret's changing lifestyle is also suggested by her accounts. In her fifties, Margaret still rode on horseback with her son's court, braving the discomfort of hours in the saddle on her increasingly arthritic frame. But, as her sixtieth birthday approached, she chose instead to travel by the less fatiguing means of a litter: a curtained frame supporting a couch or bed, drawn by horses and often used by the sick or advanced in age. When Margaret needed to move, her litter would be summoned from storage in London to cross the country to wherever she was staying.[26]

But Margaret's 'retirement' from court to Collyweston was not a turning away from the world. She continued to exercise her

---

* Modernised: 'Sheen. Sunday 24 June, in the Eighteenth Year [of Henry VII's reign]... Windsor. Monday 25... Esthampsted. Tuesday 26.' D91.17 (SJLM/1/1/2/1), p. 19.

lordship over her servants and tenants, and she became more than ever a representative of royal authority, providing hospitality and dispensing justice on her son's behalf. In effect, she became Henry's regent in the Midlands.

ON 8 SEPTEMBER 1500, EIGHT OF THE LEADING LANDOWNERS of Lincolnshire assembled in the chambers of Maxey Castle at Margaret's command. A decade-long dispute between the people of Kesteven and Holland had erupted into sacrilegious violence: a boundary cross above a holy well consecrated to St Guthlac had been 'thrown down by the diabolical effort' of those within Margaret's lordship.[27] Margaret had empanelled a royal commission to settle the matter, and commanded her noble and knightly commissioners to tour the local fenland 'on horseback… on foot and sometimes in boats' to resolve the dispute once and for all. After four days, the commission reported their findings and Margaret gave her judgement: the frontier was delineated, restoration made of a contested marsh to a neighbouring abbey, and the miscreants who had torn down the boundary cross were banished. She then dispatched her decision under her own seal to the royal chancery.[28]

This was only one of Margaret's local judgements. After becoming a vowess, she increasingly assumed vice-regal legal oversight in her territories, effectively acting as a court representing royal interests and enforcing effective administration of justice, usually through the arbitration of disputes. Her judicial workload increased so much that she had to build both a council house and a prison at Collyweston. The house's position on the road from the north down to London meant it often hosted prisoners travelling south for trial, and Margaret's servants were regularly commissioned to guard them as they moved.[29] Margaret also kept a keen eye out for signs of treason in the locality. In January 1500, a prior of Stoneleigh in Warwickshire was summoned before her with one 'Master Butler' to answer questions regarding treasonable words they had unwisely spoken about the battle at Blackheath in 1497.

She also took a personal interest in defamatory words spoken in a Colchester tavern about Henry VII's ancestry.[30] The most singular case brought before Margaret's council involved the vice-president of Magdalen College, Oxford, John Stokesley, who was accused in 1506 of baptising a cat to discover treasure by magical means. Stokesley had allegedly committed his 'illicit plot'[31] in Collyweston, his birthplace, which explains Margaret's involvement in a case that should ordinarily have gone before a church court.[32]

When people had the temerity to ignore Margaret's rulings, she assumed the full majesty of her status as king's mother. Among those who incited her displeasure was the East Anglian gentleman Sir John Paston, who earned Margaret's ire when he ignored the judgement of an arbitration her representatives had organised, and refused to leave a contested estate of which he had illegally taken possession. 'You,' Margaret wrote to him, pointing the finger firmly at the man she considered the guilty party, 'by mighty power, keep and withhold' the estate '...without any just title... to our marvel' and in breach of the 'full agreement made and concluded, and also put in writing.' 'We desire,' she continued, 'and also counsel you without delay... to abide' by the existing agreement. The tacit threat was that, if he failed to do so, Margaret would be forced to use her influence with the king to pursue the matter through him.[33] Margaret similarly voiced her royal authority in a letter to the mayor of Coventry, who had failed to settle a dispute with a local burgess despite Margaret's intervention. 'We will,' she wrote, 'and in the King's name command you' to bring the matter to a conclusion, 'so as no complaint be made unto us hereafter... as ye tender the King's pleasure and ours, and the due ministration of justice.'[34] What makes this letter noteworthy is that Margaret had no authority over Coventry, and was clearly acting in her son's place.

One of the most important resources at Margaret's command after 1499 was Collyweston itself. As a satellite royal court, Margaret projected the authority of her dynasty with public displays such as feasts or performances within her household. It appears that she was able to absorb the expenditure such entertainments entailed by administering her territories more effectively. At the turn of the century, she started to undertake local infrastructure works, employing a Flemish engineer to construct a tidal sluice at Boston to limit the increasing impact of floods that were causing the harbour to silt up and damaging the countryside. Embankments and drainage systems were improved and maintained through the diligence of her officers.[35] Her efforts were rewarded: in 1493–4, her Lincolnshire estates yielded her only £266, but a decade later this had risen to £399.[36]

Publicly, Margaret was the ideal vice-regal figure; privately, however, she did not enjoy ostentation for its own sake. As well as being a projection of her power, her home was also a sanctuary for those in need. This dichotomy between Margaret's outer and inner life can be read in two surviving descriptions of her household: those of Henry Parker, Lord Morley, her servant and protégé, and John Fisher, her confessor. Parker entered Margaret's service as an adolescent cupbearer in the early 1490s and raised his family within her household after marrying her great-niece Alice St John. Parker's father had been Richard III's standard bearer at Bosworth, but Margaret saw no reason to hold the father's allegiances against the promising young son, and ensured Parker was well-educated and provided for in her home. The grateful Parker recorded his reminiscences of his life in Margaret's service in a text gifted to her great-granddaughter Queen Mary I at New Year 1556.

For Parker, Margaret's home was a place of conviviality and good cheer. 'She kept so honorable a house' and 'used such humanity' to her visitors that, almost forty years after her death, Parker still fondly remembered 'her fame, her honour, her liberality, her prudence, her chastity and her excellent virtues'. In particular, he was struck by the hospitality of her dinner table, at which he regularly served. Although towards the end of meals Margaret would encourage conversation 'of some godly matter' with a bishop or her chancellor, earlier in the evening she enjoyed hearing Parker or her almoner 'read some virtuous tale', and encouraged the telling of 'tales that were honest to make her merry'.[37] Parker's memories of Margaret were those of a subordinate for a 'benign' mistress – he was particularly struck by her personal attendance on his fellow servants when they fell sick, and her remarkable memory for her attendants' names, even though there were 'two and two score' of them in her household.

By contrast, John Fisher became Margaret's confessor after 1498 and recorded his memories of her in a funeral sermon in July 1509. Theirs was a more equal relationship and, in keeping with his religious status, Fisher cast Margaret as a biblical 'Martha' of the modern age: a pious woman of learning and self-discipline, whose home was a fount of charity and good order, and whose hours were marked by religious observance and rigorous devotion. He praised Margaret as 'bounteous and liberal... merciful also and piteous' in dealing with all those with whom she came into contact, entertaining guests at her home 'according to their degree' while ensuring that 'the poor and needy specially would be relieved and comforted'. He, too, praised Margaret's 'good... remembrance' and 'ready wit', but associated her 'singular wisdom' with typical female virtues. Never 'forgetful of any kindness or service done to her', she expressed 'marvellous gentleness... unto all folks... Unkind she would not be unto no creature.'[38]

Intriguingly, both Parker and Fisher recalled Margaret proclaiming on multiple occasions in later life that she wished she could go on crusade, even if all she was capable of doing was washing the shirts of the Christian soldiers.[39] But Parker did not mention, and presumably did not know as Fisher did, that Margaret also expressed her faith by wearing hair shirts and girdles beneath her fine clothes; nor that she spent hours bending her arthritic knees in private prayer. Nor that many of the fine foods Parker saw delivered to her table ('how honourably she was served', he noted, 'I think few kings better'[40]) went uneaten by his mistress, who preferred 'sober temperance in meats and drinks... keeping always her straight measure and often dining as little as any creature might'.[41] Since Fisher enjoyed a rare, perhaps unique, insight into Margaret's inner spiritual life, it is natural that his account focused on her piety, whereas Henry Parker, whose experience of his mistress was public facing, remembered her for her outward displays of liberality.[42]

Sometimes, Margaret's generosity put her at odds with wider social norms, and even with Henry. Collyweston regularly hosted

Margaret's friends, especially women, and when they found themselves in need, Margaret herself stepped in to protect them.[43] In 1499, her niece Anne St John fled her unhappy marriage to the eccentric and adulterous Lord Henry Clifford and sought shelter at Margaret's home. Anne was the daughter of Margaret's half-brother John and she arrived at Collyweston with two daughters and three servants in tow. They lived with Margaret for eight months while the couple's separation was discussed.[44] Anne ultimately returned to Lord Clifford, but she and Margaret stayed in touch through exchanges of messages and gifts.[45]

Similarly afflicted with challenging husbands, Lady Jane Guildford and Katherine, countess of Devon received financial support from Margaret for themselves and their children when their spouses dragged them into financial or political misfortune. Both women lived mainly at court as servants of Queen Elizabeth, but Jane in particular had a long history with Margaret: she and her brother, Nicholas Vaux, grew up in Margaret's household. The Vaux family had suffered terribly for its Lancastrian allegiance in the Wars of the Roses: their father died at the Battle of Tewkesbury in 1471 and was attainted by Edward IV, stripping his children of their inheritance. Their mother followed Queen Marguerite of Anjou into imprisonment and exile. By February 1478, Dowager Lady Vaux claimed to have 'none earthly thing for her and her children to live upon'.[46] Margaret's charity towards Jane and Nicholas was thus essential to their survival, and never forgotten. In a pedigree written for Nicholas later, it was proudly proclaimed that he 'flourished... in the household of Margaret Countess of Richmond'.[47]

As well as providing a sanctuary for these women and others who resided for extended periods in her home, Margaret also offered legal assistance where necessary.[48] In 1502, Lady Elizabeth Scrope, a regular resident at Collyweston, was barred from taking possession of lands by her stepson.[49] Margaret had an arbitration panel set up under her own chamberlain, Sir Roger Ormeston, who bound Elizabeth's stepson by substantial financial obligations to accept its decision.[50]

But it was not only the high-born who were helped at

Collyweston. In December 1504, Margaret made provision for 'a woman that Hugh Latimer had a child by'.[51] Latimer was one of Margaret's servants, and the unnamed woman with whom he fathered a child was supported by Margaret through her labour and the fortnight following. Margaret also arranged and funded transport to Stamford for both the woman and her new-born baby. What then became of mother and child thereafter is unclear. In the early new year of 1504, 'a poor child' was abandoned at Margaret's doorstep, and Margaret paid for it to be nursed while sending one of her servants to inquire 'for the mother of the child', although apparently without success.[52]

In an era when political allegiances had incited unprecedented bloodshed and morality was publicly expressed, Margaret demonstrated a surprising capacity to navigate moral ambiguities. 'She was not vengeful nor cruel,' wrote John Fisher, 'but ready anon to forget and to forgive injuries done unto her at the least desire or motion made unto her.'[53] Lady Scrope and Henry Parker were from zealously Yorkist families, as was Margaret's carver, Ralph Bigod, whose refusal to hear censure of his one-time master Richard III was infamous. Yet all were patronised by Margaret, and she praised Bigod for remaining 'ever more so true a servant' to the late king.[54]

Margaret also forbore, apparently, to pass judgement on her friends' disordered private lives: Bigod, Margaret's cherished stepson James Stanley and probably Lady Scrope all had illegitimate children, and Jane Guildford had a notably close relationship with a male friend after her husband's death.[55] Despite James Stanley being a priest (and later bishop of Ely), he had at least three children with his housekeeper at Somersham, Huntingdonshire. Intriguingly, James Stanley's only daughter was named Margaret, and was born around 1480, meaning it is possible that James's stepmother acted as her godmother. The existence of Margaret Stanley and her brothers was well known within the family, and she married the Lancashire gentleman Henry Halsall, who served in Scotland with James's brother George in 1497. He was even ultimately knighted by him. Margaret Stanley-Halsall predeceased her father but both of her brothers were made executors of their father's will.[56] James's sexual indiscretions did not prevent him being a close ally of Margaret in many of her endeavours, nor her from using his palace at Hatfield as a second home in the last years of her life.[57]

These relationships grew more important to Margaret after she left the royal court and saw less of the royal family, and, on at least one occasion, Margaret chose to protect a friend in defiance of her son's wishes. In February 1499, Cecily of York was widowed by the death of Margaret's half-brother John, Lord Welles. John and Cecily had lived at court with Margaret and her family ever since Bosworth, and in his will John defined himself by his kinship and allegiance to Henry. He proudly proclaimed himself 'uncle to the king... and brother to the right noble Princess Margaret Countess of Richmond, natural and dear mother to our said sovereign lord king'.[58] As a sign of his incorporation into the Tudor clan, John was buried in what was to become a family mausoleum, in the Lady Chapel at Westminster Abbey where ultimately Margaret, Henry and Elizabeth would also be buried. But, despite the closeness that Cecily and John had enjoyed with the royal family, her remarriage in 1502 caused a rupture with Henry and Elizabeth.

Cecily's second husband was a lowly squire, Thomas Kyme of Friskney in Lincolnshire, and – probably because of Kyme's status – Cecily married without Henry's permission. For the sister-in-law of the king to stoop so low – and to thus circumvent any plans Henry himself might have had for her remarriage – insulted royal honour. Henry banished Cecily and attempted to occupy the Welles estates that she had inherited from John. Perhaps Elizabeth of York also found her sister's match degrading, as she made no sisterly efforts to protect Cecily from the king's wrath. Instead, it fell to Margaret to shelter her. Margaret welcomed Cecily and her new husband at Collyweston while she negotiated personally with Henry to protect some of Cecily's estates. Riders were dispatched to gather the necessary paperwork to support Margaret's efforts, and in 1503 a settlement was agreed between Cecily and the crown. Although Cecily had to surrender certain Lincolnshire manors to Henry, and promise him the remainder of her estates for ten years after her death, she was permitted to hold most of her lands for her lifetime. Her husband was pardoned any fines for occupying her lands, and did not have to pay a potentially bankrupting fee for illicit remarriage. Cecily thus got off far more lightly than her aunt Katherine Woodville, dowager duchess of Buckingham and Bedford, whose penalty for a disparaging remarriage was so financially stringent that, even after her death, her son was almost crippled by it.[59]

Margaret evidently felt no resentment towards Cecily for remarrying after her brother's death. Cecily continued to regularly visit Collyweston after 1502, and had a special chamber reserved for her at Croydon Palace (which Margaret used as a secondary base) in 1506. In 1504, no doubt at Margaret's suggestion, Cecily enrolled in St Katherine's Guild in Stamford.[60] Theirs was a friendship that endured until Cecily's death in August 1507. She died in Margaret's home and was nursed through her last illness, then honourably buried, at Margaret's expense.[61]

However, Margaret's disagreement with Henry over the treatment of Cecily Welles was an unusual friction in a relationship that was largely harmonious. Henry implicitly trusted his mother to see to his interests. 'I know well,' he wrote in a letter to her in September 1503, 'that I am as much bound… [to you] as any creature living, for the great and singular motherly love and affection that it hath pleased you at all times to bear towards me.'[62] In turn, Margaret was an unfailing servant: 'I and all that God has given me,' she told him, 'is and shall ever [be] at your will and commandment.'[63] Even when she lived at a distance from him, Margaret's first loyalty would always be to her son.

21

'All that God has given me'[1]

✳

In summer 1499, the Tower of London was the hushed eye of a tempest of clandestine activity. In dark corners, secret tokens were exchanged – coins bitten and bent in half, metal tags cut from hoods, a book of prophecy and letter cipher smuggled into the Tower to create coded messages. A servant of the lieutenant of the Tower even managed to sneak in a file and hammer, for a prisoner 'to cut and break the iron bar of the window of his prison, and… break and unloose the chains wherewith he was bound'.[2] The focus of these covert activities was a turret in which two highly sensitive prisoners were stacked one cell on top of the other: below, the unfortunate Perkin Warbeck chipped away at the shackles chaining him to the wall; above, the child-like Edward, earl of Warwick gleefully contemplated his imminent escape. Warwick had been a prisoner for more than half his life. Margaret's one-time ward and son of George, duke of Clarence was twenty-four but, as Polydore Vergil put it, he had been so long 'removed from the sight of man and beast that he could not easily tell a chicken from a goose'.[3] Despite Warwick's unsuitability for rule, he was still the male heir of York and for the past year and a half his right to the throne had been resurrected by those 'professing to be versed in prophecies'. Referring to their books of divination, they whispered to their merchant neighbours 'that the bear would shortly beat his chains within the city of London'.[4] The chained bear was the Warwick coat of arms. Soon, these plotters insisted, Warwick would be free to rule.

The English were obsessed with prophecies; the Welsh even more so.[5] Along with a taste for Welsh rhymers and Llanthony cheese, Henry had inherited his ancestors' proclivity for fortune-telling.[6] His account books saw frequent payments to astronomers or priests for 'making a prognostication'.[7] Margaret was not immune to these acts of divination, buying an astronomical calendar for herself in 1506, but her real interest in prophecy probably lay in its power to influence minds.[8] Both she and Henry had circulated the story of holy King Henry VI's prediction of the Tudor accession, and promoted his cult as a saint to bolster the Lancastrian association with the present ruling dynasty. Margaret also saw the benefits to be gleaned from assertions of Henry's mythic descent from Cadwaladr, and of the circumstances surrounding Prince Arthur's birth at Winchester. But the English impulse to prophesy could also work against the Tudors, as the whispers about Warwick's restoration demonstrated. Henry's spies in the capital had learned by summer 1499 that the chained-bear prophecies were not merely being repeated, they were motivating citizens to actively conspire for Warwick.

Already that year, Henry had had to quash more than one pretender inspired by visions of future greatness. Among the reeds and mosquitoes of Cambridge, the teenage son of a cordwainer had dreamed that he was anointed king. Groomed by a local priest, this 'new mawmet' [false idol] called himself the earl of Warwick, hoping to become a second Lambert Simnel. Instead, the earl of Oxford had him arrested and Henry convicted him of treason. On Shrove Tuesday 1499, the boy was hanged in his shirt at St Thomas-a-Watering on the pilgrim's route to Canterbury,* and left dangling until the Saturday following, when his corpse was cut down to assuage the 'annoyance of the way passers'.[9]

More seriously, the week after Midsummer 1499, the earl of Warwick's cousin Edmund de la Pole, earl of Suffolk suddenly fled the realm without royal approval.† Headstrong, arrogant

---

* The first rest stop on the pilgrim's road from London. It is now the junction of Old Kent Road and Albany Road.
† Edmund de la Pole's mother was Elizabeth, sister of Edward IV, Richard III and George, duke of Clarence.

and touchy, Suffolk had suffered one indignity after another under the Tudor regime. 'Oppressed by debt', he had been pursued through the courts for a death resulting from a brawl in late 1498.[10] Other courtiers were able to escape the public humiliation of trial, but Suffolk was indicted for murder at Westminster Hall by Reynald Bray. Unable to endure this dishonour at the hands of a low-born upstart, Suffolk fled to St Omer in the Habsburg Netherlands, presumably en route to the court of the duchess of Burgundy, to once again raise the spectre of a Yorkist coup. Acting swiftly to prevent Suffolk securing sanctuary on the Continent, Henry threatened Flanders with a trade embargo if the Yorkist was permitted to stay. Meanwhile, two English messengers, one Henry's master of the ordnance, Sir Richard Guildford, were sent directly to Suffolk to warn him that if he did not return peaceably to England now, 'he may never look to recover nor come [home] again'.[11] Chastened and perhaps a little disappointed with his reception on the Continent, Suffolk accepted Henry's offer of grace. But he was not fully reconciled.

The danger of asking what the future held, of course, was that you might learn something unpleasant. In spring 1499, not long after Queen Elizabeth had delivered her latest child – a prince named Edmund, probably at Margaret's request[12] – Henry made the mistake of asking a fortune-telling priest when he would die. The priest had allegedly foretold the deaths of Edward IV and Richard III, and Henry sought reassurance about the future of his family. 'According to common report,' as the Spanish ambassador heard, Henry was warned 'that his life would be in great danger during the whole year.' He must beware of the warring factions within his kingdom.[13] Not wishing the prophecy to inspire further conspiracy among his subjects, Henry swore the priest to secrecy, but inevitably word seeped out. The priest escaped retribution but one of those heard repeating his prediction was thrown in prison.[14] The prophecy was less of a concern for Henry than the fact the Spanish ambassador heard of it, and relayed it to his rulers. For the greatest danger to Henry's family at this time was not his own mortality, since there were now three princes and two princesses to continue the dynasty. Henry's worst fear was that political uncertainty in England would doom the alliance that had been the lynchpin of his international policy for over a decade: the Anglo-Spanish treaty, which was to be cemented by the marriage of the Infanta Catalina (Katherine) of Aragon to Prince Arthur.

In September 1499, Margaret's eldest grandchild would be thirteen. Should Henry's terrible prophecy come to pass, Arthur would not be old enough to rule independently, but he could succeed with the help of a council. And he was certainly old enough to marry. Although Arthur had been growing to manhood in the solitude of his court at Ludlow, Margaret probably kept a close watch over his development through the reports of the kinsmen and friends she maintained in his household. Her nephew Sir Richard Pole was Arthur's chamberlain, and her protégé William Smith, bishop of Lincoln, served on both Arthur's and Margaret's councils. She even had a source among Arthur's youthful companions, as within their number was John, Lord Grey of Powys, whose mother often resided with Margaret at Collyweston. From them Margaret gathered that Arthur had the same innate capacity for learning that she and Henry had demonstrated in their youth. Unlike Margaret, he also had excellent Latin. The prince did not regularly attend the royal court, but he had visited occasionally, allowing Margaret to see for herself how he combined the best attributes of the Houses of York and Lancaster: he had the height and copper hair of his mother's kin; and the circumspection, concentration and lean features of his father. In him, the warring roses were unified.

In May 1499, Arthur took his first steps onto the international political stage, marking the most significant advance in the Anglo-Spanish union in years. At Whitsunday (19 May) 1499, in the chapel of Bewdley, Hertfordshire, he was married by proxy to Katherine of Aragon. Margaret was not present – nor, indeed, was the bride, who was represented by her notoriously gluttonous ambassador Rodrigo González de la Puebla – but some of Margaret's most influential allies were in attendance. Bishop Smith was a witness and Sir Richard Pole was the lynchpin of the whole ceremony, binding the hands of Arthur and De Puebla as they vowed the 'indissoluble marriage' of Arthur to Katherine.[15] For all the apparent certainty of the rhetoric, the union was still very much dissoluble and, until Katherine actually reached England and consummated the marriage, there was still a danger that this alliance could collapse.

Aware of the high stakes involved, Margaret did everything in her power to bring the match to fruition, often working alongside Queen Elizabeth. In several of Rodrigo De Puebla's reports to Ferdinand and Isabella, he referred to 'the Queen and the Mother of the King' acting in concert: both were present during a four-hour private audience held by De Puebla and Henry in July 1498, during which letters were presented from their potential in-laws. For some months, both Margaret and Elizabeth provided gentle encouragement for Princess Katherine's coming to England 'as soon as possible' in letters to Queen Isabella, as well as in audiences with the Spanish ambassador. 'The earlier she comes, they say, the easier will she learn the language and assume the customs of the country.'[16] They also provided valuable insights into these native customs for the future Princess of Wales, advising that she practise her French, since English 'ladies do not understand Latin' (in which Katherine was proficient) 'and much less, Spanish'. Knowing that Queen Isabella was teetotal, they also suggested Katherine grow accustomed to drinking wine, as English water was not generally safe to drink.[17] De Puebla's bitter rival, the Spanish ambassador to Scotland Don Pedro de Ayala, disagreed with his compatriot on almost everything but he too described Margaret and Elizabeth as presenting a united front in international affairs.[18]

But, despite their efforts, and even after the proxy marriage of Arthur and Katherine, still the princess did not set sail. The treaty had promised that Katherine would arrive before Arthur's fourteenth year was over, but that deadline loomed ever closer with no sign of progress. This hesitancy to send Katherine was partly inspired – and could certainly be justified – by the lingering dynastic threats in England. The royal family had attempted to allay these concerns without success. After Perkin Warbeck briefly escaped Henry's custody in 1498, the king had taken care to alert the Spanish ambassador 'the same hour that he was arrested', and had allowed him to visit the pretender in prison so he could see for himself that Warbeck was kept so tightly he saw 'neither sun nor moon'.[19] Henry's swift and merciless treatment of the Cambridgeshire 'mawmet', and eagerness to repatriate Edmund de la Pole, were similarly intended to reassure the Spanish. Now the latest dynastic threat – the conspiracy swirling around Warwick within the Tower of London – was growing sufficiently menacing that it also needed to be crushed.

Henry and his closest advisers – among whom, according to the Spanish ambassador Pedro de Ayala, was Margaret – had probably been monitoring the Warwick conspiracy for some time, and certainly knew of it by early August 1499 when one of the plotters confessed. The scheme was so elaborate that at first it sounded highly improbable: the plotters intended to ransack the royal treasury, seize the Tower, fire the royal ordnance with its own gunpowder and escape overseas in a wool ship to raise an insurrection against Henry.[20] Confident that the plot posed no immediate threat, Henry and his counsellors watched and waited, gathering enough information to implicate the leading conspirators and eradicate them. They particularly sought to snare Warwick and his accomplice Perkin Warbeck.

However, when it appeared that the continued existence of these pretenders posed a threat to the Anglo-Spanish match, the trap was sprung. In November, Warwick, Warbeck and their co-conspirators were arrested and condemned as traitors. On 29 November, Warwick enjoyed the relative mercy of a short walk to Tower Hill followed by beheading, but Warbeck and the other lower-born plotters were sent to Tyburn. Warbeck's execution on Saturday 23 November drew enormous crowds and, while it was generally agreed that he must die, popular opinion opposed him receiving the tortuous traitor's death of hanging, drawing and quartering.[21] As a compromise, he was sentenced merely to hang. In his scaffold speech Warbeck declared 'that he never was the person which he was named [i.e. Richard of York]… but a stranger born' overseas. Perhaps he hoped the confession would save him, but his luck had run out. The pretender who had bedevilled Margaret's family for almost a decade was executed.[22]

Margaret is unlikely to have felt much remorse for Warbeck's death, but the execution of the unworldly Warwick may have troubled her. Politically, his removal could be, and was, justified for it ensured that – as De Puebla put it – not 'a drop of doubtful royal blood' remained in the kingdom.[23] Henry's own physician-astrologer, William Parron, wrote in a manuscript of that year that, 'it is expedient that one man should die for the people and the whole nation perish not'.[24] But morally Warwick's death was highly ambiguous, and Margaret is likely to have felt that ambiguity more than Henry. Warwick's sister, Margaret Pole, was a long-standing friend, married to Margaret's nephew Richard Pole and at the time of Warwick's death five months pregnant. As Margaret had herself once been Warwick's guardian, she may also have regretted the necessary tragedy of his fate.

Moreover, with her encyclopaedic knowledge of noble ancestry, Margaret knew that De Puebla was wrong. A considerable stock of 'doubtful royal blood' continued to pulse through the veins of England's courtiers: Henry's full-blood relatives were dwindling almost to non-existence, but among the cousins of Elizabeth of York were many young bucks perfecting their martial skills in tournaments, whose Yorkist descent could be revived if they grew frustrated with the Tudor regime. These noble youths inclined to be haughty and ambitious, like Edmund, duke of Suffolk and his brother Richard de la Pole; Thomas Grey, marquess of Dorset; Henry Bourchier, earl of Essex; William Courtenay, earl of Devon. Fortunately, as a new century dawned, these potential Yorkist agitators seemed to be reconciled to Henry's rule. 'England has never before been so tranquil and obedient as at present,' wrote De Puebla in January 1500.[25]

Yet political stability could not insulate Margaret's family from all danger. That year, her long-held terror, the plague, returned to England. Polydore Vergil claimed the sickness killed 30,000 in London, an inflated sum that nonetheless testifies to the very real sense of threat to the population at large.[26] Those who could afford it, including the royal family, fled the contagion that was rife in the cities. Prince Arthur was far removed at Ludlow, his sisters and Prince Henry safe in Eltham, and the infant Prince Edmund was immediately sent to the rural retreat of the bishop of Ely at Hatfield. Country air, it was believed, was safest at such times.

While Margaret probably remained at Collyweston,[27] Henry and Elizabeth fled the realm to escape the sickness. They crossed the English Channel on 8 May 1500, hoping to capitalise on their relative domestic security by holding a diplomatic meeting with Duke Philip of Burgundy in the Calais Pale.[28]

They returned to the devastating news that the son born to them only sixteen months earlier – Prince Edmund – had died. It is possible that Edmund was a victim of the sickness sweeping the country. Henry paid over £242 for the prince's burial, with a stately procession through London to Westminster Abbey, where Prince Edmund was buried beside his sister Elizabeth at the tomb of Edward the Confessor.[29] It seemed more imperative than ever to protect the future of the dynasty, and press forward with Arthur's marriage.

KATHERINE FINALLY SET FOOT ON ENGLISH SOIL ON THE afternoon of 2 October 1501. She had been a long time coming. It was six months since Margaret had first begun to prepare Coldharbour to accommodate the Spanish entourage attending Katherine, which was originally scheduled to reach London on 25 May. As well as improvements to the fabric of her palace, Margaret also ensured there was a supply of 'oranges, sugar and honey' so any of her guests with a sweet tooth could savour a taste of home.[30] Meanwhile, Margaret and Elizabeth had consulted about which Englishmen and -women should best serve the new Princess of Wales when she surrendered her Spanish household, compiling a 'remembrance' that listed her intended servants. This included experienced and reliable women like Margaret's good friend Elizabeth, duchess of Norfolk, who was to be Katherine's chief English companion when she landed, and Lady Jane Guildford, who was seconded from her usual duties with Princesses Mary and Margaret.[31] Some positions on the 'remembrance' were left blank, awaiting further discussion between Margaret and Elizabeth.[32]

But, in late May 1501, Katherine had still been in Granada, at the southernmost tip of her parents' territories. The Muslim population of the kingdom of Granada had been in rebellion since 1499, and Ferdinand had to suppress the rising before the Infanta could leave for England. Then Katherine caught a fever. Then Isabella had a fever. By the time Ferdinand returned from quashing the Moorish rebellion to bid his daughter farewell, Katherine's fever had intensified. Her journey north through the shimmering Spanish heat was punctuated by frequent pauses to rest and recuperate. Even once the princess boarded a ship at Laredo, she was driven back to port by fierce storms.[33] To prevent further delays, Henry 'sent one of his best captains, Stephen Butt' to steer Katherine's fleet to England.[34] Little wonder that, by the time word arrived in England that Katherine had finally boarded a vessel that had successfully weighed anchor from Spain, Margaret deemed the event sufficiently noteworthy to commemorate it in her Book of Hours: 'This day... my lady Princess took her ship towards England in the year of our lord 1501.'[35] It was now twelve years since Katherine's marriage to Arthur had first been arranged.

In the end, only six days separated Margaret's record of Katherine's departure from Spain and her landing in England, at Plymouth, at three o'clock in the afternoon of 2 October 1501. There the duchess of Norfolk and 'a goodly company... of countesses, baronesses and many other honourable gentlewomen' finally met their new princess, and shortly after so too did Henry and Arthur. They were so eager to see Katherine that they raced to her accommodation at Dogmersfield in Hampshire while she was still recovering from her journey. Mildly startled, Katherine did credit to her princely upbringing and greeted her father-in-law and husband with 'great joy and gladness', celebrating throughout the afternoon and on into the evening. Arthur and Katherine communicated in Latin, using the attendant bishops as interpreters when needed. After supper, Katherine 'and her ladies let call their minstrels and with right goodly behaviour and manner they solaced themselves with the disports of dancing'. Although at some point that day Arthur and Katherine were, again, 'spousally ensured' to each other, the prince refrained from taking his young wife by the hand in the dance, and instead chastely partnered Lady Jane Guildford.[36] Then, Arthur bade his bride farewell and rode with

Henry back towards London, to tell Elizabeth and Margaret 'how he liked [Katherine's] person and behavior', while Katherine made a more leisurely progress, showing herself to her future subjects as she wound towards the capital.[37]

On the day that Katherine finally entered London, 12 November, Margaret joined Henry, Elizabeth, Thomas and her granddaughters to observe the princess's entrance from a distance. 'Festivities such as never before were witnessed in England' were laid on for Katherine, with six dramatic pageants arranged to entertain her as she proceeded through the cramped city streets towards St Paul's Cathedral from Lambeth.[38] Margaret was positioned close to the penultimate pageant, opposite the Standard conduit in Cheapside, inside the home of William Geoffrey, a haberdasher who had been accorded the honour of hosting them for the afternoon. There, 'privily and secretly' from within a lady's chamber, Margaret peered out as the citizens of London gathered around a remarkable display of dynastic heraldry: a 'temple' constructed on top of the conduit, in which a giant red rose as tall as a man was flanked by the Tudor dragon and Richmond greyhound. Burning wax tapers illuminated the pageant, surrounded by golden-winged angels who sang throughout 'with a sweet and solemn noise'. 'Above, in windows, leads, gutters and battlements,' wrote the author of the *Receyt of the Ladye Kateryne*, the official record of the pageants, 'stood many of the Yeomen of the Guard and also beneath in the street the servants of' the nobility, 'with other divers [people] to a great and a huge number on both the sides of the street.' To protect the onlookers from 'the spring of the horsemen' as Katherine's entourage approached, a railed platform had been constructed two feet above the pavement for the wealthier citizens.[39]

Katherine was accompanied into the City over London Bridge by the leading noblemen of the realm, including her brother-in-law, ten-year-old Prince Henry, Margaret's ward the duke of Buckingham and stepson Lord Strange.[40] Since all the pageants through which she was hurried included lengthy speeches in English, which Katherine could not understand, she was probably glad of the extraordinary visual imagery of the tableaux. Built into the street furniture of conduits and bridges, the pageants were platforms for the costumed performers and astonishing scenic backdrops full of moving parts and painted imagery. Being well-educated, Katherine may have grasped some of the occasionally obscure classical, astronomical and biblical allusions of the performances, which were constructed around her progress from an earthly realm to the celestial, encountering various saints and stars on the journey.

From Master Geoffrey's chamber at Cheapside, Margaret caught her first glimpse of Katherine late in the afternoon, riding 'upon a great mule richly trapped after the manner of Spain'.[41] Cheers erupting from the Great Conduit marked the approach of the princess, preceding the shouts and stamps of the city officials and royal heralds, who 'divided the common people right orderly' to create a passage for her. Tinkling silver bells on the horse harness of the earl of Essex's men were drowned out by the blast of Spanish trumpets, shawms and sackbuts. And only after the leading citizens of London, the noblemen of England and of Spain and the bishops had passed by could Margaret properly see Katherine, flanked on one hand by Prince Henry, and on the other by a legate of Rome. She was dressed in the Spanish fashion, her features somewhat obscured by a little cardinal's hat perched atop a carnation-coloured coif. Visible to all, however, was her long auburn hair, which hung down around her shoulders.

Katherine's Spanish apparel was a calculated choice that proudly proclaimed her nationality, ensuring all who saw her knew that the English royal family had gained a vital international partner. Katherine also made a subtle reference to her parents' recent military success in the far south of Spain: riding in chariots towards the back of her train were two attendants whom the author of the *Receyt* described as 'not the fairest women of the company'.[42] Probably, they were Granadans, and may have been the same enslaved young women who were listed among Katherine's attendants in Spanish household accounts. The London lawyer Thomas More, an eyewitness, described Katherine's retinue as containing 'Ethiopians' – a catch-all term used by many white Europeans for people of colour. The notice paid by both More and the author of the *Receyt* to these attendants' clothing, which More associated with ghostly winding sheets and misinterpreted as bare feet, suggests the women were probably dressed in the traditional Granadan fashion of sandals and amalfas, to emphasise the domination of Katherine's family over Muslim Granada.[43]

Katherine's entourage paused in front of the royal vantage point in William Geoffrey's house, to watch the pageants and be stared at by her in-laws. By now, though, daylight was fading and Katherine was ushered on to the last pageant and her accommodation in the Bishop's Palace beside St Paul's Cathedral. From her first distant sighting of Katherine, Margaret could appraise the princess's composure and beauty, but she only really learned about the young woman who would one day be Queen of England when Katherine called at Baynards Castle to meet Elizabeth the following day, Saturday 13 November. Margaret encountered a formidably well-educated princess, capable of conversing comfortably in Latin as well as Italian (although still not English), and as well schooled in devotional works as the feminine art of embroidery. Katherine had spent most of her life travelling, celebrating sixteen Christmases in Spain, in thirteen different cities. For the last two years, her primary homes had been the Alhambra in Granada and the Alcázar in Seville, where she enjoyed the architecture and culture of the Muslims her parents had slaughtered and enslaved. Despite growing up in the dry heat of southern Spain, Katherine's fair skin testified to a life spent behind veils and under marble walkways. Her hair was as copper-coloured as Arthur's and she shared with him, too, the customary royal accomplishments of falconry, horse riding, hunting, music and dancing – although unlike Arthur her earliest steed had been a mule, not a horse.

As for her character, that probably took some time to emerge. Like Margaret, perhaps even more so, Katherine had been schooled from infancy in physical and emotional self-restraint. Her mother, Isabella, was known to be an intensely loving and humorous individual, prone to outbursts of joy; when reunited with her eldest daughter once she hugged her child so hard they both fell to the ground. But this open nature was eclipsed by deep bouts of depression and jealousy. Katherine would ultimately demonstrate a depth of resolve and passion to rival her mother's, but there was likely little sign of it when she met Margaret in 1501.[44] Nonetheless, everyone was delighted with Katherine. She seemed the perfect companion to their precious Prince Arthur. He wrote to his new parents-in-law insisting that he 'had never felt so much joy in his life as when he beheld the sweet face of his bride. No woman in the world could be more agreeable to him.'[45]

The couple were formally married at St Paul's Cathedral two days after Katherine's arrival, on 14 November. Bride and groom both wore white satin, and so many people attended that the author of the *Receyt* reported that, wherever you looked, you could 'behold nothing but visages'.[46] After a celebratory banquet in the Bishop's Palace, a specially chosen group of ladies including Elizabeth, duchess of Norfolk and Lady Jane Guildford was dispatched to prepare the marital 'chamber and bed'. The preparations apparently took two or three hours, during which Katherine herself was 'reverently laid and reposed' in the bed, then the earl of Oxford accompanied Arthur to the bedchamber and 'the day, thus with joy, mirth and gladness deduced to its end'.[47]

While the young couple recovered on the morning after the wedding, Margaret and Thomas took charge of court affairs. Margaret hosted a dinner for the Spanish at Coldharbour, after which Thomas escorted them to supper in his lodgings. That afternoon the whole court travelled upriver to Westminster for the chief diversions of the wedding celebrations: the tournaments. The royal jousts – watched enthusiastically by Margaret, her namesake granddaughter and her grandson Prince Henry – occupied an entire week, except for one notably wet Saturday when rain stopped play. Margaret's youngest granddaughter, Princess Mary, only five years old, sat through the first day but was spared the others.[48]

This pageantry was merely an appetiser, however, for the last course of the wedding feast: the court's first visit to the newly built Richmond Palace. They arrived 'very late, in the silence of the evening' on Friday 26 November, gaining their first glimpse of the 'mighty brick wall' and towers looming above the River Thames by the light of 300 torches. The palace had been built to replace the fire-damaged Sheen Palace, the works overseen by the same Prior Ingleby of the Charterhouse who had once saved

Perkin Warbeck's life.[49] The palace was named Richmond in honour of Henry's comital title – a name that reflected honour on 'Margaret R', the famed countess of Richmond who had valiantly defended her son's right to the estate. The palace was almost a love letter from son to parent, an expression in tile and timber, freestone and marble, glazed, painted, tapestried and limed, of the ascendancy of Margaret's family – and a legacy that would survive her to be enjoyed, they hoped, long into the future by Arthur and Katherine's children and grandchildren. In this 'bright and shining star of building' and 'earthly and second paradise', this 'beauteous exemplar of all proper lodgings' (as the author of the *Receyt* breathlessly described it), Katherine enjoyed her last hours with her Spanish attendants. Here they danced in 'pleasant' chambers and wandered through passages inlaid with badges of gold, showing roses and portcullises. It was almost December and the herb gardens with their intricate patterns of knots and painted beasts were beaded with frost, but there were plenty of entertainments to distract them indoors: chess, backgammon, dice, cards, bowling, archery and tennis. The palace also provided for Margaret's devotional activities: to the left of Henry's chapel, and next to that of Elizabeth and her attendants, she had her own private closet.[50]

On the penultimate day of their visit, the Spanish entertained their hosts with bass dances in the hall and a remarkable performance by a tightrope-walker who leaped about while juggling tennis balls and dancing with bells, even throwing 'himself suddenly from the rope' to 'hang by the toes, sometimes by the teeth'.[51] As a parting extravagance, white doves and birds were released into the great hall, causing 'great laughter and disport', as rabbits skittered between the courtiers' feet.

On Monday 29 November, Margaret watched Katherine bid farewell to her Spanish attendants, handing over letters and messages to take home to her parents. It was likely Katherine would never see her beloved mother and father again – a fact that made the princess understandably 'pensive'. To assuage her melancholy, Henry summoned Katherine and her ladies to the magnificent new library he had constructed, encouraging her to take solace in the manuscripts and printed works there in Latin, French and English. He also arranged for his jeweller to visit, and encouraged Katherine to choose whichever jewel best pleased her to take away for herself. Then her Spanish ladies had their choice, and finally her English attendants.[52]

Perhaps Margaret saw in Katherine a foreshadowing of what was to come: her own two precious granddaughters must also leave their families for foreign shores when they married. Already preparations were underway for the next alliance to ensure the family's security: on 24 January 1502, Princess Margaret was betrothed to King James IV of Scotland.[53] Although a proxy marriage was swiftly held, Margaret and Elizabeth did all they could to delay her departure. Legally, the twelve-year-old Princess Margaret could immediately marry her twenty-eight-year-old husband, but her mother and grandmother insisted that the princess ought to be 'married much later than other young ladies' because she suffered from a slight build and weak constitution.[54] If the princess was sent 'directly to Scotland… they fear the King of Scots would not wait' (i.e. to consummate the marriage), 'but injure her, and endanger her health'.[55] By coincidence, the age difference between the princess and King James was almost exactly the same as Margaret's had been to Edmund Tudor. She had good reason to fear the result of sending a child-bride to the home of her adult husband too early. An eighteen-month deferral was put in place, delaying Princess Margaret's departure until summer 1503.

Sexual activity was a concern for all the royal children. Arthur and Katherine were in their mid-teens, but Henry, Elizabeth and presumably Margaret, too, were reluctant to let the young couple embark on a full marital life together, far removed from parental supervision at Ludlow. There was concern that Arthur might over-indulge his lust for his wife and thus harm his developing constitution – and potentially also hers. For this reason, Henry had intended to keep Arthur and Katherine at his court for a year after marriage, and possibly even to insist that they maintain separate households for another year after that.[56] But, by late December, Arthur sought to return to the government of Wales, and it was evident that he and Katherine did not wish to be parted. The elders bowed to the wishes of the couple and, on 21 December 1501, Katherine and Arthur left his family and set out for Ludlow Castle, taking with them Margaret's nephew Sir Richard Pole and his wife, Lady Margaret Pole. No doubt the king's mother hoped that, at some safe moment within the next few years, the union would be blessed with children – great-grandchildren to continue the family far into the future.

22

'A manifold grief'[1]

✳

Through foul rain and bitter winds, Nicholas Aughton spurred his horse towards Collyweston. In the three years or so he had been in Margaret's service, Aughton had grown accustomed to long journeys as he ferried important messages from his mistress to bishops and lords. England was no friend to the medieval messenger, prey to roads that were more mud than stone and dependent on the maintenance of bridges by local benefactors. It was not unknown for the ruts in roads to fill with rainwater and drown the unwary traveller. But no task Aughton had faced before had been as serious – nor confronted with such dire inclemency – as this. The roads east from Ludlow Castle verged on impassable, wagons mired in mud so deep that oxen were needed to pull them loose. And the news that Aughton brought Margaret was the worst imaginable.[2]

Her grandson Prince Arthur was dying. It was not clear at first how serious the illness that afflicted him that spring was, nor even its precise cause. The author of the *Receyt* simply called it 'a lamentable and... most pitiful disease'. It may have been cancer, or tuberculosis. There was suspicion that Arthur had over-indulged his sexual appetites with his new wife and, being young and tender, his constitution could not withstand his activities. Such a fate, it was said, had also befallen Katherine's brother Juan, and he had been three years older than Arthur when he married. All the worst anxieties that Margaret and Elizabeth had shared for Princess Margaret – that marriage too swiftly consummated would injure her – had instead befallen Prince Arthur. Was there guilt that they had been looking in the wrong direction?

Margaret's grandchildren had been much on her mind that spring. On 17 March, she had sent a small token in the shape of a 'boat royal' to her granddaughter Princess Margaret, now proudly titled 'the lady of Scotland', and in April she was preparing a little keepsake of a golden garter for her grandsons, one for Arthur and one for Henry. She expected Arthur to recover. But, steadily and inexorably, 'the deadly corruption did utterly vanquish and overcome... the lively spirits of this noble prince'.[3] On 2 April 1502, after only five months of marriage, Prince Arthur died. The future that Margaret, and all England, had envisaged for a decade and a half was swept away in an instant.[4]

AT GREENWICH, FAR TO THE SOUTH, HENRY WAS ROUSED FROM sleep before his accustomed hour on Tuesday 5 April. At the door of his chamber was his confessor, a grey-habited and austere Franciscan friar. After making his customary obeisance, the confessor immediately quoted a sobering Latin text: *Si bona de manu Dei suscipimus, mala autem quare non sustineamus?* It was a quotation from the Book of Job: *If we have received good things at the hand of God, why should we not also endure evil?* Margaret could scarcely have put it better herself. But even the pessimistic Beaufort worldview could hardly have prepared the family for this. The bright hope of the Tudor dynasty, snuffed out in an instant. It was Margaret's nephew, Arthur's chamberlain Sir Richard Pole, who had sent word of the prince's death to the king, the messenger covering 150 miles in little more than two days.

As soon as Henry was informed, he called his wife to his chamber and broke the news to Elizabeth himself in private, 'saying that he and his queen would take the painful sorrows together'.[5] In the report of this tragedy left by the author of the *Receyt*, we learn much about the dynamic of the royal couple's relationship: that Henry would only trust his distress to his wife and that, despite the extremity of her grief, Elizabeth demonstrated a remarkable capacity for selfless support – a characteristic that suggests why she was so loved and respected by both Henry and Margaret. Instead of giving way to her 'natural and painful sorrow' at the loss of her son, Elizabeth's first impulse was to soothe her husband. She offered him 'full great and constant comfortable words', beseeching him to 'remember the welfare of his own noble person' before all else. She recognised that the loss of Arthur was not merely a personal bereavement, but the destruction of their carefully tended hopes for the future. Nonetheless, she reminded Henry of the good fortune that had brought them all to the crown, through Margaret: 'My lady his mother had never no more children but him only, and... God by his Grace had ever preserved [Henry] and brought him where that he was.' Moreover, 'God had lent them yet a fair, goodly and towardly young prince and two fair princesses', who could continue the dynasty. 'And we [are] both young enough', Elizabeth concluded, to have more children yet. Given how seriously Elizabeth's health had been endangered by childbirth, this was a courageous suggestion.[6]

Having done her duty and comforted her husband, Elizabeth returned to her own chamber, and it was only there, doors closed to outer eyes, that she permitted herself to surrender to her grief. The 'natural and motherly remembrance of that great loss smote her so sorrowful to the heart that those that were about her' were seriously alarmed. Henry was sent for, and now he became the comforter. 'Of true, gentle and faithful love in good haste [he] came and relieved her.' It is a truly poignant insight into their marriage.[7]

At Collyweston, Margaret was geographically closer to Ludlow, but the record of her book of accounts suggests that she received the news of Arthur's death later the same day that Henry was informed at Greenwich.[8] Even in the extremes of bereavement, royal protocol must be followed. Just like Elizabeth, Margaret's first instinct was to comfort Henry. Nicholas Aughton barely paused at Collyweston before he was back on horseback and making for Greenwich. In his wake came more of Margaret's men.[9] Precisely what messages they bore to Margaret's 'dearest and only desired joy in this world' are lost.[10] All the same, what little 'good and most loving writing' she could provide was surely appreciated by her 'most humble and loving son'.[11]

Once assured of Henry's wellbeing, Margaret sought out her connections at Ludlow to learn more about the cause of Arthur's death, and the state of his young widow. Her groom, Richard Carre, was dispatched as emissary to the prince's household, now suddenly consumed with preparations for Arthur's funeral. Perhaps Margaret offered advice on the topic. Few in England could match her experience of royal bereavement.

Arthur's body remained at Ludlow for three weeks before, having been disembowelled, embalmed and wrapped in a winding sheet, it was removed to Worcester Cathedral on the afternoon of St George's Day (23 April). Tradition, and appalling weather conditions – 'the foulest, cold, windy and rainy day... that I have seen' reported one of the entourage that slowly made its way to Worcester – meant none of Arthur's family were in attendance at his burial on 1 May. But the occasion was still commemorated with all the sombre pageantry that the Tudor dynasty could muster.[12] More than a thousand lights flickered around Arthur's corpse in the cathedral, their heat stirring the damp air and unfurling the banners that encircled him: those of the king his father, the queen his mother, Katherine's royal Spanish parents, of the Prince of Wales, of Cadwaladr, of the lost French territories of old English kings, Normandy and Guienne, and the rightful lands of the heir to the throne, Cornwall and Chester. All representations of what Arthur should have inherited. All now symbols of hope, unfulfilled. 'To have seen the weepings,' at the funeral, wrote the eyewitness author of the *Receyt*, '... he had a hard heart that wept not.'[13]

When Richard Carre returned to Collyweston after the funeral, he brought Margaret the troubling news that Katherine, too, was sick.[14] In her grief and worry, Margaret was comforted by the network of kin, friends and neighbours she had built over generations. Lady Jane Guildford's mother, Lady Katherine Vaux, sent her servant to Margaret to offer support. Elizabeth's sister Cecily also hurried to Collyweston – Margaret paid for the costs of her servants and horses in journeying there.[15] And, when she had no friends at hand, Margaret attempted to distract herself with the daily business of managing her estates. She still personally signed every page of her household accounts. Perhaps, with her world rocked to its foundation, Margaret found comfort in the continuity and control of financial affairs. She could not hold sickness at bay, but she could maintain her ledger.[16]

While Margaret waited to hear if Katherine recovered, the succession to the throne hung in uneasy stasis. If Katherine survived and turned out to be pregnant, her child would be the heir to the crown. If not, then the excitable ten-year-old Prince Henry, still romping in his nursery in the south-east, would don the mantle of Prince of Wales. But rumours were already circulating that the chances of Katherine being pregnant were slim. Among the princess's Spanish attendants, it was suspected that her marriage to Arthur had never even been consummated. Katherine's close confidante, Francisca de Cáceres, who was responsible for dressing and undressing the princess, had explicitly told the other ladies in her service 'that nothing had passed between Arthur and his wife' on their wedding night, 'which surprised everyone and made them laugh at him'.[17] Katherine's doctor believed that Arthur's illness meant he 'had been denied the strength necessary to know a woman, as if he was a cold piece of stone' – or so his nephew remembered him reporting, almost three decades later.[18] Indeed, Katherine's chief attendant, Doña Elvira, was so convinced that Katherine remained a virgin at Arthur's death that she reported the fact to Queen Isabella that summer.[19]

Yet there was a curious disconnect between the impressions of the Spanish and English attendants of the couple: while the Spanish appeared certain of Katherine's virginity, Arthur's English servants were equally convinced that the marriage had been consummated. Arthur's servant Anthony Willoughby long remembered the jubilant prince emerging from his marital chamber, pink-cheeked and full of bravado. 'Willoughby,' Arthur had announced, 'bring me a cup of ale, for I have been this night in the midst of Spain... it is good pastime to have a wife.'[20] Lady Jane Guildford, who was one of the last attendants to leave the couple on their wedding night and among the first to greet them the following morning, was adamant even decades later that the couple had 'carnal cognition together as man and wife'.[21] Indeed, Lady Jane recalled that Queen Elizabeth, Katherine and 'many other nobles and honourable ladies divers times' discussed how the prince and princess had lain 'together in bed as man and wife all alone 5 or 6 nights after the said marriage'. One of these noble ladies must surely have been Margaret.

The root of this stark difference in the reports of the Spanish and English may have lain in the sexual inexperience of bride and groom, and their resulting difference of expectations. Contemporary medical theory was still dominated by the classical Greek and Roman authors Galen and Hippocrates, now filtered through the distorting lens of Christianity. The Catholic Church held that the only morally acceptable motivation for sexual intercourse was procreation within marriage, but for conception to occur both parties had to play their part. Due to a quirk of Hippo-Galenic theory, which maintained that both men *and* women produced semen-like 'seed', it was believed that a child could only be conceived if both parties emitted their 'seed' – in other words, reached orgasm. It is easy to imagine a scenario in which an adolescent boy believed he had consummated a marriage because he fulfilled the Galenic bargain, while his female partner was left unsatisfied. Since both Katherine and Arthur had grown up in chaste, morally rigorous courts – Katherine kept away from almost all male company, Arthur observing only the sexually continent partnership of his parents with little female interaction – naïvety and misunderstanding were almost inevitable.

Whatever the reality of these marital relations, Henry and Elizabeth took no chances with the health of their daughter-in-law and any potential offspring. As soon as Katherine was sufficiently well to travel, they removed her from 'that unhealthy place' (as Queen Isabella described Ludlow). Elizabeth personally dispatched an invalid's litter, bedecked in mourning black, to bring the princess by easy stages to London.[22] Thus, in a trundling horse-drawn car, its black fringes swaying along the road, the dowager Princess of Wales was brought back to the city she had left in triumph a matter of months ago, still only sixteen, in a strange land and already a widow. It was a circumstance with which

Margaret could readily empathise. In one key area, however, she and the princess differed. Time soon revealed that Katherine was not pregnant.

Even before Katherine had settled into her new quarters in Durham House on the Strand in London, King Henry had already turned his attention to the challenge of extricating his dynasty from this disaster, and resurrecting the Anglo-Spanish alliance. Within five weeks of Arthur's death, Ferdinand and Isabella had sent instructions to their ambassador to negotiate with the English, with the contradictory aims of either recalling Katherine to Spain with a refunded marriage portion, or arranging her marriage to Prince Henry. Despite considerable debate about the financial settlement, the latter course was ultimately pursued and on 23 June 1503 a treaty agreeing the marriage of Katherine and Henry, now invested as Prince of Wales, was sealed at Richmond Palace. Three days before Henry's twelfth birthday, on 25 June, he was betrothed to the now seventeen-year-old Princess Katherine. Before the marriage could progress any further, however, the royal families had to await a papal dispensation to deal with the minor inconvenience of a prince marrying his late brother's widow, which created a bond of consanguinity between the pair. As King Henry enjoyed good relations with the Pope, no difficulties were foreseen.

Thus, Prince Henry, who as of Easter 1502 was a younger son growing up in his sisters' nursery, became within a matter of months the heir to the throne and betrothed. Margaret recognised her grandson's newly elevated position, referring to him now in her household accounts as 'my lord prince' and issuing a steady stream of gifts and messages.[23] She probably enjoyed a more intimate relationship with Henry than she had with Arthur, since the younger prince had grown up close to or within the queen's household, where Margaret had so long resided. When a Venetian ambassador had visited the family in autumn 1497, he had found Arthur with the king and leading ministers in one chamber, while Prince Henry kept company with Margaret and Elizabeth in a separate hall.[24] Perhaps, therefore, Margaret counselled her son in the very different policy he pursued towards the new Prince of Wales. Unlike Prince Arthur, the young Henry was not dispatched to far-away

Ludlow Castle to learn government first-hand. Until adolescence he would continue to live in the same household as his sisters, attended by a staff largely made up of the same women who had served him since infancy. Among his attendants were the women who had rocked the cradles of the prince and princesses when they were new-borns: Frideswide Puttenham and Margery Gower, who may have been a relative of Margaret's lady-in-waiting Jane Gower. Even once the prince was old enough to have his own household, the king would continue to keep him close within the royal court, and there too both he and Margaret had spies to keep watch over the boy's progress. Among Prince Henry's cupbearers was Henry Guildford, a couple of years his senior and the son of Lady Jane Guildford.[25]

Given recent losses, the vigilance of Margaret's family towards the new heir was understandable. But there was additional need for caution after Arthur's death. For, by 1502, Prince Henry was not the only potential heir on people's minds. Edmund de la Pole, the disaffected hothead with Yorkist blood,* had once again fled the realm in August 1501, this time to rendezvous with his fugitive brother Richard at the court of Emperor Maximilian in Aachen. While Arthur lived and the Anglo-Spanish alliance held, Edmund represented little threat to Margaret's family. But now the succession to the English throne was endangered, and the union with Spain in limbo until Henry and Katherine married, Edmund loomed large in royal anxieties.

The king acted swiftly to extinguish the threat and Arthur's corpse was not yet in its grave before Henry moved against de la Pole and his associates. Men of previously unquestioned loyalty now found themselves roused from their homes and thrown into prison cells. The lieutenant of Guînes in the Calais Pale, Sir James Tyrell, was arrested with his son. Tyrell had once been a Ricardian stalwart, and had made the cardinal error of welcoming the fugitive Edmund to his territories two years earlier. The day after Arthur's funeral, 2 May 1502, Tyrell was convicted of treason at the London Guildhall and within a week he had been beheaded.

---

* Edmund was Elizabeth of York's cousin, the son of Elizabeth, duchess of Suffolk.

On 8 May, Tyrell's son was arraigned before Thomas Stanley at White Hall, similarly to be condemned – although ultimately he received a pardon.[26] Laying further Yorkist ghosts to rest, during Tyrell's incarceration he allegedly confessed to the murder of the Princes in the Tower twenty years earlier. But, although this suspiciously well-timed confession was reported by both Polydore Vergil and Thomas More, it was never published.

Tyrell's long service for Richard III made his collusion in de la Pole's treasonable activities credible, but altogether more startling was the arrest of Sir William Courtenay in April 1502. Courtenay and de la Pole were both young hotheads and jousting companions, but William had given no previous signs of disloyalty. Indeed, he had shared Henry's exile, been made a Knight of the Bath and married Queen Elizabeth's sister Katherine. Courtenay's royal connection may have harmed rather than helped his cause – similar proximity to the Tudors had made Sir William Stanley's minor treason appear more egregious. In December 1502, Courtenay was included in an attainder that outlawed de la Pole and his allies, and he would remain a prisoner for the rest of Henry's life.[27]

Katherine Courtenay, meanwhile, suffered considerably from her husband's downfall. She had to be financially supported by the queen, and only three months after William's arrest suffered the further loss of her son Edward. All the child's funeral expenses were met by Elizabeth. Margaret, too, provided regular donations to Katherine and her children, to mitigate their dire financial straits.[28] She may also have inspired the princess to follow her example in later life, for, when Courtenay eventually died in 1511, Katherine chose to live as a vowess in her West Country estates, where she exercised considerable regional authority.[29] However heavy-handed Henry's actions seemed, they were at least vindicated. For the time being, the threat of the de la Pole pretender was neutralised.

IN PERIODS OF MOURNING, THE FRIENDS AND FAMILY WHO survive take on a renewed importance in the mind of the living.

Thus, having suffered the loss of her grandson, Margaret sought solace not only in her own family but also in her Stanley relatives. Although the lack of surviving accounts for Margaret's household between 1499 and 1502 means it is impossible to know if she had maintained contact with the Stanleys in the years immediately after her vow of independence, it is clear that in the wake of Arthur's death Margaret was in frequent communication with Thomas and the Stanleys. Indeed, Thomas was among the first to contact Margaret in the weeks after Arthur's death, dispatching a servant to Collyweston, presumably to offer words of sympathy.[30] The couple continued to exchange messages and New Year gifts, and in September 1502 Margaret treated her husband's servants to a post-hunt banquet in Stamford.[31]

Margaret was always a generous almsgiver and pious benefactor. In the summer after Arthur's death, she made a progress through her territories in the East Midlands, making offerings at several shrines: twelve pence to the head of St John the Baptist beside Bourne, where Margaret and Harry Stafford had spent the early years of their marriage; three shillings four pence at Peterborough for the Virgin Mary and 'St Oswald's Arm'. Notably, however, she reserved her largest offerings for Trinity Sunday,* and for the feast day of St Thomas the Apostle (3 July) – the namesake saint of both her husband and his grandson.[32] Although Margaret customarily made offerings on the feast day of St Thomas Becket (29 December), St Thomas the Apostle was not one of her usual beneficiaries, and her charity was probably given in remembrance of her Stanley relatives.

When Margaret returned to Collyweston after her progress on 28 July, Thomas and his teenage grandson, Sir Tom Stanley, joined her there. Over the following weeks, Margaret indulged the young Tom with cash to gamble at table games with his grandfather.[33] Tom was a similar age to Prince Arthur, and perhaps Margaret found solace in the company of a young man who recalled her lost grandson. She had taken a personal interest in

---

* The first Sunday after Pentecost, which celebrated the Holy Trinity: God the Father, God the Son and God the Holy Ghost.

Tom for some time, betrothing him to her niece Elizabeth Welles in 1498 – a significant display of trust, given that Elizabeth, and any heirs she produced, had the royal blood of the Plantagenets running through their veins.* Tragically, Margaret's hope of uniting these families was thwarted by the early death of the bride. In 1505, Tom instead married Anne Hastings, the granddaughter of William, Lord Hastings, who had been summarily executed by Richard, duke of Gloucester in 1483. Their only surviving daughter was named Margaret, suggesting she may have been one of the many godchildren of Tom's step-grandmother.

Although now in his seventieth year, and despite his separation from the king's mother, Thomas Stanley continued to serve Henry faithfully as councillor and constable of England. In May 1502, he had presided at the trials of the suspected de la Pole traitors at Westminster. In the months after Arthur's death, Thomas also suffered personal bereavement: his eldest son, George, Lord Strange, died in the same month as his granddaughter Elynor Stanley, in December 1503. George's death, after a banquet at Derby House in London,† was sudden: he left no will and there were later suggestions he had been poisoned.[34] The precise cause of his death, and that of his daughter Elynor, is unclear, but Elynor was cared for in her last illness at Collyweston by Margaret's household. Perhaps Margaret herself sat at the bedside of the invalid Elynor, 'in [her] sickness... comforting... and ministering unto [her] with her own hands'.[35] She certainly took considerable trouble to provide a lavish funeral for the child, paying four men to 'bear her to the church', where she was laid to rest in a place of honour in the chancel, close to the altar.[36] Margaret had not been able to see her grandson in his last sickness, and perhaps the duty of properly tending to Elynor offered some consolation.

A year that had seen more than its fair share of grief and trouble ended with hope for the family. During the summer, as Elizabeth and Henry visited his childhood home at Raglan and his dear friends the Herberts, the queen had celebrated her quickening – the first

---

* Elizabeth's mother was the queen's sister Cecily Welles, from whom her royal descent came.
† Now the College of Arms.

movements of a child in her womb.[37] In the wake of Arthur's death, Elizabeth and Henry had wasted no time replenishing the Tudor stockpile of heirs. The arrival of the new prince or princess was anticipated early the following year and, although geographically distant, Margaret ensured she stayed in communication with the queen's household as the pregnancy progressed, rewarding Elizabeth's servants throughout October and December, and the royal midwife Alice Massy on 4 November.[38] She also sent Ralph Bigod with a New Year gift of gold coins for the queen, and – with considerable effort – transported a wild boar to the king as a Christmas entertainment.[39] Then, at Collyweston, she awaited news of the birth of her latest grandchild.

23

'Blessed are the Dead'[1]

✳

Although it fell at a gloomy time of year, Candlemas Day was a festival of light. Celebrated on 2 February, it honoured the churching of the Virgin Mary after the birth of Jesus and in past years Margaret and Elizabeth had gone on procession together to celebrate it, carrying flaming wax tapers through their homes to banish the shadows. Indeed, one could argue that the queen represented a similar purifying light amid the murky politics of the court. However, in 1503, Margaret made her Lady Day offering alone while Queen Elizabeth gave birth.[2]

Elizabeth and Henry had intended their latest child to be born in the comfortable surroundings of Richmond Palace, but Elizabeth went into labour early so was forced to stay at the more forbidding Tower of London. Her child, a girl, was born on 2 February, and hastily christened two days later. Margaret's latest granddaughter was named Katherine, likely in honour of either Katherine of Aragon or the queen's sister.

Soon after the birth, it was clear that all was not well. Elizabeth may have developed puerperal fever, the post-partum infection that causes fever, chills and crippling abdominal pain. Curing the sickness was beyond the powers of Elizabeth's experienced midwife Alice Massy – or indeed anyone in 1503 – but in desperation King Henry dispatched a servant to locate one Doctor Hallyswurth to aid the queen. There was an anxious wait, through day and night, before Hallyswurth arrived at the Tower. When he could not cure the queen, another physician was summoned from

Plymouth – but it made no difference.³ On the morning of 11 February 1503, Elizabeth died. A week later, her infant daughter followed her to the grave.

Elizabeth's death, wrote one contemporary, 'was as heavy and dolorous to the king's highness as hath been seen or heard of'.⁴ Ever conscious of his duty to the ritual of monarchy, Henry appointed a council to oversee the arrangements for Elizabeth's funeral, under the direction of his old friend Sir Richard Guildford and the earl of Surrey, lord treasurer of his household. Then he 'privily departed to a solitary place to pass his sorrows and would no man should resort to him... And then were rung the bells of London, every one'.⁵

No *man* should resort to him, certainly. But one person was sure to be admitted: his mother. Even before the queen's death, Margaret had quit Collyweston and sped southwards. Margaret's absence from the royal family's Christmas festivities suggests that she had not intended to be at her daughter-in-law's bedside for this birth, but, as soon as news of Elizabeth's sickness reached her, she knew her place was with her son. The record of her journey south with her small entourage has an air of panic to it, at odds with the usual stately record of her travels that appear in her household accounts. Margaret was evidently under-prepared for the cold conditions, and at Kettering an attendant was sent back to retrieve a counterpane for her 'little bed'. Provision also had to be made for a chafing dish, fire shovel and bellows, and for Margaret's mantle. Later on, between Northampton and Stony Stratford, a bridge had to be mended at Margaret's own expense before she could continue her journey.⁶

While Margaret was still on the road, Elizabeth was laid to rest at Westminster Abbey. Her funeral car was drawn by six horses draped in black velvet so long that you could only see their eyes and hooves, and at every corner was 'a banner of Our Lady borne by a knight, all white in token that [Elizabeth had] died in childbed'.⁷ The queen was attended on her last journey by the ladies who had served her so faithfully: her sisters Anne and Katherine, Lady Jane Guildford, Margaret's niece Eleanor St John, Lady Katherine Bray and Lady Herbert. Thomas Stanley rode ahead of the funeral bier, his face lit by the 5,000 torches that surrounded the queen's cortège. Elizabeth was laid to rest in the Lady Chapel, not far from her dead children at St Edward's shrine.

By St David's Day (1 March), Margaret and Henry were reunited at Richmond.[8] Margaret found the court grief-stricken and stripped of colour. Henry, who had previously favoured the tawny-coloured garments beloved of European princes, now wore a long, black gown, furred with black budge*, worn over doublets and jackets of the same. The royal children, too, wore black, their pale faces and red hair offering a stark contrast with their sombre attire.[9] Even the paupers and lepers in the streets wore black gowns, granted to them by Henry as a penitential act for his wife's soul.

Medieval mourning was public – royal mourning even more so – and to don anything but the requisite colour was highly disrespectful. However, the death of the queen had clearly not been anticipated, so the mourning livery required for Elizabeth's household was not ready in time for her vigil. It had been almost twenty years since the last queen consort died – Richard III's wife, Anne Neville – and Henry had then been living in French exile. Perhaps he was uncertain how to deal with Englishwomen's mourning attire, or was simply overwhelmed by the business attendant on a queen's death. To relieve her son of this burden, Margaret stepped in and drew up ordinances regulating mourning clothing for all court ladies from the queen down to her relatively lowly gentlewomen – and including, of course, the king's mother, who was to be dressed in 'everything like to the queen'.[10] Margaret's role in crafting royal ordinances has been exaggerated in the centuries since her death. The only royal ordinance that can, in fact, be attributed to Margaret with any certainty is this one for mourning dress, created between 25 August 1502 and 24 August 1503, in response to the deaths of Prince Arthur and Queen Elizabeth. The manuscript containing the ordinance is clearly entitled:

---
* Lamb's skin with the wool dressed outwards.

Reformation of apparel for princesses and great estates... for the time of mourning made by the right high mighty and excellent princess Margaret Countess of Richmond.... Mother to our most dread sovereign lord King Henry the VIIth.[11]

This image of the 'dread sovereign' was one Henry continued to project to the outer world even as he grieved for his queen. But, in the private chambers of the palace, as Margaret studied her son, she must have been concerned. Now forty-six, Henry was showing his age: not long ago a Spanish ambassador reported that he had aged twenty years in two weeks.[12] The shock of losing both his heir and wife within less than a year was weakening his faltering constitution. That March, Margaret closely monitored Henry's health, making a number of payments to his most intimate servants, who attended him even in his 'secretest' chambers: Henry's groom of the stool, Hugh Denys, and also Denys's wife, Mary; various grooms and pages of the privy chamber, including Richard Weston; and Henry's barber Piers Barbur and physician Thomas Fraunces.[13] Margaret may have been simply thanking them for their attendance on Henry at such a difficult time, but perhaps she was also rewarding them for sharing insights that she could not gain herself. For Henry concealed his grief behind closed doors, refusing to admit weakness or distress publicly.

While she was at Richmond, Margaret must also have attempted to comfort her grandchildren, who had so suddenly lost their cherished mother. An extraordinary vignette of royal private life at this time is preserved inside an illuminated manuscript known as 'the Vaux Passional'.[14] This contemporary work, once owned by Lady Jane Guildford (née Vaux), ruminated on death and the passion of Christ. Given its date and provenance, one illuminated scene almost certainly represents the surviving royal children, who were under Lady Guildford's care. Within it we find an opulent bedchamber with a roaring fire; a red-haired boy has thrown himself across the empty bed, apparently lost in despair, while on the floor beside him two girls in black hoods sit weaving at little hand looms. The smaller of the girls, her back to us, appears to glance at the boy, while the other studiously ignores him.

Prince Henry was already known to be volatile, emotional and impetuous – the same characteristics that had made his grandfather Edward IV such a dynamic monarch. It is easy to imagine him giving way to his sorrow like the boy in the 'Passional', and it is equally plausible that his father played the part of the king in this image. It is telling that King Henry is represented apart from the bedchamber scene, not grieving with his children but instead seated on a throne in kingly robes, surrounded by courtiers. As far as he was concerned, the realm must be ruled regardless of private heartache.

Margaret probably shared her son's instinct to bury her grief in practical action, but it cost them both. Margaret was now in her sixtieth year and the strain of bereavement alongside her lengthy winter journey had taken their toll. Two weeks after rushing to Richmond, she fell ill herself, requiring her physician William Hilmer to provide 'medicines and other necessaries'.[15] Her friends were worried, sending her provisions and rejuvenating gifts to aid her recovery: rose water, fortified wines and walnuts in syrup.[16] The abbess of Syon even sent Margaret some butter, whose consumption was usually forbidden during Lent. For Margaret to contradict a religious fast, abetted by an abbess, strongly suggests she was sick.[17]

Fortunately, the illness proved not to be serious. By 22 March, Margaret was well enough to leave the palace and make the short journey across the river to visit the monasteries of Syon and Charterhouse.[18] Whether fully recovered or not, she was determined to be useful to her son. Henry was deeply concerned about the external threat represented by Edmund de la Pole, especially now he had no hope of producing more heirs to shore up his own dynasty in the immediate future. As such, the international alliances Henry had brokered in recent years were vital to protect the realm, particularly the Anglo-Scottish Treaty that prevented enemies sneaking into England through the back door. So, even though both Margaret and Elizabeth had been anxious to delay the union as long as possible, Henry decided that Princess Margaret's marriage to James IV of Scotland would go ahead that summer.

Margaret took responsibility for one of the most important stages of the weeks-long ritual of the wedding ceremonials: the moment when the princess would leave her own family and formally enter the keeping of the Scots. Reflecting her transition from England to Scotland, this would take place halfway between the kings' seats of power, at Margaret's palace of Collyweston in the English Midlands. The location for the event had long been planned, and Margaret had already begun improvement works to properly accommodate the two courts. But, with a summer date now confirmed and her family recuperating as best they could, Margaret hurried home in mid-April to ready the palace with renewed urgency. There must be no suggestion that the Tudor dynasty had been weakened by the loss of its queen.

ON 5 JULY 1503, HENRY, HIS DAUGHTER AND 'A GREAT MULTITUDE of lords and other noble persons' arrived at Collyweston to see the fruits of Margaret's labours – and that of the myriad labourers who had worked against the clock to prepare the palace to her exacting standards.[19] The royal party trotted through battlemented gateways to take their ease beneath freshly leaded roofs and newly installed bay windows. When the princess rested, she probably did so on the 'great bed' that had taken a team of Cambridge embroiderers seven weeks to make, its richly textured bedding carried over water and land all the way from London via Spalding, Boston and Huntington. To set the stage appropriately, Margaret had called in favours from her wealthiest friends and relatives, borrowing plate from Henry to adorn her cupboards and wall hangings from Richard Fox, bishop of Winchester. Already a patron of a famed chapel choir, Margaret sought out additional singers from Cambridge and Westminster; and to set the tone of Anglo-Scottish concord she provided royal minstrels (English) and a royal bagpiper (presumably Scottish).[20]

At the heart of this pageantry was Margaret's granddaughter, almost fourteen years old but slight and pale, like Margaret herself. The princess may still have shown signs of the sorrowful last few months. In her wedding trousseau, beside gaudy crimson velvets, green satin and cloth of gold were packed the mourning clothes she had been wearing since February.[21] Young as the princess was, Margaret had to believe she was ready to leave her family and become a queen. She had been given the best possible preparation. Like her two surviving siblings, Mary and Henry, Princess Margaret had been brought up in the royal nursery under Elizabeth's close supervision – and with Margaret's eye upon her too. The royal children had shared tutors – in French, dancing, the lute, and in reading and writing. Latin and martial arts were left to Henry alone, repeating through the generations the pattern of inferior female education that Margaret had suffered. But all the siblings had been able to access the extensive royal library with its chronicles and histories, classical, Christian and mythic. All three children were to demonstrate a wilful impetuosity and impulse for the romantic in their adult lives – behaviour far more akin to that of their Yorkist forebears than their self-controlled Tudor–Beaufort kin. Elizabeth might be gone, but her influence lingered in her children.[22] All the same, young Margaret faced a challenging transition. She was marrying a thirty-year-old man she had never met, who was famous for his luxuriant mane of hair, his reckless love of fighting and a sexual voraciousness that had already produced seven illegitimate children. The princess's grandmother probably hoped that King James's many mistresses would distract him from consummating his marriage for a while longer, and indeed young Margaret would not conceive her first child until three years after her wedding.[23]

After fêting the new Queen of the Scots for three days, the English court gathered to bid young Margaret farewell. She received a royal blessing from her father – the form of her grand-mother's leave-taking is unrecorded – then, with no outward show of sorrow, she bade goodbye to her old life. In the entourage that accompanied her a mile further along the road was Thomas Stanley, who kissed her goodbye and returned to Collyweston to relate to her grandmother how the Scottish queen had fared after her leave-taking.[24] Although she would never see her grand-daughter in person again, Margaret kept up a frequent exchange of messengers with the Scottish court, and stayed informed about the queen through her niece Lady Eleanor Verney and Eleanor's husband, Sir Ralph,* who joined the Scottish court.[25]

The letters between the two Margarets have not survived, but one sent by the Queen of Scots to her father the September after her arrival in Scotland suggests that, although she felt homesick, she was pressing on with her family duty. She provided a report on her new husband's current court favourites, which she knew could be to English advantage. She signed off, 'with a wish I would I were with your grace now, and many times more… Our Lord have you in his keeping. Written with the hand of your humble daughter Margaret.'[26]

Perhaps Henry found the loss of his daughter harder than expected. Multiple times that summer, he and his mother exchanged messages through their servants, and while perambulating the Midlands he returned to Collyweston twice more that July to visit her.[27] Then he turned his horse from the last place he had seen his daughter, and rode away.

CLOSE TO THE FIRST ANNIVERSARY OF HER GRANDDAUGHTER'S departure, in high summer 1504, one of the last remaining links between Margaret and her identity as someone other than the king's mother was severed. On 21 July 1504, a large party of horsemen drew up at the gates of Collyweston led by Margaret's step-grandson Sir Tom Stanley. Later the same day, a vicar in Stamford was rewarded by Margaret's cofferer 'for stilling of waters' to make medicine – perhaps to aid recovery from shock. A blow against which Margaret had long been steeling herself had finally struck. Thomas Stanley was dying.[28]

Thomas had probably been unwell for some time. In March 1504, he was holed up at his principal seat in Lancashire, from where he exchanged messages with his ex-wife. It may have

---

* Eleanor Verney née Pole was the daughter of Margaret's half-sister Edith St John. Her husband, Ralph, was the Queen of Scots's chamberlain.

been news of his declining health that propelled Margaret into a remarkably energetic pilgrimage in the following months. From April until the end of June, she toured most of the religious sites of Lincolnshire and Norfolk, visiting shrines at Crowland, Lynne, Walsingham, Wisbech, Castle Acre and Peterborough. Notably, she made an offering at the shrine dedicated to St Thomas at Westacre, perhaps praying for the recovery of her husband of thirty years. Given her own advanced age and unreliable constitution, something extraordinary must have brought on this flurry of movement.[29] As recently as February, she had required 'divers spices and medicines [to be] ministered', and throughout the year payments appear in Margaret's accounts for 'divers herbs' and rewards to the king's physician, Master Fraunces, suggesting that her health continued to be delicate.[30] Even from the comfort of a litter, Margaret's lengthy tour of the East Anglian shrines would have been bone-achingly laborious.

Just over a week after Tom Stanley's visit to Collyweston, on 29 July 1504, Thomas Stanley died at Lathom. He had written his will the day before, but it contained no personal bequests to 'my lady my wife', merely stating that he hoped his executors would let her 'peaceably enjoy' her territories.[31] He did, however, include Margaret's 'personage' in a family mausoleum he direct-ed his executors to build, with prayers instructed for her soul.* Word of Thomas's death reached Margaret at Collyweston on 3 August, borne by his servant George Rygmadon. Immediately, she dispatched a trusted groom, Richard Aderton, with a full purse to instruct the many orders of friars in Stamford to say Masses for Thomas's soul: Greyfriars, White Friars, Black Friars, Austin Friars, nuns, the canons of Newstead, priests of the local alms-house and Benedictine monks. Seven hundred yards of saye (a type of woollen cloth) were dyed black for her household. Then, Margaret set out to visit a local holy well. Holy wells were often associated with St Winifred, an important saint to both Henry (who shared his Welsh ancestry with the saint) and the Stanleys, who were major patrons of the Holywell of St Winifred in North

---

* Margaret chose instead to be buried with Henry and Elizabeth at Westminster.

Wales. Margaret's choice of pilgrimage site was a judicious one, honouring both her late husband and her son, the king.[32]

The loss of Thomas must have been significant for Margaret. For all their troubles, the couple had shared a unique and lasting relationship, and, even after their separation, outward respect and probably some real affection had lingered between the pair. Long after Margaret became a vowess, Thomas continued to be referred to respectfully in Margaret's accounts as 'my lord'.[33] But, painful as the loss of Thomas was – painful as all her recent griefs must have been – Margaret was able to bear them.[34] The one person she could not stand to lose was her son. If Henry were to die soon – with no queen, no European marital alliance and (it would soon emerge) little consensus around the succession – Margaret's family would be more vulnerable than ever. But just as important was the political and emotional reality that, ever since Henry's return to her life in 1485, and especially in the wake of their recent bereavements, mother and son had grown to depend on one another.

Not long after Thomas's death, Margaret resolved to leave Collyweston and move back closer to the royal court. Although she had done important work representing Tudor interests in the Midlands and enjoyed her independence, at Collyweston she was geographically isolated from her family. In autumn 1504, as Henry toured the portside towns of Hampshire and Sussex, Margaret relied on her groom Nicholas Aughton to relay messages to her son: gruelling twelve-day round trips that made the relay of information painfully slow.[35] As Margaret grew older and less physically able to travel, she may have feared that, if there were another family emergency, she could not respond in time. The desperate scramble across winter-rimed roads she undertook as Elizabeth lay dying would have been profoundly distressing and Margaret had no desire to repeat such a trial if Henry or her grandchildren fell ill. So, Margaret decided to leave the place that had been her home for six years and move instead into two palaces closer to southern seats of power: the bishop of Ely's manor at Hatfield and the archbishop of Canterbury's palace of Croydon. Croydon was within thirteen miles of the palaces of Eltham, Greenwich and Richmond – and a similar distance from Westminster itself. Hatfield, lying to the north of London, was close to her son's Essex and Oxfordshire hunting grounds, and to the road northwards with its access to Cambridge and her Midlands estates.

In part because they were so often in one another's company, and in part perhaps because of a shared suspicion, few of Henry and Margaret's personal letters survive. But those that do reveal the degree of their mutual reliance. Henry respected Margaret's judgement so highly and wished to displease her so little that when he considered promoting her confessor John Fisher to a bishopric in 1504 – an act that would take Fisher away from his duties to Margaret – Henry insisted that 'without your pleasure known I will not move him nor tempt him therein'. 'I have in my days promoted many a man unadvisedly,' he added ruefully, 'and I would now make some recompense.'[36] To his mother, Henry could admit his failings, certain that she would never share his confidences beyond their private circle. It was around this time that Margaret also took up a domestic act of devotion that she perhaps inherited from Elizabeth: that of sewing Henry's shirts. This undertaking, which would have demanded she peer through her golden spectacles to see the fine needle and small stitches, formed a physical bond between them even when they were apart.[37] Through force of maternal willpower, Margaret strove to keep her son safe. But, as the events of the past three years had demonstrated, to the medieval mind nothing was more certain than death – and even a king could not outrun mortality forever.[38]

24

'Change of worlds'[1]

✳

About the last day of September 1504, the Flintshire administrator, and one-time co-conspirator of Margaret's, Sir Hugh
Conway, convened a secret meeting at the home of the deputy
lieutenant of Calais to debate the succession. Since becoming
treasurer of this last fragile strip of English-held France some
weeks earlier, Conway had grown increasingly concerned about
what would befall Calais, the royal family and – most importantly
– himself when Henry VII died, an event that appeared to be growing ever closer. At some uncertain date not long before Conway's
Calais meeting, Henry had fallen ill at his manor of Wanstead.[2] The
nature of his illness is as mysterious as its precise timing, but it was
sufficiently serious that some of the 'great personages' of the realm
had assembled to discuss the succession. Conway had witnessed
this gathering and, even weeks after the king's apparent recovery,
he noted that Henry still seemed 'but a weak man and sickly'.[3] As
Conway informed his colleagues at the furtive gathering in Calais,
a book of prophecy had come into his possession that foretold that
Henry 'shall no longer reign than did King Edward [IV], which…
was but 22 years and little more'.[4] If the prophecy were true,
Henry would be dead within three years.

Such prophecies were no idle concern for Henry VII, and when
one of Conway's associates broke their covenant of secrecy and
informed the king about the Calais meeting, he immediately inves-
tigated. Given her status within Henry's regime at this time and her
existing connection with Conway, it is highly likely Margaret too

was informed. As more details of Conway's activities emerged, it transpired that his book of prophecy was the very least of Henry and Margaret's issues. The Calais meeting was just the latest in a series of discussions Conway had held with leading figures in the Henrician regime, to ascertain their loyalties in the event of the king's death. And, in one interview after another, Conway had learned – as now Henry and presumably Margaret did – that even after two decades of Tudor rule, few were wholly committed to the dynasty. As Henry lay on his sickbed at Wanstead, Conway had heard the 'great personages' whispering about who should succeed him in the event of his death:

> Some of them spake of my lord of Buckingham, saying that he was a noble man and would be a royal ruler. Other there were that spake... of your traitor Edmund de la Pole. But none of them... spake of my lord prince [Henry].[5]

Even Sir Nicholas Vaux, the lieutenant of Guînes fortress, who boasted of his upbringing in Margaret's home, had confided in Conway that, when the king died, he intended to retreat to a stronghold and 'make [his] peace however the world turn' – in other words, reach an accommodation with whichever regime held power.[6]

This was of grave concern to Margaret, who had witnessed first-hand the events of 1483, when apparent consensus for an ordered succession to the reign of a strong and popular sovereign had dissolved into chaos and murder following that king's death. Indeed, she must have been painfully conscious that the last time a prince had peaceably inherited his father's throne had been a generation before she was even born, in 1422, when the nine-month-old King Henry VI acceded after the death of his father Henry V. The calamities of his reign hardly needed reciting. Little wonder, perhaps, that the prospect of another child-king was unwelcome, and in 1504 Prince Henry was only slightly older than Edward V had been in 1483. Who was to say, indeed, that Conway was wrong to doubt Prince Henry's prospects? If the king died soon, the prince would be old enough to inherit the throne but not to defend it.

Edmund de la Pole and the duke of Buckingham might revive the Plantagenet–Buckingham treasons of their ancestors. As Margaret's one-time ward, Buckingham was assiduous in his attentions to his old guardian, sending Margaret gifts of bucks in hunting season and paying her a personal visit at Collyweston in October 1504.[7] But precedent had proven that even lengthy bonds of kinship might be betrayed when opportunity and ambition were roused.

Moreover, while Henry had proven an effective ruler, he was gaining an ugly reputation for avarice and suspicion. The old Beaufort traits that had destroyed Margaret's father were reborn in her son, much to her dismay. When describing his mistress, John Fisher noted that 'avarice and covetousness she most hated, and sorrowed it full much in all persons – but especially in any that belonged unto her'.[8] And Henry had undoubtedly become a miser, choking his subjects into submission with their own purse strings. It may have been Henry's recollection of the financial treasons of his own supporters under Richard III that motivated his rapacity: between 1483 and 1485, Margaret, Reynald Bray and their confederates had undermined royal authority and siphoned away royal funds for Henry's cause, and the money they thus assembled enabled Henry to invade and kill his rival. Money was power. It provided for public assertions of authority. It bought soldiers for war, the ships to carry them, their weapons, their armour. Without money, Henry might well reason, his enemies were weakened. But so, of course, was he. Perhaps this was why, in the wake of endless challenges from pretenders, repeated invasions, treasonous meetings and threats to dynastic security, Henry turned more and more to financial manipulation as a means of political control. Good behaviour was guaranteed with eye-watering monetary bonds and recognisances,* friends and relatives who stood surety becoming enmeshed in murky webs of financial manipulation. Polydore Vergil believed that Henry purposefully exacted heavy penalties in order to weaken his wealthy and noble subjects so they could not oppose him. But this was just the beginning of Henry's fiscal repressions.

---

* Recognisances are financial bonds of good behaviour.

By the middle of the first decade of the sixteenth century, offices that ought to have gone to worthy recipients were being sold, and so too was royal favour in lawsuits. Henry's feudal rights to the wardship of under-age heirs, the marriage of his tenants' widows and fees for inheriting estates were scrupulously asserted and even minor transgressions punished with heavy fines. Among Henry's targets was Margaret's old ward Edward Stafford, duke of Buckingham, who had the double misfortune to be a royal ward who came of age under Henry VII, with a mother who illegally remarried.* The £7,000 debt he thus accrued was felt, by Buckingham, to be tantamount to extortion.[9] But Henry always had his suspicions about Buckingham – his father was a byword for treachery – so the restraining leash was at least politically justifiable. What was most uncomfortable for Margaret was that her son increasingly inflicted his mercenary attentions on their leading supporters.

Among those who Hugh Conway reported were, at best, equivocal in their allegiance to the dynasty were its own stalwarts: loyal servants who had shared Henry's exile and continued to enjoy his confidence, whose homes he visited and whose female relatives were deeply rooted in Margaret's social life – but whom he nonetheless persecuted financially. Sir Richard Guildford had endured attainder, exile and risked bodily harm in support of Henry Tudor. But his military abilities, which saw him created master of the ordnance at the Tower of London, were not matched by economic discipline. Creditors dating back to the reign of Edward IV continually resurfaced to menace him, and in June 1505 Henry had to arrest Richard for non-payment of debts and a failure to return ordnance accounts. Richard spent some time in the Fleet prison and ultimately could only save himself from dishonourable prosecution by retiring from public life. In April 1506, he left his children with his wife, Jane, and set out on pilgrimage to Jerusalem. He died in the Holy Land five months later, leaving Jane struggling to unravel his finances and pay off his creditors. To do so, she was forced to borrow money from two of Margaret's accountants, and failed to pay back either of them.[10]

---

* Katherine Woodville, duchess of Buckingham and Bedford.

Jane was not the only one of Henry's victims who sought Margaret's assistance. In 1507, George Neville, Lord Bergavenny was indicted for illegal retaining (taking men into one's service, potentially for military action). He was fined a staggering £100,000 and forbidden to enter south-eastern territories in which he held land without Henry's permission.[11] Bergavenny sought – unsuccessfully – to placate the king through the intercession of his mother, sending Margaret gifts of a greyhound (the symbol of her Richmond title) and goshawk.[12] But illegal retaining like Lord Bergavenny's was a major concern of Henry's, and he would brook no defiance, even from offenders of proven loyalty. Margaret's stepsons James and Edward Stanley were both indicted for illegal retaining in 1506, and the whole family bound in recognisances for good behaviour. The indictment against Edward was even annotated in Henry's own meticulous hand.[13]

In the wake of William Stanley's betrayal, perhaps Henry did not trust old ties of service to keep his closest allies loyal. Stanley's successor in the sensitive office of chamberlain was one of Henry's most long-standing supporters, Giles Daubeney. But that did not stop Henry punishing his friend Daubeney when he was discovered to have been embezzling funds during his time as lieutenant of Calais. Henry forced Daubeney to repay £2,000 and surrender his French pension. In the will Daubeney wrote eighteen months later, he noted bitterly that, 'it pleased the kings highness whose true servant I have been these 26 years and above to charge me... the sum of £2,000'.[14] Hugh Conway had been confident that Daubeney would remain 'as true to the king's grace as any man living' as long as Henry was in good health – but he added the salutary coda that 'it hath been seen in times past that change of worlds hath caused change of minds'.[15] Henry would, no doubt, have argued that his actions were justified. These men had done wrong. But many must have agreed with Giles Daubeney that the punishment they suffered for financial misconduct was unduly heavy given their otherwise blameless records.

And perhaps, like her contemporaries, Margaret chose to blame malign forces around Henry for his behaviour. Popular opinion held that Reynald Bray and John Morton, bishop of Ely 'corrupted the king's character' and encouraged Henry's tendency towards avarice, earning them 'much hatred' and 'grudge of the people'.[16] Since his earliest days in Margaret's service, Bray had shown himself to be a meticulous and unyielding financial officer. It was precisely these qualities that made him so valuable to the Tudor regime. He was the natural choice to run Henry's newly formed Council Learned in the Law, a shadowy court founded in 1499, whose sole purpose was to fill royal coffers under the guise of protecting Henry's prerogative. Yet, while Bray and Morton undoubtedly enacted Henry's financial privations, they probably did not instigate them. Indeed, they may have constrained his worst impulses. Polydore Vergil asserted that Bray was one of the only people who could chastise the king when he went astray, and that he and Morton had 'restrained royal power' when it inclined to excess.[17] This could explain why Henry's penny-pinching got so much worse after both men were replaced by less scrupulous royal advisers. Morton had died in 1500, and Bray followed him to the grave in August 1504. (Margaret maintained contact with her faithful servant until the end, dispatching her groom Richard Carre with a message in late July.)[18]

Bray's place as leading adviser, and chief officer of the Council Learned in the Law, was taken by someone for whom Margaret had rather less affection: his protégé, the Northamptonshire lawyer Richard Empson. Empson and his Sussex-born colleague Edmund Dudley were to become infamous for the imagination, efficiency and cruelty of their enforcement of the king's fiscal policies. As far back as 1497, Empson had been named one of the king's 'low-born and evil counsellors' by the Cornish rebels, and that low birth offended contemporary sensibilities as much as his morality.[19] Like Bray, Empson and Dudley were both educated gentlemen, but they were very far below the status of noble-born advisers that fifteenth-century minds accepted as satellites of their king. Henry seemed to delight in elevating these relatively lowly individuals to honourable positions: within two years, Dudley went from Speaker of the Commons in 1504 to president of the king's council, becoming the first layman to hold the position. As

Henry's early influences died away, Empson and Dudley stepped eagerly into their vacant seats.

Their authority over the king was not unrivalled, however. Henry maintained his suspicion of single over-mighty counsellors. His old companions in exile, Bishop Richard Fox and Thomas Lovell, continued to exercise influence as keeper of the privy seal and treasurer of the chamber respectively. Others had risen in royal favour: Margaret's flamboyant Stanley relation Thomas Savage, archbishop of York* (who died in 1507) and Henry's eloquent secretary Thomas Ruthall had both impressed the king with their diplomatic service and domestic counsel. But it was a sign of Empson and Dudley's dominance that this pair of lowly lawyers could inflict their financial wounds on the leading counsellors of the king – and even on Margaret.

To support her Cambridge foundation of Christ's College, Margaret persuaded Henry to grant her Creek Abbey in Norfolk. However, the deal was negotiated by Edmund Dudley, who received a cut of the profits of the exchange. The royal grant was made without payment of routine official fees, but Margaret was nonetheless forced to pay a staggering £466 (plus change) for the grant.[†] Margaret clearly felt the fault for this lay not with Henry but with Edmund Dudley, who acted as intermediary for the exchange and personally profited. She must have bitterly resented having rewarded Dudley sixty-six shillings in June 'for his diligent labour... for getting the abbey' when she discovered the high price she was expected to pay for his efforts.[20]

But, for all Margaret's alleged unease with avarice, she was not above similarly high-handed behaviour towards her own servants for financial infractions. She brought legal action against several of her officers for debt, including her cofferer James Clarell who 'should have been imprisoned' over £59 that he owed his mistress. For good measure, Margaret also sued Clarell's surety, Thomas Haselwode. Even after Margaret's officers were dead, she did not scruple from pursuing their widows and executors, most

---

* Thomas Savage was the nephew of Thomas Stanley. His mother, Katherine, was Thomas's sister.
† More than £308,000 in modern money.

glaringly her northern chamberlain Roger Ormeston. Ormeston was fiercely loyal and bequeathed Margaret a standing cup in his will, but, nonetheless, she sued his widow for a debt of £22* in 1506.[21] The 'wonderful ready remembrance' that John Fisher praised in Margaret had its dark side in her as it did in Henry. Perhaps what made Margaret most uneasy about Henry's rapacity was the knowledge that, had she been in his position, she might have behaved exactly the same.

Thus, whether due to disinclination or manipulation, Henry proved incapable of restraining his mercenary impulses – even if it endangered the succession by alienating popular opinion. However, the revelation in autumn 1504 of Sir Hugh Conway's clandestine discussions concerning the succession appears to have jolted him into reconsidering his position as a widower. If the existence of a single male heir caused such uncertainty, Henry would improve the family's chances of survival by creating more. So, not long after the third anniversary of Elizabeth's death, in spring 1505, Henry chose to remarry.

THE ONE ADVANTAGE OF BEING A NOTORIOUS MISER WAS THAT Henry was believed by most European powers to be phenomenally rich – and that was a highly desirable commodity in a bridegroom. Throughout Europe, he was renowned for the magnificence of his court and for the vast reserves of cash he had stockpiled during his twenty-year reign. In 1505, Margaret's son was forty-eight, which was a perfectly respectable age to remarry. Thus, when Henry let it be known that he was looking for a new queen, he received several tantalising offers: Queen Giovanna of Naples, the twenty-eight-year-old niece of Ferdinand of Aragon, was recently widowed and Ferdinand hoped to entice Henry to maintain the Anglo-Spanish alliance by reuniting their families. The Holy Roman Emperor Maximilian, having forgiven Henry for his abandonment

---

* This was the equivalent of 733 days' wages for skilled labour in 1510 (and £14,580 in modern money) – a not inconsiderable sum.

of their joint invasion of France, offered his widowed daughter Marguerite of Austria, the twenty-four-year-old governor of the Netherlands. Even Henry's one-time nemesis Louis XII of France proposed his teenage cousin Marguerite d'Angoulême.[22]

Henry approached the task of finding a bride with the same meticulous eye for detail that he applied to his accounts. Margaret was with him at Richmond in May 1505 when he instructed an English embassy bound for Spain to investigate Queen Giovanna of Naples as a potential bride.[23] Perhaps she even helped Henry draw up the exhaustive, twenty-four-point list of inquiries about the lady, which covered everything from Giovanna's wealth and character to the minutest details of her personal appearance: 'The fashion of her nose and the height and breadth of her forehead.' The ambassadors were to approach as close to the queen as possible so they might 'mark whether there appear any hair about her lips or not' and 'feel the condition of her breath, whether it be sweet or… if they feel any savour of spices, rosewater or musk'. The royal inquiry into the size of the queen's feet and 'her breasts… whether they be big or small' smacks more of Henry's personal tastes than anything else.[24]

In less intimate questions of politics, it is likely that Henry welcomed his mother's advice about his remarriage. She had, after all, arranged an exceptionally successful first union. Nonetheless, the difference in circumstances must have been plain to Margaret: before, she had been a parent negotiating the marriage of a powerless child. Now, her son was a king forging international alliances with the weight of a dynasty on his shoulders. At most, Margaret was her son's chief adviser. Soon, she might lose even that status. When a new queen arrived in the kingdom, Margaret's pre-eminent position would inevitably be diminished by the presence of a European princess as her daughter-in-law.

By Christmas 1505, however, Henry had closed one avenue of international cooperation: the Anglo-Spanish alliance had collapsed. In November 1504, Katherine's mother, Isabella of Castile, had died, ending the union of Spain that endured throughout her marriage to Ferdinand of Aragon. Castile was supposed to pass to her elder daughter, Joanna, who was living in the Low Countries with her husband, Philip the Fair of Burgundy. However, Ferdinand insisted that Isabella's dying wish was for him to rule Castile in Joanna's place. Since Ferdinand was already in Spain, he had the advantage over his daughter. Nonetheless, Philip was determined to assert the rights of his wife – and, through her, himself. Since Philip was sheltering Edmund de la Pole, an extension of his powers into Iberia was bad news for Henry and Margaret. War looked imminent as Philip readied a fleet to sail for Castile. The last thing Henry wanted at a time of domestic uncertainty was to be dragged into a Spanish war that offered no material advantage – and Prince Henry's betrothal to Katherine of Aragon threatened to entangle them. Suddenly the union with Katherine was a lot less appealing and, the day before Prince Henry's fourteenth birthday (27 June 1505), he formally repudiated his betrothal.

Bereft of her marital status and surrounded by faction-ridden Spanish attendants, Katherine was left in limbo: living close to, and sometimes within, the royal court, but no longer part of the family. At Christmas 1505, the king invited Katherine to join himself, Princess Mary and Prince Henry at court, but it must have been an uncomfortable festive season for the Spanish princess. The mood was not helped by an accident at Epiphany (6 January) 1506, when, 'by negligence of a page of the king's chamber', Henry's private apartment at Richmond almost burned to the ground. Many costly 'carpets, rich beds' and tapestries were destroyed – a vexing beginning to the year for this penny-counting king, and an alarming one for the royal children and Margaret.[25] Only a few days later, however, a messenger arrived at the royal court from the West Country with news that completely altered the diplomatic landscape.

IN THE FIRST WEEKS OF 1506, A HURRICANE ROARED OFF THE Atlantic and scourged the south coast of England. As far east as Croydon, Margaret felt its effects: houses and trees were overturned, thatch and tiles torn from their rooftops, and the rain fell so heavily that cattle and sheep were drowned. At St Paul's

Cathedral, in the heart of London, the weathercock atop its spire, shaped like an eagle, was ripped from its socket and blown the entire length of the churchyard, eventually coming to land with a destructive clang on the penthouse at the sign of the Black Eagle.[26] This curious concatenation of one eagle destroying another was taken by superstitious minds as a sign that Emperor Maximilian, whose sigil was an eagle, would suffer loss in the year ahead.[27] Meanwhile, in the English Channel, the storm blasted the fleet of Philip and Joanna of Burgundy as it sailed for Castile. Their forty ships were soon scattered or wrecked, their flagship almost destroyed when its mainsail snapped in half and the vessel caught fire. Somehow, though, the monarchs themselves survived and limped ashore in Dorset, barefoot, singed and sodden.[28]

Word of their landfall on 16 January was brought to Margaret shortly after she had taken delivery of clothing: a consignment of silken belts to loop at the waist of her fine velvet gowns, and hair shirts to be concealed beneath and chafe her bare flesh. She had received, too, a welcome update on the wellbeing of her grand-daughter the Queen of Scots from one of her attendants in the north.[29] And then a messenger hotfoot from her son, advising her that Henry was now the effective gaoler of the rulers of Burgundy and Castile. Margaret did not need the significance of this reversal explained to her. With Philip and Joanna in his control, Henry could surely dictate the terms of any alliance they made: insist on the return of Edmund de la Pole, gain economic concessions for English merchants trading with the Low Countries and negotiate the most advantageous marriages for his family. Presuming, of course, that the proud young Philip did not take against his custodian. Having spent years as a hostage in European courts, no one knew better than Henry how to win the hearts of his prisoners. He immediately dispatched Prince Henry to escort the monarchs to court, while he oversaw preparations for their welcome at Windsor Castle. The family must appear both desirable allies and unquestioned rulers.

The Burgundian party was escorted to the castle by fourteen-year-old Prince Henry on Saturday 31 January, via a route that offered the best prospect of the fine medieval fortress on its clifftop. The question of precedence was a tricky one, since Philip insisted he was king of Castile, but technically he held the inferior title of duke of Burgundy. Philip was famous throughout Europe for his chivalry, so Henry took pains to prove himself the equal of his cultured guest. When they came face to face, Philip graciously placed himself in a subordinate position to Henry and doffed his hat like a servant. Henry returned the courtesy and embraced Philip as a brother-king. Then they walked, arm in arm, into the galleries of Windsor, which Henry had painstakingly decorated with the richest items possible to impress his guest. Henry might have a reputation as a hoarder, but he knew when to spend. His own ambassadors had been unimpressed when they visited Queen Giovanna of Naples in summer 1505 and were conveyed through chambers with bare walls to the queen's presence. Such paucity, even in the lower corridors of a palace, suggested either poverty or miserliness.[30]

The English court was probably a little surprised when Philip arrived at Windsor without his wife, who had been left behind in Hampshire. This confirmed rumours that, although Philip and Joanna's relationship had begun with affection and produced six children, by 1506 it had disintegrated into animosity and neglect. It was reported that, even as their ship burned and tossed on the waves, Philip had clung to his courtiers – who hated Joanna – leaving the queen to weep at his feet.[31] Joanna only eventually made an appearance at Windsor once business was almost concluded, on 10 February, and arrived 'so secretly... by the backside of the castle' that she might have been completely overlooked.[32] Having barely been permitted to greet the king and reunite with her sister Katherine for the first time in years, Joanna was bundled away into obscurity again. This 'sudden and hasty departure' was remarked, although Henry restrained himself from commenting on it, thinking 'he ought not to interfere between husband and wife'.[33] Perhaps, however, it reminded Henry how fortunate he had been in his own harmonious marriage.

After little more than a week of public entertainments and diplomatic wooing behind closed doors, Henry and Philip concluded an alliance, which was sealed amid much pageantry in St George's Chapel at Windsor on Monday 9 February. Unsurprisingly, considering the power in which Henry held Philip, the terms of the treaty were substantially in England's favour and disadvantaged Dutch traders angrily renamed it the 'wicked alliance' (*intercursus malus*). At Henry's insistence, the agreement demanded the surrender of Edmund de la Pole. On 16 March 1506, the pretender was transferred into English custody at Calais, whence he was moved to the Tower of London, where he would remain imprisoned until his death thirteen years later.[34] On 20 March, as a symbol of their lasting national friendship and a first step towards Henry's remarriage, the king of England was betrothed to Philip's sister Marguerite, archduchess of Savoy – with extensive financial provisions, naturally.[35] Although the marriage never came to pass, Henry's political alliance remained in place. And, in return for these considerable advantages, Henry pledged little more than to support Philip and Joanna's claim to the Castilian throne. This definitively severed his alliance with Ferdinand, but was of little material help to the couple. On 25 September 1506, having failed to wrench control of Castile from Ferdinand, Philip died of typhoid at Burgos. His unfortunate queen, Joanna, was thrust back onto the marriage market and, in hopes of maintaining the Anglo-Burgundian alliance and gaining a desirable bride, Henry suggested himself as a groom. But this union, too, never progressed beyond discussion. Ultimately, Henry would remain a bachelor for the rest of his life.

Margaret herself had played no role in the events at Windsor. She was probably too unwell to attend – late in January she took delivery of the cure-all, aqua vita[36] – but she followed proceedings closely from Croydon, gaining first-hand reports from three of her servants who visited the court 'at divers times' in February. Henry's courtiers returned the favour and among those sharing updates were Henry's servant Garrard Osborne and Margaret's step-grandson Tom Stanley, now earl of Derby.[37] To ensure the family's triumph was commemorated more enduringly, Margaret also commissioned a written description of the 'Reception of Philip, King of Castile', possibly by her confessor John Fisher. Still not satisfied, she insisted the description was updated a few weeks later, and this document is our most important source for the diplomatic events at Windsor, which proved vital to restoring the security of their family.[38]

Margaret's concern to produce a fulsome account of the Burgundian visit was not only to publicise her son's success in achieving a highly favourable treaty; it was also to advertise the abilities of her grandchildren on the international stage. For, while the Burgundian court was riven with internal disharmony, Margaret's family impressed with their unity and chivalric behaviour. Prince Henry took a leading role, conversing with the Burgundians in fluent French and growing so close to Philip that 'one would imagine', wrote an eyewitness, 'that they were really brothers or best friends'.[39] Now in his teens, Prince Henry took after his handsome Yorkist grandfather, Edward IV, growing tall and sturdy, with a halo of golden red hair and rosy cheeks. Within a couple of years, he would outgrow his father. 'There is no finer youth in the world', wrote the Spanish ambassador Rodrigo González de la Puebla.[40] At the climax of events at Windsor, the sealing of the Anglo-Burgundian alliance in St George's Chapel, the prince was manoeuvred into the spotlight as, in a chivalric exchange, Philip became a Knight of the Garter and Prince Henry was invested into the Burgundian Order of the Golden Fleece.[41] No one could argue now, surely, that the line of succession to the throne of England was not clear.

Margaret's youngest grandchild, nine-year-old Princess Mary, had also demonstrated tact and accomplishment beyond her years. She had been present during an uncomfortable exchange between Philip and his sister-in-law Katherine. Henry had asked the princesses to dance for their guests while he and Philip conversed, but Katherine had eagerly pressed Philip to join them. Philip made his excuses once, then twice, and finally lashed out at Katherine, demanding that she desist. The atmosphere soured and it took all the ingénue charms of Princess Mary to restore a measure of tranquillity. As she plucked at the strings of her lute and turned her pale fingers to the keys of her clavichord,* tensions dissipated. One

---

* A soft-toned keyboard instrument.

onlooker reported that Mary 'played very well, and she was of all folks there greatly praised that [despite] her youth in everything she behaved herself so very well'. Better, evidently, than it was felt that Katherine had conducted herself.[42]

The positive impression that Mary left on the Burgundian court was pivotal, for during his discussions with Philip, Henry had intimated that perhaps his daughter was a suitable match for Philip and Joanna's six-year-old heir Charles.[43] This was extraordinarily ambitious. Charles was probably the most sought-after prince in Europe, his inheritance stretching from the Low Countries and Holy Roman Empire into the kingdoms of Castile and Aragon, and across the Atlantic to the New World with all its riches. After Philip's sudden death in September 1506, Charles's guardians would challenge the terms of the alliance. Eventually, however, Henry triumphed. On 21 December 1507, Mary and Charles were betrothed.[44]

After the Burgundian court had departed, Margaret rewarded both her grandchildren for their achievements. Prince Henry was presented with a magnificent steed already caparisoned in embroidered black velvet harness and 'Venice gold', with gilt flowers studded into the leatherwork.[45] Mary, who clearly appreciated music, was invited to Croydon with her minstrels, and Margaret in turn visited her granddaughter in the nursery at Eltham. In June, Margaret delivered Mary the high-status gift of a buck – perhaps she had inherited the family love of hunting.[46] Margaret was conscious that her grandchildren had lost their mother at a sensitive age, and tried to involve herself in their lives, playing something of a maternal role. She took care to reward their servants, some of whom were trusted friends of both Elizabeth and Margaret, including Lady Jane Guildford, Elizabeth Denton, Mary Denys and the enigmatic 'Great Elizabeth'.[47]

But not everyone believed that Margaret's involvement in her grandchildren's upbringing was benign. Writing in 1508, the Spanish ambassador Gutierre Gòmez de Fuensalida claimed that Henry and Margaret's attentions towards the prince were crushing his natural ebullience, treating him more like a princess than a future king:

[Prince Henry] was never permitted to go out of the palace, except for exercise through a private door leading into the park. At these times he was surrounded by the persons specially appointed by the king as his tutors and companions, and no one else dared, on his life, to approach him. He took his meals alone, and spent most of his day in his own room, which had no other entrance than through the king's bedchamber. He was in complete subjection to his father and his grandmother and never opened his mouth in public except to answer a question from one of them.[48]

Fuensalida's report must, however, be taken with a pinch of salt. It was written expressly to excuse himself from having failed to gain a private audience with the prince and thus progress his mission. Fuensalida's colleague the duke de Estrada interpreted royal concern for the prince's upbringing more positively, believing that King Henry wanted to mould his son in his own image: 'Formerly the king did not like to take the Prince of Wales with him [to court], in order not to interrupt his studies,' Estrada reported, but now he kept him close 'to improve him... If he lives ten years longer [the king] will leave the prince furnished with good habits, and with immense riches.'[49]

In fact, it seems Prince Henry enjoyed a reasonable degree of liberty at the royal court. Among his 'specially appointed' companions were roistering jousters like Charles Brandon and the earl of Kent, with whom he spent many hours outside his own room, improving his skills in the tiltyard and parklands. Margaret's choice of gifts to Prince Henry supported these activities: after the expensively caparisoned horse she gave him in March 1506, in 1507 Margaret gave the prince a cloth of gold saddle and harness, and golden garters for Henry to wear in the tiltyard.[50] She is unlikely to have bestowed such expensive and ostentatious gifts if the king was opposed to his son participating in these princely, but potentially dangerous, pursuits.

But, although Margaret spoilt her grandchildren with gifts and visits, it is perhaps legitimate to ask if, as they grew to maturity, she felt a pang of redundancy? For decades, Margaret had been the matriarch not only of her own family but of a network of friends, relatives and dependents who looked to her for guidance. There were few areas of English life where she could not offer her wisdom. But now Henry was growing into a Renaissance prince, and Mary intended for a marriage of unrivalled international prestige. What could Margaret really teach them? They belonged to the era of the New World, she to the long-ago age of the Hundred Years War. Even her knowledge of the Wars of the Roses, valuable as it had once proven, was growing irrelevant. She was one of its last survivors.

Yet, although the life of a European princess was beyond Margaret's realm of experience, in other areas of political and public life – quieter, less ostentatious corners – she had already begun to carve out a niche for herself that was revolutionary. Perhaps her legacy would not extend as globally as her grandchildren's would, but, within her own sphere, she would exert influence as few women had before.

25

'More precious than gold'[1]

✳

On the eve of St Bartholomew's Day (23 August) 1506, a gentleman in his middle years shook off the dirt of London as he arrived at Hatfield Palace. In Richard Pynson's saddlebags, or perhaps tightly bound to a wagon behind him, was a bundle of books. These were not costly manuscripts like the handsome volumes in the libraries of the royal family, but printed, by Pynson himself, in his shop at 'the sign of the George' on the north side of Fleet Street. Like the many other book bundles that Pynson had brought to Margaret in the last few years, they were destined to be distributed throughout her household, to young scholars and neighbouring religious orders. Remarkably, some of the works Pynson had printed were written by Margaret herself.[2]

Print shops like Pynson's were a familiar sight in the cities of England. Beyond London, where they clustered around St Paul's Cathedral, they were to be found everywhere from Exeter to York, often run by foreign-born men like Pynson, for the book trade was international. But the ubiquity of print shops belied their novelty. When Margaret was born, the moveable printing press had only just been invented, in 1440 by the German craftsman Johannes Gutenberg. Business rapidly boomed and in 1476 William Caxton installed the first printing press in London.

Margaret's attitude towards printing, as to scholarship in general, was unusual. Blessed with an easy facility for learning, she never lost her sense that education was valuable for its own sake, and that it should therefore be disseminated as widely as possible.

Indeed, she felt a duty to propagate it. Her motivation and means of doing so, however, were firmly within the context of her time. For Margaret and her contemporaries, the source and purpose of education were religious: people learned their letters from religious texts, including the most basic 'horn books' from which children read aloud their prayers as well as the alphabet. As many as half of all books printed at this time were religious in their subject matter and many were in Latin, the language of the Church. Margaret would also have understood the purpose of education as moral: to enable people to understand their place in the (Christian) world, and to ready their souls for the afterlife. It was generally accepted that some period of that afterlife would be spent in Purgatory, from which one could only escape by good works and the benevolent prayers of others. The provision of education – like healthcare – was thus a moral duty for the wealthy, but it was also transactional. The founding of schools, colleges, almshouses and hospitals was repaid by the prayers of the scholars or patients using these facilities, for the spiritual benefit of the benefactor, whose time in Purgatory was thereby lessened.

Margaret was not motivated, however, solely by this quest for prayers. She sought to elevate her less fortunate contemporaries by enabling them to access the educational tools that she enjoyed. She knew that as a wealthy, literate woman she was exceptionally fortunate, since she could afford to buy religious texts, hand-written and illuminated, imported from overseas, and she understood works in French and – with some effort – simple Latin. Most of her son's subjects could only speak English or Welsh, and many could not read, which debarred them from the texts that provided her with spiritual comfort and enlightenment. That injustice rankled with her. But now the new technology of the printing press offered the opportunity to spread written works to the masses. A prayer book could be bought for as little as three pence – a day's wage for an unskilled labourer.[3] Even those who could not afford the books, or who could not read them, could have the works read aloud to them. Her son chose to employ Richard Pynson's services to print parliamentary statutes and ordinances of war, but Margaret commissioned Pynson, and other printers, to produce works that would illuminate the lives of her contemporaries.[4]

Margaret's patronage of printers began shortly after her son's accession and possibly as early as 1486, when William Caxton printed the *Speculum vite Christi*, a devotional life of Jesus translated by the Carthusian monk Nicholas Love.[5] Three years later, Caxton translated and printed the romance *Blanchardin and Eglantine* at Margaret's instigation – she had bought a copy of the work in its original French some years before. As well as Caxton and Pynson, Margaret also patronised the printer Wynkyn de Worde, who in 1494 printed the *Scala Perfectionis* at her commission. The subject matter of how to live a good religious life as a temporal lord was an important one to Margaret. By 1507, de Worde was Margaret's nominated printer, and produced several works for her including a life of the virgin-saint Ursula.

In her promotion of spiritual wellbeing, Margaret followed in the footsteps of earlier fifteenth-century noblewomen who were posthumously famed for their piety, most notably her own grandmother Margaret Holland, duchess of Clarence, who had been an early supporter of the Bridgettine order of Syon and instigated the dissemination of copies of a life of St Jerome. Many fifteenth-century noblewomen sponsored the Carthusian order, which prioritised English-language preaching and texts, including Cecily, duchess of York, Richard III's queen, Anne Neville, and Anne, duchess of Buckingham. But while these noblewomen were essentially conservative and private in their religion, Margaret sought to promote spiritual devotion beyond the walls of her home.[6]

One of her early religious projects was the cult of the Devotion to the Holy Name of Jesus. Originally a fourteenth-century English movement confined to closed religious communities and the nobility, this cult promoted the idea that there was intrinsic sacred power to the act of reciting Jesus' name. In the early years of her marriage to Thomas Stanley, Margaret commissioned a prayer book for her husband in which reverence for the Holy Name is evident. Such private devotional gifts were not uncommon for noblewomen, but, by 1493, Margaret was promoting the cult on a much wider scale. She commissioned Henry Hornby, the dean of her chapel at Collyweston, to write an office* of the Holy Name, which she then had printed by Richard Pynson. It was the first time this liturgy appeared in print, and such was Margaret's 'intense zeal' for the veneration of the Holy Name that in 1494 the Borgia Pope Alexander VI granted papal indulgences to encourage the celebration of its feast, at Margaret's request and with her personally named as patron.⁷ But even this level of popular promotion was less ambitious than Margaret's later-life educational work. For, shortly after Pynson printed the office of the Holy Name, Margaret met the man who transformed her advancement of learning.

John Fisher was a talented and uncompromising Yorkshire-born priest who, by 1495, had become proctor of Cambridge University. It was in this capacity that he first encountered Margaret, dining with her in the royal court at Greenwich, which he was visiting on university business. Although Fisher came to court as a petitioner and was young enough to be her son (indeed, a good decade younger than Henry), he so impressed Margaret that she quickly became his patron and appointed him her confessor. In 1504, he was made bishop of Rochester and chancellor of Cambridge University, in no small part thanks to Margaret's influence. While privately conversing in the sanctity of Margaret's closet, Fisher gently but unwaveringly stoked his patron's ambition. At his urging, Margaret used her privileged access to religious resources and transformed her private spiritual exercises into major works of religious devotion.

Margaret often visited religious houses like Syon Abbey on the Thames to enjoy their extensive libraries, and with her confessor's encouragement she began translating their works as a spiritual exercise. However, the religious knowledge that Margaret gained from these texts was inaccessible to most people, so in 1502 she took a radical step to circulate the books in print and translation. She urged a Cambridge fellow called William Atkinson to translate an enormously popular work on the importance of the Mass called

* An office is a liturgy of prayers.

De Imitatione Christi, or the *Imitatio*, from Latin into English, making it available to a wider audience. Margaret commissioned Pynson to publish the first three books of the *Imitatio*, which Atkinson had translated in 1503, stamping her authority on the title page with a woodcut of a crowned portcullis. The fourth book of the *Imitatio*, however, was little known in England, so Margaret undertook to translate it from French herself. In 1504, Pynson printed Margaret's translation, making her the first Englishwoman to appear in print.

Another book followed: *The Mirror of gold for the sinful soul** came hot off the presses from Paris, where it had been translated from its original Latin into French. Each of its seven chapters provided a meditation for the days of the week, leading sinners to repentance. It was again the French text that Margaret translated and Pynson printed in 1506. Margaret not only commissioned the translation and publication of these works, she also purchased large numbers of the books herself, which she paid to be bound by her servant Lenard of the Vestry and gifted to others. The sheer quantity of texts that she bought from Pynson gives some idea of the breadth of their dissemination: in November 1503, 76 copies of the *Imitatio* were bound by Lenard, and in December 100 printed books carried to Collyweston. A hundred volumes were also dispatched to Syon and, at New Year 1507, fifty books 'which my lady's grace translated out of French into English' brought by Pynson to Hatfield.[8] Margaret was not concerned with innovation for its own sake, but her recognition of the opportunity for mass dissemination that the printing press represented was astute.

Margaret and John Fisher also worked together on Margaret's most famous educational legacy: the foundation of her two Cambridge colleges, Christ's and St John's. Margaret was not the first noblewoman to found a university college: in the fourteenth century, Elizabeth, Lady Clare transformed University Hall in Cambridge into Clare College, while her friend Marie de Valence, countess of Pembroke founded Pembroke College. More

---

* *Speculum aureum animae peccatricis.* Fisher suggested that Margaret translated *several* works into English, but so far only these two texts, which Margaret undertook to print, have been found.

recently, Marguerite of Anjou had established a Queen's College in Cambridge.* By 1498, Margaret was funding two 'readerships' (professorships) in theology, one each at Cambridge and Oxford. However, Cambridge was geographically closer to Collyweston and had been supported by Henry VI, and it received the lion's share of Margaret's patronage.† In 1506, statutes were drawn up for 'Christs College', with Margaret providing for twelve fellows, of which six must be from nominated northern counties, and forty-eight scholars, of whom twenty-three must also come from the north. This stipulation owed something to Fisher's northern roots, and to Margaret's adopted Stanley family, but it was also a reflection of the poverty of northern England, for Margaret stipulated that she wanted to prioritise those 'in greater need'.[9] Margaret also converted the hospital of St John, which was in the control of her stepson James Stanley as bishop of Ely, into a college of the same name. Although neither college was complete by the time Margaret died – indeed, St John's was not formally founded until two years after her death – she ensured their financial stability with meticulously arranged endowments.[10]

John Fisher said that Margaret undertook her educational projects so 'that at length there should be born from this undertaking theologians who might communicate the fruit of their studies to the people'.[11] The ripples of her own good fortune would spread out into the country at large. For this reason, she insisted that the fellows of her colleges, and of other preacherships that she created at Cambridge, must deliver a set number of sermons publicly and in English, so their message was conveyed to the widest possible audience.

Margaret had a firmness of conviction that lent her a clear sense of purpose. She knew that as a noblewoman her duties were to God, her family and to the dependents whose lives she held in her power – in that order. Her legacy would be measured in how successfully she had protected, preserved and ideally improved the status of these responsibilities. Through her educational works she

---

* There was also a Queen's College, Oxford, founded by Philippa of Hainault, the queen of Edward III.
† Henry VI founded King's College, Cambridge.

had, she hoped, widened the pool of dependants whose lives were bettered by her actions, and who would thus be brought closer to God and into greater allegiance to her family. But, as hard as Margaret strove for this legacy, her first priority remained to care for her son. And in the New Year of 1507 – that very year that Hugh Conway's prophecy had once asserted would be the king's last – all her efforts had to be focused on that primary concern.

THERE WAS NOTHING, AT FIRST, TO INDICATE HOW SERIOUSLY ill Henry would become. But, shortly after his fiftieth birthday on 28 January 1507, some suggestion of sickness – a sore throat, huskiness to Henry's voice – summoned Margaret to her son's side. Early in February they were still together at Richmond, idly gambling at the card table and enjoying the Lenten gifts of baked lampreys and perch that Margaret was sent by the abbess of Syon and abbot of Gloucester. But, shortly after St David's Day (1 March), when Margaret and Henry rewarded the Welshmen in their service, Henry's throat grew so swollen he could barely swallow, and the severe pain extended up to his ears. He became feverish. His brow beaded with sweat, while his body was racked with chills. Eventually his breathing became laboured and he could take neither drink nor food.[12]

Fearing for her son's life, Margaret's short visit became a sick-bed vigil. She would not leave Henry's side. Her faithful grooms were dispatched back to Hatfield to fetch Margaret's ladies-in-waiting Margaret Stukeley and Perrot Doryn, who arrived with more supplies for the king's mother.[13] Margaret was sufficiently worried that she also ordered her servant John Holt to inform two of Henry's oldest friends, Thomas Savage, archbishop of York and John de Vere, earl of Oxford about the king's illness. From this mission, Holt rode on to Margaret's confessor, John Fisher, who promptly joined the household at Richmond. Did Margaret confide in Fisher, as she could in no other, her fears for her son's life?[14]

Margaret did everything in her power to help Henry. As she sat at his bedside, money flew from her coffers to good causes across the south-east, in the hopes that these acts of mercy would persuade God to save her son's life, or at the very least to spare his soul the agonies of Purgatory. Anchorites received reward, the needy gained alms and prisoners of London both male and female had their fees paid and were freed. And, just as she had in the wake of Elizabeth's death, Margaret rewarded and privately communicated with the king's closest servants. Payments went to Henry's closest body servant, the groom of the stool Hugh Denys, and a gift, too, for the groom of the chamber Richard Weston. The king's physicians, naturally, received a considerable bonus.[15] Now more than ever Margaret required the good service of these attendants – and also their silence. If word of the severity of Henry's illness escaped the walls of Richmond Palace, it might raise the spectre of rebellion, or prompt fresh pretenders to claim the Tudor crown. Flower buds in the Richmond Palace gardens burst into life, blooming months earlier than usual in the mild, dry weather, but inside the redbrick walls, Margaret watched in desperation as Henry ordered one of the under-clerks of the signet to write his will.[16] By now he had not eaten or drunk in six days, and 'his life was despaired of'.[17]

As he believed himself to be dying in March 1507, Henry repented his merciless financial exactions. Like Margaret, he sought remission of his sins through acts of charity, and ordered his servants to throw open the gates of prisons and pour coins into the eager palms of the poor. Two priests in royal service – Thomas Wolsey and Robert Fisher – were ordered to recite Mass after Mass for the king's soul, 7,209 altogether.[18] And eventually, around Easter, Margaret and Henry's prayers were answered. The swelling in the king's throat diminished, enabling him to finally take on liquid and then food. By 7 April, the Wednesday in Easter week, Henry was well enough to receive the Spanish ambassador Rodrigo González de la Puebla, who spent two hours in the royal chamber, discussing ongoing negotiations for an alliance.[19] Margaret set out on a thanksgiving pilgrimage to St Albans Abbey, perhaps fulfilling a vow she had made during Henry's illness. A new horse was purchased for her litter, and the king's own courser men accompanied her as she laid offerings of gold on the altar and presented money to an 'old monk' and anchorite within the town.[20]

Good fortune followed Henry's return to health. Towards the end of March, news had arrived from Scotland that Margaret's granddaughter the Queen of Scots had given birth to her first child, a son named James after its father. The messenger, Thomas Shirley, was richly rewarded by both Margaret and Henry for bringing such happy 'tidings'. Shortly after Margaret returned from St Albans, on 11 April, the Stanley servant Henry Conway arrived with news of another safe delivery: the wife of Margaret's grandson Tom, earl of Derby had also had a child and named her Margaret.[21] By late summer 1507, Henry was well enough to ride out hunting and hawking, and his mother could observe that, after months of lean sickness, her son was growing a little stout.[22]

Less pleasing to Margaret, and ominously for his good intentions, as soon as Henry recovered his strength, he also resumed communication with Empson and Dudley.[23] He might release prisoners and dole out alms in mortal extremis, but fundamentally his policy towards his subjects was unchanged. He still sought to bind them by fear and finance, not love.

AFTER HENRY'S INITIAL RECOVERY IN SPRING 1507, HE AND Margaret re-established a habit from the early years of his reign, with Margaret once again her son's shadow within the peripatetic royal court. In the following months, she trailed Henry from Westminster to Cambridge and Ely, before – trusting in his wellbeing – she briefly retired to Hatfield and left him to enjoy his customary summer hunting trip.[24] During 1508, she was often at court, seven months in all, longer than she had spent there in a decade. But, in Henry's early years as king, Margaret had exercised her vigilance against external threats. Now, she focused her energies on the less tangible challenges of maintaining her son's wavering health and tarnished reputation, and quieting the unease both engendered within the court. Henry's constitution had been substantially weakened by age, stress and repeated bouts of ill health. Spring 1508 once again saw him fall into a dangerous decline, only for the summer to bring restoration.[25]

Margaret was in her mid-sixties, and these cycles of sickness with their intense spikes of anxiety, mental efforts to limit political fallout and physical demands of removing from her home to take care of Henry, took their toll. On 10 May 1507, while staying with Henry at the Tower, Margaret required 'honey for a medicine', in August 1507 she took another delivery of aqua vita and in February 1508 there were repeated payments to her physician William Hilmer for 'certain medicines' for 'my lady'.[26] Compounding her concern for her son, tragic messages arrived from Scotland that caused relapses in Henry's illness. In July 1508, Margaret's granddaughter lost her first child to sickness and only months later gave birth to a daughter who died within a few hours. It was a devastating reminder of how swiftly and cruelly generations could be snatched away, and of the dynastic insecurity bedevilling their family.[27]

The one advantage that came from Henry's sequences of ill health was that, in the king's absence, the prince was able to display himself to his subjects. Thus, the process of winning hearts and minds necessary for his safe accession could get underway. In March and April 1508, while the king disingenuously pleaded 'a touch of gout' and retreated with Margaret away from the noise and bustle of the court, Prince Henry took his father's seat in the royal hall to dine among his lords.[28] On St George's Day (23 April), the prince processed at the head of the Knights of the Garter in Windsor Castle, symbolically embodying the chivalric ideals of the order. But, unlike his father, the prince did not merely represent knighthood from a safe distance. In spring and summer 1508, the sixteen-year-old participated in a succession of tournaments around London, displaying his formidable horsemanship and precision while 'running at the ring'. In one contest, he even accidentally broke the arm of his fellow competitor the earl of Kent.[29] Aware of the benefit to their regime of her grandson demonstrating such military skills as he bonded with his 'comrades in arms', Margaret sent the prince more than £33 to fund these martial activities.[30]

But Margaret's concern for her son's declining health was still paramount. By summer 1508, Bernard André reported that Henry was still 'greatly taxed and emaciated [from] his previous prolonged malady'.[31] It was a bad time for the king to be unwell. On 13 June, the morning of Pentecost, a lunar eclipse was prophesied and, since eclipses were believed to presage the downfalls of regimes and deaths of kings, there must have been an uncomfortable wait for the phenomenon. Fortunately, the eclipse occurred before dawn and thus went largely unnoticed. But the season remained unbearably hot and, as temperatures rose, fever appeared in the fetid, close alleyways of London. The sluggish Thames began to stink and plague broke out in the capital. Even when the weather broke with a burst of thunder, the pestilence could not be contained, and soon it was clear that this was one of the most serious epidemics to have struck England in twenty years: the sweating sickness had returned.[32]

When it was apparent how dangerous this plague was, Henry and Margaret leaped into action. They divided their households, splintering into separate, small entourages to seek sanctuary in their courtiers' manor houses, far removed from the populous Thameside palaces. These measures were taken only just in time. Two of Henry's closest companions, his chamberlain Sir Charles Somerset* and Richard Fox, were both laid low by the sickness. Both, mercifully, survived. Thousands did not. In August, a public supplication was made by the priests of St Paul's Cathedral, pleading with God to end the ravages of plague. Henry issued an edict forbidding anyone coming from London to visit him, and prohibiting his courtiers from entering the capital. Margaret, meanwhile, decamped with a reduced household from Hatfield to Tongges, the Hertfordshire manor now known as Theobalds.† There, she hoarded a treasure trove of medicines against the plague. A groom of her spicery was dispatched to fetch 'drugs and other

---

* Somerset replaced Giles Daubeney after the latter's death from a strangury (a painful bladder disorder) on 21 May 1508.
† Tongges was owned by Cecily Bedell, the wife of Margaret's treasurer William.

necessary medicines' to sustain her; William Hilmer bought her 'a pot with treacle* of Genoa'; and one of Prince Henry's servants sourced curatives including choice ginger and a mysterious powder kept in a tin pot.[33]

In June that year, Margaret wrote her will, having 'called to our remembrance the unstableness of this transitory world'. The only inevitabilities were 'that every creature here living is mortal, and the time and place of death to every creature uncertain'.[34] She was primarily concerned with the religious arrangements for her funeral, and for the sustenance of her household servants should she die suddenly. She directed her executors, led by Richard Fox, John Fisher and Charles Somerset, to ensure her household was maintained for three months after her death, with all the attendants therein 'kept together' receiving their 'meat, drink and other things convenient'. In the hope that he would survive her, she named 'our dear son' Henry as supervisor of her will, 'for the singular love that we bear and ever have born unto his highness... and for the singular trust that we have' in him.[35]

By their swift actions, both Margaret and Henry survived this spell of sweating sickness. Not long after the twenty-third anniversary of Henry's accession, in late August 1508, the king returned to Greenwich Palace, and Margaret to Hatfield. The plague receded. Normal life resumed. But perhaps Margaret felt that niggling fear that always accompanied moments of calm or joy. Two years in a row, spring had brought her son to the brink of death, and confronted Margaret with his mortality. The new year would repeat this pattern – for the last time.

---

* 'Treacle' or 'mithridatum' was a cure-all medicine.

26

'Smoke and shadow'[1]

※

St George's Day (23 April) 1509 brought the great of the land to court in Richmond, among them the grave but gentle archbishop of Canterbury, William Warham. Having enjoyed a little dinner at royal expense – the archbishop was famed for his frugality – Warham found himself looking up into the smiling face of the esquire of the body, Richard Weston. Since moving from Elizabeth's service, Weston had served Henry faithfully, and in recent weeks had become a constant presence in the palace chambers. He arrived now to summon Warham, along with certain other leading royal advisers, to the king's secret chamber. Weston bade Warham to come and speak – Weston checked himself before continuing, still smiling – he ought to come to the king.[2]

But, within the secret chamber to which Weston led him, Warham did not find Henry. Instead, he was confronted by a wall of grim-faced royal counsellors, headed by Richard Fox. Fox looked as pale and gaunt as death at the best of times, and was still emaciated from the sweating sickness that had almost killed him the previous summer. A small coterie of fellow Garter luminaries surrounded him, almost certainly including Margaret, her pinched features gleaming within her black headdress. Thus, Warham was informed that two days ago, an hour before midnight on Saturday 21 April, King Henry had died. The event Margaret had feared since her son had quickened in her womb fifty-two years earlier had finally come to pass. And she was helping to conceal it.

*

Margaret had spent the first four months of 1509 between fear and hope. She was confident enough in Henry's health to spend Christmas away from him at Hatfield.[3] As she had every Christmastide for the past eight years, she alternated between enjoying the entertainments provided by her yellow-suited Lord of Misrule and the more serious business of preparing for her death, drawing up her legacies and estimates for likely funeral expenses. She may have been ill herself, for she required her physician William Hilmer to prepare 'certain medicines' for her in January.[4] Any concern for her own wellbeing was laid aside, however, by word of a downturn in Henry's health. In mid-January, she hurried to her son's side, following him from Richmond Palace to the health-giving open heathland of Hanworth Park, to the west of London.

Although Henry's sickness had returned, it did not yet fully consume Margaret's attentions. Ever the mindful patron, she was vexed by the poor state of repair of Chertsey Bridge as she travelled, and on 1 February gave Mary Denys twenty shillings to put towards its reparation.[5] Once past the February anniversaries of the death and birth of Queen Elizabeth – dates always acknowledged by Henry, when Margaret feared some relapse – she felt able to attend to Lenten religious acts. She dispatched gifts of baked bream to her fellow observant fasters and undertook a pilgrimage as far as St Albans. There, she met with Thomas Stanley's grandson Tom, earl of Derby, who was staying nearby with his sister and young children, Margaret and John. Tom's countess, Anne, was heavily pregnant and may have remained at the family seat in Lathom, where she gave birth on 10 May to Tom's future heir.[6] Throughout her journey, Margaret maintained regular contact with the royal court, through the servants of her grandchildren and of Katherine of Aragon, and via her usual trusted emissaries: Richard Aderton and Nicholas Aughton.[7]

Perhaps Margaret hoped that her visit to the shrines of St Albans could restore her son's health, but early April brought Aughton rushing to her door with terrible news. Henry had collapsed.

Bedridden, he lay sick at Richmond, unable to eat or drink, his body wracked by pain. Margaret hurried to her son, enlisting a barge with eight oars to row her from Coldharbour to Putney, then on to Richmond. She settled in for a long stay, bringing with her kitchen staff and utensils.[8] Ten days later, Reginald 'my lady's idiot' was summoned from Hatfield to join her with his keeper Laurence Bonde, presumably to comfort Margaret during this desperate period.[9] For it was now clear that her son was, finally, dying. Not that Henry was ready yet to accept it.

Still clinging to hope of recovery, Henry bartered for his life with God. He promised his confessor 'with great sorrow and great repentance... a true amendment of all his' wrongdoings, called for 10,000 Masses for his soul and a general pardon for his subjects. Even as his will was drawn up on 31 March, still he prayed for remission. If he survived, he swore to God, he would reform his officers and ensure justice was executed honestly rather than for financial gain. With that promise in his heart, he crept on agonised knees across the tiled floor of his chapel closet at Easter. Even as his appetite failed, the meat 'loathsome' in his mouth, still he hoped. By 19 April, he could no longer make it to Mass and had to have the sacrament wafer brought to him in his bed. Weeping, and hitting his cramped hands against the protruding bones of his ribcage, he kissed the ornate vessel in which the sacrament was contained over and over again.

Henry's death was 'a blessed end' in that he fulfilled all the requisite duties to enter Heaven: he clutched a crucifix to his chest, called out to Jesus and received the sacrament of extreme unction. But it was not an easy death, and Margaret endured the sight of her son surrendering, unwilling and agonised, to his own mortality. In John Fisher's funeral sermon for Henry, he described the king making 'so many tears, so many callings for mercies' during the twenty-seven hours that 'he lay continually abiding the sharp assaults of death'. Like Margaret, Henry believed that invoking Jesus' name had sacred influence, so in his last hours, 'with all his might and power he called upon the name of our lord... *Et nomen domini invocui. O* my blessed Jhesu, o my most merciful Jhesu, o my lord and creator Jhesu. *O domine libera animam meam.*

O my lord deliver my soul...' As the darkness gathered outside the windows of Richmond Palace, Margaret heard her son mutter the words: 'Deliver my soul from these deadly pains, deliver my soul from this corruptible body, deliver my soul from the bonds of sin, deliver my soul from my mortal enemies, deliver my soul... deliver my soul...'[10]

And finally, an hour before midnight on 21 April 1509, God did.

THE DAY BEFORE HENRY DIED, A CURIOUS PAYMENT WAS rendered in Margaret's household accounts: her groom of the chamber, Hugh Worsley, received expenses for going to London 'to cause Mr Polydore to come to Richmond'.[11] Why did Margaret seek to summon her son's historian, Polydore Vergil, to court now? Perhaps it was to fulfil his religious role, for beside his literary accomplishments Polydore was also a priest and papal agent. Or maybe Margaret wanted him to bear witness to the end of her son's rule and the accession of her grandson. If he was a witness to the first hours of the new regime, Polydore was privy to a secret that was kept from some of the closest advisers of Henry VII. For around Henry's cooling body, finally released from its terrible struggle, a political coup was underway.

Henry's death two nights before St George's Day afforded his surviving counsellors a brief window of opportunity. Margaret more than anyone wanted to ensure her grandson Prince Henry acceded the throne safely, but no one living in 1509 could remember a smooth succession. The last two had triggered bloodshed and political chaos – even the peaceful accession of the infant Henry VI, all the way back in 1422, following the death of Henry V, had necessitated the politically fraught process of establishing a regency council to rule during the child-king's infancy.* John de Vere, earl of Oxford was sufficiently anxious about the turmoil that might follow the king's death that on 10 April he wrote his own will, despite 'being in good health and perfect mind, not...

---

* He was, and remains, the youngest king in English history at nine months old.

diseased with any bodily sickness'. Like Margaret, he had lived through the Wars of the Roses and knew 'well the uncertainty and unstableness of this wretched life'.[12] It was almost five years since Hugh Conway had overheard leading advisers debating the succession and Margaret knew that, to manoeuvre her seventeen-year-old grandson safely onto the throne, she could not leave affairs to chance.

It was not the first time that Margaret had needed to suppress grief in favour of action. Even the greatest loss of all, of her child, could not be dwelt on. She must act, and fortunately she had allies among the royal counsellors who stood with her at Henry's deathbed. Many were long-term adherents of her son, their service stretching all the way back to Henry's days as a penniless exile on the Continent: Richard Fox, Thomas Lovell, Charles Somerset. Over the years since, Margaret had built personal relationships with these men, their families and households. But potential rivals lurked everywhere, especially among the relatives of the late Queen Elizabeth. The younger brother of Edmund de la Pole, Richard, known as the 'White Rose', still flitted between the courts of European princes. His cousin Thomas Grey, marquess of Dorset was a young man who excelled in the tournament and had been accorded the honour of leading the jousts for Arthur and Katherine's wedding. Nonetheless, King Henry had suspected him of Yorkist conspiracy and late in 1508 consigned him to prison. Margaret was close to Dorset's wife, Eleanor St John (daughter of her half-brother Oliver), who was a frequent visitor to Margaret's home and recipient of monetary rewards.[13] Perhaps, then, it had been Margaret's intercession that persuaded Henry to pardon Dorset in January 1509, although he remained imprisoned three months later.

Dorset and Edmund de la Pole were captive at Henry's death, but other potential rivals walked free. Among the most immediately concerning were the Staffords, Margaret's one-time wards whose distant blood claim could easily be revived. Henry VII never fully trusted the duke of Buckingham, whose fractious relationship with his younger brother Lord Henry Stafford augured ill for any familial loyalty. Margaret knew Buckingham and Lord

Stafford from their childhoods, and seems to have shared her son's disquiet. There was something in the Stafford blood that lent itself to conspiracy. Among the servants of Buckingham's arrogant, rabble-rousing brother-in-law the earl of Northumberland, it was already confidently asserted that, when Henry died, Buckingham and Northumberland would rule as protectors while dominating young Henry VIII, and split England between them.[14]

But Margaret's greatest challenge was not suppressing external threats, it was the long shadow of Henry's rule. The past decade of creeping injustice and fiscal control had made his regime deeply unpopular, and Prince Henry could easily be tainted by association. Still only seventeen at his father's death, he might easily be led by malign forces – or sheer inexperience – to maintain Henry VII's resented style of kingship, risking rising discontent and potentially even rebellion. Polydore Vergil wrote that, because of the prince's youth, Margaret 'began to take precautions' from the earliest moments of his reign in order 'that the reins of government would at the outset be in the hands of excellent men'.[15]

But Margaret did not only seek to surround her grandson with the right people. She also wanted to change the public perception of their family. As the chronicler Edward Hall put it, Margaret needed 'to shift the noise' against them and 'appease the people' with a clear statement of change.[16] Unfortunately, so many leading officers of Henry's regime had benefited from his financial exactions and harsh justice that almost everyone at court was implicated – including Margaret herself. As much as she was truly dedicated to protecting her family, she was also undeniably concerned to divert attention from her own punitive activities so she could maintain a pre-eminent status. Someone must answer for her son's exactions, clearly, but it must not be the late king himself and it must not be Prince Henry – and, as far as Margaret was concerned, it must not be her either.

Here, Margaret was helped by the court factionalism that had arisen in the last years of her son's life, when the ascent of Empson and Dudley had caused fault lines to fracture her son's government. The unprecedented promotion of these parvenu lawyers seriously affronted counsellors like Fox and Lovell, whose loyalty to Henry

VII was of long-standing and whose rewards were both hard-won and sparing. In recent months, there had been subtle indications that the two factions were beginning to move against one another. Hugh Denys, a known associate of Edmund Dudley and once ubiquitous presence at court, had virtually disappeared. Denys had suffered a bout of sweating sickness the previous summer, and was still not fully recovered by spring 1509. In his absence, Richard Fox had manoeuvred his own ally, Richard Weston, into the royal chambers with their ready access to the king and potential to influence affairs. Unlike Denys, Weston had quietly but consistently opposed Empson and Dudley's financial exactions, and was noted by one knight in 1503 as a reliable ally of Fox and Lovell.[17] While Fox was moving his chess pieces within the royal household, Empson and Dudley were gearing up for more direct action: they had primed their supporters in Northamptonshire and the south-east to come to them when summoned, armed and armoured. If necessary, when Henry VII died, they would seize control of government by force.[18] From the precedent of previous coups, it was evident that whichever faction triumphed, the other would lose influence – and potentially also their lives.

In this high-stakes political game, Margaret had a singular advantage: she held no formal office, and represented no clear faction beyond her familial attachment to the dynasty of her son and grandson. Her personal political preference was probably for a coalition led by Bishop Fox, but she was pragmatic enough to recognise that his triumph was far from certain. So, as late as April 1509, she was still prepared to work instead with Empson and Dudley. In effect, she had assumed the traditional tactic of her late husband.

The evidence for Margaret's thinking during this crucial period, as for so much of her activity, lies in her household accounts. They demonstrate, unsurprisingly, that Margaret's relationship with Fox was close and long-standing. There are numerous payments over the years to her messengers for their visits to the bishop.[19] Thomas Lovell also appears a number of times: in July 1507, Margaret stayed with the Lovells for long enough to present rewards to their kitchen offices on departure, and the following November

Thomas's wife Isabel visited Margaret at Hatfield with Margaret's niece Eleanor, marquess of Dorset.[20]

Where Margaret had contact with an influential male politician, she often cultivated relationships with his family too. Thus, there are numerous rewards in her accounts to both Hugh and Mary Denys, as well as to Richard Weston and his wife, Anne Sandys. The king's mother was sufficiently acquainted with the Westons that she gave their first child a christening gift in March 1507, and another gift the following year. It is possible that this child was Margaret's godchild, as Richard and Anne Weston had a daughter called Margaret whose birthdate is unknown. It is also possible, although hard evidence is lacking, that Margaret had an even longer relationship with the family, and that Richard's father, Edmund Weston, was among the Lincolnshire rebels whom Margaret persuaded to support Henry in 1483–5. On Henry's accession, Edmund was swiftly elevated to the position of captain, keeper and governor of Guernsey and the lesser Channel Islands – a militarily sensitive appointment suggestive of prior acquaintance.[21]

But, if Margaret had been entirely committed to Fox's faction in the last months of her son's life, one might expect her to have avoided contact with Empson and Dudley. Yet the accounts reveal the opposite. As recently as Lent, Margaret had sent them both gifts of bream: fished from her rivers, baked in her ovens and conveyed at her own expense to the doors of their homes. The few other recipients of this gift were Margaret's stepson James Stanley; Perkin Warbeck's widow, Lady Katherine Gordon; Mary Denys – and Bishop Fox.[22] Margaret's dealings with Richard Empson had otherwise been essentially professional, although a subtle shift in her accounting in 1504 from payments to 'the king's attorney' to simply 'Master Empson' may suggest a closer working relationship. With Dudley, Margaret had more interaction, because of his role as intermediary in securing Creek Abbey as an endowment for Christ's College – a part that would have won him little favour, given the high price she ultimately paid for it. Nonetheless, there were exchanges between her and Dudley going back several years, with their servants received frequently at each other's homes. In September 1504, Margaret had even dispatched a message to Elizabeth, Dudley's wife, perhaps after the birth of their son John.[23]

Perhaps, by courting both sides of the divide towards the end of Henry's life, Margaret viewed herself as playing the traditional, female role of intermediary, attempting to keep the peace. Or perhaps she had already committed to Bishop Fox's faction and merely sought to lull Empson, Dudley and their ally Denys into a false sense of security. But, given her decades of political activity, not to mention her marriage to the notoriously equivocal Thomas Stanley, the most likely explanation for Margaret's activities was that she played both sides so that, whoever emerged the victor, she could safeguard the interests of herself and her own family.

As it transpired, when Henry died on 21 April, one faction held a clear advantage, for Fox and his friends were at Henry's deathbed. Empson, Dudley, the Staffords and other potential rivals were not. Denys's supplanting by Richard Weston meant that Empson and Dudley were deprived of insider intelligence in these vital hours. Thus, Fox could seize the initiative while his rivals were ignorant that the king was even dead. He entreated his allies – and surely Margaret – to join him in concealing Henry's death so that a coup could be launched against Empson and Dudley, removing them from the political landscape altogether. They would be cast as wicked counsellors who had subverted justice and abused their power over the king. Henry VII's good name would be preserved and the reign of the new King Henry VIII could begin by sweeping away injustice. Since this achieved precisely Margaret's objective of 'shifting the noise' from her own family, she too committed to the conspiracy. Given her constant proximity to Henry during his illness, it would have been impossible for her to be excluded.

So, for two days, while Fox and his allies made the last manoeuvres for their coup, the pretence was maintained that Henry was still alive. As his corpse lay in his chamber, on Sunday 22 April, an offering was made at the high altar of the royal chapel in his name. On the morning of St George's Day, heralds loudly proclaimed the 'largesse' of the king, and Prince Henry continued to dine publicly as if he was still the heir to the throne. Margaret's servants played their part in this subterfuge. On 22 April, she dispatched two trusted grooms, Robert Fremingham and Robert Hilton, downriver to the royal wardrobe in London to fetch 'certain black cloth' with which Margaret and her ladies could have mourning clothes made. It was a simple task, but Fremingham and Hilton made it last six days, presumably so their return journey through the city bearing a cartload of mourning black would not attract the attention of any sharp-eyed citizens in the pay of Empson and Dudley until after Fox's coup was achieved.[24]

In the meantime, many leading noblemen and bishops arrived at court to celebrate St George's Day with the Order of the Garter, of which Richard Fox himself was prelate. Notably absent were the Staffords, and Empson and Dudley. A select few of these attendees – carefully chosen after consultation between Margaret, Fox and the plotters – were led by Richard Weston into the secret chamber of King Henry, and there informed of his death. Having thus been inducted into the coup, they then trooped back out into public view as outwardly merry as they had gone in. The following morning, shortly after dawn, soldiers beat at the doors of Empson's and Dudley's homes and, caught unawares, the lawyers were carted off to the Tower. Lord Henry Stafford, too, was seized and imprisoned.

The success of the coup against Empson and Dudley can be read in the pages of the *Great Chronicle of London*, written shortly after Henry VII's death. Praise is lavished on that 'fortunate prince' Henry VII, in whom was 'all virtue'. His only vice was a tendency to avarice incited by 'Empson and Dudley... to their own lucre and advantage', which 'caused his grace to bear the wit and blame of all their ill doing'.[25] Thus, with scapegoats for the old regime incarcerated and Henry VII's good name preserved, proclamation was finally made that the king had died. Long live the new king. Long live King Henry VIII.

27

'A golden world'[1]

*

On 3 May 1509, Margaret was rowed downriver to the Tower of London, for once her customary black-clad form merely one among many. According to the mourning ordinances she had written six years earlier, Margaret was surrounded by figures concealed beneath black hoods and long black trains, among them her St John nieces Alice Parker and Anne Clifford, and the faithful attendants now of decades' standing, Lady Jane Guildford, Edith Fowler and Alice Stanhope. In all, ten of Margaret's gentlewomen and twenty-seven men attended her in their mourning livery.[2] Their presence must have been a comfort to Margaret in these difficult days. While her teenage grandson rode through the City of London in the bright spring sunshine to take up residence at the Tower and begin his life as king, Margaret had remained in the hushed confines of Richmond Palace, entombed in a world of Death.

As chief executor of her son's will and leading organiser of his funeral, for the past fortnight she had remained close to where Henry's embalmed corpse lay in state – in his great chamber, his hall and finally the chapel royal at Richmond. She sifted through the same dismal post-mortem administration that had followed the deaths of her husbands and her mother – this time with the additional stress of executing the exacting demands of a monarch. Henry VII's last will and testament ran to thirty-seven pages, longer than that of any other English medieval king.[3]

But, when Margaret stepped ashore at the Tower dock in May, she entered a new world. The court of the teenage King Henry

VIII was a place of glittering chivalry, display and romance. The wild divergence in Margaret's and her grandson's experience during the transition to Henry VIII's reign is evident in their surviving documents. As monarch, Henry VIII spent his early days dispatching announcements of his accession to Justices of the Peace and foreign princes. Plans were immediately underway for his coronation – a ceremony that would cost a staggering amount of money. Payments for cloth of gold and silk numbered into the high hundreds of pounds. Jewels worth £150 were purchased by his newly appointed groom of the stool, and childhood friend, William Compton, and then set in gold at a cost of over £142 by John Vanvtrike, goldsmith to Margaret and the late king. On 8 July, the master of the great wardrobe, Andrew Windsor, received £3,000 towards his outlay on coronation expenses, with an additional £2,322 at the end of August.[4]

At Richmond, meanwhile, beneath black-cloth canopies, Margaret and the leading members of the royal council – many of them also Henry VII's executors – had been signing their names to sheet after sheet of paperwork as they organised the late king's funeral. Not every authorisation for payment contains the signature of all the royal executors – some days Thomas Lovell was absent, on others John Fisher was not in attendance – but on every page of signatures, there is 'Margaret R'. With the same meticulous attention that she and her son had always focused on administrative tasks, Margaret signed her name to payments to religious houses, or for heraldic displays around the royal hearse – for the timber construction of the hearse itself – £500-worth of torches, and 330 poor men to accompany them. Every last penny was accounted for, down to the £2,895, 11s and 2d received by Andrew Windsor for the funeral expenses of the royal household.[5] Little wonder that, at the end of May, Margaret needed to buy a new penner,* inkhorn, parchment and vellum.[6]

Thus, throughout April and May, Margaret's was a black world of death and sorrow; her grandson's one of celebration and liberty. On 8 May, only a fortnight after the Spanish ambassador Fuensalida

---

* A writing case for pens.

had been assured by a royal councillor that Henry VIII would not consider marrying Katherine of Aragon because 'it would burden his conscience to marry his brother's widow', the king decided to do precisely that. A delighted Katherine joined Henry, Princess Mary and their '*grauntdame*' Margaret at the Tower of London as messages were dispatched to Spain to formalise the agreement as quickly as possible. Only a month later, the couple would be married.[7] Not for the new king the endless rounds of marital bartering that his father insisted were necessary. He wanted to be wed, and – probably even more – he wanted a Spanish alliance that would enable him to imitate his ancestor King Henry V and ride to war with France in gleaming plate armour. In June, he would be eighteen, old enough to risk his strong, sturdy body in battle – or so at least he believed. Margaret and the royal council continued to advise caution. The swiftly conducted marriage was probably a delaying tactic on the part of Henry VIII's advisers – the king could have a wife, to distract him a little longer from warmongering.

Although the Spanish ambassador Fuensalida named only the male counsellors involved in negotiating the marriage, Margaret must have played a leading part in arranging the union. Her approval was unnecessary but, as a proficient matchmaker, she could act the emollient negotiator between her inexperienced but headstrong grandson and his guarded, politically minded council. Margaret clearly approved of Henry's choice of bride – during almost a decade of acquaintance, she had been impressed by Katherine's patient stoicism in the face of marital purgatory. The dynastic uncertainties of the past seven years had also encouraged Margaret to believe that hastening the production of an heir was no bad thing. Once Henry and Katherine had a prince, the king could have his war.

The day after Henry VIII's marriage was agreed, his father's corpse began its journey from the chapel of Richmond Palace to its final resting place beside his own beloved queen, at Westminster Abbey. Throughout the three days of funeral ceremony, as the city of London reverberated with requiems, clouds of incense rising over the procession of the royal court to St Paul's Cathedral and then on to Westminster, Margaret remained with her grandson

inside the Tower. Had she joined the crowds pressing eagerly along
the route of the funeral cortège, she would have been confronted
with the eerie sight of two spectres of her son: one a life-like carved
and painted wooden effigy in robes of estate, its sunken cheeks a
testament to the king's harrowing last days, but its slightly lopsided
smile and raised eyebrow suggesting the charm and humour that
Polydore Vergil described in Margaret's son. A little way ahead of
this effigy rode a tall, slender figure in the king's suit of armour,
the royal battle-axe held with its head downward, resting on his
foot. Sir Edward Howard, the second son of the earl of Surrey
and stepfather of Margaret's protégé Henry Parker, had been afforded the honour of riding in the king's harness, which would
later be offered up at the altar – a visible symbol of the restoration
of the Howard family, and of the martial victories of this king of
England, the last to win his throne in battle.[8]

Margaret's purpose for fifty years had been the preservation
of her son. She had served his material interests in life and now,
parted by Death, she continued to strive for his soul. She entrusted
the delicate task of delivering her son's funeral sermon at St Paul's
Cathedral to her own confessor, John Fisher. Neither she nor
Henry VII had appreciated vain praise, and even dead she would
not permit him to be extolled beyond his measure. She trusted
Fisher to elicit prayer and compassion for King Henry from his
audience without muddling his purpose with excessive praise. As
was her wont, Margaret insisted on a full record of events: both
a description of the 'honourable services done about King Henry
VII in coming of his corpse from thence to Westminster', delivered
by her yeoman Robert Merbury, and a copy of Fisher's sermon.[9] By
now it was clear that Margaret was assembling these archives –
just as she had commissioned a memorial of King Philip of Castile's
visit – not only for her own interest, but for posterity. She sought
to store and even disseminate the papers, just as she had spread
her translations of moral works. On 22 May, she paid one of her
servants to carry Fisher's sermon to her printer, Wynkyn de Worde,
at his print shop on Fleet Street in London. At her 'special request',
de Worde printed the sermon so that all who took the inexpensive
text in their hands would be encouraged to pray for the late king.

Thus, Fisher's words reached far beyond the audience who heard his eulogy in person.[10]

With Margaret's son entombed at Westminster Abbey, she moved with Henry VIII, Mary, Katherine and the rest of their court to the garden palace of Greenwich to make preparations for Henry and Katherine's wedding on 11 June and joint coronation a fortnight later. Shortly after moving in, Margaret made alterations that suggest she was struggling physically. Even though her harbinger, George Fraunces, had gone ahead to ready her lodgings before her arrival on 15 May, it was necessary for Margaret to have a featherbed moved downriver from her Coldharbour mansion to the palace on 22 May. She may have been suffering from arthritis or rheumatism – John Fisher recalled his benefactor enduring 'most painful cramps so grievously vexing her' hands towards the end of her life.[11] Perhaps finding the royal court's food was also too much for her diminished appetite, on 31 May further payments were made for the movement of her privy kitchen 'stuff' from the Tower: butter, eggs, frying pan, kitchen pots and fuel duly bobbed along the River Thames in her wake.[12]

Details of Henry and Katherine's marriage are scant, but it is likely Margaret and her granddaughter formed part of the wedding party on 11 June. The union took place in the oratory of the friary church of Greenwich, with Katherine wearing white, her auburn hair hanging virginally loose.[13] Margaret may have presented the bride with a wedding gift, for at some point between May and June she gifted Katherine 'a girdle [belt] of gold containing 29 links and a great pomander at one end', which she had originally planned to bequeath to her granddaughter the Queen of Scots.[14] Katherine had officially been absorbed into the Tudor royal family. Now there was just the small matter of crowning her and her new husband.

MIDSUMMER'S EVE, AND 'ALL ENGLAND [WAS] IN ECSTASIES' TO celebrate the coronation of Henry VIII and Queen Katherine.[15] From a rented house in Cheapside, Margaret looked out across a gilded world.[16] The close, dusty streets of London had been transformed that afternoon.[17] Where once timber buildings loomed, now the heavy weight of tapestries hung like battle standards, rippling with foliage and mythical creatures. Through the clouds of incense, Margaret might have been able to make out the glimmering stalls of goldsmiths and the silver crosses and censers of priests, their metalwork catching the sunlight as they swung between shafts of light and shadow. It was a bright morning, but clouds overhead threatened rain. With her ingrained pessimism, perhaps Margaret awaited the downfall with more certainty than her companion that day, her thirteen-year-old granddaughter Princess Mary. It was the first time Mary had witnessed a coronation. It was Margaret's fourth.* It would also be her last.

Henry VIII seemed determined to outdo every previous celebration Margaret had seen. Golden embroidery, knotwork, chains and clothing were everywhere. Even the noble horses were adorned with costly goldwork trappings and silken reins. Margaret would have been happy to see her friend Margaret Pole in attendance. She had been raised from her impoverished circumstances at Syon to chief lady of the queen's household. Most magnificent of all were the king and queen themselves: Henry, five days shy of his eighteenth birthday, weighed down by ermine-furred robes of crimson velvet, his broad chest a shimmering rainbow of precious stones: diamonds, rubies, emeralds, great pearls and other gems.

As a statement of intent, ahead of the king rode two men in the robes of the duchies of Gascony and Normandy, and his children of honour wore the twinkling blue and gold *fleur de lys* of the French monarchy. This allusion to the territories over which the kings of England had once held dominion signalled Henry's determination to win the lands back. One might almost imagine Margaret rolling her eyes at this vain military posturing. How many times in her life had she watched men ride to futile war with France? How many thousands of lives had been lost as a result? And what had been gained from all their efforts? Or perhaps this is an imaginary leap too far. In her sixty-sixth year, perhaps

---

* Richard III and Anne Neville, Henry VII, Elizabeth of York, Henry VIII and Katherine of Aragon. Margaret probably did not attend Edward IV's 1461 coronation.

Margaret's commitment to the cause of English dominion over the French crown was as committed as that of the councillors into whose Hundred Years War she had been born.

Such ghosts of Margaret's past were everywhere, even on this day celebrating new beginnings. The last double coronation Margaret had witnessed was Richard III and Anne Neville's. Did she see in her grandson eerie shadows of his royal forebears, the men and women whose blood now coursed through his veins? Was there something in his rounded jawline to recall the blessed Henry VI, or was his youthful plumpness and auburn hair more reminiscent of Elizabeth of York? Did she catch, in his shrewd blue eyes, a glint of his late father – of Margaret herself – her own parents, or what she might imagine of her long-dead father's features? Perhaps she saw passing shades of lost but still beloved relatives: her half-brother John Welles, Jasper Tudor, the myriad St Johns and Plantagenets. Was there something of the height of Edmund Tudor – had he been tall? With no surviving portrait and almost five decades' distance, perhaps Margaret could not recall. There was no escaping one resemblance, however. In the 'features of his body, his goodly personage, his amiable visage [and] princely countenance', Henry powerfully resembled his grandfather Edward IV.[18] For Margaret, that similarity may not have been wholly comfortable. Might her grandson also imitate the less desirable features of Edward: his lust, his greed, his cruel streak?

Before Queen Katherine could approach Margaret and Mary's position in Cheapside, the threatening clouds burst. Hammering rain beat down on the roofs of the city and the queen was forced to dismount her litter and shelter under the awning of a draper's stall.

THROUGHOUT THE CELEBRATIONS FOR HENRY AND KATHERINE'S coronation, Margaret maintained a dignified distance. While the king and queen banqueted with their court, Margaret dined separately, and watched their activities 'in a place appointed on the right side of Westminster Hall'. She was attended by her cupbearer, Henry Parker.[19] Parker had been a constant presence in Margaret's household for years, and had become officially part of her family when he married her niece Alice St John. They and their two daughters were clearly held in great affection by their mistress, so it was fitting that Parker was in attendance for what would be Margaret's last court appearance – and that he is our chief source for her death.[20]

According to Henry Parker, among the many dishes served to Margaret during this coronation feast was a cygnet: a swan not yet a year old whose sweet flesh had not had the chance to gain the brackish, fishy taste of its elders. These were royal birds, many owned by Margaret herself, and according to legend when they neared death and their grey feathers had given way to pure white plumage, they would sing so sweetly 'that they teach us not to grieve at the fate of death' but to 'depart joyfully from the troubles of the present world.'[21] Parker blamed this dish for a sickness that overcame Margaret later that afternoon. Removed to her apartments in Cheneygate beside Westminster Abbey, she lay sick for five days. It was soon clear that her aged body could not withstand the assault of illness, possibly food poisoning. Her health had been declining in recent years, but in the struggle to care for her son and to ensure the safe accession of her grandson, she had buried her own pains and weaknesses. Now, however, her task was done. Like the swan, she sought only to be 'freed from this body of death, and to be with Christ'.[22] Her attendants provided 'certain waters and powders' to alleviate her discomfort.[23] Little else could be done.

Even as she lay dying, Margaret strove to fulfil her duties as a noblewoman. For someone who subscribed to the view that 'the time and place of death' was 'to every creature uncertain', Margaret had made every possible attempt in the past year to be braced against that uncertainty. She had repeatedly rewritten her will, and even calculated her likely funeral expenses – as it transpired, slightly over-estimating them.[24] She now made alterations to the legacies she had written in February at Hatfield, to reflect the changed circumstances of the new reign. The rest of the document containing Margaret's bequests is studiously neat, with ample space for each entry and Margaret's steady signature marking her assent to every bequest. But those for her grandchildren, updated towards the end of her life, have been struck through by one of Margaret's clerks, the bequests jumbled around and rewritten with additional notes squeezed between existing entries in an uncharacteristically disordered manner. Evidently, Margaret felt that the personal legacies she had made to 'my lord the prince' and 'the princess' Katherine were insufficient for their new status, so their titles were upgraded in the document to 'king' and 'queen,' and they were bequeathed six 'of my best cups of gold with their covers'.* It is a sign of the haste with which these bequests were made that Margaret did not bother specifying exactly which were her best cups for the king and queen, whereas in February she had carefully described all the items in her will.[25] The remainder of Margaret's will was left largely unaltered.

Evidence of Margaret's painful decline in those last days is provided by a scrap of paper that was placed amongst her will and legacies and lies now in St John's College archives in Cambridge. It is a note concerning an estate in Bassingbourne, Cambridgeshire, which she purchased as an endowment for Christ's College the previous January. Unlike the twenty or so firm, clear signatures that Margaret signed on the rest of her will, this note is signed with a cramped, shaky and effortful 'Margaret R', the pen pressing too hard and smudging the 'g', and rendering the 'R' barely recognisable. The line that extends beneath her signature is completely uneven and breaks halfway through. It is the writing of someone whose hands, as John Fisher noted, are crippled by pain, and whose body was wracked by sickness. But it is a testament to the fact that, even as Margaret's physical self was collapsing, her mind was still acute.[26]

Henry Parker recorded that, on the morning of St Peter's Day (29 June), the day after her grandson's eighteenth birthday, Margaret felt herself to be dying. The servants attending her, including Parker and probably his wife, Alice, were distraught to see 'death so haste upon her and that she must needs depart from them... Then wept they marvellously.'[27] Margaret summoned 'her ghostly father', probably John Fisher, so she could receive the

---

* The five best to Henry, the next best to Katherine.

sacrament and hear Mass. Parker claimed that, as Bishop Fisher 'lifted up the precious host this worthy lady expired... The last thing that ever she saw, as I do think, was God in his essence.'[28] For a woman of Margaret's profound belief, it was truly 'a fortunate and godly end'.

For Margaret, death was by this time a release. It ended her physical suffering and arrived, with extraordinary timeliness, only after her grandson had attained the crown, adulthood and a queen. For Margaret's servants, friends and family, however, her death was a profound loss. John Fisher claimed that, when knowledge of Margaret's demise trickled from her chamber in Westminster to the country at large, it provoked a wave of grief:

> [Then] wept her ladies and kinswomen to whom she was full kind, wept her poor gentlewomen whom she had loved so tenderly before, wept her chamberers to whom she was full dear, wept her chaplains and priests, wept her other true and faithful servants... All England for her death had cause of weeping.[29]

DEATH, AS MARGARET KNEW ALL TOO WELL FROM HER OWN experience, meant dispersal – and with that a deluge of administrative effort. Furniture and furnishings must be inventoried, packed up and conveyed to legatees; servants provided with six months wages – as Margaret had insisted – and then dispatched to find other masters. Money, in gold and silver, in jewels and manuscripts, and often in its less tangible but far more lucrative forms of lands, buildings, animals, rents and road tolls, must be accounted for and if necessary siphoned into the repayment of debts or the provision of religious bequests. Margaret's total assets came to a staggering £14,724 – almost ten million pounds in today's money.* To distribute this as she wished, Margaret had appointed John Fisher as her chief executor, to be assisted by a team of leading royal counsellors: Richard Fox, Charles Somerset,

---

* £9,758,550.39 to be precise.

Thomas Lovell, Sir Henry Marney.* They were joined by a trusted trio of her household administrators: her nephew and chamberlain, Sir John St John, her chancellor Henry Hornby and the controller of her household Sir Hugh Ashton.

As a wealthy Christian patron, Margaret had made extensive, detailed provision for her post-mortem wishes relating to educational and religious bequests: a chantry chapel was to be founded at her parents' burial place in Wimborne Minster, its expenses covered by a grant of West Country estates. That was a relatively straightforward task for her executors. The endowments to fund Christ's College in Cambridge ran to several pages of Margaret's wills and legacies. The provision for St John's College was far less advanced, and would cause John Fisher considerable trouble in the years to come. Perhaps he had an easier task than her faithful footman and messenger Nicholas Aughton, however, who had to oversee the capture of Margaret's swans on the River Thames for inventory purposes.[30]

Dispersed, too, were the specific legacies that Margaret had assigned to her closest relatives and attendants – many of whom had served her for decades by the time she died. A number of these servants received landed trusts to enjoy for life, including the widowed Edith Fowler and the husband and wife pair Richard and Margaret Stukeley. To Lady Jane Guildford, who was still struggling to extricate herself and her children from the financial disasters of her impecunious husband, Margaret left cold hard cash. She knew it was needed. More tangible items once owned by Margaret would be found in the houses of her survivors for many years to come, providing an abiding reminder of her. The priests tending to the needs of the students of St John's and Christ's College performed their rites surrounded by plate, jewels, vestments, altar cloths, books and hangings that had once adorned her private chapel. Among the gleaming gold and silver treasuries of the wealthy subjects of Henry VIII could be found golden pots and cups engraved with her portcullis crest, red rose or daisy marguerites: John Fisher, Charles Somerset, Margaret's chancellor

---

* A friend of Henry VIII's, Marney was appointed Chancellor of the Duchy of Lancaster in May 1509.

Henry Hornby and her nephew Sir John St John all received such bequests. Sir John's library bore another memento of Margaret – a manuscript of the *Canterbury Tales* in English, while a manuscript of John Gower's English works resided in the home of his daughter Alice Parker. Unsurprisingly, given their closeness to Margaret in life, the Parkers were the beneficiaries of several bequests, the most useful of which was probably the bedroom suite that Henry and Alice had shared in Margaret's household: a curtained bed with white damask curtains and counterpane, a canopy of cloth of gold on crimson velvet, wall hangings embroidered with clusters of grapes and foliage and an array of other furnishings – carpet, velvet cushions, blankets, sheets, a featherbed, bolster and pillows.[31]

The most extraordinary memorial to Margaret is the gilt bronze effigy sculpted by Pietro Torrigiano that lies atop her tomb in Westminster Abbey. The effigy, like Torrigiano's nearby sculptures representing Henry VII and Elizabeth of York, shows Margaret life size and with vivid realism. The lined, open-eyed face is so realistic that it was likely modelled on Margaret's death mask. Possibly originally painted, but now faded almost to black, the effigy shows Margaret lying at prayer, her wrinkled, papery hands pressed firmly together. She is dressed as she was for her last decade of life, in her familiar vowess headdress, wimple and long mantle, and surrounded by her heraldic symbols: the portcullis and Tudor rose embroidered on the cushions beneath her head and a Beaufort yale lying at her feet.

It is extremely life-like, but it is static, calm. It does not reveal Margaret's dynamism or her sense of responsibility and duty, which abided until her last days. A more human memento is provided by Henry Parker, in an account he wrote for his friend, Margaret's great-granddaughter, Queen Mary I. Parker's writing is occasionally hyperbolic, as befits a humanist eager to demonstrate his learning to an educated prince. He compares Margaret not only to the Saxon queens Æthelflæd and Maud* but also to male classical figures including Seneca, Socrates and Titus Vaspasianus. Decades after the death of his patron, Parker still recalled her

---

* Wife of King Henry I.

'benign nature' and 'humanity' to those below her; a lingering affection for someone who took the effort to know the names of every one of her 'two and twenty score' (that is, 440) servants, personally visiting them when they were sick and ensuring they left her side content. Parker's final words of praise for 'this precious marguerite… our fair flower' are moving. 'Her fame,' he wrote, 'her honour, her liberality, her prudence, her chastity and her excellent virtues shall be commended for' 'as long as the sea hath fishes, and the sky twinkling stars.'[32] She was, he believed, 'a clear light to all the world to follow'.[33]

Epilogue

✳

The timing of Margaret's death was an apt conclusion to a life so deeply invested in the cause of her family. To see her only son's only son ascend the English throne was the realisation of her highest hopes – hopes that she once may have believed to be mere fantasies. It is an incredible achievement, especially given the challenges that Margaret and her descendants faced.

It has been my intention in this book to relate Margaret's life as she experienced it, not looking back from a time when she enjoyed the comfort of being the king's mother or *Grantdame*, but looking forwards, from the perspective of the mother of a fatherless infant whose prospects were so often endangered by her political circumstances. Margaret is justly celebrated as a capable political operator, but what struck me in telling her story in this way is how seldom she acted with any clear political allegiance – despite her reputation as a 'Lancastrian' – and how often, in the first forty years of her life, she got things wrong.

She chose to marry Edmund Tudor because of a vision from St Nicholas, and that choice led her into the deepest and most mortal danger: early widowhood and traumatic childbirth in a plague-stricken war zone with none of her familiar supports around her. Having manoeuvred herself into a stable personal and political position, during the turmoil of 1469–71 she flitted between factions according to her own, sometimes misguided, sense of which was ascendant. First, she made peace with Edward IV, then betrayed him in favour of his brother Clarence, then courted Edward once more, then abandoned him for Henry VI, and finally she renounced Henry's supporters, even though they included her closest relatives and forced her only child into exile. Her equivocal allegiance was far from exceptional, but its ruthless pragmatism is matched in this period only by its ineptitude. She was fortunate indeed to survive into Edward's second reign with any hope of restoration. She was chastened by her experiences of conspiracies, and it is little wonder that for the next decade she trod a more cautious path, consistently warning her son Henry not to trust the ruling regime, but to instead maintain his exile and the status quo. Only the instability of Richard III's coup made her revert to her old, politicking ways – again, with disastrous consequences. Had Henry Tudor's 1485 invasion failed – had Richard not chosen (courageously, but fatally) to launch an attack on his enemy at Bosworth – had the sweating sickness that walked ashore with her son also claimed his life – we might remember Margaret as an ineffectual bungler. Without the Tudor-inspired resources of Polydore Vergil, Bernard André, many civic chroniclers and (most crucially) Margaret's own household accounts, we might scarcely remember her at all.

Margaret weathered these self-made storms in part because of the people with whom she surrounded herself – her mother, in-laws, cousins, servants, half-siblings, husbands and later son and grandchildren. Even more, though, she survived because of her own perseverance and fortitude. I hope that in my version of Margaret's tale I have illuminated both Margaret's character and the world of supporters who encircled her. I hope to have peopled that world in a way that contextualises her: as a princess, a lord, a king's mother, a duchess's daughter, a patron, a founder, a counsellor, an administrator, a sister, a cousin, a mistress, a benefactor, a wife, a vowess, a friend. Not only does contextualising Margaret in this way deepen our understanding of her character and choices, it renders her achievements all the more remarkable. Although she sought to assert precedents, her role as king's mother and chief royal counsellor was unique. Her later-life ability to turn misfortune into opportunity was unparalleled.

Without Margaret Beaufort, we would have had no Henry VII, no Henry VIII and therefore no Tudor dynasty. Some might argue that would be an improvement, but it would certainly have made for an utterly different world from the one we live in today. Despite being a product of her times, forged in the furnace of the most turbulent era in English history, Margaret was not merely a survivor, but quietly, unassumingly, revolutionary.

Acknowledgements

I come from a family full to the brim with men. I have four brothers, my paternal grandmother had nine; the generations on both sides have been sorely lacking in sisters – honourable mention here, of course, to Hilary Kay, Lily Johnson, Jeannie Scott and Mary Taylor. I was blessed to grow up with a present, loving and endlessly supportive Dad. I'm blessed that another one is raising my daughter with me. But, with all apologies, lads, this book is dedicated to the women who have made me.

This is not the first biography of Margaret, and I must acknowledge my debt to Margaret's historians who have come before me, especially Michael K. Jones and Malcolm Underwood, whose magisterial work is a pathfinder for any researcher on this topic. The publication of Margaret's household accounts in transcription by Susan Powell arrived late in my research, but was of enormous assistance: a work of considerable scholarship and labour, it made the task of uncovering the humanity of a woman in the last decade of her life no simpler, but certainly a great deal quicker. Having wanted to write about Margaret for over twenty years, I am enormously grateful that I had the opportunity thanks to my agent, Georgina Capel, and the brilliant team at HoZ. Especial thanks for the guiding editorial hands of Richard Milbank and Georgina Blackwell.

The pandemic, combined with pregnancy, made accessing research materials very challenging, so I want to express my sincere thanks to the archivists who have digitised sources to make them accessible remotely, and to the historians who provided me with research when I could not reach it in person. In particular, I am indebted to Joanna Laynesmith for providing invaluable feedback on a first draft of the book, and for sharing recent research by the Ricardian Society. My sincere gratitude goes to those who preserve Margaret's legacy in the archives of Westminster Abbey, the National Archives, British Library and St John's College, Cambridge, especially Tracy Deakin and Lynsey Darby. Thanks also to Jean Follett of the Friends of Woking Palace, James Meek, Sean Cunningham, Rachel Delman, Katherine J. Lewis, James Wright, Sylvia Soberton, Suzannah Lipscomb, Micheline White, Nathen Armin, Kelcey Wilson-Lee, Melita Thomas, Nikki Clark, Joanne Paul, Keith Dowen. Thanks to Jan Smith for an extremely valuable conversation about maternal trauma. And to Helen Carr for advice, Imogen Hermes Gower for the chats about fifteenth-century women, and to my early readers Siorna Ashby, Leanne O'Boyle, Rosanna Heverin-West, Ali Tudor and John Gregor. Thanks especially to Christina J. Faraday and Frances Rothwell Hughes for their Cambridge-based support activities. If I have forgotten anyone, I crave forgiveness. The supervisors of my PhD, Catherine Fletcher and Ruth Selman, have been more than understanding at my slow progress while distracted by offspring and book. Thanks to AHRC too for supporting my CDP studentship. And thank you to Lucy Nicholas for enabling me to overcome some of my own ineptitude at Latin. Like Margaret, I really wish I had made more effort with it as a child.

I wrote this book in very difficult circumstances during which I relied, like Margaret, on my own patchwork of family and friends. Without that network it would have been impossible for me to get through the past six years, let alone finish this book. Special mention as always, then, to Keith, Anne and Joe, as well as Luke, Sophie, Irene, Anne, Steve, Mick, Jenna, Al, Law, Sarah, Faith, Frankie, Fiona, Laura M, Laura KdW, Fran, Alex, Amy, Lucy, Lachlan, Tina, Jen, Tim, Gloria, Sofia, Emily, Dougal, Benji and Benjy, my many incredible teachers especially Mr Waldren, HistoryRiot and all my friends in the world of historical interpretation, the Trailblazers cast, Wadham College Tea Society, Bedford NCT group, Brighton parents, and my wider Bristolian and Geordie families by blood and in affection. And, always motivating me, Claire.

ACKNOWLEDGEMENTS

Like Margaret, I drew inspiration from the women who went before me. My great-aunt Margaret 'Jeannie' Scott was the first person in either of my families to attend university, and discovering more about her through the books she left behind while writing this one was a salutary reminder that stories of women's brilliance, persistence and quiet courage hide everywhere in plain sight.

Certain people, of course, made this book infinitely more difficult to finish, of whom the chief culprit is my daughter. Thank you for making me miss most of my deadlines, dearest one. You truly are 'all my worldly joy'.

Lastly, I feel I should thank Margaret herself. Partly because I think she may have sent a plague to test me while I was writing, and I'm quite afraid of her. Mainly, though, because she inspired me with her story when I was a nerdy teenager, which opened up the world of women's history to me, and she has continued to fascinate me throughout the research and writing of this book. I hope that this contribution to the expanding body of work on her does justice to Margaret as a woman as well as a political player irrespective of her gender, and that it inspires future historians to learn more about Margaret and the women who surrounded her.

Abbreviations

André (Hobbins): Bernard André and Daniel Hobbins (trans.), *The Life of Henry VII* (New York, 2011).

André (Sutton): Bernard André and Dana F. Sutton (ed. and trans.), *Annales regni Henrici Septimi (1504/5 and 1507/8): A hypertext critical edition*, https://philological.cal.bham.ac.uk/andreannals/2e.html

Benet: G. L. Harriss and M. A. Harriss (eds.), *John Benet's Chronicle for the years 1400 to 1462* (London, 1972).

BL: British Library.

Chrimes: S. B. Chrimes, *Henry VII* (New Haven, 1999).

CCC: Nicholas Pronay and John Cox (ed. and trans.), *The Crowland chronicle continuations, 1459–1486* (London, 1986).

Commines: Andrew R. Scobie (ed.), *The memoirs of Philippe de Commines, Lord of Argenton: containing the histories of Louis XI and Charles VIII kings of France and of Charles the Bold, duke of Burgundy to which is added, The scandalous chronicle, or Secret history of Louis XI, by Jean de Troyes,* 2 vols (London, 1855–6).

CPR: *Calendar of the Patent Rolls, preserved in the Public Record Office.*

CSP Milan: Allen B. Hinds (ed.), *Calendar of State Papers and Manuscripts in the Archives and Collections of Milan 1385–1618* (London, 1912), www.british-history.ac.uk/cal-state-papers/milan/1385-1618

CSP Spain: G. A. Bergenroth (ed.), *Calendar of State Papers, Spain, Volume 1, 1485–1509* (London, 1862), www.british-history.ac.uk/cal-state-papers/spain/vol1

CSP Venice: Rawdon Brown (ed.), *Calendar of State Papers Relating To English Affairs in the Archives of Venice, Volume 1, 1202–1509* (London, 1864), www.british-history.ac.uk/cal-state-papers/venice/vol1

***Excerpta Historica*:** Samuel Bentley (ed.), *Excerpta Historica or Illustrations of English History* (London, 1831).

Ford, 'Itinerary': Lisa L. Ford, 'Appendix I: Itinerary for Henry/Privy Seal', in *Conciliar Politics and Administration in the Reign of Henry VII*, unpublished PhD thesis, University of St Andrews, 2001, https://core.ac.uk/download/pdf/30319489.pdf

Gairdner, 'Letters and Papers Illustrative': James Gairdner (ed.), *Letters and Papers Illustrative of the Reigns of Richard III and Henry VII* (London, 1861), www.google.co.uk/books/edition/Letters_and_Papers_Illustrative_of_the_R/L8e2O2BoXWwC?hl=en&gbpv=0

Great Chronicle: A. H. Thomas and I. D. Thornley (eds.), *The Great Chronicle of London* (Gloucester, 1983).

Hall: Edward Hall and Richard Ellis Grafton, *Hall's Chronicle; containing the history of England, during the reign of Henry the Fourth, and the succeeding monarchs, to the end of the reign of Henry the Eighth, in which are particularly described the manners and customs of those periods. Carefully collated with the editions of 1548 and 1550* (London, 1809).

Henry Parker: Marie Axton and James P. Carley (eds.), 'Appendix 7: The Account of the Miracles of the Sacrament', in *Triumphs of English: Henry Parker, Lord Morley: Translator to the Tudor court / new essays in interpretation* (London, 2000).

Household Ordinances: *A collection of ordinances and regulations for the government of the Royal Household, made in divers reigns, from King Edward II to King William and Queen Mary* (London, 1790).

Ingulph: Henry T. Riley (trans.), *Ingulph's Chronicle of the Abbey of Croyland with the Continuations by Peter of Blois and Anonymous Writers* (London, 1854).

Jones and Underwood: Michael K. Jones and Malcolm G. Underwood, *The King's Mother: Lady Margaret Beaufort, Countess of Richmond and Derby* (Cambridge, 1995).

Leland: John Leland and Thomas Hearne (ed.), *Joannis Lelandi antiquarii De rebus Britannicis Collectanea cum Thomae Hearnii Praefatione Notis et Indice ad Editionem primam*, Vol. IV (London, 1774), https://babel.hathitrust.org/cgi/pt?id=uc1.31175035526816;view=1up;seq=263

Materials: William Campbell (ed.), *Materials for a History of the Reign of Henry VII from Original Documents Preserved in the Public Record Office*, 2 vols (London, 1877).

Memorials: James Gairdner (ed.), *Memorials of King Henry the Seventh: Rerum Britannicarum mediaevi scriptores, or, Chronicles and Memorials of Great Britain and Ireland during the Middle Ages*, 2 vols (London, 1858), www.google.co.uk/books/edition/Historia_Regis_Henrici_Septimi/ixxZAAA AcAAJ?q=&gbpv=o#f=false

'Mornynge Remembraunce': John Fisher and John E. B. Mayor (ed.), *The English works of John Fisher, Bishop of Rochester Part I* (London, 1876).

ODNB: Oxford Dictionary of National Biography: www.oxforddnb.com

Pollard: A. F. Pollard (ed.), *The Reign of Henry VII from Contemporary Sources*, 3 vols. (London, 1913–14).

Powell, *Household Accounts*: Susan Powell (ed.), *The Household Accounts of Lady Margaret Beaufort (1443–1509). From the Archives of St John's College, Cambridge* (Oxford, 2022).

Parliament Rolls: Chris Given-Wilson *et al.* (eds.), *Parliament Rolls of Medieval England, British History Online*, www.british-history.ac.uk/no-series/parliament-rolls-medieval

Vergil: Polydore Vergil and Dana F. Sutton (ed. and trans.), *Anglica Historia (1555 version): A hypertext critical edition*, www.philological.bham.ac.uk/polverg/

SJLM: The Records of Lady Margaret Beaufort, St Johns's College archives, University of Cambridge. (Modern reference system.)

Stevenson, *Letters & Papers*: Joseph Stevenson (ed.), *Letters & Papers Illustrative of the Wars of the English in France During the Reign of Henry the Sixth, King of England*, 2 vols (London, 1861–4).

TNA: The National Archives.

TNA, E36/210: The Queen's Book, March 1502–March 1503, *Chamber Books of Henry VII and Henry VIII*, www.tudorchamberbooks.org/edition/manuscript/E36_210/folio

TNA, E36/214: The Chamber Books of Henry VII (Payment Book), October 1505–1 May 1509 (*Chamber Books of Henry VII and Henry VIII*), www.tudorchamberbooks.org/edition/manuscript/E36_214/folio

TNA, E36/215: The Chamber Books of Henry VII (Payment Book), April 1509–Oct 1518, *Chamber Books of Henry VII and Henry VIII*, www.tudorchamberbooks.org/edition/manuscript/E36_215/folio

TNA, E101/414/6: The Chamber Books of Henry VII (Payment Book), October 1497–1 October 1499, *Chamber Books of Henry VII and Henry VIII*, www.tudorchamberbooks.org/edition/manuscript/E101_414_16/folio

'Vitellius A XVI': Charles Lethbridge Kingsford (ed.), 'Vitellius A XVI' in *Chronicles of London* (Oxford, 1905).

WAM: Westminster Abbey Muniments archive.

Warkworth: James Orchard Halliwell (ed.), *A Chronicle of The First Thirteen Years Of The Reign Of King Edward The Fourth, by John Warkworth* (London, 1839).

Endnotes

CHAPTER 1

1 Ingulph, p. 399.
2 There was, however, some debate about the year in which Margaret was born. The seventeenth-century antiquarian William Dugdale suggested Margaret was born in 1441, but the Book of Hours recording Margaret's birth clearly notes the year as 'A[nno]o D[omi]ni Mo CCCCmo XLIIJ' (1443). BL MS Royal MS 2 A XVIII, f. 30r. See Jones and Underwood, p. 34.
3 BL MS Royal MS 2 A XVIII, f. 30r.
4 Basin was a Norman bishop writing in Lancastrian-controlled territory during the Hundred Years War. Thomas Basin, *Histoire de Charles VII éditée et traduite par Charles Samaran, Tome Ier: 1407–1444* (Paris, 1933), pp. 281–3. The Crowland Chronicle also comments on John's pride, saying he was 'puffed up by the great applause of the populace'. Ingulph, p. 398.
5 Basin, *Histoire de Charles VII*, pp. 281–3.
6 Jones and Underwood, p. 21.
7 *Excerpta Historica*, pp. 152–3; Jones and Underwood, pp. 22–5.
8 Juliet Barker, *Conquest: The English Kingdom of France, 1417–1450* (London, 2010), pp. 22–3.
9 'Historical Memoranda of John Stowe: The manner of making Knights of the Bath', in John Stowe and James Gairdner (ed.), *Three Fifteenth-Century Chronicles with Historical Memoranda by John Stowe* (London, 1880), British History Online, www.british-history.ac.uk/camden-record-soc/vol28/pp106-113; accessed 7 February 2019.

10 Jones and Underwood, p. 27.
11 Maxwell-Lyte H. C. et al. (ed.), *Calendar of the Patent Rolls, preserved in the Public Record Office: Henry VI, Vol. IV, 1441–1446* (London, 1908), p. 515; Ingulph, p. 398.
12 Janet Backhouse, 'Patronage and Commemoration in the Beaufort Hours', in Kathryn A. Smith and Carol H. Krinsky (eds.), *Tributes to Lucy Freeman Sandler: Studies in Illuminated Manuscripts* (London / Turnhout, 2007), p. 335.
13 Ingulph, pp. 388–9.
14 Harris Nicolas (ed.), *Proceedings and Ordinances of the Privy Council of England* (London, 1834), V, p. 288.
15 Ibid., pp. 252, 254–5. For the terms of Somerset's appointment see pp. 229–35; 251–7. For the lack of noble support by 1443 see G. L. Harriss, *Cardinal Beaufort: a study of Lancastrian ascendancy and decline* (Oxford, 1988), pp. 332–7.
16 Nicolas, *Proceedings and Ordinances*, pp. 225–6.
17 Ibid., pp. 411, 413. For the whole letter, ibid., pp. 409–14. The 'remarkable' heat of summer 1443 is described by Ingulph, p. 399.
18 Traditionally, Margaret's birth site has been identified as Bletsoe, but her mother's movements at this time are not recorded. John was certainly at Corfe Castle in summer 1444, as the Crowland Chronicler notes. Ingulph, p. 399.
19 Basin, *Histoire de Charles VII*, p. 281.
20 Ingulph, p. 399.

21 Basin, *Histoire de Charles VII*, pp. 283–5.
22 Ingulph, p. 399.
23 Alexander Murray, *Suicide in the Middle Ages, Volume 1: The Violent Against Themselves* (Oxford / New York, 1998), pp. 3, 151–2; idem, *Suicide in the Middle Ages, Volume 2: The Curse on Self-Murder* (Oxford / New York, 2000), pp. 42, 46, 67, 345–6.
24 Jones and Underwood, p. 30.

CHAPTER 2

1 'Mornynge Remembraunce', p. 292.
2 Tacyn was married at Bletsoe, and Reginald's home at Bletchley was only a day's ride away. Jones and Underwood, p. 32.
3 M. K. Jones, 'The Beaufort Family and the War in France, 1421–50', unpublished PhD thesis, University of Bristol, 1982, pp. 9–10, 16.
4 Maxwell-Lyte H. C. et al. (ed.), *Calendar of the Patent Rolls, preserved in the Public Record Office: Henry VI, Vol. IV, 1441–1446* (London, 1908), pp. 268, 269, 276, 281.
5 *Excerpta Historica*, p. 4; CPR,1441–1446, p. 283.
6 Jones and Underwood, p. 32. BL MS Royal MS 2 A XVIII, f. 1v.
7 Jones and Underwood, p. 32.
8 Ibid., p. 30.
9 Christine de Pizan and Sarah Lawson (trans.), *The Treasure of the City of Ladies of The Book of the Three Virtues* (London, 2003), p. 110.
10 Lionel also had a number of daughters. Maxwell-Lyte H. C. et al. (ed.), *Calendar of the Patent Rolls, preserved in the Public Record Office: Henry VI, Vol. V, 1446–52* (London, 1909), p. 44.
11 Frederick Pollock and Frederic William Maitland, *The History of English Law Before the Time of Edward I: Volume 2* (Cambridge, 1911) p. 390.
12 On this central contradiction between femaleness and lordship see Barbara J. Harris, *English Aristocratic Women: 1450–1550: Marriage and Family, Property and Careers* (Oxford, 2002), pp. 8–11.
13 Ingulph, p. 400.
14 'Mornynge Remembraunce', p. 292.
15 Later in life, Margaret 'full often complained that in her youth she had not given her[self] to the understanding of Latin, wherein she had [only] a little perceiving'. Ibid.
16 See for instance *The Book of the Knight of the Tower*, an advice text written by the Frenchman Geoffroy de la Tour Landry for his daughters in 1371. William Caxton (trans.) and M. Y. Offord (ed.), *The Book of the Knight of the Tower* (London / New York / Toronto, 1971), p. 122.
17 'Mornynge Remembraunce', p. 290.
18 See for instance Pizan, *Treasure of the City of Ladies*, p. 145.
19 Ibid., pp. 110–2.
20 Ibid., p. 110.
21 Ibid., p. 111.
22 'Henry VI: November 1450', Parliament Rolls, item 16, www.british-history.ac.uk/no-series/parliament-rolls-medieval/november-1450; accessed 18 December 2024.

CHAPTER 3

1 'Mornynge Remembraunce', p. 293.
2 This was the estimated population early in the sixteenth century. In 1377, the population had been closer to forty thousand. Eric Ives, *The Reformation Experience: Living Through the Turbulent 16th Century* (Lion Hudson, 2012), p. 14.
3 John Major and Archibald Constable (ed.), *A History of Greater Britain as well England as Scotland compiled from the Ancient Authorities* (Edinburgh, 1892), p. 21.
4 Jones and Underwood, p. 38.
5 'Mornynge Remembraunce', p. 293.
6 Ibid., pp. 292–3.
7 For Catherine and Owen's relationship see Ralph A. Griffiths and Roger S. Thomas, *The Making of the*

Tudor Dynasty (Gloucester, 1985), pp. 26–33; for Katherine de la Pole see 'Rymer's Foedera with Syllabus: November 1440', in Rymer's *Foedera* Volume 10, ed. Thomas Rymer (London, 1739–1745), pp. 817–834. British History Online www.british-history.ac.uk/rymer-foedera/vol10/pp817-834; accessed 24 February 2017.

8 'Mornynge Remembraunce', p. 293.

9 Benet, p. 209.

10 G. du Fresne de Beaucourt (ed.), *Chronique de Mathieuu d'Escouchy: nouvelle édition* (Paris, 1864), II, pp. 39–43.

11 'Bale's Chronicle', in Ralph Flenley (ed.), *Six Town Chronicles of England* (Oxford, 1911) p. 140.

12 Rachel Podd, 'Reconsidering maternal mortality in medieval England: aristocratic Englishwomen, c.1236–1503', *Continuity and Change*, 35 (2020), pp. 115–137.

13 They may have arrived in September 1455. Griffiths and Thomas, p. 44.

14 That Margaret conceived a child so young was exceptional, especially in the Middle Ages when it seems menstruation and puberty started later. Most modern girls start puberty at ten, and menstruate on average at thirteen. Bioarchaeolgical evidence and late medieval literature suggests contemporaries first menstruated around fifteen, with puberty continuing to twenty. Podd, 'Reconsidering maternal mortality in medieval England', pp. 115–137.

15 Howell T. Evans, *Wales and the Wars of the Roses* (Cambridge, 1915), pp. 16–20.

16 Initially, because of native Welsh activities. See Griffiths and Thomas, pp. 44–6.

17 Jones and Underwood, pp. 147, 177; Cambridge, Fitzwilliam Museum, MS 261. Among the contents of this manuscript are 'Bishop of Arusiens, 'a litil booke the whiche traytied and rehercd many goode thinges neceffaries for the infirmite and

grete fekeneffe called peftilence' and 'a nobyll tretyfe made by a Right Worthy Phyfician named Maifter John Burdeux [sic] agaynes the malady of the peftilence'.

18 John Fisher and John Lewis (eds.), 'Oration made at Cambridge, 1506', in *The Life of Dr. John Fisher, Bishop of Rochester in the Reign of King Henry VIII, with an appendix of illustrative documents and papers*, vol 2 (London, 1855), p. 265.

19 Podd, 'Reconsidering maternal mortality in medieval England', pp. 124, 127; Barbara J. Harris, *English Aristocratic Women: 1450–1550: Marriage and Family, Property and Careers* (Oxford, 2002), p. 277, n. 33 calculated the rate of maternal mortality as high as 2.5 per cent per birth.

20 Henrietta Lesyer, *Medieval Women: A Social History of Women in England, 450–1500* (London, 2002), pp. 125–6.

21 Harris, *English Aristocratic Women*, p. 102.

22 My thanks to James Meek for sharing the results of the archaeological investigation at Pembroke Castle with me. 'Pembroke Castle: Geophysical Survey 2016', https://castlestudiestrust.org/docs/Pembroke_Castle_Geophysical%20_Survey_FINAL.pdf; accessed 27 February 2019.

23 Leland, p. 249; 'Ryalle Boke', F. Grose (ed.), *The Antiquarian Repertory: a miscellaneous assemblage of topography, history, biography, customs and manners. Intended to illustrate and preserve several valuable remains of old times*, 1 (London, 1807), pp. 304–5; Christine de Pizan and Sarah Lawson (trans.), *The Treasure of the City of Ladies of The Book of the Three Virtues* (London, 2003), p. 137; Janelle Day Jenstad, 'Lying-in Like a Countess: The Lisle Letters, the Cecil Family, and A Chaste Maid in Cheapside', *Journal of Medieval and Early Modern Studies*, 34, ii (2004), pp. 374–5; Harris, *English Aristocratic Women*, p. 103.

24 Leland, p. 249.

25 Jenstad, 'Lying-in Like a Countess,' pp. 374–5.

26 Monica H. Green (ed.), *The Trotula: An English Translation of the Medieval Compendium of Women's Medicine* (Philadelphia, 2002), p. 80.

27 Ibid., p. 79.

28 Ibid., pp. 77, 81.

29 Ibid., p. 82.

30 Leyser, *Medieval Women*, p. 128.

31 CSP Spain, no. 210, www.british -history.ac.uk/cal-state-papers/spain /vol1/pp167-180; accessed 26 February 2019.

32 'Tam mirabiliter natus, atque in lucem editus a nobilissima principe genetrice tua, nunc praesenti; quae tum annum non implevit quartum decimum... ipsaque (ut cernimus) non magnae staturae faemina est at multo tunc (ut asseritur) minoris fuit, adeo ut miraculum cunctis videbatur in illis annis, et in illa corporis parvitate gnatum aliquem.' Fisher, 'Oration', p. 265.

33 Harris, *English Aristocratic Women*, p. 276, n. 3. eighty-seven per cent of the noble couples she examined for the period 1450–1550 had children.

CHAPTER 4

1 TNA, PRO B 11/7/2.

2 It has been suggested that Margaret could have married Jasper Tudor, and there were certainly advantages to such a match: the Tudor–Beaufort alliance would be maintained, and Jasper's estate enriched by Margaret's inheritance. But Margaret and Jasper are unlikely to have considered the option since, although marriage to a spouse's sibling was not unknown, it was uncommon, and indeed in religious circles it was deemed tantamount to incest. Marriage created a new bond of kinship between in-laws called 'affinity', so according to contemporary thought Margaret and Jasper were siblings from the moment of her marriage to Edmund. The noble class was so inward-looking that the Church

had imposed controls on it marrying within itself, establishing in 1215 that marriage was forbidden within four degrees of consanguinity (i.e. if a couple shared a great-grandparent). Philip Niles, 'Baptism and the Naming of Children in Late Medieval England', *Medieval Prosopography*, 3, i (1982), pp. 102–3; Robert Cirivilleri, 'Marriage and canon law: Consanguinity, affinity and the medieval church (996–1215)', unpublished MA thesis, San Jose State University, 2000, https:// scholarworks.sjsu.edu/cgi/viewcontent .cgi?article=2978&context=etd_theses; accessed 8 May 2019.

3 The dates of birth of the Stafford children are not recorded, but the duke and duchess married by October 1424, and Harry was their second son.

4 Stourton was connected to the dowager duchess of Somerset's Beaufort and Welles husbands, and his name appears in various legal documents for both her and Margaret over several decades. Even after Stourton died, his descendants continued to counsel Margaret, acting as trustees of a document for her in 1472. D56.205 (SJLM/4/2/3); Colin Richmond and L. S. Woodger, 'John Stourton II (1400–62), of Stourton, Wilts.', *History of Parliament Online*, www.historyofparliamentonline.org /volume/1386-1421/member/stourton -john-ii-1400-62; accessed 11 January 2024.

5 John Chandler (ed.), *John Leland's Itinerary: Travels in Tudor England* (Gloucester, 1993), p. 289 for a description of the surrounding countryside.

6 Edith was certainly married before 1458, as her son was born that year or 1459. She may have met Geoffrey through Margaret, as he was a councillor of Jasper Tudor in Wales. They later lived at Whittington in Buckinghamshire.

7 As well as Richard, Edith and Geoffrey were parents to Eleanor Pole (later Verney) and Henry. Hazel Pierce, 'The King's Cousin: The Life,

Career and Welsh Connection of Sir Richard Pole, 1458–1504', *Welsh History Review = Cylchgrawn Hanes Cymru*, 19, ii (1998), pp. 190–2.

8   Ralph A. Griffiths, *The Reign of King Henry VI: The Exercise of Royal Authority, 1422–1461* (London, 1981), p. 804.

9   Ralph A. Griffiths and Roger S. Thomas, *The Making of the Tudor Dynasty* (Gloucester, 1985), pp. 49–50.

10   TNA, PROB 11/7/2; WAM 5472, ff. 23v, 58r; WAM 12189, f. 46v; Jones and Underwood, pp. 95–6.

11   D56.195 (SJLM/3/2/1): Harry and Margaret's servants in 1466 are listed at WAM 12181, f. 42 v.

12   'Gregory's Chronicle: 1451–1460', in James Gairdner (ed.), *The Historical Collections of a Citizen of London in the Fifteenth Century* (London, 1876), pp. 196–210. British History Online www.british-history.ac.uk /camden-record-soc/vol17/pp196 -210; accessed 20 February 2023.

13   Griffiths and Thomas, *Tudor Dynasty*, pp. 50–1.

14   John Silvester Davies (ed.), *An English Chronicle of the Reigns of Richard II, Henry IV, Henry V and Henry VI, written before the year 1471* (London, 1856), p. 96.

15   'Gregory's Chronicle'.

16   Ingulph, p. 426. I discussed the casualties of Towton with Keith A. Dowen, curator of arms and armour for the Wallace Collection and lead member of the Palm Sunday Field project that is revising our understanding of this battle. The mythology of Towton (which began almost as soon as it finished, thanks to the earl of Warwick and his allies' propagandic communications with the Continent) has subverted our notion of what was possible in medieval warfare. This was undoubtedly a very bloody battle with high numbers of participants, but could not have involved the numbers that are commonly stated. Casualties into the low thousands appears possible.

17   'Henry VI: November 1459', Parliament Rolls, www.british-history .ac.uk/no-series/parliament-rolls -medieval/november-1459; accessed 29 April 2019.

18   Both Lady Hampden and Lady Hungerford would ultimately be widowed by the Wars of the Roses. Several other noblewomen were also monitored by Edward IV's appointees in 1461. Margaret's kinsman John Stourton served on a commission to arrest Margaret Botreaux, Lady Hungerford in January 1462. Maxwell-Lyte H. C. et al. (ed.), *Calendar of the Patent Rolls preserved in the Public Record Office, 1461–1467. Edward IV* (London, 1897), p. 101. The wife of another prominent Lancastrian, Philippa Tiptoft, Lady Roos was arrested in June 1461 (mistakenly under the name 'Elizabeth' in the patent roll) and put into the guardianship of her (Yorkist) brother and two others in December. Ibid. pp. 33, 87, 181, 184. For wider context see Lauren Johnson, 'The Impact of the Wars of the Roses on Noblewomen', unpublished MSt thesis, University of Oxford, 2007.

19   Great Chronicle, p. 199.

20   Anne Crawford, 'Victims of attainder: the Howard and de Vere women in the late fifteenth century', *Reading Medieval Studies*, 15 (1989), pp. 62–3.

21   Griffiths and Thomas, *Tudor Dynasty*, pp. 57–8.

22   Maxwell-Lyte H. C. et al. (ed.) *CPR, 1461–1467, Edward IV*, pp. 6, 24, 196, 298; 'Edward IV: November 1461', item 15, Parliament Rolls, www .british-history.ac.uk/no-series/parlia ment-rolls-medieval/november-1461; accessed 8 May 2019.

23   CPR, 1461–7, p. 12; 'Edward IV: November 1461', item 15, Parliament Rolls.

24   CPR, 1461–7, pp. 114, 197, 71, 130.

25   Lauren Johnson, 'The Impact of the Wars of the Roses on Noblewomen', unpublished Mst thesis (Oxford University, 2007), pp. 36–7.

26 C. L. Scofield, 'Henry, duke of Somerset, and Edward IV', *English Historical Review*, 21 (1906), pp. 301–2.

27 CPR, 1461–7, pp. 362–3.

28 WAM 12181, ff. 50, 52v; Jones and Underwood, pp. 47, 139.

CHAPTER 5

1 Christine de Pizan and Sarah Lawson (trans.), *The Treasure of the City of Ladies of The Book of the Three Virtues* (London, 2003), p. 32.

2 The major sources for Margaret's household at Woking are her books of accounts, especially WAM 5472 and WAM 12182–90. Elizabeth Jackson appears in accounts made at Bourne, for instance WAM 12181, f. 42v (1466). For her attendance on Margaret see for example WAM 5472, f. 8v. For household livery: ibid., f. 22v. There are myriad references to Margaret's dealings with merchants, for instance f. 43.

3 WAM 5472, ff. 21v, 23v, 24v, 33, 41, 41v; Carole Rawcliffe, *The Staffords, Earls of Stafford and Dukes of Buckingham, 1394–1521* (Cambridge, 1978), pp. 71, 94, 96.

4 For their journeys to and from London together see for example WAM 5472, f. 9. For other referenced payments: WAM 5472, ff. 21, 24v, 26v, 37v, 40, 43v, 58.

5 Great Chronicle, p. 325.

6 Bray's account book survives in the archives of Westminster Abbey, WAM 5472. His clear, vernacular handwriting is a blessed relief compared with the Latin scrawls of some of Margaret's other servants. For more on Bray see M. M. Condon, 'From caitiff and villein to Pater Patriae: Reynold Bray and the profits of office' in Hicks, Michael (ed.), *Profit, piety and the professions in late medieval England* (Gloucester, 1990), pp. 137–68.

7 WAM 5472, ff. 23v, 24, 57v, 58; WAM 12186, ff. 43–45v.

8 WAM 5472, f. 8v.

9 WAM 6658, 6660. These were the confraternities of the order of the Holy Trinity at Knaresborough and of the hospital at Burton Lazars.

10 This riding household is named in WAM 12185, f. 40.

11 WAM 12185, ff. 31–42v, 45.

12 PROB 11/7/2.

13 WAM 12185, f. 42v. They arrived home on 8 November, at night. Ibid., f. 53v.

14 WAM 5472, f. 21v.

15 WAM 5472, ff. 22, 22v, 24, 24v; WAM 12186, f. 42.

16 This description was written by the contemporary Burgundian chronicler Philippe de Commines, who met Edward in 1470–1. Commines, I, p. 192.

17 WAM 5472, f. 22; WAM 12186, f. 42.

18 WAM 5472, ff. 19, 19v, 26v, 27.

19 Harry rewarded the officers of his mother's household for attending him during his illness. WAM 5472, ff. 30–30v.

20 Jones and Underwood, p. 143.

CHAPTER 6

1 'Mornynge Remembraunce', p. 285.

2 (13 July 1469.) WAM 5472, f. 41.

3 Great Chronicle, p. 207.

4 Warkworth, p. 12.

5 'Bale's Chronicle', in Ralph Flenley (ed.), *Six Town Chronicles of England* (Oxford, 1911), p. 144.

6 Elizabeth's date of birth is disputed, and she may only have been a year older than Edward. See Susan Higginbotham, *The Woodvilles* (Stroud, 2013), p. 14. My thanks to Joanna Laynesmith for bringing this to my attention.

7 For Edward and Elizabeth's marriage see Michael Hicks, *Edward V: The Prince in the Tower* (Stroud, 2003), pp. 37–48.

8 Katherine Neville was the aunt of Warwick and Edward IV – and indeed of Sir Harry Stafford. Stevenson, *Letters & Papers*, Vol. 2, Part 2, p. 783.

9 WAM 5472, f. 38.

10 'The articles and causes for the assembling of Robin of Redesdale', in Margaret Lucille Kekewich (ed.), *The Politics of Fifteenth Century England: John Vale's Book* (Stroud, 1995), pp. 212–15.
11 WAM 5472, f. 41v.
12 D. H. Thomas, *The Herberts of Raglan and the Battle of Edgecote 1469* (Enfield, 1994), pp. 56–71.
13 TNA, PROB 11/5/430.
14 WAM 5472, f. 41v.
15 Ibid.
16 Ibid., f. 42v.
17 Ibid., ff. 43, 44v.
18 Ibid., f. 43v; WAM 12184, f. 3.
19 WAM 5472, f. 45v; WAM 12184, f. 11.
20 Jones and Underwood, p. 50; Hicks Michael, *False, Fleeting, Perjur'd Clarence: George, Duke of Clarence 1449–78* (Gloucester, 1980), pp. 57–8.
21 James Gairdner (ed.), *The Paston Letters 1422–1509 AD. A Reprint of the Edition of 1872–5* (Edinburgh, 1910), II, p. 390.
22 WAM 5472, ff. 44, 45, 46, 46v, 47v, 57.
23 Ibid., ff. 46, 46v, 47.
24 See chapter 20 for Margaret's continued close relationship with Anne and her daughter.
25 Warkworth, p. 8.
26 Harry's itinerary and attendants are listed in WAM 12184, ff. 41–7.
27 Warkworth, p. 8.
28 WAM 12184, f. 48.
29 Hall, p. 277.
30 The battle was later given the name 'Losecoat Field'. See Nicholas Bennett, 'The Road to Losecoat Field', *The Ricardian*, 30 (2020).
31 WAM 12184, f. 52.
32 Ibid., ff. 59–77.

CHAPTER 7

1 Nicholas O'Flanagan, bishop of Elphin, quoted in Joanna Laynesmith, 'The King's Mother', *History Today*, 56, iii (2006).
2 WAM 12183, f. 13.

3 According to the Burgundian chronicler Philippe de Commines, Clarence's sister Margaret sent a mysterious lady to Calais in 1470 to woo the duke home. Commines I, pp. 188–9; John Bruce (ed.), *Historie of the arrivall of Edward IV in England and the finall recouerye of his kingdomes from Henry VI A.D. M.CCCC.-LXXI* (London, 1838), p. 10.
4 J. L. Laynesmith, *Cecily Duchess of York* (London / New York, 2017), p. 128.
5 Ibid.
6 WAM 12183 ff. 19–19v; Vergil, 'Edward IV', c. 10, https://philological.cal.bham.ac.uk/polverg/24eng.html; accessed 19 December 2024.
7 WAM 12183 f. 25; Hicks, Michael, *False, Fleeting, Perjur'd Clarence: George, Duke of Clarence 1449–78* (Gloucester, 1980), p. 96.
8 During the 1469 rebellions, Jacquetta was accused by one of Warwick's esquires, Thomas Wake, of using images of lead for sorcery. She was cleared of the charges after Edward IV was restored, in February 1470. Lucia Diaz Pascual, 'Luxembourg, Jaquetta de, duchess of Bedford and Countess Rivers (c.1416–1472)', ODNB, https://doi.org/10.1093/ref:odnb/101258; accessed 20 February 2023.
9 Hicks, Michael, *Clarence*, pp. 96, 99; Jones and Underwood, pp. 116, 119.
10 D. H. Thomas, *The Herberts of Raglan and the Battle of Edgecote 1469* (Enfield, 1994), p. 75.
11 WAM 12183, ff. 20–23.
12 Arrivall, p. 2.
13 WAM 12189, f. 58.
14 Some of Harry's men rode from Reading to Newbury at the start of April to continue discussions with Edmund. WAM 12183, ff. 40–40v. For context see Jones and Underwood, pp. 54–5.
15 WAM 12183, ff. 44v–45.
16 WAM 12183, f. 50v.
17 Hannes Kleineke, 'Gerhard von Wesel's Newsletter from

England, 17 April 1471', *The Ricardian*, 16 (2006), p. 81.
18 WAM 12183, f. 50; D56.158 (SJLM/4/2/2).
19 Ibid.
20 Warkworth, pp. 38–9; WAM 12183, f. 51.
21 Warkworth, p. 40.
22 Warkworth, p. 21; Arrivall, p. 38.
23 Vergil, 'Edward IV', c. 19.
24 André (Hobbins), p. 13.
25 TNA, PROB 11/7/2.
26 WAM 32407, ff. 5v, 7v. For arrangements for Harry's burial and religious rites, ibid., ff. 11v, 19v. Jones and Underwood, pp. 96–7, 144.

CHAPTER 8

1 Christine de Pizan and Sarah Lawson (trans.), *The Treasure of the City of Ladies of The Book of the Three Virtues* (London, 2003), p. 38.
2 D56.200 (SJLM/4/3/2/1).
3 Bray was still noting payments for Harry's debts in his book of expenses in 1473–4. See WAM 32407, ff. 5v, 7v. For arrangements for Harry's burial and religious rites, ibid., ff. 11v, 19v; TNA, PROB 11/7/2.
4 Lord John Stourton and two other Stourton relatives acted as witnesses, while Margaret's feofees (trustees) included Thomas Bourchier, cardinal and archbishop of Canterbury, Robert Stillington, bishop of Bath and Wells, Reynald Bray, Harry's brother John Stafford, earl of Wiltshire, and stepfather Sir Walter Blount, Lord Mountjoy. D56.195 (SJLM/3/2/1); D56.205 (SJLM/4/2/3).
5 Anne, countess of Warwick survived until 1492, outliving both of her sons-in-law. Lauren Johnson, 'The Impact of the Wars of the Roses on Noblewomen', unpublished MSt thesis, University of Oxford, 2007, pp. 23–4. Similarly, Warwick's nephew George Neville was deprived of his rights in 1478 to prevent him reclaiming any of the Neville lands. Michael Hicks, *Richard III: The Self-Made King* (New Haven / London, 2019), p. 185;

'Edward IV: October 1472, Second Roll', Parliament Rolls, items 20–4: www.british-history.ac.uk/no-series /parliament-rolls-medieval/october -1472-second-roll; accessed 5 July 2019.
6 I follow the interpretation of events provided by Hicks, Michael, 'The Last Days of Elizabeth Countess of Oxford', *The English Historical Review*, vol. 103, no. 406 (1988), pp. 76–95. For an alternative – but, to my mind, less persuasive – interpretation of Richard's interactions with Elizabeth, see David Johnson, 'Coercion or Compliance: Richard, duke of Gloucester and Elizabeth, countess of Oxford', *The Ricardian*, 34 (2024), pp. 73–93. See also Hicks, Michael, *Richard III*, pp. 121–4; A. Crawford, 'Victims of attainder: the Howard and de Vere women in the late fifteenth century', *Reading Medieval Studies*, vol. 15 (University of Reading Graduate Centre for Medieval Studies, 1989), pp. 65–6.
7 Richard met a doughtier opponent in Lady Margaret Hungerford, several of whose estates he eventually also secured in 1474. See Hicks, Michael, *Richard III*, pp. 62–3, 120–1.
8 James Gairdner (ed.), *The Paston Letters 1422–1509 AD. A Reprint of the Edition of 1872–5* (Edinburgh, 1910), III, pp. 5–6.
9 i.e. what needlework she could sell. Henry Ellis (ed.), *Robert Fabyan: New Chronicles of England and France* (London, 1811), p. 663.
10 Johnson, 'The Impact of the Wars of the Roses on Noblewomen', pp. 35–6; Commines, I, p. 182.
11 Michael Jones, 'Richard III and the Stanleys' in Rosemary Horrox (ed.), *Richard III and the North* (Hull, 1986), pp. 35–7.
12 D56.195 (SJLM/3/2/1); D56.205 (SJLM/4/2/3); D56.206 (SJLM/4/3/1/4); D56.200 (SJLM/4/3/2/1). The Stanleys later claimed this marriage had been arranged by Edward IV, and it coincided with the marriage of Thomas's brother Sir William Stanley to the widowed Elizabeth, countess of Worcester, another

wealthy noblewoman offering social advancement to the parvenu Stanleys. However, the king did not have the authority to choose Margaret's husband and contemporary documents clearly demonstrate Margaret's agency in concluding what was, however personal the relationship, ultimately a business arrangement. Maxwell-Lyte H. C. et al. (ed.), *Calendar of the Patent Rolls preserved in the Public Record Office, 1467–1477, Edward IV, Henry VI* (London, 1900), p. 297; Jones and Underwood, p. 14.

13   Anne left Margaret 'a book of English of Legenda Sanctorum, a book of French called Lucun, another book of French of the Epistles and Gospels and a primer [prayer book] with clasps of silver and gilt covered with purple velvet'. Anne died by 31 October 1480, when her will was proved. TNA, PROB 11/7/7.

14   By 2 June, Margaret had reached Bewsey in Lancashire. D56.195 (SJLM/3/2/1).

15   WAM 32407, f. 4v.

16   John Seacome, *The History of the House of Stanley, from the Conquest to the Death of the Right Honourable Edward, Late Earl of Derby, in 1776: Containing a Genealogical & Historical Account of that Illustrious House. To which is Added, a Complete History of the Isle of Man* (London, 1821), pp. 41–52. See also www.google.co.uk/books/edition/_/dfIHAAAAMAAJ?hl=en&gbpv=0; accessed 23 May 2019.

17   Jones and Underwood, p. 146.

18   WAM 32407, f. 13v.

19   Ibid., f. 5.

20   Jones and Underwood, p. 59; Michael J. Bennett, 'Stanley, Thomas, first earl of Derby (c.1433–1504)', ODNB, https://doi.org/10.1093/ref:odnb/26278; accessed 23 May 2019.

21   D56.185 (SJLM/6/2). For context see Jones and Underwood, p. 147; J. L. Laynesmith, 'The Piety of Cecily, Duchess of York: A Reputation Reconsidered' in Hannes Kleineke

and Christian Steer (eds.), *The Yorkist Age: Proceedings of the 2011 Harlaxton Symposium* (Donington, 2013), pp. 31, 149; Charles Farris, 'The New Edwardians? Royal Piety in the Yorkist Age', in ibid., p. 59.

22   WAM, MS 39.

23   Rebecca Osawa, 'Emotional intelligence (EI) in the life and career of Lady Margaret Beaufort (1443–1509)', unpublished MA thesis, Trent University, 2011.

24   WAM 32407, ff. 3v, 8v, 9, 12, 13v.

25   Contemporary reports claimed Edward's army was 30,000 strong. In reality, it was just shy of 11,500 combatants. Charles Ross, *Edward IV* (Trowbridge, 1975), p. 221; CSP Milan, No. 277, www.british-history.ac.uk/cal-state-papers/milan/1385-1618/pp189-220; accessed 17 July 2019.

26   WAM 32407, ff. 7, 7v, 8, 8v, 9. For Edward's preparations see for example CSP Milan, nos. 277, 282. For Stanley's indenture to provide men, 'Rymer's Foedera with Syllabus: January–February 1475', www.british-history.ac.uk/rymer-foedera/vol11/pp842-852; accessed 12 July 2019.

27   'Rymer's Foedera with Syllabus: April–June 1475', www.british-history.ac.uk/rymer-foedera/vol12/pp1-14; accessed 16 July 2019.

28   The other was John, Lord Howard, the future duke of Norfolk. Commines, I, p. 253.

29   Ibid., p. 261.

30   Ibid., p. 277.

31   The dauphin Charles (later Charles VII) had murdered the duke of Burgundy on the bridge at Montereau in 1419. For the meeting at Picquigny see ibid, pp. 272–9.

32   Ibid., p. 251.

33   Vergil, 'Edward IV', c. 25. Polydore Vergil's suggestion that in 1476 Edward intended to marry Henry to Elizabeth of York must be mistaken, since one of the conditions of the Treaty of Picquigny a year earlier was for Elizabeth to marry the dauphin. Presumably Vergil misdates this episode, which occurred in 1482.

34 CSP Milan, no. 319, www
.british-history.ac.uk/cal-state-papers
/milan/1385-1618/pp189-220; accessed
17 July 2019; Great Chronicle, p. 233.
35 André (Hobbins), p. 19.
36 As reported by Polydore Vergil,
the source for Henry's near capture
and escape. Vergil, 'Edward IV', c. 25.
37 Ralph A. Griffiths and Roger S.
Thomas, *The Making of the Tudor
Dynasty* (Gloucester, 1985), pp. 82–4.

CHAPTER 9

1 John Stow, *The Annales, or a
Generall Chronicle of England,
Begun First by Maister Iohn Stow,
and after Him Continued and
Augmented with Matters Forreyne,
and Domestique, Auncient and
Moderne, Vnto the Ende of This
Present Yeere 1614 by Edmond Howes,
Gentleman* (London, 1615), p. 460.
2 William Henry Black (ed.),
'Narrative of the Marriage of
Richard Duke of York with Ann
of Norfolk, the Matrimonial Feast
and the Grand Justing [sic], AD
1477', in *Illustrations of Ancient
State and Chivalry from manuscripts
preserved in the Ashmolean Museum*
(London, 1840), pp. 27–40.
3 J. L. Laynesmith, *Cecily
Duchess of York* (London / New
York, 2017), pp. 147, 149–151.
4 Philippe de Commines recorded
how, after falling out with Edward IV
over the outcome of their intended war
with France in 1475, Charles
the Bold had 'called the King of
England Blancborgne, the son
of an archer who bore his name,
with as many invectives besides,
as could possibly be used against
any man'. Commines, I, p. 265.
5 CSP Milan, no. 313, www
.british-history.ac.uk/cal-state
-papers/milan/1385-1618/pp189
-220; accessed 17 July 2019.
6 CCC, pp. 146–7.
7 Vergil, 'Edward IV', c. 26.
8 This bizarre method of execution
was cited by Polydore Vergil, who

interviewed eyewitnesses, and Dominic
Mancini, writing in 1483: Dominic
Mancini and C. A. J. Armstrong (ed.
and trans.), *The usurpation of Richard
the Third: Dominicus Mancinus ad
Angelum Catonem De occupatione
regni Anglie per Riccardum Tercium
libellus* (Gloucester, 1984), p. 63;
Vergil, 'Edward IV', c. 26. Another
close contemporary, the Crowland
Chronicler, is more circumspect, simply
saying the execution was carried out
secretly in the Tower. CCC, p. 147.
9 This pardon survives only in some
text on the reverse of a document
granting the original earldom to
Edmund Tudor. WAM 32378.
10 'Vatican Regesta 685: 1484–1487',
in *Calendar of Papal Registers Relating
To Great Britain and Ireland: Volume
14, 1484–1492*, British History Online,
www.british-history.ac.uk/cal-papal
-registers/brit-ie/vol14/pp14-30;
accessed 31 July 2019.
11 Margaret Beauchamp's date of
birth is unrecorded, but her eldest child
was born in 1426 and her last *c*.1448
so a birthdate of around 1410 is
likely.
12 D56.158 (SJLM/4/4/2).
13 Ibid.
14 CSP Venice, no. 475, www.british
-history.ac.uk/cal-state-papers/venice
/vol1/pp141-159; accessed
5 August 2019.
15 Michael Jones, 'Richard III and
the Stanleys' in Rosemary Horrox (ed.),
*Richard III and the North. Studies
in Regional and Local History, no. 6*
(1986), p. 33; William Arthur Shaw,
*The Knights of England; a complete
record from the earliest time to the
present day of the knights of all
the orders of chivalry in England,
Scotland, and Ireland, and of knights
bachelors* (London, 1906), II, p. 18.
16 Vergil, 'Edward IV', c. 27.
17 CCC, p. 149.
18 Maxwell-Lyte H. C. et al.
(ed.), *Calendar of the Patent Rolls
preserved in the Public Record Office,
1476–85, Edward IV, Edward V,
Richard III* (London, 1901), p. 326.

CHAPTER 10

1 Thomas More and Richard S. Sylvester (ed.), *The History of King Richard III and Selections from the English and Latin Poems* (New Haven / London, 1976), p. 76.
2 Dominic Mancini and C. A. J. Armstrong (ed. and trans.), *The usurpation of Richard the Third: Dominicus Mancinus ad Angelum Catonem De occupatione regni Anglie per Riccardum Tercium libellus* (Gloucester, 1984), p. 67; CCC, p. 153.
3 More, *History of King Richard III*, p. 14.
4 Gairdner, 'Letters and Papers Illustrative', pp. 1–10; C. L. Scofield, *The life and reign of Edward the Fourth. King of England and of France and Lord of Ireland* (Croydon, 2016), II, pp. 366–8.
5 M. K. Jones, 'Sir William Stanley of Holt: Politics and Family Allegiance in the Late Fifteenth Century', *Welsh History Review*, 14 (1988), pp. 17–8; Nicholas Orme, 'The Education of Edward V', *Bulletin of the Institute of Historical Research*, 57 (1984), pp. 124, 129; Hicks, Michael, 'The Changing Role of the Woodvilles in Yorkist Politics to 1483' in C. D. Ross (ed.), *Patronage, Pedigree and Power in Later Medieval England* (Gloucester, 1979), pp. 78–9.
6 Mancini, *The usurpation of Richard the Third*, p. 75.
7 CCC, p. 155.
8 Mancini, *The usurpation of Richard the Third*, pp. 71–3, Vergil, 'Richard III', c. 1, https://philological.cal.bham.ac.uk/polverg/25eng.html; accessed 19 December 2023.
9 CCC, p. 155; Mancini, *The usurpation of Richard the Third*, p. 73; Vergil, 'Richard III', c. 1; More, *History of King Richard III*, p. 18.
10 Margaret and Harry both occasionally hosted the young duke at their own home. WAM 12182.
11 Mancini, *The usurpation of Richard the Third*, p. 75.
12 More, *History of King Richard III*, p. 8.
13 Ibid., p. 9.
14 CCC p. 157.
15 Edward spent his first five days at the Bishop's Palace by St Paul's Cathedral. CCC, p. 157.
16 CCC p. 159.
17 Mancini, *The usurpation of Richard the Third*, p. 91; Christine Carpenter (ed.), *Kingsford's Stonor Letters and Papers: 1290–1483* (Cambridge: 1996), pp. 159–160.
18 Mancini, pp. 77–9.
19 Ibid., p. 85.
20 Rosemary Horrox, *Richard III: A study in service* (Cambridge, 1989), p. 112.
21 More, *History of King Richard III*, p. 5.
22 Vergil suggested, with more dramatic flair than pragmatism, that Hastings held his secret conversations at St Paul's Cathedral. Vergil, 'Richard III,' c. 2; Mancini, *The usurpation of Richard the Third*, pp. 90–1; More, *History of King Richard III*, pp. 44–5.
23 C. S. L. Davies, 'Bishop John Morton, the Holy See, and the Accession of Henry VII', *English Historical Review*, 102 (1987), p. 4.
24 More, *History of King Richard III*, pp. 21–3; Mancini, *The usurpation of Richard the Third*, p. 85.
25 More, *History of King Richard III*, p. 45.
26 Ibid., pp. 49–50.
27 As a civil servant in the Tudor regime, More is clearly not an unbiased reporter, and indeed his relation of Richard's coup in 1483 was not intended to be taken as 'history' so much as a literary exploration of tyranny, in a classical mode. Nonetheless, More's access to eyewitness testimony makes him a valuable source for what may have been reported, and believed, at the time of events.
28 Vergil, 'Richard III,' c. 4; More, *History of King Richard III*, p. 48.
29 Mancini, *The usurpation of Richard the Third*, p. 91.

30 Great Chronicle, p. 231.
31 More, *History of King Richard III*, p. 49.
32 Ibid., p. 50.
33 'Rous Roll' in Alison Hanham, *Richard III and his Early Historians 1483–1535* (Oxford, 1975), p. 122; Great Chronicle, p. 231.
34 'Rous Roll', p. 122.
35 Michael Jones, 'Richard III and the Stanleys' in Rosemary Horrox (ed.), *Richard III and the North* (Hull, 1986), p. 33.
36 Ibid., pp.32–7.
37 A week earlier one London correspondent noted that even though a great council was held at Westminster by Richard and Buckingham, close to Elizabeth's sanctuary, 'there was none that spoke with the queen' – a noteworthy breach of royal etiquette. Carpenter, *Kingsford's Stonor Letters*, p. 160.
38 CCC p. 159; Mancini, *The usurpation of Richard the Third*, p. 89; Carpenter, *Kingford's Stonor Letters*, p. 161; 'Vitellius A XVI', p. 190; More, *History of King Richard III*, pp. 26–42.
39 Shaa went further, reviving the old stories about Edward's illegitimacy, adding suggestive allusions to his physical dissimilarity from his father. Rumour ran that Richard, duke of Gloucester 'altogether resembled his father', according to Dominic Mancini. However, popular opinion did not accept Edward IV's illegitimacy, so Richard and Buckingham let that slander drop. CCC, p. 161; Thomas Basin and J. Quicherat (ed.), *Histoire des Règnes de Charles VII et de Louis XI* (Paris, 1857), III, p. 135; Mancini, *The usurpation of Richard the Third*, pp. 95–7; Great Chronicle, pp. 231–2; 'Vitellius A XVI', p. 190; More, *History of King Richard III*, pp. 60–1, 65–8; 'Richard III: January 1484', Parliament Rolls, item1, www.british-history.ac .uk/no-series/parliament-rolls-medieval /january-1484; accessed 17 September 2019.
40 Great Chronicle, p. 232; 'Vitellius A XVI', pp. 190–1; More, *History of King Richard III*, pp. 70–9.
41 CCC, p. 159; Mancini, *The usurpation of Richard the Third*, p. 97; 'Vitellius A XVI', p. 191; More, *History of King Richard III*, pp. 79–82.
42 It is possible that some form of judgement was passed against them by the earl of Northumberland, who was in attendance, but contemporaries are unanimous in condemning the executions as unlawful. Mancini, *The usurpation of Richard the Third*, p. 93; CCC, p. 161; Vergil, c. 6; More, *History of King Richard III*, p. 58.

CHAPTER 11

1 Vergil, 'Richard III', c. 11, https: //philological.cal.bham.ac.uk/polverg /25eng.html; accessed 19 December 2023.
2 For the description of the coronation see Anne F. Sutton and P. W. Hammond (eds.), *The Coronation of Richard III: The Extant Documents* (Gloucester, 1983), pp. 160–75, 275–87.
3 John Stow, *The Annales, or a Generall Chronicle of England, Begun First by Maister Iohn Stow, and after Him Continued and Augmented with Matters Forreyne, and Domestique, Auncient and Moderne, Vnto the Ende of This Present Yeere 1614. By Edmond Howes, Gentleman* (London, 1615), p. 460; CCC p. 163; Thomas Basin and J. Quicherat (ed.), *Histoire des Règnes de Charles VII et de Louis XI* (Paris: 1857), III, p. 137. Jones and Underwood discuss Stow's source, see Jones and Underwood, p. 62.
4 Edward had been created Prince of Wales at Pontefract on 24 August, but the York celebration was a more public, ritualistic occasion. See Peter Hammond, *The Children of Richard III* (Stroud, 2018), pp. 31–2.
5 The inclusion of the Tudors in what is otherwise a predominantly Yorkist plot is an oddity, given that Margaret's kinsmen had necessarily been keeping a low profile on the Continent for the

past decade. The person most likely
to promote their involvement was
Margaret Beaufort. Stow, *The Annales*,
p. 460.
6 Great Chronicle, p. 234.
7 Dominic Mancini and C. A. J.
Armstrong (ed. and trans.), *The
usurpation of Richard the Third:
Dominicus Mancinus ad Angelum
Catonem De occupatione regni
Anglie per Riccardum Tercium
libellus* (Gloucester, 1984), p. 93.
8 Henry VII made Argentine dean of
the chapel of Windsor and physician
to his heir Prince Arthur. Peter Murray
Jones, 'Argentine, John (c.1443–1508),
physician and college head', ODNB,
https://doi.org/10.1093/ref:odnb/642;
accessed 19 December 2022.
9 Mancini, *The usurpation of
Richard the Third*, p. 93.
10 Mancini is the earliest witness to
this rumour of the princes' death, and
his account is the more reliable for
being untainted by a retrospective
desire to vilify Richard III, since he
completed his narrative before Richard
was deposed in 1485. Mancini, *The
usurpation of Richard the Third*, p. 93.
11 Stow, *The Annales*, p. 460;
CCC, p. 163; Basin, *Histoire
des Règnes*, p. 137.
12 Hall, p. 389.
13 CCC, p. 163.
14 Vergil, 'Richard III', c. 8. See
also 'Short Latin Account' in Alison
Hanham, *Richard III and his Early
Historians 1483–1535* (Oxford, 1975),
p. 108; 'Vitellius A XVI', p. 191; Great
Chronicle, p. 234; Thomas More and
Richard S. Sylvester (ed.), *The History
of King Richard III and Selections
from the English and Latin Poems*
(New Haven / London, 1976), p. 85;
Basin, *Histoire des Règnes* III, p. 137;
Commines, II, p. 63; J. Molinet and
J. A. C. Buchon (ed.), *Chroniques de
Jean Molinet, Publiés Pour Le Première
Fois, D'après Les Manuscrits De La
ioiothèque Du Roi*, Vol. 2 (Paris, 1826),
pp. 401–4, https://babel.hathitrust.org
/cgi/pt?id=ucm.5325872212&view=1up
&seq=9; accessed 3 September 2019.

15 Polydore Vergil reported that
Margaret was staying at Stanley's
home in London when she plotted
with Elizabeth Woodville, at an
indeterminate time that summer: Denis
Hay, *Polydore Vergil: Renaissance
Historian and Man of Letters* (Oxford,
1952), p. 195; Hall's Chronicle locates
Margaret in both Lathom, with
Thomas, or London that summer. It is
likely she visited both. Hall, pp. 390–1.
16 Rosemary Horrox and P. W.
Hammond (eds), *British Library
Harleian Manuscript 433. Volume
2: Second Register of Richard
III* (Trowbridge, 1980), p. 7.
17 In John Welles's parliamentary
attainder, he is listed among the Exeter
rebels. 'Richard III: January 1484',
Parliament Rolls, item 3, www.british
-history.ac.uk/no-series/parliament
-rolls-medieval/january-1484;
accessed 21 July 2019.
18 The illegitimate heir of Henry
Beaufort, duke of Somerset (executed
after the Battle of Hexham in 1464)
had also survived Edward IV's purges:
Charles Beaufort aka Somerset. He
was in exile with Henry by 1485.
19 CCC, p. 163.
20 Vergil, 'Richard III', c. 11.
21 Ibid.; Hall, pp. 390–1.
22 Rosemary Horrox, *Richard III:
A Study in Service* (Cambridge,
1989), p. 151.
23 Vergil, 'Richard III', c. 11.
Urswicke deposed in January 1486 that
he had known Henry 'well for fifteen
or sixteen years'. 'Vatican Regesta
685: 1484–1487', *Calendar of Papal
Registers Relating to Great Britain and
Ireland: Volume 14, 1484–1492*, www
.british-history.ac.uk/cal-papal-registers
/brit-ie/vol14/pp14-30; accessed 31
July 2019.
24 Hall, pp. 389–390; More,
History of Richard III, pp. 42–4.
25 Allegedly, Buckingham had been
denied the earldom of Hereford. For
this and Buckingham's motivation more
broadly, see Barbara J. Harris, *Edward
Stafford: Third Duke of Buckingham,
1478–1521* (Stanford, 1986), pp. 24–7.

26 Hall, p. 387, Great Chronicle, p. 234; Henry Ellis (ed.), *Robert Fabyan: New Chronicles of England and France* (London, 1811), p. 670. Buckingham himself was believed responsible for the murder by continental sources: C. S. L. Davies, 'Stafford, Henry, second duke of Buckingham (1455–1483)', ODNB, https://doi.org/10.1093/ref:odnb /26204; accessed 31 July 2019.

27 J. A. F. Thomson, 'Bishop Lionel Woodville and Richard III', *Bulletin of the Institute of Historical Research*, 59 (1986), pp. 132–3.

28 Vergil, 'Richard III', c. 13–14; B.-A. Pocquet du Haut-Jossé, *Francois II, duc de Bretagne et l'Angleterre (1458–1488)* (Paris, 1929), pp. 248–51.

29 Vergil, 'Richard III', c. 12.

30 William Adams, *Adam's Chronicle of Bristol* (Bristol, 1910), p. 74.

31 James Gairdner (ed.), *The Paston Letters 1422–1509 AD. A Reprint of the Edition of 1872–5* (Edinburgh, 1910), p. 308.

32 Henry Ellis, *Original letters, illustrative of English history; including numerous royal letters; from autographs in the British Museum, and one or two other collections* (London, 1827), I, p. 161.

33 Joan Kirby (ed.), *The Plumpton Letters and Papers* (Cambridge, 2010), pp. 60–1; 'Rymer's Foedera with Syllabus: July–December 1483', www .british-history.ac.uk/rymer-foedera /vol12/pp192-209; accessed 16 September 2019; Horrox, *Richard III: A Study in Service*, pp. 151–2.

34 Harris, *Edward Stafford*, pp. 29–30.

35 Buckingham's servant Ralph Bannaster, who in some sources is named Humphrey, was rewarded with the manor of Yalding in Kent. CCC, pp. 163–5; Vergil, 'Richard III', c. 13; 'Vitellius A XVI', pp. 191–2; Hugh Owen and John Brickdale Blakeway, *A History of Shrewsbury: Volume I* (London, 1825), pp. 236–40; Harris, *Edward Stafford*, p. 28.

36 CCC, p. 169; Vergil, 'Richard

III', c. 14; Haut-Jossé, *Francois II, duc de Bretagne*, pp. 249–51.

37 Thomas Stanley's influence with the king probably also saved Reynald Bray, who was granted a royal pardon in 1484. Horrox and Hammond (eds.), *Harleian 1*, pp. 61, 108; Barry Coward, *The Stanleys, lords Stanley and earls of Derby, 1385–1672: the origins, wealth and power of a landowning family* (Manchester, 1983), p. 12.

38 Vergil, 'Richard III', c. 11.

39 'Richard III: January 1484', Parliament Rolls, item 6, www.british -history.ac.uk/no-series/parliament-rolls -medieval/january-1484; accessed 17 September 2019.

40 Horrox and Hammond, *Harleian*, I, p. 173. See also ibid., pp. 169, 176, 186, 202, 203, 271.

41 William Campbell, *Materials for a History of the Reign of Henry VII from Original Documents Preserved in the Public Record Office* (London, 1873), pp. 233, 296.

42 Vergil, 'Richard III', c. 15; 'Richard III: January 1484', Parliament Rolls, item 6; Horrox and Hammond, *Harleian*, I, pp. 173, 186, 202, 271.

CHAPTER 12

1 'Richard III: January 1484', Parliament Rolls, item 3: www.british -history.ac.uk/no-series/parliament-rolls -medieval/january-1484; accessed 29 May 2020.

2 Henry Ellis (ed.), *Robert Fabyan: New Chronicles of England and France* (London, 1811), p. 672.

3 Vergil, 'Richard III', c. 17, https:// philological.cal.bham.ac.uk/polverg /25eng.html; accessed 19 December 2023.

4 Keith Dockray, *Richard III: A Sourcebook* (Stroud, 1997) p. 102.

5 CCC, p. 173; Ralph A. Griffiths and Roger S. Thomas, *The Making of the Tudor Dynasty* (Gloucester, 1985), p. 105.

6 The best source for events in this period is Polydore Vergil, who almost certainly gained his story

first-hand from those involved. Vergil, 'Richard III', c. 15.

7 Yvonne Labande-Mailfert, *Charles VIII et Son Milieu (1470–1498): La Jeunesse au Pouvoir* (Paris, 1975), pp. 33–5.

8 Vergil, 'Richard III', cc. 16, 18; Griffiths and Thomas, *Tudor Dynasty*, pp. 122–3; C. L. Scofield, 'The early life of John de Vere, thirteenth earl of Oxford', *English Historical Review*, 29 (1914).

9 Chrimes, p. 117.

10 Vergil, 'Richard III', c. 16.

11 Griffiths and Thomas, *Tudor Dynasty*, p. 120. For context, see Michael K. Jones, *Bosworth 1485: Psychology of a Battle* (Stroud, 2003), pp. 148–9.

12 Henry Ellis, *Original letters, illustrative of English history; including numerous royal letters; from autographs in the British Museum, and one or two other collections* (London, 1827), I, pp. 162–5.

13 CCC, p. 171.

14 'Rous Roll', in Alison Hanham, *Richard III and his Early Historians 1483–1535* (Oxford, 1975), p. 122.

15 'Rous Roll', pp. 122–3; CCC, p. 175.

16 As brother- and sister-in-law Richard and Anne were related in the first degree of affinity, and through Anne's first marriage in the second degree of affinity. Through shared ancestors they were also related three times over in the fourth degree of consanguinity. Richard had secured a papal dispensation only for their affinity, not their blood relationship. Michael Hicks, *Anne Neville: Queen to Richard III* (Stroud, 2013), pp. 132–4. For a contrary view, Marie Barnfield, 'Diriment Impediments, Dispensations and Divorce: Richard III and Matrimony', *The Ricardian*, 17 (2007).

17 For the validity of Richard and Anne's marriage see Michael Hicks, *Richard III*, pp. 364–5; and for Richard's intentions towards Elizabeth, CCC, p. 175; Vergil, 'Richard III', c. 17.

18 CCC, p. 175.

19 Hanham, *Richard III and his Early Historians*, p. 49.

20 CCC, p. 175.

21 Ibid.

22 'Rous Roll', p. 121; Vergil, 'Richard III', c. 17; CCC, p. 175.

23 Dockray, *Richard III: A Sourcebook*, pp. 102–3. CCC, p. 177 gives the location of this assembly.

24 Angelo Raine, *York Civic records: Vol. 1* (Wakefield, 1939), pp. 115–6.

25 CCC, p. 175.

26 Ibid.

27 Vergil, 'Richard III', c. 19.

28 Michael K. Jones, 'The Myth of 1485: did France really put Henry Tudor on the throne?', in David Grummitt (ed.), *The English Experience in France c.1450–1558: War, Diplomacy and Cultural Exchange* (Aldershot, 2002), pp. 98, 101.

29 Ibid., pp. 98–101.

30 Vergil, 'Richard III', c. 19.

31 C. S. L. Davies, 'Bishop John Morton, the Holy See, and the Accession of Henry VII', *English Historical Review*, 102 (1987), pp. 13–4.

32 Vergil, 'Richard III', c. 19.

33 The precise location of Henry's court-in-exile is unclear, but as Dorset was returned to Paris after his flight and was caught on a road through Compiègne towards Flanders (a natural path from the eastern side of capital) it is likely he departed from Château de Vincennes. The other Parisian royal base, the Louvre to the west, lay within the city walls, whose gates were locked and guarded at night. Vergil, 'Richard III', c. 19.

34 Ibid.

35 There are several payments for clothes and footwear given to 'young Cheyney' in Reynald Bray's book of accounts in 1468–9. WAM 5472, ff. 22v, 24v, 30v, 31v, 40, 46. Humphrey appears to have been with Harry Stafford when he rode into Lincolnshire with Edward IV in 1470. WAM 12184, ff. 47, 48v, 56; WAM 12183, f. 11.

36 Vergil, 'Richard III', c. 19.

37   Vergil, 'Henry VII', c. 6, https://
philological.cal.bham.ac.uk/polverg
/26eng.html; accessed 19 December
2023.
38   Vergil, 'Richard III', c. 19 does
not date Dorset's flight. I follow
Griffiths and Thomas, who suggest it
was in June, when Henry was in Paris
with Charles VIII and Richard III
left Dorset's name off a list of rebels,
probably to lure him home. Griffiths
and Thomas, *Tudor Dynasty*, p. 126.
39   Jones, 'Myth of 1485', pp. 100–1.
40   William Berkeley was married
to Katherine Stourton, and his sister
(another Katherine) married John, 3rd
baron Stourton. John and Katherine
Stourton were the grandchildren of
John Stourton, 1st baron Stourton,
who was the dowager duchess of
Somerset's cousin and adviser. G.
L. Harriss, 'Stourton family (per.
*c.*1380–1485), gentry', ODNB, https://
doi.org/10.1093/ref:odnb/52797;
accessed 9 January 2024.
41   For another regional Tudor
network, centring around John
Morton and East Anglia, see
Davies, 'Bishop John Morton'.
42   Vergil, 'Richard III', c. 19;
Jones, 'Myth of 1485', p. 102.
43   Vergil, 'Richard III', c. 19.
As I make clear in the text, Vergil
couched this stockpile as being
Bray's doing, but I think it extremely
likely he was acting on Margaret's
orders, as he had since 1483.
44   'Richard III: January 1484',
Parliament Rolls, item 6, www.british
-history.ac.uk/no-series/parliament
-rolls-medieval/january-1484; accessed
29 May 2020.
45   Christopher was later a member of
Margaret's household and council, and
his manor at Tolethorpe was only six
miles from Collyweston. Rachel Delman,
'Elite Female Constructions of Power
and Space in England, 1444–1541,'
unpublished PhD thesis, University
of Oxford, 2017, pp. 254, 256.
46   Another prominent London
merchant and associate of Reynald
Bray who probably supported Henry in

1485 was the goldsmith Edmund Shaa,
who also had some existing connection
to William Herbert. Samantha Patricia
Harper, 'London and the Crown in the
Reign of Henry VII', unpublished PhD
thesis, University of London, 2015,
pp. 63–9.
47   For Richard's insolvency
see Alex Brayson, 'The Fiscal
Policy of King Richard III of
England', *Quidditas*, 40 (2019).
48   Sean Cunningham, '"Fraudulently
Compassed Against All Right
and Conscience": Evidence of the
Defection of Richard III's Government
Officials and the Progress of Henry
Tudor's Conspiracy, 1483–1485', *The
Ricardian* 34, i (2024), pp. 57–8, 61–2.
49   Vergil, 'Richard III', c. 19.
50   John's brother Thomas Savage
seems to have been abroad during
Richard III's reign and may have acted
as the family's direct contact with Henry
Tudor. Tim Thornton, 'Savage family
(per. *c.*1369–1528), gentry', ODNB,
https://doi.org/10.1093/ref:odnb/52794;
accessed 22 January 2025.
51   A release of land late in July
was witnessed by Thomas Stanley
and his sons. Michael Jones, 'Richard
III and the Stanleys' in Rosemary
Horrox (ed.), *Richard III and
the North* (Hull, 1986) p. 34.
52   CCC, p. 179.
53   Ibid., p. 177.
54   Commines, II, p. 64.
55   Vergil, 'Richard III', c. 20; CCC,
p. 177; Commines, I, p. 397; Fabyan,
p. 672; Hicks, Michael, *Richard
III*, p. 376; Jones, 'Myth of 1485',
p. 85; Griffiths and Thomas,
Tudor Dynasty, pp. 129–131.

CHAPTER 13

1   Diego de Valera, in Michael J.
Bennett, *The Battle of Bosworth*
(Stroud, 2000), Appendix III, p. 137.
2   This was a reference to Psalm
43, which concludes with the appeal
for salvation from the deceitful and
unjust. It was commonly used at
Mass during the office of Lauds.

3   Henry Ellis (ed.), *Robert Fabyan: New Chronicles of England and France* (London, 1811), p. 672.
4   Chrimes, p. 42.
5   Ralph A. Griffiths, and Roger S. Thomas, *The Making of the Tudor Dynasty* (Gloucester, 1985), p. 135.
6   Vergil, 'Richard III', c. 20, https://philological.cal.bham.ac.uk/polverg/25eng.html; accessed 19 December 2023.
7   For details of Henry's itinerary I follow Griffiths and Thomas, *Tudor Dynasty*, pp. 134–56. Quote, p.139.
8   CCC, p. 179.
9   Vergil, 'Richard III', c. 20 claims Thomas Stanley had 'a little less than 5,000 armed men in his host', but this may reflect the entire Stanley force, including the armies of his brother and other kinsmen.
10   Savage defected from King Richard's army the night before battle, on 21 August.
11   Griffiths and Thomas, *Tudor Dynasty*, pp. 149–50.
12   Bennett, *Bosworth*, p. 89; Mike Ingram, *Richard III and the Battle of Bosworth* (Warwick, 2019), pp. 220–1.
13   He reminded Henry of this fact in a petition after Bosworth: John Brickdale Owen and Hugh Blakeway, *A History of Shrewsbury* (London, 1825), I, p. 248.
14   Vergil, 'Richard III', c. 22.
15   Ibid.
16   WAM 5472, f. 44v.
17   Christopher Gravett and Graham Turner, *Battle of Bosworth: Last Charge of the Plantagenets* (Oxford, 1999).
18   CCC, p. 181.
19   Sir Ralph Bigod joined Margaret's household by 1491 at the latest, perhaps gaining an entrée into her inner circle through his guardian John, Lord Scrope of Bolton. Lord Scrope was married to Margaret's half-sister Elizabeth St John, and also fought at Bosworth. Vergil, 'Richard III', c. 23; Henry Parker, f. 19v (p. 262); Retha M. Warnicke, 'Sir Ralph Bigod: A loyal servant to Richard III', *The Ricardian*, 6 (1984).
20   Anne F. Sutton and Livia Visser-Fuchs, *The Hours of Richard III* (Stroud, 1990), pp. 77–8.
21   Richard's Book of Hours has been digitised by Leicester Cathedral: https://leicestercathedral.org/uploads/richard-iii-book-of-hours.pdf; accessed 21 February 2023. For context to the book see Sutton and Visser-Fuchs, *The Hours of Richard III*. The page where Richard recorded his date of birth is f. 7v.
22   Vergil, 'Richard III', c. 23.
23   James Orchard Halliwell (ed.), 'The Most Pleasant Song of Lady Bessy', in *Early English Poetry, Ballads and Popular Literature of the Middle Ages* (London, 1847), p. 38.
24   Vergil, 'Richard III', c. 233.
25   Ibid.; 'Song of Lady Bessy', pp. 33, 38.
26   Vergil, 'Richard III', c. 24.
27   Ibid.
28   Translation from Bennett, *Bosworth*, Appendix III, pp. 138–9.
29   Vergil, 'Richard III', c. 24.
30   CCC, p. 181; 'Song of Lady Bessy', pp. 39–40.
31   Bennett, *Bosworth*, Appendix III, p. 137.
32   According to the Denbighshire poet Tudur Aled. Griffiths and Thomas, *Tudor Dynasty*, p. 162.
33   Vergil, 'Richard III', c. 24.
34   'Song of Lady Bessy', pp. 41–2.
35   Jo Appleby *et al.*, 'Perimortem trauma in King Richard III: a skeletal analysis', *Lancet*, 385 (2015), pp. 253–59, www.thelancet.com/action/showPdf?pii=S0140-6736%2814%2960804-7; accessed 20 November 2019.
36   Vergil, 'Richard III', c. 25.
37   Molinet, translated in Bennett, *Bosworth*, p. 139.
38   Vergil, 'Richard III', c. 25. York's civic records also record that Henry was 'proclaimed and crowned at the field of Redmore'. Angelo Raine, *York Civic records: Vol. 1* (Wakefield, 1939), p. 119.
39   BL MS, Royal MS

2 A XVIII, f. 31v.
40 Molinet, translated in
Bennett, *Bosworth*, p. 139.
41 Diego, in Bennett, *Bosworth*,
p. 138; 'Song of Lady Bessy', p. 78;
Georges Doutrepont and Omer
Jodogne (eds.), *Chroniques de Jean
Molinet* (Bruxelles, 1935), I, pp.
435–6; Vergil, 'Richard III', c. 25.
42 Doutrepont, *Molinet*, I, p. 436.

CHAPTER 14

1 BL Egerton MS 985, f. 27.
2 Materials, I, pp. 178–182, 229;
Angelo Raine, *York Civic records:
Vol. 1* (Wakefield: 1939), pp. 118–9.
3 Vergil, 'Henry VII', c. 1, https:
//philological.cal.bham.ac.uk/polverg
/26eng.html; accessed 19 December
2023; Hall, pp. 422–3; Great
Chronicle, pp. 238–9; 'Vitellius A
XVI', p. 193.
4 Materials, I, pp. 188, 201.
5 Raine, *York Civic records*, p. 120.
6 Ibid., p. 121.
7 CCC, p. 169.
8 'Vitellius A XVI', p. 193.
9 The precise date of Henry's
entry into London is debated,
variously placed anywhere between
27 August to 7 September. It is
likelier to have been later. Jones and
Underwood, p. 66; Ford, 'Itinerary'.
10 Vergil, 'Henry VII', c. 51.
11 Ibid.
12 Hall, pp. 422, 425.
13 'Mornynge Remembraunce',
pp. 305–6.
14 Ibid., p. 305.
15 Ibid., p. 306. Margaret's
anxiety that disaster would come
hot on the heels of this celebration
was not entirely misplaced. During
the celebrations at Westminster,
'there fell a scaffold with much
people [but] none slain, blessed be
God'. BL Egerton MS 985, f. 45.
16 Vergil, 'Henry VII', c. 1;
André (Hobbins), pp. 6–7.
17 Leopold George Wickham
Legg, *English Coronation Records*
(London, 1901), pp. 202–10;

BL Egerton MS 985, f. 45v.
18 Materials, I, pp. 77–8.
19 Ibid., I, pp. 76, 296.
20 Ibid., I, pp. 7, 271, 258.
21 Ibid., I, pp. 19, 190, 574.
22 'Carissimus avunculus
noster.' Materials, I, p. 102.
23 Ralph A. Griffiths and Roger S.
Thomas, *The Making of the Tudor
Dynasty* (Gloucester, 1985), p. 183.
24 BL Add MS 4712, f. 25.
25 Margaret acquired Coldharbour
in September 1485, but the grant was
not formally confirmed until March
1487. Jones and Underwood, p. 100.
26 The accounts showing payment
for repairs are transcribed in C. L.
Kingsford, 'On some London houses of
the early Tudor period', *Archaeologia
or, Miscellaneous Tracts Relating to
Antiquity*, 71 (1921), pp. 43–50.
27 Ibid.; Materials, I, p. 311.
28 J. L. Laynesmith, 'The King's
Mother', *History Today*, 56 (2006);
idem, *Cecily Duchess of York* (London
/ New York, 2017), pp. 100–1.
29 Materials, I, pp. 81, 233, 225.
30 'Hault et puissant princesse la
mere du Roy Comtesse de Richemonde
et de Derby'. BL Egerton MS 985,
f. 27.
31 Ibid., ff. 28–9.
32 The original language is 'eny other
sole persone not covert of eny husband
may do'. 'Henry VII: November 1485,
Part 1', Parliament Rolls, item 12 [17],
www.british-history.ac.uk/no-series
/parliament-rolls-medieval/november
-1485-pt-1; accessed 3 January 2025.
33 Jones and Underwood, p. 99.
34 Ibid., pp. 100–4.
35 D56.158 (SJLM/4/4/2).
36 This book of accounts from
December 1491 to March 1492 also
notes interactions with Margaret's
officers like Hugh Oldham (her receiver)
and William Croke (her auditor).
WAM 5474, ff. 26, 29. For visits to
Coldhabour and dealing with 'my
lady's matters' see ibid., ff. 5v, 21v,
25v, 26, 27v, 28v.
37 Kingsford, 'On some
London houses', p. 45.

CHAPTER 15

1   André (Hobbins), p. 37.
2   'Ceremonial of the celebration of Christmas by Henry VII', BL Egerton MS 985, ff. 27-29v.
3   Retha M. Warnicke, *Elizabeth of York and Her Six Daughters-In-Law: Fashioning Tudor Queenship 1485–1547* (New York, 2017), p. 22; Materials, I, pp. 227–8.
4   CSP Venice, no. 506, www.british-history.ac.uk/cal-state-papers/venice/vol1/pp141-159; accessed 22 February 2023; Materials, I, p. 264.
5   James Orchard Halliwell (ed.), 'The Most Pleasant Song of Lady Bessy', in *Early English Poetry, Ballads and Popular Literature of the Middle Ages* (London, 1847).
6   Rosemary Horrox, 'Elizabeth [Elizabeth of York] (1466–1503)', ODNB, https://doi:10.1093/ref:odnb/8635; accessed 30 July 2020; Arlene Naylor Okerlund, *Elizabeth of York* (New York, 2009), pp. 7–12; 'Narratives of the Arrival of Louis de Bruges, Seigneur de la Gruthuyse', *Archaeologia: Or Miscellaneous Tracts Relating to Antiquity*, 26 (1836), pp. 277–9.
7   Okerlund, *Elizabeth of York*, p. 6.
8   'Song of Lady Bessy', p. 6; Vergil, 'Henry VII', c. 17, https://philological.cal.bham.ac.uk/polverg/26eng.html; accessed 19 December 2023.
9   Livia Visser-Fuchs, 'Where did Elizabeth of York find Consolation?', *The Ricardian*, 9 (1993).
10   Alison Hanham, 'Sir George Buck and Princess Elizabeth's Letter: A Problem in Detection', *The Ricardian*, 7 (1987).
11   Marie Barnfield, 'Diriment Impediments, Dispensations and Divorce: Richard III and Matrimony', *The Ricardian*, 17 (2007), p. 97.
12   Arthur Kincaid, 'Buck and the Elizabeth of York Letter: A Reply to Dr Hanham', *The Ricardian*, 8 (1988).
13   'Vatican Regesta 685: 1484–1487', in J. A. Twemlow (ed.), *Calendar of Papal Registers Relating to Great Britain and Ireland: Volume 14, 1484–1492*, www.british-history.ac.uk/cal-papal-registers/brit-ie/vol14/pp14-30; accessed 31 July 2019.
14   C. S. L. Davies, 'Bishop John Morton, the Holy See, and the Accession of Henry VII', *English Historical Review*, 102 (1987), p. 15; Sydney Anglo, *Spectacle, Pageantry and Early Tudor Policy* (Oxford, 1997), p. 19.
15   André (Hobbins), pp. 34–5.
16   Materials, I, pp. 227, 253–4; André (Hobbins), p. 35; CCC, p. 195.
17   Joan Kirby (ed.), *The Plumpton Letters and Papers* (Cambridge, 2010), p. 64.
18   Anglo, *Spectacle, Pageantry and Early Tudor Policy*, p. 22.
19   Shannon McSheffrey, 'Henry VII and Humphrey Stafford', in idem, *Sanctuary Seekers in England, 1394–1557*, https://sanctuaryseekers.ca/2020/06/10/stafford; accessed 15 March 2025.
20   Vergil, 'Henry VII', c. 4.
21   Anglo, *Spectacle, Pageantry and Early Tudor Policy*, pp. 34–5.
22   Materials, I, p. 543.
23   Leland, p. 249.
24   For example: 'a dominant personality who expects to run the show'. Okerlund, *Elizabeth of York*, p. 90.
25   'Mornynge Remembraunce', p. 296.
26   For the debate surrounding Margaret's authorship of the ordinances see K. Staniland, 'Royal entry into the world', in D. Williams (ed.), *England in the Fifteenth Century* (Woodbridge, 1987), pp. 297–313.
27   The Constitutio survives in early thirteenth-century manuscripts. Joanna Laynesmith, 'The Order, Rules and Constructions of the House of the Most Excellent Princess Cecily, Duchess of York' in Gwilym Dodd and Craig Taylor (eds.), *Monarchy, State and Political Culture in Late Medieval England: Essays in Honour of W. Mark Ormrod* (Woodbridge, 2020), p. 169.

28 Warnicke, *Elizabeth of York and Her Six Daughters-In-Law*, p. 174; Laynesmith, 'The Order, Rules and Constructions', pp. 167–173; Staniland, 'Royal entry into the world', pp. 299–300, 303.

29 CSP Spain, no. 205, www.british-history.ac.uk/cal-state-papers/spain/vol1/pp153-167; accessed 20 September 2022.

30 Ibid.

31 Ibid., nos. 204, 210, www.british-history.ac.uk/cal-state-papers/spain/vol1/pp153-167; accessed 20 September 2022; www.british-history.ac.uk/cal-state-papers/spain/vol1/pp167-180; accessed 20 September 2022.

32 Retha M. Warnicke, 'Margaret Tudor, Countess of Richmond and Elizabeth York: Dynastic Competitors or Allies?' in Valerie Schutte (ed.), *Unexpected Heirs in Early Modern Europe: Potential Kings and Queens* (New York, 2017), pp. 42–4.

33 Materials, I, pp. 278–9.

34 TNA, SC 1/51/189.

35 Leland, p. 249.

36 André (Hobbins), pp. 37–8; Leland, p. 204.

37 Anglo, *Spectacle, Pageantry and Early Tudor Policy*, pp. 46–7; David Carlson, 'King Arthur and court poems for the birth of Arthur Tudor in 1486', *Humanistica Lovaniensia*, 36 (1987), pp. 148–59.

38 Leland, pp. 204, 207.

39 Materials, II, p. 39; Leland, pp. 204, 180–1.

40 Ibid., pp. 205–6.

41 Ibid., pp. 206–7.

CHAPTER 16

1 CSP Venice, no. 519, www.british-history.ac.uk/cal-state-papers/venice/vol1/pp141-159; accessed 5 February 2020.

2 Symonds did not name the boy in his confession. For questions about the identity of the pseudo-Warwick and Lambert Simnel see Michael J. Bennett, *Lambert Simnel and the Battle of Stoke* (Stroud, 1993), pp. 43–8.

3 'Concilia Magnae Britanniae et Hiberniae', translated in ibid., 'Appendix: Extract from Key Sources', p. 121; Vergil, 'Henry VII,' c. 5, https://philological.cal.bham.ac.uk/polverg/26eng.html; accessed 19 December 2023.

4 Vergil, 'Henry VII,' c. 7.

5 James Orchard Halliwell (ed.), *Letters of the Kings of England, now first collected from the originals in royal archives, and from other authentic sources, private as well as public* (London: 1846), I, p. 171.

6 Chrimes, p. 75.

7 Rosemary Horrox and P. W. Hammond (eds.), *British Library Harleian Manuscript 433, Volume 1, Register of Grants for the Reigns of Edward V and Richard III* (Trowbridge, 1979), pp. 177–8.

8 Vergil, 'Henry VII', c. 7.

9 Materials, II, pp. 142, 148, 221.

10 Francis Bacon and Jerry Weinberger (ed.), *The History of the Reign of King Henry the Seventh* (Ithaca / London, 1996), pp. 49–50; David Baldwin, *Elizabeth Woodville Mother of the Princes in the Tower* (Stroud, 2010), pp. 111–5.

11 Vergil, 'Henry VII', c. 6.

12 J. G. Nichols, (ed.), *A Collection of All the Wills, Now Known to Be Extant, of the Kings and Queens of England, Princes and Princesses of Wales, and Every Branch of the Blood Royal: From the Reign of William the Conqueror, to that of Henry the Seventh* (London, 1780), pp. 350–1.

13 Euan C. Roger, '"To Be Shut Up": New Evidence for the Development of Quarantine Regulations in Early-Tudor England', *Social History of Medicine*, 33, iv (2020), pp. 1077–1096.

14 Ibid.; CSP Venice, no. 116, www.british-history.ac.uk/cal-state-papers/venice/vol2/pp46-49; accessed 3 September 2020.

15 As Susan Higginbotham notes, if Elizabeth were under royal suspicion, this would be a curious choice of prison. Susan Higginbotham, *The Woodvilles: The Wars of the Roses and England's Most Infamous*

Family (Stroud, 2013), pp. 164–5.

16 This was increased to £400 in February 1490. Materials, II, pp. 273, 319; Maxwell-Lyte H. C. et al. (ed.), *Calendar of the Patent Rolls preserved in the Public Record Office, 1485–1494, Henry VII* (London, 1914), p. 302.

17 Materials, II, pp. 297, 322, 379.

18 Elizabeth's was one among a wider series of marital alliances between the families.

19 Bennett, *Lambert Simnel and the Battle of Stoke*, p. 70.

20 'Herald's Report' in ibid., p. 128.

21 Ibid.; Molinet, 'Chronique' in Bennet, *Lambert Simnel and the Battle of Stoke*, p. 131; Great Chronicle, p. 241; 'Vitellius A XVI,' p. 194; CSP Venice, no. 519, www.british-history .ac.uk/cal-state-papers/venice/vol1 /pp141-159; accessed 5 February 2020.

22 The organisation of the royal forces is related by Molinet in Bennett, *Lambert Simnel and the Battle of Stoke*, p. 131. Bennett puts the royal and rebel forces at respectively 15,000 and less than 8,000. Ibid., pp 92, 95.

23 André (Hobbins), p. 46.

24 Molinet in Bennett, *Lambert Simnel and the Battle of Stoke*, p. 131.

25 Great Chronicle, p. 241; Vergil, 'Henry VII', c. 9.

26 Topography of the battlefield is provided by 'English Heritage Battlefield Report: Stoke Field 1487' (1995), https://historicengland.org .uk/content/docs/listing/battlefields /stoke-field/; accessed 18 August 2020.

27 Ibid.; Bennet, *Lambert Simnel and the Battle of Stoke*, p. 101.

28 André (Hobbins), p. 47.

29 Bennett, *Lambert Simnel and the Battle of Stoke*, pp. 44–8.

30 Vergil, 'Henry VII', c. 9.

31 Leland, pp. 217–8.

32 BL Royal MS 2 A XVIII, f. 30v.

33 That Henry had delayed Elizabeth's coronation so long was no slight on his bride, and nor was it understood as such by contemporaries. Such an interpretation gained currency after Francis Bacon wrote his highly influential *History of King Henry VII* in 1622. Bacon suggested that Henry did not wish to crown Elizabeth at all because her Yorkist blood repulsed him, and that he deliberately delayed her coronation to diminish her dynastic claims 'lest a joint coronation of himself and his queen might give any countenance of participation of title'. But Henry was as shrewd a propagandist as his mother, and understood how unifying and popular the coronation of his queen would be. As well as demonstrating divine approval of the king's marriage and the legitimacy of his heirs, it also provided entertainment, distraction and economic benefit to those in attendance. Moreover, if – as Bacon suggested – Henry sought to subordinate Elizabeth's Yorkist royal claim to his own Lancastrian one, a joint or queen's coronation would help him to achieve this end, as subtle intimations of female inferiority ran throughout the ritual. In joint coronations, a queen's throne was always placed lower, and to the left (subordinate) side, of the king's. A queen was anointed with holy oil only in three places (twice on her breast and once on her forehead) and received a rod of office to hold alongside her royal sceptre, rather than a golden orb – the queen's rod was redolent of the staff of office of royal officers, suggesting a limited role granted to her by the king, and thus in his power to remove. Royal accounts of expenditure also suggest that Henry had not originally intended such a long delay. There had been plans afoot for Elizabeth's coronation as far back as December 1485, when Henry signed a royal writ to purchase 'coursers' for the occasion. But the pressing demands of the intervening years had forced the delay and only in autumn 1487 was there sufficient breathing space to arrange the necessary celebrations. Francis Bacon and J. Rawson Lumby (ed.), *Bacon's History of the Reign of King Henry VII* (London, 1885), pp. 12, 19, 40, www

.google.co.uk/books/edition/Bacon_s
_History_of_the_Reign_of_King_Hen
/gnCjHCH-wjoC?hl=en&gbpv=1;
accessed 1 September 2020. For
context see Retha M. Warnicke,
*Elizabeth of York and Her Six
Daughters-In-Law: Fashioning Tudor
Queenship 1485–1547* (New York,
2017), pp. 22, 37; and for earlier
preparations, Materials, I, p. 220.
34 Leland, p. 218. For what
follows see ibid., pp. 218–233.
35 Ibid., p. 225.
36 As Henry put it in a letter
sent from Newark to York on 16
June 1487, probably one of several
dispatched nationwide to disseminate
news of Henry's victory. 'York Civic
Records' in Bennett, *Lambert Simnel
and the Battle of Stoke*, p. 123.

CHAPTER 17
1 TNA, SC 1/51/189.
2 Ian Arthurson, *The Perkin Warbeck
Conspiracy 1491–9* (Stroud, 1994),
pp. 21–3, 40–5.
3 As is plain in the text, I do not
believe that Warbeck was really
Richard of York. His own testimony,
combined with the evidence of many
contemporaries and the sheer weight
of probability, tell against it. For
an alternative interpretation of the
Warbeck/Richard history, however, see
Matthew Lewis, *The Survival of the
Princes in the Tower: Murder, Mystery
and Myth* (Cheltenham, 2017);
Philippa Langley, *The Princes in the
Tower: Solving history's greatest cold
case* (Cheltenham, 2023); Anne Wroe,
Perkin: A Story of Deception (London,
2004). And for scepticism of Warbeck
discoveries in the archives, Michael
Hicks, 'Historic Doubts about
the Survival of the Princes in the
Tower after 1485', *Historical
Research: The Bulletin of the
Institute of Historical Research*,
97 (2024), pp. 437–42.
4 'Henry VII: November 1485, Part
1', Parliament Rolls, item 8, https:
//www-british-history-ac-uk.lonlib

.idm.oclc.org/no-series/parliament
-rolls-medieval/november-1485-pt-1;
accessed 21 January 2025.
5 Arlene Naylor Okerlund, *Elizabeth
of York* (New York, 2009), pp. 126–7.
6 The exact date of Cecily's
marriage is unknown, but it took
place by 1 January 1488.
7 J. W. Clay (ed.), *North Country
Wills: Being Abstracts of Wills
Relating to the Counties of York,
Nottingham, Northumberland,
Cumberland and Westmorland at
Somerset House and Lambeth Palace
1383 to 1558* (Durham, 1908), p. 68.
8 Margaret also supported Richard
and Margaret Pole's daughter, Ursula,
paying for her 'costs and exhibitions':
D91.19 (SJLM/1/1/3/3), pp. 26, 42,
56, 75, 98; D91.21 (SJLM/1/1/3/2),
pp. 105, 137, 141, 157. For Margaret's
support of Lady Pole and her children,
including 'reward to two women
nurse to my Lady Pole's two children
that were with my lady's grace at
Syon', see D91.21 (SJLM/1/1/3/2),
p. 113, 22, 24, 98, 119, 128, 153;
D91.19 (SJLM/1/1/3/3), pp. 10, 77,
96; D102.1 (SJLM/1/1/5/1), ff. 9v,
12v, 15v. For Margaret's relationship
with Margaret Pole see Sue Powell,
'Margaret Pole and Syon Abbey,'
Historical Research, 78 (2005).
9 'Henry VII: January 1497',
Parliament Rolls, item 3, www.british
-history.ac.uk/no-series/parliament
-rolls-medieval/january-1497; accessed
16 March 2022; *Excerpta Historica*,
p. 101.
10 The household accounts of
Elizabeth of York contain many
payments to Katherine and her
children, who lived at court. TNA,
E36/210, ff. 65, 70, 74, 75, 76, 83, 91,
94, 95. Margaret, too, was a patron
of Katherine's family, rewarding 'my
lady Katherine's child' with a generous
sum of money on at least one occasion.
D91.17 (SJLM/1/1/2/1), p. 217.
11 Jones and Underwood, pp. 121–2;
Rosemary Horrox, 'Parr family (per.
c.1370–1517), gentry', ODNB, https:
//doi.org/10.1093/ref:odnb/52790;

accessed 4 January 2024.

12 H. M. Colvin (ed.), *The History of the King's Works: Volume IV, 1485–1660* (Part II) (London, 1982), p. 351; Jones and Underwood, pp. 70–75.

13 CSP Spain, no. 21, www.british-history.ac.uk/cal-state-papers/spain/vol1/pp3-19; accessed 5 September 2020.

14 Ibid.

15 Leland, p. 253.

16 Ibid., pp. 252–3.

17 Dynastically speaking, Margaret was the sole heir of her father. She had a number of half-siblings.

18 TNA, SC 1/51/189.

19 Rewards to the royal children and their servants can be found at D91.20 (SJLM/1/1/3/1), pp. 123, 127; D91.21 (SJLM/1/1/3/2), pp. 92, 25, 27–8, 30, 41, 46, 110. See also below.

20 D91.20 (SJLM/1/1/3/1), pp. 48, 191.

21 The New Year gift is found in D91.20 (SJLM/1/1/3/1), p. 198. For other exchanges between Margaret and her granddaughter in Scotland see ibid., pp. 92, 123, 135, 140, 177; D91.19 (SJLM/1/1/3/3), pp. 16, 118. Rewards to the Verneys may also have been in relation to their service for Princess Margaret.

22 Sir Richard Pole was Margaret's nephew of the half-blood: his mother was her half-sister Edith St John.

23 Vergil, 'Henry VII', c. 43, https://philological.cal.bham.ac.uk/polverg/26eng.html; accessed 2 November 2022; Margaret Bowker, 'Smith [Smyth], William (d. 1514), bishop of Lincoln and a founder of Brasenose College, Oxford', ODNB, https://doi.org/10.1093/ref:odnb/25920; accessed 19 December 2024.

24 From BL Harley MS 6079, transcribed in Leland, pp. 238–242. This quotation is p. 239.

25 Leland, p. 242 and more generally pp. 238–242; Retha M. Warnicke, *Elizabeth of York and Her Six Daughters-In-Law: Fashioning Tudor Queenship 1485–1547* (New York, 2017), pp. 185–6.

26 Leland, p. 242.

27 Ibid., pp. 239–40, 243–5.

28 Ibid., pp. 254–5.

29 Lady Mary was the daughter of William Paston and Anne Beaufort, and thus granddaughter of Edmund Beaufort, duke of Somerset (d. 1455).

30 Leland, pp. 255–6.

31 For these events of 1489 see Michael J. Bennett, 'Henry VII and the Northern Rising of 1489', *English Historical Review*, 105 (1990), pp. 34–59.

32 Margaret's husband Thomas Stanley and Elizabeth's chamberlain the earl of Ormond were certainly with Henry at Hertford, so the presence of the king's mother and queen is likely. Bennett, 'Henry VII and the Northern Rising', p. 41.

33 Materials, II, 444–5.

34 Bennett, 'Henry VII and the Northern Rising', p. 42–4.

35 C. P. Wilkins, 'Woodville, Sir Edward (d. 1488)', ODNB, https://doi.org/10.1093/ref:odnb/101193; accessed 3 February 2022; 'A letter of William Paston to Sir John Paston, 13 May 1488', Pollard, I, p. 58.

36 Leland, p. 243; Pollard, I, p. 60.

37 Jones and Underwood, p. 81.

38 The timeline of Perkin Warbeck's promotion by European powers is debated. For Margaret of Burgundy's likely involvement in Warbeck's schemes before Charles VIII championed him, see Mark Ballard and C. S. L. Davies, 'Étienne Fryon: Burgundian Agent, English Royal Secretary and "Principal Counsellor" to Perkin Warbeck', *Historical Research*, 62 (1989).

CHAPTER 18

1 André (Hobbins), p. 61.

2 Great Chronicle, p. 251.

3 Michael J. Bennett, 'Stanley, Sir William (c. 1435–1495)', ODNB, https://doi-org/10.1093/ref:odnb/26282; accessed 19 May 2019.

4 Vergil, 'Henry VII', c. 28, https://philological.cal.bham.ac.uk/polverg/26eng.html; accessed 3 January 2025.

5   Hall, p. 469.
6   Jones and Underwood, p. 150;
M. K. Jones, 'Sir William Stanley of
Holt: Politics and Family Allegiance
in the Late Fifteenth Century', *Welsh
History Review*, 14 (1988), pp. 20–1.
7   Ian Arthurson, *The Perkin Warbeck
Conspiracy 1491–9* (Stroud, 1994),
p. 178.
8   For instance, the royal receiver John
Hayes of Tiverton was convicted of
misprision of treason and imprisoned
for failing to reveal a conspiracy to
put the earl of Warwick on the throne
in 1491. Robert Chamberlain and
Richard White were executed for
plotting Henry's death in league with
the French. 'Henry VII: October 1491',
items 15, 16, Parliament Rolls, www
.british-history.ac.uk/no-series
/parliament-rolls-medieval/october
-1491; accessed 1 February 2022.
9   See for example Henry's letter
to Gilbert Talbot in summer 1493.
James Orchard Halliwell (ed.), *Letters
of the Kings of England, now first
collected from the originals in royal
archives, and from other authentic
sources, private as well as public,
Vol I* (London, 1846), pp. 172–3.
10 André (Hobbins), p. 60.
11 Vergil, 'Henry VII', c.24; Chrimes,
pp. 81–3, 88–9; Arthurson, *Perkin
Warbeck*, pp. 10–13; John M. Currin,
'To traffic with war? Henry VII and
the French Campaign of 1492', in
David Grummitt (ed.), *The English
Experience in France c.1450–1558:
War, Diplomacy and Cultural
Exchange* (Aldershot, 2002), p. 118.
12 Currin, 'To traffic with
war?', pp. 113–4, 127.
13 CSP Milan, no. 456, www.british
-history.ac.uk/cal-state-papers/milan
/1385-1618/pp283-291; accessed 8
February 2022.
14 Jones and Underwood, p. 81;
Currin, 'To traffic with war?', p. 116.
15 *Excerpta Historica*, pp.
90–2; Currin, 'To traffic with
war?', pp. 110–1, 116, 119.
16 'Rymer's Foedera with Syllabus:
January–June 1492', www.british

-history.ac.uk/rymer-foedera/vol12
/pp465-482; accessed 8 February 2022.
17 Great Chronicle, p. 247;
'Vitellius A XVI', p. 197.
18 Chrimes, p. 83.
19 *Excerpta Historica*, p. 89;
Great Chronicle, pp. 247, 254–6.
20 Arthurson, *Perkin Warbeck*, p. 65.
21 Ibid., pp. 68, 73; Great
Chronicle, pp. 248–9.
22 Clifford also had a long-term
connection to the Mowbray retinue
of East Anglia. As Richard, duke of
York was by right of marriage the
Mowbray heir, this may have been
another factor in Clifford's decision
to follow the alleged duke. Arthurson,
Perkin Warbeck, p. 62.
23 Hall, p. 465; Arthurson,
Perkin Warbeck, p. 62.
24 Charles Henry Cooper, *Memoir
of Margaret Countess of Richmond
and Derby* (Cambridge, 1874), p. 48.
25 *Excerpta Historica*, p. 100;
Arthurson, *Perkin Warbeck*, p. 84.
26 Great Chronicle, p. 251;
'Vitellius A XVI', p. 200.
27 Arthurson, *Perkin Warbeck*, p. 75.
28 Vergil, 'Henry VII', cc. 26–7;
Great Chronicle, p. 256.
29 Arthurson, *Perkin
Warbeck*, p. 178.
30 Vergil, 'Henry VII', c. 27.
31 My translation from the Latin
text provided in W. A. J. Archbold,
'Sir William Stanley and Perkin
Warbeck', *English Historical
Review*, 14 (July 1889), p. 531.
32 Great Chronicle, pp. 257–8.
33 *Excerpta Historica*, pp. 101–2.
34 Arthurson, *Perkin
Warbeck*, pp. 108–18.
35 Great Chronicle, p. 260;
'Vitellius A XVI', pp. 206–7.
36 Hall, p. 471.
37 BL Add MS 7099, ff. 28–29.
38 For infant and maternal mortality,
see Retha M. Warnicke, *Elizabeth of
York and Her Six Daughters-In-Law:
Fashioning Tudor Queenship 1485–
1547* (New York, 2017), pp. 113–4.
39 Ibid., p. 115.
40 Margaret's letters, as transcribed

in Charles Henry Cooper, *Memoir of Margaret, countess of Richmond and Derby* (Cambridge, 1874), pp. 64–7.

41 Ibid., p. 67.

42 'Maria Hayward, *Dress at the Court of King Henry VIII* (Leeds, 2007)', p. 67. A gilt effigy on the princess's tomb has been removed but the rest of the monument can still be seen within Westminster Abbey. 'Elizabeth daughter of Henry VII', www.westminster–abbey.org/abbey -commemorations/royals/elizabeth -daughter-of-henry-vii; accessed 22 February 2022.

43 John Gough Nichols and John Bruce, (eds.), *Wills from Doctors' Commons: A Selection from the Wills of Eminent Persons Proved in the Prerogative Court of Canterbury, 1495–1695* (London, 1863), pp. 1–8.

44 TNA, PROB 11/10/591.

CHAPTER 19

1 Hall, p. 425.

2 Great Chronicle, pp. 261–2.

3 TNA, SC1/ 51/189.

4 The progress and its participants can be mapped in TNA, E101/414/6, ff. 38v, 39r, 41r, 42v; *Excerpta Historica*, pp. 108–9. See also Jones and Underwood, pp. 71–2; Materials, II, p. 364; 'Corfe Castle', in *An Inventory of the Historical Monuments in Dorset, Volume 2, South east*, www.british -history.ac.uk/rchme/dorset/vol2/pp52 -100; accessed 10 March 2022.

5 TNA, E101/414/6, ff. 41r, 43r. The royal accounts show repeated payments to falconers, and thanksgiving rewards for gifts of greyhounds and goshawks to Henry throughout summer 1496. TNA, E101/414/6, ff. 38v-42r.

6 This is the only dog mentioned by name in Henry's chamber books. TNA, E101/415/3, f. 26v, M. M. Condon *et al.* (eds.), *The Chamber Books of Henry VII and Henry VIII, 1485–1521*, www.tudorchamberbooks.org/edition /folio/E101_415_3_fo_026v.xml; accessed 29 January 2025.

7 D91.20 (SJLM/1/1/3/1), pp. 26, 42,

44, 46, 50, 96, 107, 162, 164, 165.

8 *Excerpta Historica*, p. 109.

9 'Dick the fool' was probably a natural fool living in the royal household, as his payments were made to a 'master'. The 'fool at Winchester' was paid directly, and was probably a local 'artificial' performer. For the distinction, see p. 249. TNA, E101/414/6, ff. 38v, 40r. 'Dik the foles master' received a monthly wage of ten shillings at December 1495, and Dick himself was clothed at royal expense, suggesting he was part of the court. *Excerpta Historica*, pp. 95, 106; BL Add MS 7099, f. 14.

10 In 1496, at the royal court see for instance *Excerpta Historica*, p. 106; TNA, E101/414/6 f. 38v. Margaret's payments for fools and players: D102.1 (SJLM/1/1/5/1), ff. 4v, 9r, 9v; D91.19 (SJLM/1/1/3/3), pp. 75, 76, 89,105. For a St Nicholas clerk, D91.20 (SJLM/1/1/3/1), p. 52.

11 Andrew Boorde and F. J. Furnivall (ed.), *The fyrst boke of the introduction of knowledge made by Andrew Borde, of physycke doctor: A compendyous regyment; or, A dyetary of helth* (London, 1870), p. 228.

12 D102.10 (SJLM/1/1/6/1), f. 9v.

13 Henry Parker, f. 21r.

14 Desiderius Erasmus and T. N. R. Rogers (ed.), *In Praise of Folly* (New York, 2003), pp. 27–9.

15 John Southworth, *Fools and Jesters at the English Court* (Stroud, 1998), pp. 64–5.

16 D91.19 (SJLM/1/1/3/3), p 75.

17 Korse, also spelled Coksey, stayed with Margaret from 3 March to 20 May. As he was always accompanied, it is possible he was a 'natural fool'. Ibid., pp. 76, 89, 102.

18 The tomb of John Beaufort and Margaret Beauchamp can still be seen in Wimborne Minster today.

19 Wimborne was not the only West Country building to benefit from Margaret's visit. After her progress with her son, Margaret endowed the church of St John the Baptist in her estate at Sampford Peverell, Devon, with a new

south aisle and porch in local sandstone and ashlar. 'Church of St John the Baptist, Sampford Peverell', Historic England, https://historicengland.org .uk/listing/the-list/list-entry/1106431; accessed 30 March 2020.

20 *Excerpta Historica*, pp. 108–9; TNA, PROB 11/11/179; H. C. Maxwell Lyte and A. S. Maskelyne, 'Inquisitions Post Mortem, Henry VII, Entries 151–200', *Calendar of Inquisitions Post Mortem: Series 2, Volume 2, Henry VII*, www.british-history.ac.uk /inquis-post-mortem/series2-vol2 /pp103-132; accessed 14 March 2022.

21 Charles Henry Cooper, *Memoir of Margaret, countess of Richmond and Derby* (Cambridge, 1874), p. 93.

22 They moved via Heytesbury, Brook and Bath. *Excerpta Historica*, p. 109.

23 Great Chronicle, p. 264.

24 Vergil, 'Henry VII', c. 32.

25 Great Chronicle, p. 264.

26 'Henry VII: January 1497', Parliament Rolls, www.british-history .ac.uk/no-series/parliament-rolls -medieval/january-1497; accessed 16 March 2022.

27 Vergil, 'Henry VII', c. 33.

28 Ian Arthurson, *The Perkin Warbeck Conspiracy 1491–9* (Stroud, 1994), p. 163.

29 Vergil, 'Henry VII', c. 34; Great Chronicle, p. 276; 'Vitellius A XVI', p. 216.

30 'Vitellius A XVI', p. 213.

31 For Margaret, Elizabeth and the children's moves at this time see Great Chronicle, p. 275–6; 'Vitellius A XVI', p. 213.

32 Vergil, 'Henry VII', c. 35.

33 'Vitellius A XVI', p. 214.

34 Great Chronicle, pp. 276–7.

35 BL Royal MS 2 A XVIII, f. 30v.

36 Great Chronicle, pp. 279–280.

37 Chrimes, p. 91; Rymer's Foedera with Syllabus: July–December 1497', www.british-history.ac.uk/rymer -foedera/vol12/pp654-671; accessed 10 March 2022.

38 'Vitellius A XVI', p. 217.

39 André (Hobbins), p. 66.

40 *Excerpta Historica*, p. 184.

41 Vergil, 'Henry VII', c. 40.

42 The untranslated letter is provided in Pollard, I, pp. 172–3.

43 CSP Venice, no. 760, www.british -history.ac.uk/cal-state-papers/venice /vol1/pp252-266; accessed 17 March 2022.

44 Great Chronicle, pp. 283–4; 'Vitellius A XVI', p. 221.

45 Arthurson, *Perkin Warbeck*, p. 192; Great Chronicle, p. 283; 'Vitellius A XVI', pp. 218–9.

46 Arthurson, *Perkin Warbeck*, pp. 195–7; CSP Venice, no. 768, www .british-history.ac.uk/cal-state-papers /venice/vol1/pp267-276; accessed 11 October 2022.

47 Vergil, 'Henry VII', c. 42.

48 In a letter of 1490 to Pope Innocent VIII. W. N. M. Beckett, 'Ingleby, John (1434?–1499), bishop of Llandaff', ODNB, https://doi.org/10.1093/ref:odnb /53110; accessed 3 January 2025.

49 Vergil, 'Henry VII', c. 42. Margaret apparently held no ill will towards the Charterhouse for its prior's intervention, and continued to make regular visits to the Carthusians and their neighbours, the nuns of Syon. Within three weeks of Warbeck's recapture, Margaret sent a servant to make an offering at the altar in the Charterhouse chapel, and on 8 July she delivered a significant sum in alms to be dispensed there. D91.17 (SJLM/1/1/2/1), p. 22. Margaret may have visited the Charterhouse earlier, but unfortunately her detailed household accounts only begin on 24 June 1498. The earliest entry for Margaret's activities finds her across the river at Sheen. Ibid., p. 19.

50 CSP Spain, no. 221, www.british -history.ac.uk/cal-state-papers/spain /vol1/pp180-195; accessed 20 September 2022.

51 Arthurson, *Perkin Warbeck*, p. 192; Great Chronicle, p. 283; 'Vitellius A XVI', pp. 218–9.

52 'Vitellius A XVI', p. 222. See also Great Chronicle, p. 286.

CHAPTER 20

1 J. Capgrave, 'The Life of St Katherine: Book 1', https://d.lib.rochester.edu/teams/publication/winstead-capgrave-the-life-of-saint-katherine. This translation is from R. Delman, 'The Vowesses, the anchoresses, and the aldermen's wives: Lady Margaret Beaufort and the Devout Society of Late Medieval Stamford', *Urban History* (2021), p. 16, n. 104.

2 Great Chronicle, p. 287.

3 M. K. Jones, 'Collyweston – an early Tudor palace' in Daniel Williams, (ed.), *England in the fifteenth-century: proceedings of the 1986 Harlaxton symposium* (Woodbridge, 1987), p. 132.

4 Margaret's vow is transcribed in Charles Henry Cooper, *Memoir of Margaret, countess of Richmond and Derby* (Cambridge, 1874), p. 97.

5 Mary C. Erler, 'Three Fifteenth-Century Vowesses' in C. M. Barron and A. F. Sutton (eds.), *Medieval London Widows, 1300–1500* (London, 1994), pp. 167–8.

6 For the following, see Delman, 'The Vowesses'.

7 The Stokes sisters both married brothers from the Browne family. Margaret Stokes acted alongside Margaret's half-sisters Edith and Elizabeth St John as godmother for a local child many years earlier. Delman, 'The Vowesses', p. 7.

8 Ibid., pp. 9–10; 'Mornynge Remembraunce', p. 294.

9 TNA, PROB/11/5/430.

10 For example, D102.10 (SJLM 1/1/6/1), p. 138.

11 Jones and Underwood, p. 162.

12 In August 1502, Henry and Elizabeth visited Walter at Raglan. Margaret Condon, Samantha Harper and James Ross, 'An Analysis of the Books and a Synopsis of Henry VII and his Life at Court' in M. M. Condon *et al.* (eds.), *The Chamber Books of Henry VII and Henry VIII, 1485–1521*, www.tudorchamberbooks.org/chamber-books-analysis-and-synopsis-2/#

_ftn175; accessed 10 March 2022.

13 Arlene Naylor Okerlund, *Elizabeth of York* (New York, 2009), p. 97.

14 D91.20 (SJLM/1/1/3/1), pp. 36, 37.

15 Delman, 'The Vowesses', p. 179.

16 F. C. Eeles, 'Two Sixteenth Century Pontificals Formerly Used in England', *Transactions of the St Paul's Ecclesiological Society*, 7 (1911–5), and for context see Erler, 'Three Fifteenth-Century Vowesses'.

17 Transcribed in Cooper, *Memoir of Margaret*, p. 97.

18 Maria Hayward, *Dress at the Court of King Henry VIII* (Leeds, 2007), pp. 150–1.

19 The Garter gown was valued at sixteen shillings. Susan Powell, 'Textiles and Dress in the Household Papers of Lady Margaret Beaufort (1443–1509), Mother of King Henry VII', in Robin Netherton and Gale R. Owen-Crocker (eds.), *Medieval Clothing and Textiles* 11 (Woodbridge, 2015), p. 151.

20 For the debate about what Margaret's 'R' stood for and why she chose it, see Sally Fisher, '"Margaret R": Lady Margaret Beaufort's Self-fashioning and Female Ambition', in Carey Fleiner and Elena Woodacre (eds.), *Virtuous or Villainess? The Image of the Royal Mother from the Early Medieval to the Early Modern Era* (New York, 2016).

21 Cooper, *Memoir of Margaret*, p. 67.

22 By comparison, Marguerite of Anjou's household was considered bloated in 1454 when she employed 120 servants, and Margaret's one-time mother-in-law Alice Chaucer, duchess of Suffolk had a considerable following of around a hundred. Delman, 'The Vowesses', p. 276.

23 D91.19 (SJLM/1/1/3/3), pp. 97I, 97II.

24 Ibid., pp. 21, 75, 89, 102, 111; D102.6 (SJLM/1/1/4/2), f. 8v.

25 Susan Powell (ed.), *The Household Accounts of Lady Margaret Beaufort (1443–1509). From the Archives of St John's College, Cambridge*

(Oxford, 2022), pp. 17–21, 35–43.

26 See for instance, D91.20 (SJLM/1 /1/3/1), p. 29.

27 W. H. Bernard Saunders and W. D. Sweeting (eds.), *Fenland Notes and Queries, Vol.* 2 (1894), p. 211, www .google.co.uk/books/edition/Fenland _Notes_Queries/O7hAAQAAMAAJ ?hl=en&gbpv=1; accessed 15 May 2024.

28 Ibid., pp. 143–7, 209–11, 294–6. For other examples of arbitration awards see Jones, 'Collyweston', pp. 137–8, and idid, n. 41; Jones and Underwood, p. 135.

29 D91.20 (SJLM/1/1/3/1), p. 20, 155, 159; Rachel Delman, 'Elite Female Constructions of Power and Space in England, 1444–1541', unpublished PhD thesis, University of Oxford, 2017, p. 171.

30 WAM 12245; Jones, 'Collyweston', p. 139.

31 'conjurationes illicitas'.

32 Her council declined to investigate the case further, and the allegations did not impede Stokesley's career. He eventually became bishop of London. William Dunn Macray (ed.), *A register of the members of St. Mary Magdalen College, Oxford, from the foundation of the college. New series* (London, 1894), https://archive.org/details /aregistermember010oxfogoog/page/n64 /mode/2up?view=theater; accessed 1 April 2022.

33 Anne Crawford (ed.), *Letters of Medieval Women* (Stroud, 2002), pp. 189–90.

34 Cooper, *Memoir of Margaret*, pp. 229–30.

35 Jones and Underwood, pp. 128–30.

36 Ibid., p. 133.

37 Henry Parker, f. 21r.

38 'Mornynge Remembraunce', pp. 290–1, 296.

39 Henry Parker, f. 21r.

40 Ibid.

41 'Mornynge Remembraunce', p. 293.

42 Malcolm G. Underwood, 'Politics and Piety in the Household of Lady Margaret Beaufort', *Journal of Ecclesiastical History,* 38, i (1987), p. 39.

43 It should be noted that those staying with Margaret for prolonged periods tended to pay for their upkeep. Nonetheless, their outgoings would have been considerably less than if they were living on their own estates.

44 D102.10 (SJLM/1/1/6/1), p. 138, Jones and Underwood, pp. 163–4.

45 D91.20 (SJLM/1/1/3/1), p. 177; D91.21 (SJLM/1/1/3/2), pp. 34, 130.

46 L. L. Ford, 'Vaux, Nicholas, first Baron Vaux (*c.*1460–1523), courtier and soldier', ODNB, https://doi-org .lonlib.idm.oclc.org/10.1093/ref:odnb /28162; accessed 15 January 2024.

47 'Floruit summa gratia apud Margaretam comitissam Richmundiae.' Ibid.

48 Among the other semi-resident 'sojourners' at Collyweston were Lady Elizabeth Scrope, Lady Katherine Bray, Lady Jane Guildford, Lady Mary Rivers (Margaret's cousin), Lady Margaret Cheyne and Princess Cecily. Margaret also maintained several wards and almsfolk. Powell, *Household Accounts*, pp. 27–9.

49 The heir of her second husband Sir Henry Wentworth.

50 Jones and Underwood, p. 163. Margaret bequeathed Lady Scrope a primer, which was later passed to Lady Scrope's sister. This may have been Richard III's Book of Hours, which had been plundered from the late king's tent after Bosworth, and in which the king's birthdate was inscribed by Richard himself. In an end flyleaf Margaret added her own inscription, requesting the book's next owner to pray for her 'in the honour of God and St Edmund'. Anne F. Sutton and Livia Visser-Fuchs, *The Hours of Richard III* (Stroud, 1990), p. 39. Margaret's flyleaf note has now been lost.

51 D91.20 (SJLM/1/1/3/1), p. 184.

52 Ibid., p. 126b.

53 'Mornynge Remembraunce', p. 291.

54 Henry Parker, f. 19v (p. 262).

55 Ralph Bigod had two illegitimate sons, Arthur and John, who were

sufficiently accepted that in his will of 1515 he asked that they be found apprenticeships 'by the sight of Agnes my wife'. Margaret may partly have been so sympathetic towards Bigod because of his personal connection to her family: he fought alongside Thomas Stanley and his son Edward in the Scottish wars of 1482, and both his mother and nephew married Margaret's half-blood relatives: his mother, Elizabeth Scrope, wed Margaret's half-brother Oliver St John, and his nephew John, Lord Scrope married Margaret's niece Elizabeth St John. J. Raine (ed.), *Testamenta Eboracensia*, Vol. 5 (York, 1884), p. 55; Retha M. Warnicke, 'Sir Ralph Bigod: A Loyal Servant to Richard III,' *The Ricardian*, 6 (1984); P. W. Hammond, 'Scrope, John, fifth Baron Scrope of Bolton (1437/8–1498)', ODNB, https://doi-org.ezproxy2.londonlibrary.co.uk/10.1093/ref:odnb/24961; accessed 3 January 2025.

Elizabeth Scrope's 1514 will bequeathed 'my bed that my Lord Marquess [of Dorset] was wont to lie in' to 'Mary, daughter in base unto Thomas Grey, Marquess of Dorset'. Presumably, Dorset's illegitimate daughter Mary was the product of an affair with Lady Scrope. Since Dorset died in 1501, any such affair must have occurred during Scrope's friendship with Margaret, and may have been known to the king's mother. TNA, PROB 11/20/19; Barbara J. Harris, *English Aristocratic Women: 1450–1550: Marriage and Family, Property and Careers* (Oxford, 2002), p. 84. Jane Guildford and Thomas Brandon left prayers and property for one another in their wills, highly unusual bequests for a man and woman with no relation. 'Will of Thomas Brandon', TNA, PROB 11/16/746. For context to Jane's will see Mary Anne Everett Wood, *Letters of Royal and Illustrious Ladies of Great Britain, Volume 2* (London, 1846), pp. 158–60.
56 TNA, PROB 11/18/137.
57 Cecily, duchess of York

also apparently winked at the indiscretions of her officers: her chaplain was accused by opponents of sodomy, heresy, riot and treason. For more see Joanna Laynesmith, 'Richard Lessy, dean of Cecily, Duchess of York's chapel (d. 1498)', *The Ricardian*, 33 (2023). For Margaret Stanley's date of birth see 'Townships: Halsall', in *A History of the County of Lancaster: Volume 3*, www.british-history.ac.uk/vch/lancs/vol3/pp191-197; accessed 3 November 2022. Margaret and her husband have a tomb within Halsall parish church. 'The parish of Halsall: Introduction, church and charities', in ibid.; D. G. Newcombe, 'Stanley, James (c.1465–1515)', ODNB, https://doi-org/10.1093/ref:odnb/26273; accessed 3 November 2022. For Margaret's time at Hatfield see for instance D91.19 (SJLM/1/1/3/3), p. 21.
58 TNA, PROB 11/11/657.
59 Jones and Underwood, p. 134.
60 Delman, 'The Vowesses', p. 10.
61 Cecily died at Hatfield, in Margaret's care. D91.19 (SJLM/1/1/3/3), p. 30, 33–5, 44.
62 Cooper, *Memoir of Margaret*, p. 91.
63 Ibid., p. 92.

CHAPTER 21

1 Margaret in a letter to Henry. Charles Henry Cooper, *Memoir of Margaret, countess of Richmond and Derby* (Cambridge, 1874), p. 92.
2 H. C. Maxwell Lyte, *The Fifty-Third Annual Report of the Deputy Keeper of the Public Records* (London, 1889), p. 34, https://babel.hathitrust.org/cgi/pt?id=mdp.39015039450567&view=1up&seq=9; accessed 3 January 2025.
3 Vergil, 'Henry VII', c. 42, https://philological.cal.bham.ac.uk/polverg/26eng.html; accessed 19 December 2023.
4 Maxwell Lyte, *Fifty-Third Annual Report*, pp. 32–3.
5 See for instance CSP Spain, no. 239,

www.british-history.ac.uk/cal-state
-papers/spain/vol1/pp199-213; accessed
20 September 2022.
6   Henry's accounts show regular
payments for Llanthony cheese.
Margaret Condon, Samantha Harper
and James Ross, 'An Analysis of the
Books and a Synopsis of Henry VII and
his Life at Court' in M. M. Condon
et al. (eds.), *The Chamber Books of
Henry VII and Henry VIII, 1485–1521*,
www.tudorchamberbooks.org/chamber
-books-analysis-and-synopsis-2/#
_ftn175; accessed 10 March 2022.
7   Among other examples,
Henry paid 'a priest for making
a prognostication' in November
1496 and 'an astronomyer for a
prognosticacon' in February 1501.
Excerpta Historica, pp. 110, 125.
8   D91.21 (SJLM/1/1/3/2), p.
125; Susan Powell, 'Lady Margaret
Beaufort and her Books', *The
Library*, 20, iii (1998), p. 207.
9   Great Chronicle, p. 289. See
also 'Vitellius A XVI', p. 225.
10   Vergil, 'Henry VII', c. 44.
11   Gairdner, Letters and Papers
Illustrative, p. 134, www.google
.co.uk/books/edition/Letters_and
_Papers_Illustrative_of_the_R
/L8e2O2BoXWwC?hl=en&gbpv=1;
accessed 20 September 2022.
12   Edmund was born on Friday 21
February. Margaret acted as Prince
Edmund's godmother, in which role
she probably had a say in his name. She
had a particular devotion to St Edmund,
the namesake of Henry's father, and
wrote in a book of hours beseeching
prayers 'in the honour of God and
St Edmund'. Anne F. Sutton and
Livia Visser-Fuchs, *The Hours of
Richard III* (Stroud, 1990), p. 39.
13   CSP Spain, no. 239, www.british
-history.ac.uk/cal-state-papers/spain
/vol1/pp199-213; accessed 20 September
2022.
14   Ian Arthurson, *The Perkin
Warbeck Conspiracy 1491–9*
(Stroud, 1994), pp. 202, 213-4.
15   CSP Spain, no. 241, www.british
-history.ac.uk/cal-state-papers/spain

/vol1/pp199-213; accessed 20
September 2022.
16   CSP Spain, no. 227, www.british
-history.ac.uk/cal-state-papers/spain
/vol1/pp195-199; accessed 20
September 2022.
17   CSP Spain, no. 203, www.british
-history.ac.uk/cal-state-papers/spain
/vol1/pp153-167; accessed 20
September 2022.
18   CSP Spain, no. 210, www.british
-history.ac.uk/cal-state-papers/spain
/vol1/pp167-180; accessed 20
September 2022.
19   CSP Spain, nos. 198, 221, www
.british-history.ac.uk/cal-state-papers
/spain/vol1/pp150-153 and www
.british-history.ac.uk/cal-state-papers
/spain/vol1/pp180-195; accessed 20
September 2022.
20   Arthurson, *Perkin Warbeck*,
pp. 205–8.
21   Jean Molinet and J. A. C. Buchon
(ed.), *Chroniques de Jean Molinet*
(Verdière, 1828), p. 121, www.google
.co.uk/books/edition/Chroniques_de
_Jean_Molinet/ck9SgWtQolMC?hl
=en&gbpv=1; accessed 30 April 2024.
22   Arthurson, *Perkin Warbeck*,
pp. 204–18.
23   CSP Spain, no. 249, www.british
-history.ac.uk/cal-state-papers/spain
/vol1/pp213-216; accessed 21
September 2022.
24   Arthurson, *Perkin Warbeck*,
p. 213.
25   CSP Spain, no. 249.
26   Vergil, 'Henry VII', c. 43.
27   Margaret's household accounts
do not survive for this period, but
as she does not appear in Henry's
chamber book of accounts she
was probably not with him and
Elizabeth.
28   CSP Spain, no. 268, www.british
-history.ac.uk/cal-state-papers/spain
/vol1/pp220-238; accessed 21
September 2022; Vergil, 'Henry
VII' c. 43; 'Vitellius A XVI', pp.
229–231; Great Chronicle, p. 292.
29   Great Chronicle, p. 294;
'Vitellius A XVI', pp. 231–2; Maria
Hayward, *Dress at the Court of King*

Henry VIII (Leeds, 2007), p. 67.

30 D102.2 (SJLM/1/1/4/1), p. 7; CSP Spain, no. 294, www.british-history .ac.uk/cal-state-papers/spain/vol1/pp253 -265; accessed 21 September 2022.

31 Gordon Kipling (ed.), *The Receyt of the Ladie Kateryne* (Oxford, 1990), pp. 5, 8.

32 D102.11 (SJLM/9/2/1).

33 Ferdinand and Isabella's excuses to Henry can be found in CSP Spain, nos. 296, 298, 299, 300, 302, 305, www.british-history.ac.uk/cal-state -papers/spain/vol1/pp253-265; accessed 21 September 2022. For context see Giles Tremlett, *Catherine of Aragon: Henry's Spanish Queen. A Biography* (London, 2010), pp. 61–9.

34 CSP Spain, no. 304, www.british -history.ac.uk/cal-state-papers/spain /vol1/pp253-265; accessed 21 September 2022.

35 Royal MS 2 A XVIII, f. 32r.

36 *Receyt*, pp. 5–8.

37 Ibid., p. 8.

38 CSP Spain, no. 268, www.british -history.ac.uk/cal-state-papers/spain /vol1/pp220-238; accessed 21 September 2022.

39 *Receyt*, pp. 28, 30–1.

40 Ibid., p. 12.

41 Ibid., p. 32.

42 Ibid., p. 33.

43 One of these enslaved women was Catalina of Motril. Lauren Johnson, 'Catalina of Motril (fl. 1501–1531)', ODNB, https://doi.org/10.1093/odnb /9780198614128.013.369157; accessed 1 September 2022.

44 Tremlett, *Catherine of Aragon*, pp. 40–8.

45 CSP Spain, nos. 280, 312, www .british-history.ac.uk/cal-state-papers /spain/vol1/pp220-238, www.british -history.ac.uk/cal-state-papers/spain /vol1/pp253-265; accessed 10 November 2022.

46 *Receyt*, p. 44.

47 Ibid., pp. 46–7.

48 Great Chronicle, p. 314.

49 W. N. M. Beckett, 'Ingleby, John (1434?–1499), bishop of Llandaff', ODNB, https://doi.org

/10.1093/ref:odnb/53110; accessed 3 January 2025.

50 Rachel Delman, 'Elite Female Constructions of Power and Space in England, 1444–1541,' unpublished PhD thesis, University of Oxford, 2017, p. 179.

51 *Receyt*, p. 75.

52 Ibid., p. 77.

53 Great Chronicle, p. 317; Vergil, 'Henry VII', c. 43.

54 CSP Spain, no. 210, www.british -history.ac.uk/cal-state-papers/spain /vol1/pp167-180; accessed 20 September 2022.

55 Ibid.

56 'Queen Katharine: 1501', no. 1, *Calendar of State Papers, Spain: Supplement to Volumes 1 and 2*, www .british-history.ac.uk/cal-state-papers /spain/supp/vols1-2/pp1-12; accessed 10 November 2022.

CHAPTER 22

1 Vergil, 'Henry VII', c. 45, https: //philological.cal.bham.ac.uk/polverg /26eng.html; accessed 19 December 2023.

2 The terrible weather in April 1502 is attested by the author of the *Receyt*, see Gordon Kipling (ed.), *The Receyt of the Ladie Kateryne* (Oxford, 1990), p. 87. For Aughton's journeys around 5 April see D91.20 (SJLM/1/1/3/1), p. 18.

3 *Receyt*, p. 79.

4 D91.20 (SJLM/1/1/3/1), p. 18.

5 *Receyt*, pp. 80–1.

6 Ibid., p. 80.

7 Ibid., pp. 80–1.

8 D91.20 (SJLM/1/1/3/1), p. 18.

9 Margaret's groom William Aderton was sent there twice. Ibid., pp. 18, 19, 23.

10 Charles Henry Cooper, *Memoir of Margaret, countess of Richmond and Derby* (Cambridge, 1874), p. 66.

11 As Henry wrote to Margaret. James Orchard Halliwell (ed.), *Letters of the Kings of England, now first collected from the originals in royal archives, and from other authentic sources, private as well as public.*

Vol. 1 (London, 1846), p. 180.

12 *Receyt*, p. 87.

13 Ibid., p. 91.

14 D91.20 (SJLM/1/1/3/1), p. 22; *Receyt*, pp. 82–6.

15 D91.20 (SJLM/1/1/3/1), pp. 22, 23.

16 Ibid., pp. 16–9, 21.

17 Giles Tremlett, *Catherine of Aragon: Henry's Spanish Queen. A Biography* (London, 2010), p. 89.

18 Ibid., p. 102.

19 CSP Spain, no. 327, www.british-history.ac.uk/cal-state-papers/spain/vol1/pp272-276; accessed 15 November 2022.

20 'Henry VIII: July 1529, 12–19', no. 5774 (3), *Letters and Papers, Foreign and Domestic, Henry VIII, Volume 4, 1524–1530*, www.british-history.ac.uk/letters-papers-hen8/vol4/pp2572-2585; accessed 28 January 2025.

21 Godfrey Anstruther, *Vaux of Harrowden: a recusant family* (Newport, 1953), p. 13, https://archive.org/details/vauxofharrowdenrooanst/page/n5/mode/2up; accessed 28 January 2025.

22 TNA, E36/210, f. 94.

23 In September 1504, she sent him a gift of hawks. D91.20 (SJLM/1/1/3/1), pp. 127, 170; D91.21 (SJLM/1/1/3/2), p. 25.

24 CSP Venice no. 754, www.british-history.ac.uk/cal-state-papers/venice/vol1/pp252-266; accessed 17 March 2022.

25 David Starkey, *Henry: Virtuous Prince* (London, 2008), pp. 172–3.

26 Great Chronicle, p. 318.

27 'Henry VII: January 1504', item 21, Parliament Rolls, www-british-history-ac-uk.lonlib.idm.oclc.org/no-series/parliament-rolls-medieval/january-1504; accessed 22 May 2024; Vergil, 'Henry VII', c. 44.

28 In Margaret's account books there are various rewards to Katherine and, on one occasion, her child: D91.17 (SJLM/1/1/2/1), p. 29; D91.20 (SJLM/1/1/3/1), p. 83; D91.21 (SJLM/1/1/3/2), pp. 25, 72; D102.1 (SJLM/1/1/5/1), f. 10v. For Queen Elizabeth's support of her sister and her children see p. 413.

29 Margaret R. Westcott, 'Katherine, countess of Devon (1479–1527), princess', ODNB, https://doi.org/10.1093/ref:odnb/70277; accessed 1 May 2024.

30 There is a reward to his servant, Henry Coney, in the week of 20 April. D91.20 (SJLM/1/1/3/1), p. 22.

31 Ibid., pp. 22, 36, 37, 40.

32 Both occasions were marked with a five-shilling donation. Ibid., pp. 30–1, 37.

33 Ibid., pp. 36, 37, 40.

34 I have not been able to trace these claims further than an inscription within the Middlesex church of Hillingdon, where Thomas Stanley held estates, quoted in John Seacome's late eighteenth-century history of the family: Thomas Stanley 'married his first son George... honourably to the heir of the Lord Strange... At an ungodly banquet, alas! He was poisoned, And at London, in St James's Garlick Hythe, lies buried.' John Seacome, *The History of the House of Stanley, from the Conquest to the Death of the Right Honourable Edward, Late Earl of Derby, in 1776* (London, 1821), p. 51. See also Google Books, www.google.co.uk/books/edition/_/df1HAAAAMAAJ?hl=en&gbpv=0; accessed 27 January 2025.

35 As Fisher noted that Margaret attended to her almspeople and servants during their last days. 'Mornynge Remembraunce', p. 297. 'And in theyr sykenes vysytynge them & confortynge them / & mynys|trynge vnto them with her owne handes.'

36 D91.20 (SJLM/1/1/3/1), pp. 125, 139, 146.

37 Margaret Condon, Samantha Harper and James Ross, 'An Analysis of the Books and a Synopsis of Henry VII and his Life at Court' in M. M. Condon *et al.* (eds.), *The Chamber Books of Henry VII and Henry VIII, 1485–1521*, www.tudorchamberbooks.org/chamber-books-analysis-and-synopsis-2/#_ftn175; accessed

10 March 2022.

38 D91.20 (SJLM/1/1/3/1), pp. 44, 45 48, 57; TNA, E36/210, f. 57.

39 Evidently the boar or its bearer, Mr Worshoppe of Collyweston, caused Margaret some trouble as she had to send Richard Carre in pursuit, to ensure the boar reached its destination on New Year's Eve. D91.20 (SJLM/1/1/3/1), pp. 53, 56, 57, 58; TNA, E36/210, f. 85.

CHAPTER 23

1 Apocalypse 14:13: one of two texts read as the Epistle during the daily Office of the Dead.

2 D91.20 (SJLM/1/1/3/1), p. 78; Retha M. Warnicke, *Elizabeth of York and Her Six Daughters-In-Law: Fashioning Tudor Queenship 1485–1547* (New York, 2017), p. 101.

3 BL Add MS 59899, f. 13v, M. M. Condon *et al.* (eds.), *The Chamber Books of Henry VII and Henry VIII, 1485–1521*, https://www.dhi.ac.uk /chamber-books/folio/LL_BL_AddMS _59899_f0013r.xml; accessed 2 December 2022.

4 'The funeral ceremonies of Queen Elizabeth', Thomas Astle and Francis Grose (ed.), *The Antiquarian Repertory: a Miscellaneous Assemblage of Topography, History, Biography, Customs, And Manners. Intended to Illustrate and Preserve Several Valuable Remains of Old Times, Volume 4* (London, 1809), p. 655, https://catalog .hathitrust.org/Record/000309420 /Home; accessed 2 December 2022.

5 Ibid., p. 655.

6 D91.20 (SJLM/1/1/3/1), p. 81.

7 Astle, *The Antiquarian Repertory*, p. 657.

8 Margaret joined her son in making a customary gift to the king's Welsh servants. D91.20 (SJLM/1/1/3/1), pp. 78–80, 85. Henry VII was certainly at Richmond on 2 March. 'Ford, Itinerary', p. 263.

9 Maria Hayward, *Dress at the Court of King Henry VIII* (Leeds, 2007), pp. 65, 80, 90–1.

10 Ibid., p. 170. Princesses (including the king's daughters, married sisters or aunts, where they existed) were to be dressed almost identically, but with 'somewhat shorter' cloak trains and tippets to their hoods.

11 Margaret paid Thomas Wriothesley, Garter King of Arms, for the 'making of a book to wear mourning clothes by' in 1507, which was probably a printed version of this ordinance. D91.19 (SJLM/1/1/3/3), p. 8. For context to the ordinance see Susan Powell, 'Textiles and Dress in the Household Papers of Lady Margaret Beaufort (1443–1509), Mother of King Henry VII', in Robin Netherton, Gale R. Owen-Crocker (eds.), *Medieval Clothing and Textiles, Volume 11* (Woodbridge, 2015), pp. 151–2. The ordinances are quoted in full in Hayward, *Dress at the Court of King Henry VIII*, p. 170.

12 CSP Spain, no. 239, www.british -history.ac.uk/cal-state-papers/spain /vol1/pp199-213; accessed 20 September 2022.

13 D91.20 (SJLM/1/1/3/1), pp. 81, 84, 85, 87.

14 'Vaux Passional', Peniarth MS 482, f. 9r. Digitised by the National Library of Wales: http://hdl.handle.net/10107 /4399684; accessed 2 December 2022.

15 D91.20 (SJLM/1/1/3/1), p. 83.

16 Lady Rivers' sister at the Minories sent rose water; Edith Burton the walnuts in syrup; Hugh Denys two bottles of wine; Lady Scrope the fortified wine. D91.20 (SJLM/1/1/3/1), pp. 85, 87, 88.

17 Ibid., p. 85.

18 Ibid., pp. 81, 83, 84, 88.

19 BL Royal MS 2 A XVIII, f. 31r.

20 D91.20 (SJLM/1/1/3/1), pp. 91, 101–6, 109–11; M. K. Jones, 'Collyweston – an early Tudor palace' in Daniel Williams (ed.), *England in the Fifteenth-Century: Proceedings of the 1986 Harlaxton symposium* (Woodbridge, 1987), pp. 134–5; Jones and Underwood, p. 85.

21 Hayward, *Dress at the Court of King Henry VIII*, p. 56.

22   David Starkey, *Henry: Virtuous Prince* (London, 2008), pp. 118–20, 172–4; Richard Glen Eaves, 'Margaret [Margaret Tudor] (1489–1541)', ODNB, https://doi.org/10.1093/ref:odnb /18052; accessed 27 January 2025.
23   Leland, pp. 279–284; CSP Spain, no. 210, www.british-history.ac.uk /cal-state-papers/spain/vol1/pp167 -180; accessed 20 September 2022.
24   Leland, pp. 265–7.
25   D91.20 (SJLM/1/1/3/1), pp. 104, 123, 163, 168, 173, 183, 198; D91.21 (SJLM/1/1/3/2), pp. 24, 92, 135, 140; D91.19 (SJLM/1/1/3/3), pp. 16, 80, 118. The Verneys visiting Margaret: 91.20 (SJLM/1/1/3/1), p. 177; D91.21 (SJLM/1/1/3/2), p. 48; D91.19 (SJLM/1 /1/3/3), pp. 21, 53; D102.1 (SJLM/1 /1/5/1), f. 5r, f. 7r.
26   Mary Anne Everett Green, *Lives of the Princesses of England from the Norman Conquest, IV* (London, 1852), p. 100, Google Books, www.google.co .uk/books/edition/Lives_of_the_Prince sses_of_England/dKFRAAAAcAAJ?hl =en&gbpv=1; accessed 09 November 2022.
27   Henry went as far north as Nottingham Castle, but was largely in Northamptonshire and Leicestershire in July. Ford, 'Itinerary', p. 263; D91.20 (SJLM/1/1/3/1), pp. 105, 106, 110, 113, 114, 117.
28   Ibid., p. 163.
29   Their exchange of messengers: Ibid., pp. 148, 150. For the pilgrimage see ibid., pp. 153–7.
30   Ibid., pp. 168, 179.
31   TNA, PROB/11/21/376.
32   Henry included St Winifred among the stone images he had carved in his chapel at Westminster. Susan Powell, 'Lady Margaret Beaufort and her Books', *The Library*, 20, iii (1998), p. 213. On 23 August 1504, Tom Stanley, now called 'my lord of Derby' in Margaret's accounts, returned to Collyweston with a retinue of forty-seven on horseback, to attend a requiem Mass at Stamford. He

stayed for two nights. D91.20 (SJLM/1/1/3/1), p. 168; Susan Powell (ed.), *The Household Accounts of Lady Margaret Beaufort (1443–1509). From the Archives of St John's College, Cambridge* (Oxford, 2022), p. 363, n. 45.
33   See for instance in 1504, D91.20 (SJLM/1/1/3/1), pp. 128, 147, 148, 150.
34   It is worth noting that, since Easter 1502, Margaret had lost a grandson, daughter-in-law, husband, stepson, step-granddaughter – and her cherished granddaughter had left the country.
35   D91.21 (SJLM/1/1/3/2), p. 175; Ford, 'Itinerary', p. 269.
36   Charles Henry Cooper, *Memoir of Margaret, countess of Richmond and Derby* (Cambridge, 1874), pp. 95–6.
37   D91.19 (SJLM/1/1/3/3), p. 16.
38   Or, as Margaret expressed it in her will of 1508: 'We… have called to our remembrance the unstableness of this transitory world and that every creature here living is mortal. And the time and place of death to every creature uncertain.' *Collegium Divi Johannis Evangelistae, 1511–1911* (Cambridge, 1911), p. 103.

CHAPTER 24

1   Gairdner, 'Letters and Papers Illustrative', p. 233.
2   In a conversation around 'the last day of September' (no year is cited), Sir Hugh Conway mentioned to friends in Calais a time 'not long since' when 'his highness was sick and lay then in his manor of Wanstead'. It is probable Conway was speaking in 1504, when he had recently taken up position as treasurer in Calais, but the itinerary of Henry VII in Ford's thesis does not note a recent stay at Wanstead. Ford suggests April or July–August 1501 as potential dates for the Wanstead visit, but this seems too far removed from Conway's conversation in 1504 to be considered 'not long since'. Possibly the king's stay was hushed up. See 'Flamank's Information', in Gairdner, 'Letters and Papers Illustrative', pp.

231–40; Ford, 'Itinerary', p. 257: n. 99; James Gairdner, 'A Supposed Conspiracy against Henry VII', *Transactions of the Royal Historical Society*, New Series, 18 (1904), p. 158; Thomas Penn, *Winter King: The Dawn of Tudor England* (London, 2011), p. 139; Nicholas Orme, 'Conway, Sir Hugh (*c.*1440–1518), royal servant', ODNB, https://doi.org/10.1093/ref:odnb/109666; accessed 27 January 2025.

3 'Flamank's Information', p. 233.

4 Ibid., pp. 233, 236.

5 Ibid., p. 233.

6 Ibid., pp. 233, 7. One of Conway's co-conspirators at Calais was Sir Sampson Norton, husband of Elizabeth Zouche, an illegitimate relative of Margaret's St John family. In September 1507, Sampson Norton sent Margaret a gift of quinces. D91.19 (SJLM/1/1/3/3), p. 33. Julian Lock, 'Norton, Sir Sampson (d. 1517)', ODNB, https://doi.org/10.1093/ref:odnb/20356; accessed 14 December 2022.

7 D91.21 (SJLM/1/1/3/2), p. 25; D91.20 (SJLM/1/1/3/1), p. 176.

8 'Mornynge Remembraunce', p. 291.

9 C. S. L. Davies, 'Stafford, Edward, third duke of Buckingham (1478–1521)', ODNB, https://doi.org/10.1093/ref:odnb/26202; accessed 14 December 2022.

10 D91.19 (SJLM/1/1/3/3), pp. 62–3, 124–5.

11 Alasdair Hawkyard, 'Neville, George, third Baron Bergavenny (*c.*1469–1535)', ODNB, https://doi.org/10.1093/ref:odnb/19935; accessed 14 December 2022.

12 D91.19 (SJLM/1/1/3/3), pp. 90, 96.

13 Margaret Condon, 'Ruling elites in the reign of Henry VII' in Charles Ross (ed.), *Patronage, Pedigree and Power in Later Medieval England* (Gloucester, 1979), p. 113. For the wider context see Sean Cunningham and T. Thornton (eds.), *Social Attitudes and Political Structures in the Fifteenth Century* (Stroud, 2000), pp. 220–42.

14 S. J. Gunn, 'The Courtiers of Henry VII', *English Historical Review*, 108 (1993), p. 30.

15 'Flamank's Information', pp. 232–3.

16 Great Chronicle, pp. 295, 325.

17 Vergil, 'Henry VII', c. 45, https://philological.cal.bham.ac.uk/polverg/26eng.html; accessed 2 November 2022.

18 D91.20 (SJLM/1/1/3/1), p. 106.

19 M. M. Condon, 'Empson, Sir Richard (*c.*1450–1510)', ODNB, https://doi.org/10.1093/ref:odnb/8799; accessed 14 February 2023.

20 D91.19 (SJLM/1/1/3/3), pp. 21–2, 52; Jones and Underwood, pp. 221–2.

21 Ibid., p. 107.

22 Chrimes, p. 238.

23 Margaret was detained at Collyweston throughout late February and March 1505: a winter illness demanded the repeated ministrations of her late husband's physician, Boniface Stanley. On her journey south, she stopped at the Minories, just beyond the City walls, visiting her old friend Elizabeth Talbot, duchess of Norfolk who resided there. Margaret and the duchess of Norfolk were almost exact contemporaries – the duchess four months older – and had grown close in the years since Henry's accession. Although she had now largely retired to the cloistral seclusion of the Minories, the duchess remained one of the leading powers in East Anglia and was a generous benefactor to Margaret's educational projects. Later that year, she sent Margaret some spectacles – one of several 'parcels' she gave Margaret, 'for a poor token of my remembrance'. D91.21 (SJLM/1/1/3/2), p. 21. Ibid., pp. 10, 12, 21, 22, 60; Jones and Underwood, p. 162.

24 Memorials, pp. 223–38.

25 Great Chronicle, p. 330.

26 Ibid., p. 330.

27 Vergil, 'Henry VII', c. 47, https://philological.cal.bham.ac.uk/polverg/26eng.html; accessed 2 November 2022.

28 M. Gachard (ed.), *Collection des Voyages des Souverains des Pays-Bas*, Vol. 1 (Brussels, 1876), pp. 408–18,

https://books.google.co.zm/books?id
=oPkUAAAAQAAJ&printsec=frontco
ver#v=onepage&q&f=false; accessed
7 December 2022; CSP Venice, nos.
864–5, www.british-history.ac.uk/cal
-state-papers/venice/vol1/pp310-327;
accessed 7 December 2022.
29 D91.21 (SJLM/1/1/3/2), pp. 92–3.
30 Memorials, pp. 224, 300.
31 Joanna later earned the offensive
nickname 'the mad'. Her mental
illness, if real, was almost certainly
exaggerated to suit the ambitions of
her husband, father and later son. For
a more detailed exploration of this
topic in its political context see Bethany
Aram, 'Juana "the Mad's" Signature:
The Problem of Invoking Royal
Authority, 1505–1507', *The Sixteenth
Century Journal*, 29, ii (1998), pp. 331–
58; Gachard, *Collection des Voyages*,
pp. 408–18. For the assertions by Philip
and his courtiers against Joanna see
CSP Venice, no. 872, www.british
-history.ac.uk/cal-state-papers/venice
/vol1/pp310-327; accessed 8 December
2022.
32 Memorials, p. 301.
33 CSP Spain, no. 553, www.british
-history.ac.uk/cal-state-papers/spain
/vol1/pp433-441; accessed 6 December
2022.
34 Memorials, p. 302.
35 Pollard, III, p. 98.
36 D91.21 (SJLM/1/1/3/2), p. 91.
37 John Holt, Richard Aderton and
Roger Radclyff visited the court on
Margaret's behalf throughout January
and February. Ibid., pp. 91, 95, 98.
38 Margaret's receipt of the two
books 'of the coming of the king of
castille' and the agreements regarding
'Edmund de la Pole' are recorded in
her accounts: Ibid., pp. 103, 108. The
record of events itself is D105.162
(SJLM/9/2/2), reprinted in *The Eagle*,
Vol 15. (Lent 1889) pp. 336–339,
www.books.google.co.uk/books?id
=BgIBAAAAYAAJ&pg=PA336&s
ource=gbstoc_r&cad=2#v=onepag
e&q&f=false [Accessed 14/07/25].
Some of this content – minus the
address to Margaret – makes up

the contemporary report printed
in Memorials, pp. 282–303.
39 My translation. Gachard,
Collection des Voyages, p. 422.
40 CSP, Spain, no. 552, www.british
-history.ac.uk/cal-state-papers/spain
/vol1/pp433-441; accessed 6 December
2022.
41 Memorials, pp. 293–9.
42 Ibid., pp. 288–9.
43 There had been suggestions of
such a union in England in late March.
See CSP Venice, nos. 872, 886, https:
//www.british-history.ac.uk/cal-state
-papers/venice/vol1/pp310-327;
accessed 28 January 2025.
44 The alliance was confirmed by
Marguerite of Savoy, Charles's regent,
on 1 October 1508. André (Sutton),
c. 6, https://philological.cal.bham.ac
.uk/andreannals/2e.html; accessed 28
January 2025.
45 D91.21 (SJLM/1/1/3/2), pp. 99–103.
46 Ibid., pp. 25, 30, 110, 114, 118.
47 D91.20 (SJLM/1/1/3/1), pp. 81, 84,
123, 138, 191; D91.21 (SJLM/1/1/3/2),
pp. 27, 30, 41, 74, 110, 118, 155.
48 David Starkey, *Henry: Virtuous
Prince* (London, 2008), p. 240.
49 CSP, Spain, no. 398, www.british
-history.ac.uk/cal-state-papers/spain
/vol1/pp328-331; accessed 13
December 2022.
50 D91.19 (SJLM/1/1/3/3), pp. 34, 57.

CHAPTER 25

1 The 1494 edition of *Scala
Perfectionis*, printed by Wynkyn de
Worde at Margaret's request, quoted
in Susan Powell, 'Lady Margaret
Beaufort and her Books', *The Library*,
20, iii (1998), p. 215, n.110.
2 D91.21 (SJLM/1/1/3/2), p. 125.
For other deliveries in person by
Pynson see ibid., pp. 123, 133, 142.
3 Eamon Duffy, *Marking the Hours:
English People and their Prayers,
1240–1570* (New Haven, 2006), p. 4.
4 Powell, 'Lady Margaret
Beaufort and her Books', p. 206.
5 Margaret left a bequest in her will
to Love's charterhouse, Mountgrace

in Yorkshire. Ibid., p. 220, n. 146.

6 Ibid., pp. 198–9.

7 Ibid., pp. 208–210.

8 Ibid., pp. 223–4.

9 Susan Powell, 'Lady Margaret Beaufort as Patron of Scholars and Scholarship' in Paul Binski and Elizabeth A. New (eds.), *Patrons and professionals in the Middle Ages: Proceedings of the 2010 Harlaxton Symposium* (Donington, 2012), p. 115.

10 More meticulous for Christ's than St John's. The latter owed its successful completion to the posthumous efforts of John Fisher.

11 Powell, 'Lady Margaret Beaufort as Patron', p. 116.

12 The description of Henry's illness is based on the NHS website symptoms for 'quinsy', a complication of tonsilitis: www.nhs.uk/conditions/tonsillitis/; accessed 21 December 2023.

13 D91.19 (SJLM/1/1/3/3), pp. 8, 9.

14 Fisher had arrived at Richmond to preach 'before the king' by Sunday 19 March: TNA, E36/214 f. 71r; D91.19 (SJLM/1/1/3/3), p. 9. On 21 March, Margaret provided Fisher with expensive black budge for his clothes: ibid., p. 12.

15 Ibid., p. 11.

16 Great Chronicle, p. 334.

17 TNA, E36/214 f. 71r; CSP Spain, no. 511, www.british-history.ac.uk/cal-state-papers/spain/vol1/pp406-414; accessed 23 November 2022.

18 TNA, E36/214 ff. 71v, 74r, 74v; Great Chronicle, p. 334.

19 CSP Spain, no. 511, www.british-history.ac.uk/cal-state-papers/spain/vol1/pp406-414; accessed 23 November 2022.

20 D91.19 (SJLM/1/1/3/3), p. 15.

21 The child may have been named in Margaret's honour. TNA, E36/214 f. 71v; D91.19 (SJLM/1/1/3/3), p. 16.

22 CSP nos. 541, 543, 552, www.british-history.ac.uk/cal-state-papers/spain/vol1/pp425-433; accessed 23 November 2022; www.british-history.ac.uk/cal-state-papers/spain/vol1/pp433-441; accessed 23 January 2023.

23 TNA, E36/214, f. 74v.

24 Margaret's movements in summer 1507 can be traced through D91.19 (SJLM/1/1/3/3), pp. 18, 19, 25, 27, 28, 30, 33, 35, 36.

25 For Margaret and Henry's movements in spring through summer 1508 see André (Sutton), cc. 15, 22, 31; ibid., pp. 76–80, 83, 85.

26 Margaret also made several payments for medicines in August 1508, against plague (see below). Ibid., pp. 18, 30, 72, 73.

27 The Queen of Scots's pregnancy was announced at the English Court on 16 June 1508. André (Sutton), cc. 28, 31. Margaret sent her granddaughter silken frontlets to comfort her. Ibid., pp. 80, 81, 82.

28 André (Sutton), cc. 15, 22; D91.19 (SJLM/1/1/3/3), pp. 79, 80.

29 André (Sutton), c. 29.

30 Ibid., c. 19. Margaret sent Prince Henry £20 on 4 April, and a further £13 6s 8d for 'running at the ring' on 7 July. D91.19 (SJLM/1/1/3/3), pp. 80, 94.

31 André (Sutton), c. 31.

32 Ibid., cc. 31–3.

33 D91.19 (SJLM/1/1/3/3), pp. 98–100; André (Sutton), cc. 33–4.

34 D6.27 (SJLM/3/1/1), p. 3. According to her lawyer and councillor Humphrey Coningsby, Margaret had read and rewritten her will every Christmas since 1501. Jones and Underwood, p. 232.

35 D6.27 (SJLM/3/1/1), pp. 3–17.

CHAPTER 26

1 'All but *fumus et umbra* [smoke and shadow]: a smoke that soon vanissheth and a shadow soon passing away'. 'Mornynge Remembraunce', p. 270.

2 Henry VII's senior herald Thomas Wriothesley reported Weston's words, including the striking out of a word beginning 'sp-', probably 'speak'. S. J. Gunn, 'The Accession of Henry VIII', *Historical Research*, 64 (1991), p. 279, n. 8.

3 D91.19 (SJLM/1/1/3/3), pp. 111–2.

4   D102.1 (SJLM/1/1/5/1), f. 4v.
5   Ibid.
6   Tom's heir was Edward Stanley. Margaret rewarded her great-grandchildren's nurses. Ibid., ff. 7v, 8r.
7   Ibid., ff. 6r, 7r–8r, 9r–9v.
8   Ibid., f. 9v.
9   Reginald was a new arrival in Margaret's household, apparently enlisted to fill the place of the late, lamented Skypp. One of Margaret's Cambridge contacts recruited him that spring. Margaret also retained another fool called John Assheton from 1509. Ibid., ff. 9r–9v.
10   D91.19 (SJLM 1/1/3/3), p. 278.
11   D102.1 (SJLM/1/1/5/1), f. 10v.
12   W. H. St J. Hope (ed.), 'The last testament and inventory of John de Veer, thirteenth earl of Oxford'. *Archaeologia*, Vol. 66 (1915), p. 311.
13   Throughout 1502–4, Margaret personally gave semi-regular gifts of money to the Lady Marquess: D91.20 (SJLM/1/1/3/1), pp. 35, 51, 78, 95, 126b, 198; D91.19 (SJLM/1/1/3/3), p. 72; D102.1 (SJLM/1/1/5/1), f. 4v – this was the most recent reward, given in March 1509. For her visits to Margaret see D91.20 (SJLM/1/1/3/1), pp. 45, 97, 157, 161; D91.19 (SJLM/1/1/3/3), p. 39. Eleanor's husband the marquess had also visited Margaret in December 1502, receiving a parting gift of 100 shillings. D91.20 (SJLM/1/1/3/1), p. 53.
14   'Henry VIII: August 1509', no. 157, *Letters and Papers, Foreign and Domestic, Henry VIII, Volume 1, 1509–1514*, www.british-history.ac.uk/letters-papers-hen8/vol1/pp71-82; accessed 14 February 2023.
15   Vergil, 'Henry VIII', c. 2: https://philological.cal.bham.ac.uk/polverg/27eng.html; accessed 28 January 2025.
16   Hall, p. 505.
17   Thomas Penn, *Winter King: The Dawn of Tudor England* (London, 2011), pp. 337–9.
18   Sir William Duffers Hardy, Sir H. C. Maxwell Lyte and Sir Francis Palgrave (eds.), *The Third Annual Report of the Deputy Keeper of the Public Records*

(London, 1842), pp. 226–8, https://www.google.co.uk/books/edition/The_1st_Annual_Report_of_the_Deputy_Keep/SFVJAQAAMAAJ?hl=en&gbpv=1; accessed 30 January 2023.
19   D91.17 (SJLM/1/1/2/1), p. 55; D91.20 (SJLM/1/1/3/1), pp. 25, 117–8, 121; D91.21 (SJLM/1/1/3/2), pp. 54, 60, 114; D91.19 (SJLM/1/1/3/3), pp. 42, 72, 89, 93, 100, 104, 107.
20   D91.19 (SJLM/1/1/3/3), pp. 24, 39, 86, 119.
21   'Sir Richard Weston (c.1465–1541), of Sutton Place, Surrey,' *The History of Parliament: the House of Commons 1509–1558*, https://www.historyofparliamentonline.org/volume/1509-1558/member/weston-sir-richard-1465-1541; accessed 1 February 2023. Margaret's relations with Weston are revealed by D91.19 (SJLM/1/1/3/3), pp. 11, 54, 85; D91.20 (SJLM/1/1/3/1), pp. 42, 86, 87; D91.21 (SJLM/1/1/3/2), pp. 26, 27, 48, 50. For the Denys family see D91.20 (SJLM/1/1/3/1), pp. 82, 84, 86, 88, 109, 184; D91.21 (SJLM/1/1/3/2), pp. 102, 104, 110; D91.19 (SJLM/1/1/3/3), pp. 11, 54; D102.1 (SJLM/1/1/5/1), ff. 4v, 6r, 8v.
22   D102.1 (SJLM/1/1/5/1), ff. 7r, 8v.
23   John Dudley's precise date of birth is unknown, but was in 1504. D91.20 (SJLM/1/1/3/1), pp. 25, 112, 126c, 137, 172, 173; D91.21 (SJLM/1/1/3/2), p. 27, 49, 72, 104, 124; D91.19 (SJLM/1/1/3/3), p. 22, 27, 28, 32, 52, 100; D102.1 (SJLM/1/1/5/1), f. 7r.
24   D102.1 (SJLM/1/1/5/1), f. 11r. The pair and a servant were paid for their 'diet' in London for six days on 28 April.
25   *Great Chronicle*, pp. 338–9.

CHAPTER 27

1   George Cavendish and Roger Lockyer (ed.), *Thomas Wolsey Late Cardinal His Life and Death Written by George Cavendish His Gentleman-Usher* (London, 1962), p. 11.
2   Including Henry Parker, Nicholas Aughton and Alice Parker's father, Sir John St John. '"Th'entierment of the

moost excellent prynce King Henry the vijth"' in 'Henry VIII: May 1509', no. 20, *Letters and Papers, Foreign and Domestic, Henry VIII, Volume 1, 1509–1514*, www.british-history.ac .uk/letters-papers-hen8/vol1/pp8-24; accessed 6 February 2023.

3   Ibid.; Margaret Condon, 'The last will of Henry VII: document and text' in Tim Tatton Brown and Richard Mortimer (eds.), *Westminster Abbey: The Lady Chapel of Henry VII* (Woodbridge, 2003).

4   TNA, E36/215, ff. 7–9, 11, 13, 15, 17, 22.

5   'Henry VIII: May 1509', no. 19, *Letters and Papers, Foreign and Domestic, Henry VIII, Volume 1, 1509–1514*, www.british-history.ac .uk/letters-papers-hen8/vol1/pp8-24; accessed 6 February 2023.

6   D102.1 (SJLM/1/1/5/1), ff. 11r, 13r.

7   Gutierre Gomez de Fuensalida and Jacobo Maria del Pilar Carlos Manuel Stuart Fitz-James, duque de Berwick (ed.), *Correspondencia de Gutierre Gomez de Fuensalida, embajador en Alemania, Flandes é Inglaterra (1496–1509)*, (Madrid, 1907), p. 516, https://archive.org/details/correspond enciadoogm/page/n9/mode/2up; accessed 22/05/24.

8   '"Th'entierment of the moost excellent prynce King Henry the vijth"'. Henry VII's funeral effigy survives at Westminster Abbey.

9   D102.1 (SJLM/1/1/5/1), f. 12r.

10   John Fisher and John E. B. Mayor, (ed.), *The English works of John Fisher, Bishop of Rochester Part I* (London, 1876), p. 268; D102.1 (SJLM/1/1/5/1), f. 13v.

11   'Mornynge Remembraunce', p. 301.

12   D102.1 (SJLM/1/1/5/1), ff. 12v, 13r, 15v.

13   Maria Hayward, *Dress at the Court of King Henry VIII* (Leeds, 2007), p. 53.

14   D6.27 (SJLM/3/1/1), p. 49. The gift was made to Katherine as 'the queen,' as part of the alterations to the legacies in Margaret's

will of 15 February 1509.

15   'Henry VIII: May 1509', no. 51, *Letters and Papers, Foreign and Domestic, Henry VIII, Volume 1, 1509–1514*, https://www.british-history .ac.uk/letters-papers-hen8/vol1/pp24-34; accessed 28 January 2025.

16   D102.1 (SJLM/1/1/5/1), f. 17r.

17   For details of the coronation procession on Midsummer Eve see Hall, pp. 507–9.

18   Ibid., p. 508.

19   Henry Parker, ff. 23r, 23v.

20   D91.19 (SJLM/1/1/3/3), pp. 21, 75, 89, 97 I, 97 II, 102, 111; D102.6 (SJLM/1/1/4/2), f. 8v.

21   Thomas Wright (ed.), *The historical works of Giraldus Cambrensis. Containing the topography of Ireland, and the History of the conquest of Ireland* (London, 1863), p. 39; Henry Parker, f. 23v.

22   Wright, *Giraldus Cambrensis*, p. 39.

23   D102.1 (SJLM/1/1/5/1), f. 15r.

24   D4.7 (SJLM/3/1/4), pp. 31–8; 'Appendix 4', Jones and Underwood, p. 289.

25   For instance, John Fisher was promised 'a pair of gilt pots compassed about like a hop engraved with portcullises and marguerites'. D6.27 (SJLM/3/1/1), pp. 49–51.

26   Ibid., p. 1a.

27   'Mornynge Remembraunce', pp. 301–2.

28   Henry Parker, f. 23v.

29   'Mornynge Remembraunce,' p. 302.

30   Jones and Underwood, p. 239.

31   A. C. Seward and Thomas George Bonney (eds.), *The St John's College Quatercentenary Volume: Collegium Divi Johannis Evangelistae, 1511–1911* (Cambridge, 1911), pp. 103–26.

32   Henry Parker, f. 23r.

33   Ibid., f. 2r.

Select Bibliography

Manuscripts

British Library:
- Egerton MS 985. Ceremonials and heraldic proceedings from the fifteenth century.
- Add MS 4712. Articles and ordinances of the royal household.

Cambridge:
- Fitzwilliam Museum MS261. Book against the pestilence.
- St Johns College Library MS N.24. Book of Hours.

Archives of St John's College, Cambridge:
(Note that, although the reference system of the archive has been updated in recent years to one beginning 'SJLM', many historians of Margaret still cite according to the old system beginning 'D'. For clarity, I cite both references.)
- D4.5 (SJLM/3/1/3). A contemporary copy of the will of Lady Margaret, with certain corrections.
- D6.27 (SJLM/3/1/1). A signed draft copy of Lady Margaret's will, annotated with additions and corrections in various hands.
- D56.158 (SJLM/4/4/2). Agreement between Lady Margaret and Thomas Lord Stanley, in the presence of Edward IV, 1482.
- D56.160.1 (SJLM/4/4/4). 'Great Grant' to Margaret by Henry VII.
- D56.185 (SJLM/6/2). Admission of Margaret and Thomas Stanley to the confraternity of the Carthusian Order.
- D56.186 (SJLM/4/2/2). Will of Sir Henry Stafford.
- D56.189 (SJLM/4/3/1/3). Grant, Thomas Lord Stanley to Lady Margaret, of lands in Moldesdale, Flintshire, and Beaumaris, Anglesey.
- D56.195 (SJLM/3/2/1). Declaration of uses by Lady Margaret of a grant dated 22 May 1472 related to the performance of her will.
- D56.199 (SJLM/4/2/1). Confirmation of Surrey lands and Woking manor.
- D56.200 (SJLM/4/3/2/1). Marriage settlement of Margaret Beaufort and Thomas Stanley, 1472.
- D56.205 (SJLM/4/2/3). Grant by Margaret of certain estates to trustees for her will, 1472.
- D56.206 (SJLM/4/3/1/4). Letters of attorney from Lady Margaret to Gilbert Gilpin and Thomas Atkyns, to take seisin of lands outlined in SJLM/4/3/1/3.

- D91.4 (SJLM/2/2/2). Inventory of Wardrobe of Robes, Hatfield 1509.
- D91.10 (SJLM/2/3/3/4). A list of jewels belonging to the Lady Margaret in the keeping of Mistress Fowler.
- D91.16 (SJLM 1/1/1/1). Accounts of William Bedell, treasurer of Lady Margaret's household, 1506–7.
- D91.17 (SJLM 1/1/2/1). The account of James Clarell, cofferer to the Lady Margaret, 1498–9.
- D91.19 (SJLM 1/1/3/3). Account of Miles Worsley treasurer of the chamber to Lady Margaret, 1507–9.
- D91.20 (SJLM 1/1/3/1). The account of Miles Worsley, cofferer to Lady Margaret, 1502–5.
- D91.21 (SJLM 1/1/3/2). Accounts of Miles Worsley cofferer to Lady Margaret, for the household at Croydon and Hatfield, 1504–7.
- D102.1 (SJLM/1/1/5/1). Account of the treasurer of the Lady Margaret's chamber, Robert Fremyngham, 1509.
- D102.2 (SJLM/1/1/4/1). Account of Sir Roger Ormeston, of expenses on behalf of Lady Margaret, mostly the repair and equipment of the house of Coldharbour.
- D102.4 (SJLM/2/3/1/2). Inventory of the wardrobe of the beds.
- D102.10 (SJLM 1/1/6/1). Book of receipts and deliverances.
- D102.11 (SJLM/9/2/1). List of Officers and Servants: Elizabeth of York.
- D102.13 (SJLM/2/3/2/2). Inventory of furniture and vestments of the Lady Margaret's chapel.
- D102.18 (SJLM/2/3/1/4). An inventory of my lady's goods found within her closet by her bed chamber.
- D105.162 (SJLM/9/2/2). Reception of Philip, King of Castile. (Also available in print and digitised in *The Eagle*, 15 (1889), www.books.google.co.uk /books?id=BgIBAAAAYAAJ&pg=PA336&source=gbstoc_r&cad=2#v =onepage&q&f=false)

The National Archives:

- PRO 31/9/1. Regista Brevium: Julius II to Leo X (including letters to Margaret Beaufort.)
- PROB 11. Prerogative Court of Canterbury wills.
- SC 1/51. Ancient Correspondence of the Chancery and the Exchequer.

Westminster Abbey:

- MS39. Beaufort prayer book.
- WAM 12181–12190. Household accounts of Sir Harry Stafford, 1466/71.
- WAM 12245. Confession of treason spoken before Margaret, Collyweston, 1500.
- WAM 16016. A signed letter from Margaret to Reynald Bray, concerning Walter Stukland, c.1499/1503.
- WAM 16018. Memorandum of Reynald Bray for accounts of Margaret's household, c.1493/1503.
- WAM 3172. Concerning lands in Essex, with signature 'Margaret R', temp. Henry VII.
- WAM 32378. Draft of pardon from Edward IV to Henry Tudor, written on dorse of patent of creation of Edmund Tudor as earl of Richmond.
- WAM 32407. Miscellaneous receipts and expenses of Reynald Bray as receiver for Thomas Stanley, 1473/4.
- WAM 5742. Miscellaneous receipts and expenses of Reynald Bray as receiver of Harry Stafford, 1468/9.

- WAM 5474. Accounts of Thomas Stanley, 1491/2.
- WAM 6658. Admission of Margaret Beaufort, Sir Harry Stafford and Henry Tudor to the confraternity of the order of the Holy Trinity, Knaresborough, 1465.
- WAM 6660. Admission of Margaret Beaufort, Sir Harry Stafford and Henry Tudor to the confraternity of the hospital at Burton Lazars, 1466.

Digitised manuscripts

BL MS Royal MS 2 A XVIII. Digitised by the British Library, www.bl.uk/manuscripts/FullDisplay.aspx?ref=Royal_MS_2_A_XVIII; accessed 21 November 2018.

Condon, M. M. *et al.* (eds.), *The Chamber Books of Henry VII and Henry VIII, 1485–1521*, www.tudorchamberbooks.org
- BL Add MS. 7099 Oct 1492–1509 (Antiquarian copy), www.tudorchamberbooks.org/edition/manuscript/BL_Add_MS_7099/folio
- BL Add MS 59899, www.tudorchamberbooks.org/edition/manuscript/BL_Add_MS_59899/folio
- TNA, E36/210. The Queen's Book, March 1502–March 1503, www.tudorchamberbooks.org/edition/manuscript/E36_210/folio
- TNA, E36/214. Payment Book, October 1505–1 May 1509, www.tudorchamberbooks.org/edition/manuscript/E36_214/folio
- TNA, E36/215. Payment Book, April 1509–Oct 1518, www.tudorchamberbooks.org/edition/manuscript/E36_215/folio
- TNA, E101/414/6. Payment Book, October 1497–1 October 1499, www.tudorchamberbooks.org/edition/manuscript/E101_414_16/folio

'Richard III's Book of Hours', Lambeth Palace Library MS 474. Digitised by Leicester Cathedral, https://leicestercathedral.org/uploads/richard-iii-book-of-hours.pdf

'Vaux Passional', Peniarth MS 482. Digitised by the National Library of Wales, http://hdl.handle.net/10107/4399684

Primary sources
(Where sources are online, dates of access are provided in endnotes.)

A collection of ordinances and regulations for the government of the Royal Household, made in divers reigns, from King Edward II to King William and Queen Mary (London, 1790).

Adams, William, *Adam's Chronicle of Bristol* (Bristol, 1910).

André, Bernard and Daniel Hobbins (trans.), *The Life of Henry VII* (New York, 2011).

André, Bernard and Dana F. Sutton (ed. and trans.), *Annales regni Henrici Septimi (1504/5 and 1507/08): A hypertext critical edition*, https://philological.cal.bham.ac.uk/andreannals/2e.html

Astle, Thomas and Francis Grose (ed.), *The Antiquarian Repertory: a Miscellaneous Assemblage of Topography, History, Biography, Customs, And Manners*, 4 vols (London, 1807–9), HathiTrust, https://catalog.hathitrust.org/Record/000309420

Axton, Marie and James P. Carley (eds.), 'Appendix 7: The Account of the Miracles of the Sacrament', in *Triumphs of English: Henry Parker, Lord Morley: Translator to the Tudor court / new essays in interpretation* (London, 2000).

Bacon, Francis and J. Rawson Lumby (eds.), *Bacon's History of the Reign of King Henry VII* (London, 1885), www.google.co.uk/books/edition/Bacon_s _History_of_the_Reign_of_King_Hen/gnCjHCH/wjoC?hl=en&gbpv=1.

Basin, Thomas and Charles Samaran (ed.), *Histoire de Charles VII: Tome Premier, 1407/1444* (Paris, 1933).

Basin, Thomas and J. Quicherat (ed.), *Histoire des Règnes de Charles VII et de Louis XI*, Vol 3 (Paris, 1857).

Beaucourt, G. du Fresne de (ed.), *Chronique de Mathieu d'Escouchy: nouvelle édition* (Paris, 1864), Vol. 2.

Bentley, Samuel (ed.), *Excerpta Historica or Illustrations of English History* (London, 1831).

Bergenroth, G. A. (ed.), *Calendar of State Papers, Spain, Volume 1, 1485/1509* (London, 1862), British History Online, www.british-history.ac.uk/search /series/cal/state/papers/spain
 – *Calendar of State Papers, Spain: Supplement to Volumes 1 and 2* (London, 1868), British History Online, www.british-history.ac.uk/cal-state-papers /spain/supp/vols1-2

Black, William Henry (ed.), 'Narrative of the Marriage of Richard duke of York with Ann of Norfolk, the Matrimonial Feast and the Grand Justing [sic], AD 1477' in *Illustrations of Ancient State and Chivalry from manuscripts preserved in the Ashmolean Museum* (London, 1840).

Boorde, Andrew and F. J. Furnivall (eds.), *The fyrst boke of the introduction of knowledge made by Andrew Borde, of physycke doctor: A compendyous regyment; or, A dyetary of helth* (London, 1870).

Brewer, J. S. (ed.), *Letters and Papers, Foreign and Domestic, Henry VIII, Volume 4, 1524–1530* (London, 1875), British History Online, www.british-history.ac .uk/letters-papers-hen8/vol4
 – *Letters and Papers, Foreign and Domestic, Henry VIII, Volume 1, 1509– 1514* (London, 1920), British History Online, www.british-history.ac.uk /letters-papers-hen8/vol1

Bruce, John (ed.), *Historie of the arrivall of Edward IV in England and the finall recouerye of his kingdomes from Henry VI A.D. M.CCCC.LXXI* (London, 1838).

Campbell, William (ed.), *Materials for a History of the Reign of Henry VII. from Original Documents Preserved in the Public Record Office*, 2 vols (London, 1877).

Carpenter, Christine (ed.), *Kingsford's Stonor Letters and Papers: 1290–1483* (Cambridge, 1996).

Cavendish, George and Roger Lockyer (eds.), *Thomas Wolsey Late Cardinal His Life and Death Written by George Cavendish His Gentleman-Usher* (London, 1962).

Caxton, William and M. Y. Offord (trans. and ed.), *The Book of the Knight of the Tower* (London, 1971).

Chandler, John (ed.), *John Leland's Itinerary: Travels in Tudor England* (Gloucester, 1993).

Clay, J. W. (ed.), *North Country Wills: Being Abstracts of Wills Relating to the Counties of York, Nottingham, Northumberland, Cumberland and Westmorland at Somerset House and Lambeth Palace 1383 to 1558* (Durham, 1908).

Condon, Margaret, 'The last will of Henry VII: document and text' in Tim Tatton Brown and Richard Mortimer (eds.), *Westminster Abbey: The Lady Chapel of Henry VII* (Woodbridge, 2003).

Crawford, Anne (ed.), *Letters of Medieval Women* (Stroud, 2002).

Davies, John Silvester (ed.), *An English Chronicle of the Reigns of Richard II, Henry IV, Henry V and Henry VI, written before the year 1471* (London, 1856).

Devon, Frederick (ed.), *Issues of the Exchequer being a collection of payments made out of His Majesty's revenue, from King Henry III to King Henry VI inclusive* (London, 1837), HathiTrust, https://babel.hathitrust.org/cgi/pt?id=mdp.39015032130380&seq=7

Dockray, Keith, *Richard III: A Sourcebook* (Stroud, 1997).

Doutrepont, Georges and Omer Jodogne (eds.), *Chroniques de Jean Molinet*, 3 vols (Bruxelles, 1935–7).

Ellis, Henry (ed.), *Robert Fabyan: New Chronicles of England and France* (London, 1811).

– *Original letters, illustrative of English history; including numerous royal letters; from autographs in the British Museum, and one or two other collections*, Vol 1 (London, 1827), HathiTrust, https://babel.hathitrust.org/cgi/pt?id=uc1.31158012631122&view=1up&seq=7

Erasmus, Desiderius and T. N. R. Rogers (eds.), *In Praise of Folly* (New York, 2003).

Fisher, John and John Lewis (eds.), 'Oration made at Cambridge, 1506', in *The Life of Dr. John Fisher, Bishop of Rochester in the Reign of King Henry VIII, with an appendix of illustrative documents and papers*, vol 2 (London, 1855).

Fisher, John and John E. B. Mayor (eds.), *The English works of John Fisher, Bishop of Rochester Part I* (London, 1876).

Flenley, Ralph (ed.), 'Bale's Chronicle', in *Six Town Chronicles of England* (Oxford, 1911).

Gachard, M. (ed.), *Collection des Voyages des Souverains des Pays-Bas*, Vol. 1 (Brussels, 1876), Google Books, https://books.google.co.zm/books?id=oPkUA AAAQAAJ&printsec=frontcover#v=onepage&q&f=false

Gairdner, James (ed.), *Memorials of King Henry the Seventh: Rerum Britannicarum mediaevi scriptores, or, Chronicles and memorials of Great Britain and Ireland during the Middle Ages* (London, 1858), Google Books, www.google.co.uk/books/edition/Historia_Regis_Henrici_Septimi/ixxZAAA AcAAJ?q=&gbpv=0#f=false

– *Letters and Papers Illustrative of the Reigns of Richard III and Henry VII* (London, 1861), Google Books, www.google.co.uk/books/edition/Letters_and _Papers_Illustrative_of_the_R/L8e2O2BoXWwC?hl=en&gbpv=0

– *The Historical Collections of a Citizen of London in the Fifteenth Century* (London, 1876), British History Online, www.british-history.ac.uk/camden /record/soc/

– 'Historical Memoranda of John Stowe: The manner of making Knights of the Bath', in *Three Fifteenth-Century Chronicles with Historical Memoranda by John Stowe* (London, 1880), British History Online, www .british-history.ac.uk/camden/record/soc/vol28/pp106/113

– *The Paston Letters 1422–1509 AD*, 4 vols (Edinburgh, 1910).

Giles, Joannes Allen *Incerti scriptoris Chronicon Angliæ de regnis trium regum Lancastriensium, Henrici IV, Henrici V, et Henrici VI* (London, 1848).

Given-Wilson, Chris *et al.*, *Parliament Rolls of Medieval England* (Woodbridge, 2005), British History Online, www.british-history.ac.uk/no/series/parliament /rolls/medieval

Gomez de Fuensalida, Gutierre and Jacobo Maria del Pilar Carlos Manuel Stuart Fitz-James Berwick (eds.), *Correspondencia de Gutierre Gomez de Fuensalida, embajador en Alemania, Flandes é Inglaterra (1496/1509)* (Madrid, 1907), Internet Archive, https://archive.org/details/correspondenciadoogm/page/n9 /mode/2up

Green, Monica H. (ed.), *The Trotula: An English Translation of the Medieval Compendium of Women's Medicine* (Philadelphia, 2002).

Grose, F. (ed.), *The Antiquarian Repertory: a miscellaneous assemblage of topography, history, biography, customs and manners. Intended to illustrate and preserve several valuable remains of old times*, Vol. 1 (London, 1807).

Halliwell, James Orchard (ed.), *A Chronicle of The First Thirteen Years of The Reign of King Edward The Fourth, by John Warkworth* (London, 1839), Hathitrust, https://babel.hathitrust.org/cgi/pt?id=uva.x001618188;view=1up ;seq=7

 – *Letters of the Kings of England, now first collected from the originals in royal archives, and from other authentic sources, private as well as public*, Vol I (London, 1846), HathiTrust, https://babel.hathitrust.org/cgi/pt?id =msu.31293009879051&view=1up&seq=219

 – 'The Most Pleasant Song of Lady Bessy', in *Early English Poetry, Ballads and Popular Literature of the Middle Ages* (London, 1847).

Hall, Edward and Richard Ellis Grafton, *Hall's Chronicle; containing the history of England, during the reign of Henry the Fourth, and the succeeding monarchs, to the end of the reign of Henry the Eighth, in which are particularly described the manners and customs of those periods. Carefully collated with the editions of 1548 and 1550* (London, 1809).

Hardy, William Duffers, H. C. Maxwell Lyte and Francis Palgrave (eds.), *The Third Annual Report of the Deputy Keeper of the Public Records* (London, 1842), Google Books, www.google.co.uk/books/edition/The_1st_Annual_Report_of _the_Deputy_Keep/SFVJAQAAMAAJ?hl=en&gbpv=1

Harriss, G. L. and M. A. Harriss (eds.), *John Benet's Chronicle for the years 1400 to 1462* (London, 1972).

Haut-Jossé, B. A. Pocquet du, *Francois II, duc de Bretagne, et l'Angleterre (1458– 1488)* (Paris, 1929).

Horrox, Rosemary and P. W. Hammond (eds.), *British Library Harleian Manuscript 433*, 3 vols. (Trowbridge, 1979–82).

Hope, W. H. Saint John (ed.), 'The last testament and inventory of John de Veer, thirteenth earl of Oxford', *Archaeologia*, 66 (1915).

Kekewich, Margaret Lucille (ed.), *The Politics of Fifteenth Century England: John Vale's Book* (Stroud, 1995).

Kipling, Gordon (ed.), *The Receyt of the Ladie Kateryne* (Oxford, 1990).

Kingsford, Charles Lethbridge (ed.), 'Vitellius A XVI' in *Chronicles of London* (Oxford, 1905).

Kirby, Joan (ed.), *The Plumpton Letters and Papers* (Cambridge, 2010).

Legg, Leopold George Wickham, *English Coronation Records* (London, 1901).

Leland, John and Thomas Hearne (eds.) *Joannis Lelandi antiquarii, De rebus Britannicis Collectanea cum Thomae Hearnii Praefatione Notis et Indice ad Editionem primam*, Vol IV (London, 1774), HathiTrust, https://babel.ha thitrust.org/cgi/pt?id=uc1.31175035526816;view=1up;seq=263

Macray, William Dunn (ed.), *A register of the members of St. Mary Magdalen College, Oxford, from the foundation of the college* (London, 1894), Internet Archives, https://archive.org/details/aregistermember010xfogoog/page/n64 /mode/2up?view=theater

Major, John and Archibald Constable (eds.), *A History of Greater Britain as well England as Scotland compiled from the Ancient Authorities* (Edinburgh, 1892).

Mancini, Dominic and C. A. J. Armstrong (ed. and trans.), *The usurpation of Richard the Third: Dominicus Mancinus ad Angelum Catonem, De occupatione regni Anglie per Riccardum Tercium libellus* (Gloucester, 1984).

Maxwell Lyte, H. C., *The Fifty-Third Annual Report of the Deputy Keeper of the Public Records* (London, 1889), HathiTrust, https://babel.hathitrust.org/cgi /pt?id=mdp.39015039450567&view=1up&seq=9

Maxwell Lyte, H. C. et al. (ed.), *Calendar of the Patent Rolls preserved in the Public Record Office, 1461–1467, Edward IV* (London, 1897).

- *Calendar of the Patent Rolls preserved in the Public Record Office, 1467–1477, Edward IV Henry VI* (London, 1900).
- *Calendar of the Patent Rolls preserved in the Public Record Office, 1476–85, Edward IV, Edward V, Richard III* (London, 1901).
- *Calendar of the Patent Rolls, preserved in the Public Record Office, Henry VI, 1422–1461*, 6 vols (London, 1901–10).
- *Calendar of the Patent Rolls preserved in the Public Record Office, 1485–1494, Henry VII* (London, 1914).

Maxwell Lyte, H. C. and A. S. Maskelyne, 'Inquisitions Post Mortem, Henry VII, Entries 151–200', *Calendar of Inquisitions Post Mortem: Series 2, Volume 2, Henry VII*, British History Online, www.british-history.ac.uk/inquis-post-mortem/series2-vol2/pp103-132

Molinet, J. and J. A. C. Buchon (eds.), *Chroniques de Jean Molinet, Publiés Pour Le Première Fois, D'après Les Manuscrits De La Bibliothèque Du Roi*, Vol. 2 (Paris, 1826), HathiTrust, https://babel.hathitrust.org/cgi/pt?id=ucm.53258 72212&view=1up&seq=9
- ibid, vol. 5 (Paris, 1828), Google Books, www.google.co.uk/books/edition /Chroniques_de_Jean_Molinet/ck9SgWtQolMC?hl=en&gbpv=1

More, Thomas and C. H. Miller *et al.* (eds.), *Latin Poems: The Yale Edition of The Complete Works of St. Thomas More*, Vol 3, part 2 (New Haven / London, 1984).

More, Thomas and Richard S. Sylvester (eds.), *The History of King Richard III and Selections from the English and Latin Poems* (New Haven / London, 1976).

'Narratives of the Arrival of Louis de Bruges, Seigneur de la Gruthuyse,' *Archaeologia: Or Miscellaneous Tracts Relating to Antiquity*, 26 (1836), Google Books, www.google.co.uk/books/edition/Archaeologia_Or_Miscellaneous_Tracts _Rel/R1pEAAAAcAAJ

Nicolas, Harris (ed.), *Proceedings and ordinances of the Privy Council of England*, 7 vols (London, 1834–7).

Nichols, J. G. (ed.), *A Collection of All the Wills, Now Known to Be Extant, of the Kings and Queens of England, Princes and Princesses of Wales, And Every Branch of the Blood Royal: From the Reign of William the Conqueror, to that of Henry the Seventh* (London, 1780), HathiTrust, https://catalog.hathitrust .org/Record/009025844
- *Chronicle of the Grey Friars of London Camden Society Old Series: Volume 53* (London, 1852), British History Online, www.british-history .ac.uk/camden/record/soc/vol53

Nichols, John Gough and John Bruce (eds.), *Wills from Doctors' Commons: A Selection from the Wills of Eminent Persons Proved in the Prerogative Court of Canterbury, 1495–1695* (London, 1863).

Pizan, Christine de and Sarah Lawson (trans.), *The Treasure of the City of Ladies, or The Book of the Three Virtues* (London, 2003).

Pollard, A. F. (ed.), *The Reign of Henry VII from Contemporary Sources*, 3 vols. (London, 1913–14).

Powell, Susan (ed.), *The Household Accounts of Lady Margaret Beaufort (1443–1509). From the Archives of St John's College, Cambridge* (Oxford, 2022).

Raine, Angelo, *York Civic records: Vol. 1* (Wakefield, 1939).

Raine, J. (ed.), *Testamenta Eboracensia*, Vol 5 (York, 1884), Google Books: www .google.co.uk/books/edition/Testamenta_Eboracensia/olY4AQAAMAAJ?hl =en&gbpv=1

Riley, Henry T. (trans.), *Ingulph's Chronicle of the Abbey of Croyland with the Continuations by Peter of Blois and Anonymous Writers* (London, 1854).

Rymer, Thomas (ed.), 'Rymer's Foedera with Syllabus, Vols. 8–12' (London, 1739–45), British History Online, www.british-history.ac.uk/rymer/foedera

'The Meeting of Henry VII and the King of Castile', *The Eagle* 15 (Lent 1889) pp. 336–9, www.joh.cam.ac.uk/sites/default/files/Eagle/Eagle%20Volumes/1880s/1889/Eagle_1889_Lent.pdf

Seward, A. C. and Thomas George Bonney (eds.), *The St John's College Quatercentenary Volume: Collegium Divi Johannis Evangelistae, 1511–1911* (Cambridge, 1911).

Scobie, Andrew R. (ed.), *The memoirs of Philippe de Commines, Lord of Argenton: containing the histories of Louis XI and Charles VIII kings of France and of Charles the Bold, duke of Burgundy to which is added, The scandalous chronicle, or Secret history of Louis XI, by Jean de Troyes*, 2 vols (London, 1855–6).

Stevenson, Joseph (ed.), *Letters and Papers Illustrative of the Wars of the English in France During the Reign of Henry the Sixth, King of England*, 2 vols (London, 1861–4).

Stow, John, *The Annales, or a Generall Chronicle of England, Begun First by Maister Iohn Stow, and after Him Continued and Augmented with Matters Forreyne, and Domestique, Auncient and Moderne, Vnto the Ende of This Present Yeere 1614 by Edmond Howes, Gentleman* (London, 1615).

Sutton, Anne F. and P. W. Hammond (eds.), *The Coronation of Richard III: The Extant Documents* (Gloucester, 1983).

Sutton, Anne F. and Livia Visser-Fuchs, *The Hours of Richard III* (Stroud, 1990).

Thomas, A. H. and I. D. Thornley (eds.), *The Great Chronicle of London* (Gloucester, 1983).

'Vatican Regesta 685: 1484–1487', in *Calendar of Papal Registers Relating to Great Britain and Ireland: Volume 14, 1484–1492*, British History Online, www.british-history.ac.uk/cal/papal/registers/brit/ie/vol14/

Vergil, Polydore and Dana F. Sutton (eds.), *Anglica Historia (1555 version): A hypertext critical edition*, Philological Museum, www.philological.bham.ac.uk/polverg/

Wood, Mary Anne Everett (ed.), *Letters of Royal and Illustrious Ladies of Great Britain*. Volume 2 (London, 1846), Google Books, http://books.google.com/books?id=xOoIAAAAIAAJ&oe=UTF/8

Wright, Thomas (ed.), *The historical works of Giraldus Cambrensis. Containing the topography of Ireland, and the History of the conquest of Ireland* (London, 1863).

Major online resources

British History Online: Version 5.0, www.british-history.ac.uk
History of Parliament Online: www.historyofparliamentonline.org
Oxford Dictionary of National Biography: www.oxforddnb.com

Secondary Sources

Anglo, Sydney, *Spectacle, Pageantry and Early Tudor Policy* (Oxford, 1997).

Anstruther, Godfrey, *Vaux of Harrowden: a recusant family* (Newport, 1953), Internet Archive, https://archive.org/details/vauxofharrowdenrooanst/page/n5/mode/2up

Arthurson, Ian, *The Perkin Warbeck Conspiracy 1491–9* (Stroud, 1994).

Backhouse, Janet, 'Patronage and Commemoration in the Beaufort Hours', in Kathryn A. Smith and Carol H. Krinsky (eds.), *Tributes to Lucy Freeman Sandler: Studies in Illuminated Manuscripts* (London / Turnhout, 2007).

Bennett, Michael J., *Lambert Simnel and the Battle of Stoke* (Stroud, 1993).
– *The Battle of Bosworth* (Stroud, 2000).
Colvin, H. M. (ed.), *The History of the King's Works: Volume IV, 1485–1660 (Part II)* (London, 1982).
Condon, Margaret, 'Ruling elites in the reign of Henry VII', in Charles Ross (ed.), *Patronage, Pedigree and Power in Later Medieval England* (Gloucester, 1979).
– 'An anachronism with intent? Henry VII's Council Ordinance of 1491–2' in R. A. Griffiths and J. Sherborne (eds.), *Kings and Nobles in the Later Middle Ages: A Tribute to Charles Ross* (Gloucester, 1986).
– 'From caitiff and villain to Pater Patriae: Reynold Bray and the profits of office', in Michael Hicks (ed.), *Profit, Piety, and the Professions in Later Medieval England* (Gloucester, 1990).
Cooper, Charles Henry, *Memoir of Margaret, countess of Richmond and Derby* (Cambridge, 1874).
Coward, Barry, *The Stanleys, lords Stanley and earls of Derby, 1385–1672: The origins, wealth and power of a landowning family* (Manchester, 1983).
Cunningham, S., 'Henry VII, Sir Thomas Butler and the Stanley family', in T. Thornton (ed.), *Social Attitudes and Political Structures in the Fifteenth Century* (Stroud, 2000).
Currin, John M., 'To traffic with war? Henry VII and the French Campaign of 1492', in David Grummitt (ed.), *The English Experience in France c.1450–1558: War, Diplomacy and Cultural Exchange* (Aldershot, 2002).
Duffy, Eamon, *Marking the Hours: English People and their Prayers, 1240–1570* (New Haven, 2006).
Erler, Mary C., 'Three Fifteenth-Century Vowesses', in C. M. Barron and A. F. Sutton (eds.), *Medieval London Widows, 1300–1500* (London, 1994).
Evans, Howell T., *Wales and the Wars of the Roses* (Cambridge, 1915).
Farrer, William and J. Brownbill (eds.), *A History of the County of Lancaster: Volume 3* (London: 1907), British History Online, www.british-history.ac.uk /vch/lancs/vol3/pp191/197
Farris, Charles, 'The New Edwardians? Royal Piety in the Yorkist Age', in Hannes Kleineke and Christian Steer (eds.), *The Yorkist Age: Proceedings of the 2011 Harlaxton Symposium* (Donington, 2013).
Fisher, Sally, '"Margaret R": Lady Margaret Beaufort's Self-fashioning and Female Ambition', in Carey Fleiner and Elena Woodacre (eds.), *Virtuous or Villainess? The Image of the Royal Mother from the Early Medieval to the Early Modern Era* (New York, 2016).
Gravett, Christopher and Graham Turner, *Battle of Bosworth: Last Charge of the Plantagenets* (Oxford, 1999).
Griffiths, Ralph A., *The Reign of King Henry VI: The Exercise of Royal Authority, 1422–1461* (London, 1981).
Griffiths, Ralph A. and Roger S. Thomas, *The Making of the Tudor Dynasty* (Gloucester, 1985).
Green, Mary Anne Everett, *Lives of the Princesses of England from the Norman Conquest*, Vol 4 (London, 1852), Google Books: https://www.google.co .uk/books/edition/Lives_of_the_Princesses_of_England/dKFRAAAAcAAJ ?hl=en&gbpv=1
Hammond, Peter, *The Children of Richard III* (Stroud, 2018).
Hanham, Alison, *Richard III and his Early Historians 1483–1535* (Oxford, 1975).
Harris, Barbara J., *English Aristocratic Women: 1450–1550: Marriage and Family, Property and Careers* (Oxford, 2002).
– *Edward Stafford: Third Duke of Buckingham, 1478–1521* (Stanford, 1986).
Harriss, G. L., *Cardinal Beaufort: A study of Lancastrian ascendancy and decline* (Oxford, 1988).

Hay, Denis, *Polydore Vergil: Renaissance Historian and Man of Letters* (Oxford, 1952).

Hayward, Maria, *Dress at the Court of King Henry VIII* (Leeds, 2007).

Hicks, M. A., 'The Changing Role of the Woodvilles in Yorkist Politics to 1483', in C. D. Ross (ed.), *Patronage, Pedigree and Power in Later Medieval England* (Gloucester, 1979).

– *False, Fleeting, Perjur'd Clarence: George, Duke of Clarence 1449–78* (Gloucester, 1980).

– *Edward V: The Prince in the Tower* (Stroud, 2003).

– *Anne Neville: Queen to Richard III* (Stroud, 2013).

– *Richard III: The Self-Made King* (New Haven / London, 2019).

Higginbotham, Susan, *The Woodvilles* (Stroud, 2013).

Horrox, Rosemary, *Richard III: A Study in Service* (Cambridge, 1989).

Ingram, Mike, *Richard III and the Battle of Bosworth* (Warwick, 2019).

Ives, Eric, *The Reformation Experience: Living Through the Turbulent 16th Century* (Oxford, 2012).

Jones, Michael, 'John Beaufort, duke of Somerset and the French Expedition of 1443', in Ralph A. Griffiths (ed.), *Patronage, the Crown and the Provinces in Later Medieval England* (Stroud, 1981).

– 'Richard III and the Stanleys', in Rosemary Horrox (ed.), *Richard III and the North* (Hull, 1986).

Jones, M. K., 'Collyweston – an early Tudor palace', in Daniel Williams (ed.), *England in the Fifteenth-Century: Proceedings of the 1986 Harlaxton symposium* (Woodbridge,1987).

– 'The Myth of 1485: did France really put Henry Tudor on the throne?', in David Grummitt (ed.), *The English Experience in France c.1450–1558: War, Diplomacy and Cultural Exchange: War, Diplomacy and Cultural Exchange* (Aldershot, 2002).

– *Bosworth 1485: Psychology of a Battle* (Stroud, 2003).

Labande-Mailfert, Yvonne, *Charles VIII et Son Milieu (1470–1498): La Jeunesse au Pouvoir* (Paris, 1975).

Laynesmith, J. L., *Cecily Duchess of York* (London / New York, 2017).

– 'The Piety of Cecily, Duchess of York: A Reputation Reconsidered', in Hannes Kleineke and Christian Steer (eds.), *The Yorkist Age: Proceedings of the 2011 Harlaxton Symposium* (Donington, 2013).

– 'The Order, Rules and Constructions of the House of the Most Excellent Princess Cecily, Duchess of York', in Gwilym Dodd and Craig Taylor (eds.), *Monarchy, State and Political Culture in Late Medieval England: Essays in Honour of W. Mark Ormrod* (Woodbridge, 2020).

Lesyer, Henrietta, *Medieval Women: A Social History of Women in England, 450–1500* (London, 2002).

McKenna, John W., 'Piety and Propaganda: The Cult of King Henry VI' in Beryl Rowland (ed.), *Chaucer and Middle English Studies in Honour of Rossell Hope Robbins* (London: 1974).

McSheffrey, Shannon, 'Henry VII and Humphrey Stafford', in idem, *Sanctuary Seekers in England, 1394–1557,* https://sanctuaryseekers.ca/2020/06/10/stafford

Murray, Alexander, *Suicide in the Middle Ages*, 2 vols. (Oxford, 1998–2000).

Okerlund, Arlene Naylor, *Elizabeth of York* (New York, 2009).

Owen, John Brickdale and Hugh Blakeway, *A History of Shrewsbury*, 2 vols (London, 1825).

Penn, Thomas, *Winter King: The Dawn of Tudor England* (London, 2011).

Pollock, Frederick and Frederic William Maitland, *The History of English Law Before the Time of Edward I*, Vol. 2 (Cambridge, 1911).

Powell, Susan, 'Lady Margaret Beaufort as Patron of Scholars and Scholarship', in Paul Binski and Elizabeth A. New (eds.), *Patrons and professionals in the Middle Ages: Proceedings of the 2010 Harlaxton Symposium* (Donington, 2012).

Powell, Susan, 'Textiles and Dress in the Household Papers of Lady Margaret Beaufort (1443–1509), Mother of King Henry VII', in Robin Netherton and Gale R. Owen-Crocker (eds.), *Medieval Clothing and Textiles*, 11 (Woodbridge, 2025).

Rawcliffe, Carole, *The Staffords, Earls of Stafford and Dukes of Buckingham, 1394–1521* (Cambridge, 1978).

Ross, Charles, *Edward IV* (Trowbridge, 1975)

Saunders, W. H. Bernard and W. D. Sweeting (eds.), *Fenland Notes and Queries*, Vol. 2 (1894).

Scofield, C. L., *The life and reign of Edward the Fourth. King of England and of France and Lord of Ireland*, 2 vols (Croydon, 2016).

Shaw, William Arthur, *The Knights of England; a complete record from the earliest time to the present day of the knights of all the orders of chivalry in England, Scotland, and Ireland, and of knights bachelors*, Vol. 2 (London, 1906).

Southworth, John, *Fools and Jesters at the English Court* (Stroud, 1998).

Starkey, David, *Henry: Virtuous Prince* (London, 2008).
  – 'Intimacy and Innovation: The rise of the Privy Chamber, 1485/1547', in David Starkey *et al.*, *The English Court: From the Wars of the Roses to the Civil War* (London, 1987).

Thomas, D. H., *The Herberts of Raglan and the Battle of Edgecote 1469* (Enfield, 1994).

Tremlett, Giles, *Catherine of Aragon: Henry's Spanish Queen. A Biography* (London, 2010).

Seacome, John, *The History of the House of Stanley, from the Conquest to the Death of the Right Honourable Edward, Late Earl of Derby, in 1776* (London, 1821), Google Books, www.google.co.uk/books/edition/_/df1HAA AAMAAJ?hl=en&gbpv=0

Warnicke, Retha M., *Elizabeth of York and Her Six Daughters-In-Law: Fashioning Tudor Queenship 1485–1547* (New York, 2017).
  – 'Margaret Tudor, Countess of Richmond and Elizabeth York: Dynastic Competitors or Allies?', in Valerie Schutte (ed.), *Unexpected Heirs in Early Modern Europe: Potential Kings and Queens* (New York, 2017).

Articles

Appleby, Jo *et al.*, 'Perimortem trauma in King Richard III: a skeletal analysis', *Lancet*, 385 (2015).

Aram, Bethany, 'Juana "the Mad's" Signature: The Problem of Invoking Royal Authority, 1505–1507', *The Sixteenth Century Journal*, 29, ii (1998).

Ballard, Mark and C. S. L. Davies, 'Étienne Fryon: Burgundian Agent, English Royal Secretary and "Principal Counsellor" to Perkin Warbeck', *Historical Research*, 62 (1989).

Barnfield, Marie, 'Diriment Impediments, Dispensations and Divorce: Richard III and Matrimony', *The Ricardian*, 17 (2007).

Bennett, Michael J., 'Henry VII and the Northern Rising of 1489', *English Historical Review*, 105 (1990).

Brayson, Alex, 'The Fiscal Policy of King Richard III of England', *Quidditas*, 40 (2019).

Carlson, David, 'King Arthur and court poems for the birth of Arthur Tudor in 1486', *Humanistica Lovaniensia*, 36 (1987).

Crawford, Anne, 'Victims of attainder: the Howard and de Vere women in the late fifteenth century', *Reading Medieval Studies*, 15 (1989).

Cunningham, Sean, '"Fraudulently Compassed Against All Right and Conscience": Evidence of the Defection of Richard III's Government Officials and the Progress of Henry Tudor's Conspiracy, 1483–1485', *Ricardian* 34, i (2024).

Davies, C. S. L., 'Bishop John Morton, the Holy See, and the Accession of Henry VII', *English Historical Review*, 102 (1987).

Dawson, Ian, 'Anne Herbert: A Life in the Wars of the Roses', *The Historian*, 121 (2014).

Delman, Rachel M., 'The Vowesses, the Anchoresses, and the Aldermen's Wives: Lady Margaret Beaufort and the Devout Society of Late Medieval Stamford', *Urban History*, 49, ii (2021).

Eeles, F. C., 'Two Sixteenth Century Pontificals Formerly Used in England', *Transactions of the St Paul's Ecclesiological Society*, 7 (1911–15).

Griffiths, R. A., 'Queen Katherine de Valois and a missing statue of the realm', *Law Quarterly Review*, 93 (1977).

Gunn, S. J., 'The Accession of Henry VIII', *Historical Research*, 64 (1991).
 – 'The Courtiers of Henry VII', *English Historical Review*, 108 (1993).

Hanham, Alison, 'Sir George Buck and Princess Elizabeth's Letter: A Problem in Detection', *The Ricardian*, 7 (1987).

Hicks, Michael, 'The Last Days of Elizabeth Countess of Oxford', *English Historical Review*, 103 (1988).
 – 'Historic Doubts about the Survival of the Princes in the Tower after 1485', *Historical Research*, 97 (2024).

Jenstad, Janelle Day, 'Lying-in Like a Countess: The Lisle Letters, the Cecil Family, and A Chaste Maid in Cheapside', *Journal of Medieval and Early Modern Studies*, 34, ii (2004).

Johnson, David, 'Coercion or Compliance: Richard, duke of Gloucester and Elizabeth, Countess of Oxford', *The Ricardian*, 34 (2024).

Jones, M. K., 'Sir William Stanley of Holt: Politics and Family Allegiance in the Late Fifteenth Century', *Welsh History Review*, 14 (1988).

Kingsford, C. L., 'On some London houses of the Early Tudor Period', *Archaeologia*, 71 (1921).

Kincaid, Arthur, 'Buck and the Elizabeth of York Letter: A Reply to Dr Hanham', *The Ricardian*, 8 (1988).

Laynesmith, Joanna, 'The King's Mother', *History Today*, 56, iii (2006).
 – 'Richard Lessy, dean of Cecily, Duchess of York's chapel (d. 1498)', *The Ricardian*, 33 (2023).

Niles, Philip, 'Baptism and the Naming of Children in Late Medieval England', *Medieval Prosopography*, 3, i (1982).

Orme, Nicholas, 'The Education of Edward V', *Bulletin of the Institute of Historical Research*, 57 (1984).

Pierce, Hazel, 'The King's Cousin: The Life, Career and Welsh Connection of Sir Richard Pole, 1458–1504', *Welsh History Review = Cylchgrawn Hanes Cymru*, 19, ii (1998).

Podd, Rachel, 'Reconsidering maternal mortality in medieval England: aristocratic Englishwomen, *c.*1236–1503', *Continuity and Change*, 35, ii (2020).

Powell, Susan, 'Margaret Pole and Syon Abbey', *Historical Research*, 78 (2005).
 – 'Textiles and Dress in the Household Papers of Lady Margaret Beaufort (1443–1509), Mother of King Henry VII', *Medieval Clothing and Textiles*, 11 (2015).

Roger, Euan C., '"To Be Shut Up": New Evidence for the Development of Quarantine Regulations in Early-Tudor England', *Social History of Medicine*, 33, iv (2020).

Scofield, C. L., 'Henry, duke of Somerset, and Edward IV', *English Historical Review*, 21 (1906).

– 'The early life of John de Vere, thirteenth earl of Oxford', *English Historical Review*, 29 (1914).

Thomson, J. A. F., 'Bishop Lionel Woodville and Richard III', *Bulletin of the Institute of Historical Research*, 59 (1986).

Thorpe, Deborah, '"I Haue Ben Crised and Besy": Illness and Resilience in the Fifteenth-Century Stonor Letters', *The Mediaeval Journal*, 5, ii (2015).

Underwood, Malcolm G., 'Politics and Piety in the Household of Lady Margaret Beaufort', *Journal of Ecclesiastical History*, 38, i (1987.)

Visser-Fuchs, Livia, 'Where did Elizabeth of York find Consolation?', *The Ricardian*, 9 (1993).

Warnicke, Retha M., 'Sir Ralph Bigod: A loyal servant to Richard III', *The Ricardian*, 6 (1984).

Unpublished theses

Cirivilleri, Robert, 'Marriage and canon law: Consanguinity, affinity and the medieval church: (996–1215)', unpublished MA thesis, San Jose State University, 2000.

Delman, Rachel, 'Elite Female Constructions of Power and Space in England, 1444–1541,' unpublished PhD thesis, University of Oxford, 2017.

Ford, Lisa L., 'Conciliar Politics and Administration in the Reign of Henry VII', unpublished PhD thesis, University of St Andrews, 2001.

Harper, Samantha Patricia, 'London and the Crown in the Reign of Henry VII', unpublished PhD thesis, University of London, 2015.

Johnson, Lauren, 'The Impact of the Wars of the Roses on Noblewomen', unpublished MSt thesis, University of Oxford, 2007.

Jones, M. K., 'The Beaufort Family and the War in France, 1421–50', unpublished PhD thesis, University of Bristol, 1982.

Osawa, Rebecca, 'Emotional intelligence (EI) in the life and career of Lady Margaret Beaufort (1443–1509),' unpublished MA thesis, Trent University, 2011.

Image Credits

For each page of the plate section, credits are listed for images in clockwise order.

Page 1
St John's College Cambridge / Wikiedia Commons

Page 2
Bibliothèque nationale de France, Département des Manuscrits, Latin 1158
From the British Library archive / Bridgeman Images
Dean and Chapter of Westminster, London

Page 3
Granger – Historical Picture Archive / Alamy
From the British Library archive / Bridgeman Images
Image courtesy of Sarah Morris (The Tudor Travel Guide)

Page 4
British Library
St John's College, Cambridge

Page 5
Print Collector / Getty Images
Print Collector / Getty Images
Hulton Archive / Getty Images
Peter Horree / Alamy

Page 6
The Picture Art Collection / Alamy
piemags / Alamy
Heritage Images / Getty Images
Royal Collection

Page 7
St John's College, Cambridge
The National Archives
St John's College, Cambridge

Page 8
Werner Forman / Getty Images
Angelo Hornak / Getty Images
PA Images / Alamy

Index

marriage to Margaret Beaufort
41–53, 42n, 55–60, 94, 96, 97,
98, 139, 270, 271, 305
Readeption and 76–86
Buckingham, Henry Stafford, duke of
x, 108–9, 118–24, 127–36, 140–5,
163, 170, 208, 352–3, 357
Buckingham, Humphrey Stafford,
duke of x, xiv, 41, 43–8, 52, 52n,
56, 57, 134
Buckingham and Bedford, Katherine
Woodville, duchess of x, xvi, 118,
143, 279, 322n
Bulkeley, Robert 240, 243
Burdet, Thomas 107
Burgundy x, 67, 67n, 76, 80, 82,
100–101, 104, 108, 111, 158, 197,
211, 214, 224, 228, 232, 235,
237, 239, 244, 259–60, 282, 287,
328–30
Burgh, Sir Thomas 73
Burton Lazars 62–3
Bush, John 62–3
Butt, Stephen 288

C

Cáceres, Francisca de 300
Cadwaladr 183, 281, 299
Caernarfon Castle 35
Calais xvi, 34, 65, 68, 71, 75, 102,
149, 151–2, 161, 161n, 287,
319–20, 323, 331
Cambridge University 2, 39, 133, 138,
226, 242, 248, 252, 252n, 325,
339–41, 341n, 366, 368
Canterbury 11, 101, 126, 281,
317, 348
Carmeliano, Pietro 204
Carre, Richard 299, 324
Carthusian order 98–9, 98n, 338
Castillon, Battle of (1453) 33
Catesby, William 123
Catherine de Valois, Queen of
England xv, 14, 32, 103
Catholic Church x, 301
Cato, archbishop of Vienne, Angelo
133

Caxton, William 192, 336, 338
Cecily of York, Princess xi, 139, 198,
205, 222, 248
Charles the Bold, duke of Burgundy x,
67n, 76, 82–3, 100, 101, 104, 111,
211, 215, 333
Charles VIII, King of France 150, 151,
156–7, 220, 231, 235, 237
Château de l'Hermine 105
Château of Largoët 103–4
Chaucer, Geoffrey: *Canterbury Tales*
369
Chertsey Bridge 349
Cheyne, Lady Frideswide 250, 250n
Cheyne, Humphrey 132, 139, 158
Cheyne, John 132, 139–40, 145, 172,
174, 205
Christ's College, Cambridge 325, 355,
366, 368
Clare College, Cambridge 341
Clare, Elizabeth, Lady 340
Clarell, James 271, 325
Clarence, George, duke of xi, xiv, xvi,
92, 136, 186, 199, 205, 206, 208,
223, 228, 280, 281n
Henry Tudor wardship and 70
imprisonment and death, Tower of
London 107–109, 127, 211–12
Lincolnshire Rebellion (1470) and
73–5, 371–2
marriage xi, 68
Readeption and 76, 77, 79, 80,
81, 82
Clarence, Isabel Neville, duchess of
xvi, 67, 68, 92, 107, 108
Clarence, Margaret Holland, countess
of Somerset and duchess of xi,
11–12, 21, 91n, 189, 338
Clarence, Thomas, duke of xi, 12, 13
Clifford, Anne St John, Lady
276, 358
Clifford, Henry, Lord 213, 276
Clifford, Robert 239–41, 243
Coldharbour 185–6, 190, 222, 254–5,
287, 292, 350, 362
Colet, Henry 161
Collyweston 265–8, 270–9, 283, 287,
296, 298–9, 305–9, 313–17, 321,

L

Lamphey Palace 35, 37
Landais, Pierre 105, 149–51, 159
Langton, Thomas 155
Lathom Castle 97, 100, 111, 143,
    163–4, 166, 167–8, 173, 180, 190,
    244, 246, 268, 316, 349
Latimer, Hugh 277
Le Ryall 28, 57, 89
Leo of Rozmital 200
Lessy, Richard 110
Lewis of Caerleon 132, 138–9, 144,
    163, 170
Lincoln Cathedral 216
Lincoln, John de la Pole, earl of xii,
    137, 184, 184n, 205, 207–208,
    214, 215
Lincoln, Margaret, countess of 199
Lincolnshire Rebellion (1470) 73–5
Lobe (fool) 249–50
Londoño, Sancho de 200, 201
Louis XI, King of France 76, 87,
    101–102, 103, 111, 133
Louis XII, King of France 327
Love, Nicholas 338
Lovell, Francis, Viscount xiii, 197,
    207, 208, 214, 215, 230
Lovell, Isabel 355
Lovell, Thomas 162, 201, 325, 352,
    353–5, 359, 368
Low Countries x, 28, 67n, 206, 215,
    219, 228, 234, 235, 238, 239, 240,
    327, 329, 333
Ludlow Castle 46, 115, 227, 243,
    254, 283, 286, 294, 295, 296, 298,
    299, 301, 302–3
Lynne, Alice 266

M

Magdalen College, Oxford 273
Maine 15, 17
Maltravers, Earl 205
Mancini, Dominic 118, 118n, 121,
    124, 125, 132–3
Maredudd, Rhys Fawr ap 174
Margaret of Antioch, St 38–9

Margaret Tudor, Queen of Scotland
    225–6, 229, 245, 254, 278, 294,
    296–7, 311, 312–14, 344
Margaret of York, duchess of
    Burgundy x, 67, 77, 108, 211–12
Marguerite d'Angoulême,
    Princess 327, 331
Marguerite of Anjou, Queen of
    England xiii, 5, 26–7, 29, 34, 43,
    45, 47, 49, 77, 80–3, 86,
    95, 122, 149, 169, 252n, 267, 276,
    341
Marguerite of Austria 327
Marie of Burgundy 108, 111, 211
Marie, duchess of Bourbon 13
Market Deeping, manor of 15, 23
Marney, Sir Henry 368, 368n
Mary I, Queen of England 274, 369
Mary Tudor 225, 247, 254, 287, 292,
    314, 328, 332–3, 335, 360, 362,
    363, 364
Massy, Alice 307, 308
Matienson, Fray Johannes de 200,
    201
'mawmet', Cambridgeshire 281, 285
Maxey Castle 21, 23, 25, 26, 34, 36,
    44, 47, 55, 74, 135, 161, 266, 272
Maximilian, Holy Roman Emperor
    111, 228, 228n, 235–9, 303,
    326–7, 329
Meaux, siege of (1422) 14
Medina del Campo, Treaty of (1489)
    224, 283, 284, 302
Merbury, Robert 361
Merchants of the Staple 161
Meres, Thomas 162
Merevale Abbey 169
Mirror of gold for the sinful soul, The
    340
Mitton, Thomas 168
Molinet, Jean 172, 174, 215
Mordaunt, Sir John 227
More, Thomas xiii, 119, 124–5,
    290–1, 304
Morgan, John 163, 164
Morley, Henry Parker, Lord 170, 274,
    277, 361, 364–7, 369–70
Mortimer's Cross, battle of (1461) 48